W9-BWV-867

Nebraska Symposium on Motivation 1984

Volume 32

University of Nebraska Press
Lincoln and London 1985

Nebraska Symposium on Motivation 1984

Psychology and Gender

Richard A. Dienstbier — *Series Editor*
Theo B. Sonderegger — *Volume Editor*

Presenters

Anne Anastasi — *Professor Emeritus of Psychology Fordham University*

Anke A. Ehrhardt — *College of Physicians and Surgeons of Columbia University and New York State Psychiatric Institute*

Janet T. Spence — *Ashbel Smith Professor of Psychology and Educational Psychology University of Texas at Austin*

Jacquelynne Eccles — *Associate Professor of Psychology University of Michigan*

Virginia E. O'Leary — *Deputy Executive Officer for Public Affairs, American Psychological Association*

Sandra Lipsitz Bem — *Professor of Psychology and Director of Women's Studies Cornell University*

Joan C. Martin — *Professor and Research Coordinator, Department of Psychiatry and Behavioral Science, University of Washington, Seattle*

Judith Rodin — *Professor of Psychology and Psychiatry, Yale University*

ய௱

*Nebraska Symposium on
Motivation, 1984,* is Volume 32
in the series on
CURRENT THEORY AND
RESEARCH IN MOTIVATION

Copyright 1985 by the University of Nebraska Press
International Standard Book Number 0-8032-4152-6 (Clothbound)
International Standard Book Number 0-8032-9150-7 (Paperbound)

The paper in this book meets the guidelines for permanence and durability of the
Committee on Production Guidelines for Book Longevity of the Council on Library
Resources.

"The Library of Congress has cataloged this serial publication as follows:"
Nebraska Symposium on Motivation.
   Nebraska Symposium on Motivation. [Papers] v. [1]–1953–
   Lincoln, University of Nebraska Press.
       v. illus., diagrs. 22 cm. annual.
   Vol. 1 issued by the symposium under its earlier name: Current Theory and Research
in Motivation.
   Symposia sponsored by the Dept. of Psychology of the University of Nebraska.

   1. Motivation (Psychology)

BF683.N4   159.4082   53-11655

Library of Congress

Preface

*L*ike all volumes of the *Nebraska Symposium on Motivation* published since the early 1970s, this volume is devoted entirely to a single topic. It focuses on issues of gender.

The volume editor for this edition is Professor Theo Sonderegger. Professor Sonderegger, like all the volume editors of the recent past, has assumed the major responsibility for successfully drawing together the people who are the contributors to this volume and deserves the credit. My sincere thanks to her.

The Symposium series is supported largely by funds donated to the University of Nebraska Foundation by the late Professor Cora L. Friedline in memory of Professor Harry K. Wolfe. This Symposium volume, like those of the recent past, is dedicated to the memory of Professor Wolfe, who brought psychology to the University of Nebraska. After studying with Professor Wilhelm Wundt, Professor Wolfe returned to Nebraska, his native state, to establish the first undergraduate laboratory of psychology in the nation. As a student at Nebraska, Professor Friedline studied psychology under Professor Wolfe. The editors are grateful to the late Professor Friedline for her bequest and to the officers of the University of Nebraska Foundation for their continued interest in and support of this series.

RICHARD A. DIENSTBIER
Series Editor

Contents

Introduction

*T*he zeitgeist is ready, at last, for all psychologists to include gender in their studies of human behavior. Although "gender gap" is a catch phrase used widely by the popular and scientific press, gender-related issues are understood by relatively few, and the questions raised are many. For the past 32 years the topics of the Nebraska Symposium on Motivation have reflected major theoretical concerns in psychology, and this volume continues the tradition with the topic "psychology and gender." Nineteen eighty-four is a particularly appropriate year! Fortunately, the significance of gender-related issues became apparent to many scholars some time ago, and in this volume we reap benefits from those who have translated their concern into research. Eight of the foremost researchers in the area of psychology and gender share their findings in this Symposium. The two separate Symposium sessions focused on different aspects of this multifaceted topic. The four papers of the initial fall session addressed the issue of sex differences from a broad range of perspectives, whereas the four papers of the spring session focused on gender as a variable.

The methodological tactic of reducing secondary variance by creating a new independent variable has been practiced for years. Unfortunately, so has the tactic of ignoring data that do not fit the theory. The literature is filled with examples of both techniques, the latter being especially used with data obtained from females in some of the early work on achievement motivation. Now that gender has become important and widely studied as an independent variable, relevant studies in all areas of psychology are beginning to appear, as well as reanalyses of earlier work that reveal previously missed insights.

In the first paper of this Symposium Professor Anne Anastasi examines the relation between cognitive and affective aspects of behavior as an aid to understanding individual differences, a topic on which she has published widely. Her position is that a broad spectrum of affective variables influences the cognitive development of the individual and that "effects of cognitive and affective characteristics may be mutual and reciprocal rather than unidirectional."

Her paper reviews effects of transient affective states on task performance, learning, and memory and suggests a possible mechanism for cumulative effects. Failure, for instance, can recall earlier failure experiences, thereby reinforcing and perpetuating an unpleasant feeling state; success produces a corresponding effect. Next she examines the cumulative effects of more enduring dispositions — personality traits — upon the development of abilities. There is evidence here also of a reciprocal relationship between personality and intellect. Professor Anastasi points out, however, that finding significant relations between affect and cognitive development represents only a first step; the more difficult step is to find the mechanism whereby affective components may alter cognitive development.

To understand the etiology of mechanisms for long-term effects, she examines relevant literature on motivation, learning, and human performance, concentrating on time-on-task, attention control, and environmental mastery. She also reviews the contributions of heredity and environment. Now as 25 years ago, she feels that the question of "how" — that is, the mechanism or the modus operandi of these influences — will be more productive than the question of which differences are hereditary and which are acquired.

On the basis of these considerations, she points out some implications for sex differences. One implication includes interactions between physical and attitudinal variables. Physical characteristics may provide initial advantages for each sex that are perpetuated through sex-role stereotypes well beyond the point where they are relevant. Another implication concerns motivational variables that have been shown to be related to the development of aptitudes. Sex differences in math aptitude tests demonstrated in one study were greatly reduced when math-course-taking behavior was controlled.

Professor Anastasi's concluding comments are challenging to behavioral scientists. As attitudes about the sex appropriateness of behaviors change, she feels, sex differences in aptitudes will show corresponding changes. The restructuring of society with respect to the positions of women and men will thus "provide one more natural quasi-experiment to investigate the etiology of human behavior—

one more opportunity to try to learn how the individual differences come about."

Gender-related behavior from a biosocial perspective is the focus of Professor Anke Ehrhardt's paper. Both prenatal and postnatal influences affect gender-related behavior, and the prenatal effects of sex hormones are of particular interest to this Symposium participant. She believes it is imperative that behavioral scientists be familiar with basic principles of neuroendocrinology, since there is so much knowledge about hormonal effects upon developing central nervous system (CNS). She also feels much can be learned from studies of children exposed to abnormal levels of hormones. She emphasizes, however, that "potential hormonal influences need to be integrated into an interactive model that takes into account both constitutional and social-environmental factors," and she provides information to support her approach.

Hormones can modify some behaviors differentially via the CNS. Exposure of the developing CNS to sex hormones during prenatal/ neonatal periods has been called "organizational" (permanent influence on the CNS differentiation), while exposure in the adult has been labeled "activational" (activation of behavior preorganized during development). "The important principle of the interactional or reciprocal relationship between hormones and environment is that environmental conditions can affect hormonal levels." Professor Ehrhardt provides many examples of principles learned from nonhuman research and contends that we must also employ the sophisticated methodology that now exists for hormone measures and look at clearly defined behavior rather than at global and complex units— "and one must never forget that biological markers are as modifiable as behavioral events."

This researcher believes gender identity is a crucial aspect of an individual's development. Only recently has the best prognosticator of gender identity been found to be the assigned sex of rearing. After presenting a wealth of clinical evidence on this topic, Professor Ehrhardt turns her attention to sexually dimorphic behavior, or gender-role behavior, emphasizing that there are more similarities than differences in the behavior of males and females.

In her work on behavior, she elects to study two activities where sex differences have most consistently been found—"nurturing" and "rough-and-tumble" behavior. She describes a series of studies, some in conjunction with her colleague Professor John Money, in which they looked at the effects of atypical amounts of sex hormones upon these two behaviors in nonhumans (rhesus monkeys) and in human subjects. Examples from her work include data from an ongoing project with human females exposed prenatally to diethlystilbestrol (DES), a synthetic estrogen. Both the reproductive systems and the behavior of daughters of these women appear to be affected.

In her concluding remarks, Professor Ehrhardt reiterates that work on gender-related behavior has been hampered by a model that posits biology versus learning. A biosocial perspective that includes constitutional and environmental factors in an interactional model, in her view, will be most productive in understanding such issues as the development of gender identity and gender-related behavior.

Professor Janet Spence begins her paper by questioning the meanings of the words "masculinity" and "femininity," or "masculine" and "feminine," as used in a variety of situations. The words appear to have two types of meaning—empirical, for example as labels, or as theoretical constructs "that refer to a fundamental property or aspect of the individual's self-concept that is not directly observable." Used in the latter fashion the terms are bipolar opposites, and a bipolar femininity/masculinity factor is the implicit assumption. Conventional theories are predicated on this implicit assumption, which then permits assessment of an individual's standing on a continuum of masculine and feminine qualities.

Next Professor Spence reviews conventional theories of masculinity and femininity and discusses the Personal Attributes Questionnaire (PAQ), which she developed; the Bem Sex Role Inventory (BSRI); the assumptions on which these instruments are based; and empirical data collected using them. Her concern is not with the empirical evidence collected but with interpretations of the PAQ and BSRI as measures of masculinity and femininity rather than as measures of "what their manifest content indicates, namely two constellations of personality characteristics." (Professor Spence and Professor Bem reviewed one another's papers before publication.)

She believes that a new theoretical approach is needed and proposes one that links the self-concepts of masculinity and femininity to the concept of gender identity. She makes it clear that she conceives of masculinity and femininity as "separate but basically incompatible, paralleling the dimorphism of biological sex" and cautions that her approach may surprise those who have believed that demonstrations of the statistical independence of scores on the PAQ and BSRI scales are evidence that the concepts of masculinity and femininity are orthogonal.

She argues that since gender identity, defined in the traditional sense, has been established by the age of 2½ to 3 years, it serves as an unarticulated self-concept that guides the development of gender-related qualities. As an individual grows, other factors take over the development of sex-typed characteristics and behaviors so that there is considerable diversity within each sex for gender-congruent or gender-incongruent behaviors. Empirical data, according to Professor Spence, suggest that the gender-differentiating phenomena are multidimensional. "A multifactorial model of gender-related phenomena implies that individuals' standings on each of these dimensions must be independently assessed" rather than measured by a single all-purpose instrument or by a collection of instruments as one pleases. She cautions that appropriate measuring techniques must be applied before useful tests can be made of theoretical implications of gender-related phenomena.

Sex differences in achievement patterns have long interested Professor Jacquelynne Eccles and provide the topic of her paper. Her three goals here are to review specific sex differences in achievement behaviors, to present a theory explaining these differences, and to describe a study designed to evaluate the theory. After reviewing the many ways achievement has been operationalized, she limits her discussion to specific achievement behaviors that reflect or are linked to real-life achievement choices—for example, scores on standardized academic or aptitude tests and school course grades.

After an extensive review of achievement-behavior studies, she concludes that no sex differences are found for course grades or indexes of persistence on laboratory tasks; that small but consistent differences favoring males (older children or beyond) are found on tests of mathematical reasoning and scientific knowledge; and that less consistent differences favoring females are sometimes found on tests of language skills, literature knowledge, music, and art. However, fairly consistent differences emerge on persistence and single-minded pursuit of high levels of adult occupational achievement, achievement-related activity scores in childhood and adulthood, high-school course enrollment patterns, and occupational choice.

Professor Eccles and her colleagues then propose an expectancy/value model of achievement choice to explain some of the differences they found. The model uses the construct of value to provide a line between the model and the variable of self. A major component is choice. Socialization experiences, according to the theory, shape individual differences as mediators of choice, particularly in the academic domain. By focusing on choice of an experience rather than its avoidance, the theory provides a more positive perspective on women's achievement. The model also portrays the choices of females as valuable to their own right rather than as a reflection or distortion of male values or choices.

To test the model, Professor Eccles and her colleagues conducted an extensive cross-sectional, longitudinal study using math and English course participation as task choices. Rather than suggesting that females have some type of math deficit, the findings show that females and males place different subjective values on tasks such as math and English and that their values are influenced by different factors.

This work shows that achievement patterns in females and males are modifiable; values associated with tasks may be changed by appropriate role models, information, parental beliefs regarding children's math aptitude, and career guidance. Professor Eccles feels that better career guidance may help young women develop their talents by changing the values attached to various school subjects, such as math, as well as by eliminating some of the stereotypes that both girls and boys hold regarding math-related occupations.

The first paper of the second session was given by Professor Virginia O'Leary. Creation of an attributional framework within which the persistence of beliefs in sex differences can be understood is the goal of Professor O'Leary and her coauthor, Professor Ranald Hansen. Sex biases favoring men affect outcomes in the laboratory, in clinical practice, and in criteria for mental health. Belief in sex differences, furthermore, persists despite evidence that behavioral similarities are greater than behavioral differences between sexes. These perceptions originate in the perceiver (subject sex differences) or in response to the sex of the perceived person (stimulus sex differences). Attribution theory, by focusing on people's explanations of other people's behavior, appears to these authors to be a good method of understanding the persistence of beliefs in sex differences.

Three aspects of explanation found in attribution theory are locus of the cause, perceiver's translation of observed behavior into personality traits, and use of attributions in relation to performance. After a review of relevant attribution theory, the authors describe a series of their own experiments relating these three aspects of attributional explanation to sex. Only a few of their findings are described here. From their work on locus of cause, they found what they call the "bargain-basement effect"; that is, perceivers make attributions using the least information (the least complex cognitive strategy) that will permit a confident inference. Perceivers also find that men's reactions to a stimulus more compellingly reflect the properties of the stimulus than do those of women. Society regards men's behavior as the "benchmark." A woman's behavior will be seen as stimulus-provoked if it is the same as a man's, but it will be attributed to her disposition if different. From their experiments on sex-determined trait inferences, they concluded not that perceivers are more likely to infer a woman's than a man's traits from behavior, but that the traits inferred from similar behaviors—for example, masculine/feminine—will be different.

Work concerning attributions about success and achievement has shown that both male and female perceivers agree that a man's successful performance on a task more likely is due to ability and a woman's is due to luck. Professors O'Leary and Hansen say that it also seems reasonable that "sex differences in the perceived causes of success will provide different reactions to it." Effort may be viewed as compensating for low ability in women or as resulting from intrinsic motivation that persists even if not rewarded. The opposite is true for men. The implication that follows from attributions about effort is that "Trying hurts women more than men; success helps men more than women."

The authors conclude that they have created an attributional framework that can be used to understand the persistence of beliefs in sex differences. They remind us, however, that the tendency to attribute men's behavior to stimulus properties more than women's may be the result of "automatic" or "mindless" cognitive processing that may be construed as an attributional fact rather than as the processing procedure. Attributional "facts," they caution, may appear to be true and hard to challenge. While the authors believe that they have developed a theoretical framework for understanding the persistence of sex differences, as yet there is no "magic bullet to shatter those beliefs."

Professor Sandra Bem reviews her work since she first began publishing on gender schemata and androgyny in the early 1970s. Her Symposium paper provides an opportunity to present her work from a 1984 perspective and at the same time to respond to studies by others prompted by her work. She defines the central questions of her research as, "How does the culture transform male and female infants into masculine and feminine adults? How does it create the many gender differences in behavior, motivation, and self-concept that transcend the dictates of biology?"

In discussing the psychology of the individual as it pertains to gender, Professor Bem comments on two important gender-differentiation sources, biology and the contemporary environment. She emphasizes that it is the interaction of biology with culture and not culture per se that determines how similar or how different males and females actually are. She points out that "if the many gender-differentiated practices that abound in our culture were ever to be eliminated, then males and females could finally begin to be as similar as their biology allows."

After reviewing existing theories of sex typing, she proposes that we still need a theory to explain how and why children so frequently use sex as a cognitive organizing principle. This principle is the basis for her gender schema theory, which proposes that "sex typing derives in large measure from gender-schematic processing, from a generalized readiness on the part of the child to encode and to organize information—including information about the self—according to the culture's definitions of maleness and femaleness." She provides several empirical examples to illustrate the link between sex typing and gender-schematic processing.

At this point Professor Bem makes a historical comment about the concept of psychological androgeny. When she began her work in the early 1970s, psychology assumed that sex typing was not only normal but desirable, and the concept of an androgynous individual was "undefined and unarticulated." Her work on androgyny in 1971 began with the development of the Bem Sex Role Inventory (BSRI). She believes that individuals with androgynous or "blended" personalities, as identified by the BSRI, can provide a contrast group for comparison with sex-typed groups and can help her clarify sex typing through gender-schematic processing. Besides tracing the development of the BSRI, she comments on some of the research in which it has been used, as well as on the Spence-Helmreich view of the BSRI.

After an extensive review of several of her studies of gender-schematic processing, she offers some strategies for parents who wish to raise a gender-aschematic child in a gender-schematic society. Not only does she suggest strategies, but she recounts several delightful anecdotes about applications of these techniques in her own family. Initially parents can allow their children to learn about sex differences without learning culture's sex-linked views. Simultaneously, they can provide their children with alternative schemata to use in interpreting "culture's sex-linked associative network when they do learn it."

She concludes her paper with a candid discussion of the politics of gender research and reconsiders the concept of androgyny in the light of gender schema theory. She feels that if society would stop "projecting gender into situations irrelevant to genitalia" then the fact that one is male or female would be accepted as unselfconsciously as the fact of being human. Artificial constraints of gender schematizing upon individual differences would be eliminated. "The feminist prescription, then, is not that the individual be androgynous, but that the society be gender aschematic."

"Perinatal psychoactive drug use with its effects upon gender, development, and function in the offspring" is the topic of Professor Joan Martin's paper and is obviously an area where gender is of extreme importance. Studies of compromised functioning in offspring following maternal and sometimes paternal exposure to noxious extrinsic agents before or during the perinatal period have increased dramatically. Work in this area has led to development of a new discipline, behavioral teratology, which this paper represents along with the discipline of psychology.

The United States population, including gravid women, is overmedicated, according to Professor Martin. For example, in 1977 women took an average of 6.4 prescription drugs and 3.2 nonprescription (over-the-counter) drugs during pregnancy. She presents current statistics on drug use, especially the drugs on which the paper focuses: two stimulants (nicotine and amphetamines) and two sedative-hypnotics (alcohol and barbiturates). Possible mechanisms through which use of these drugs and other extrinsic agents before or at any time during pregnancy may affect the fetus are illustrated. Since for ethical and legal reasons one cannot experiment with drugs on pregnant women, she reviews the advantages and limitations of the use of animal models in behavioral teratology. The review includes the principles of teratology and methodological design issues.

In an extensive series of investigations begun in 1967, Professor Martin and her colleagues found that nicotine administered to rats during pregnancy and lactation affects offspring's development, growth, and function. In another series of studies, metamphetamine administration appeared to produce similar but even greater effects, possibly irreversible, under the experimental conditions used.

Barbiturate studies included use of the shorter-acting drug pentobarbital and the longer-acting phenobarbital. Administration of pentobarbital to pregnant rats produced progeny with lighter brain
weights, transient hyperactivity, and lower efficiency in escaping
electric shock. Phenobarbital administration resulted in offspring
with poorer neonatal survival and higher activity rates. Alcohol is the
most frequently abused drug in this country. When administered in
utero, it produced progeny that were hyperactive, had poorer stress
tolerance (to shock), and were slower to learn simple tasks. In discussing the implications of her findings, Professor Martin states that
"it is difficult to find any merit for the ingestion of even moderate
quantities of the psychoactive drugs nicotine, alcohol, and amphetamine during pregnancy."

She concludes her paper with a discussion of sex-ratio changes following parental drug exposure, a controversial topic. Theoretically, a
shift in sex ratios could occur through either maternal or paternal
psychoactive drug use, according to Professor Martin, although this
is not always reported in perinatal drug studies. (Many people, even
in the psychological community, are not aware of this effect.) She
describes sex-ratio changes that have been found as a consequence of
use of the drugs discussed in her paper. Although the evidence is
viewed as inconclusive, sex-ratio alterations appear to favor females
when gravid animals, including humans, ingest drugs. The evidence
for paternal effects is weaker. Professor Martin believes that carefully
controlled studies designed to study this phenomenon per se, using
different drugs and drug combinations across a range of doses in
several animal models, will be needed to provide a definitive answer
to this important question.

Studies of variables associated with eating are found throughout
the Nebraska Symposium on Motivation series beginning with the
first paper in 1953. Professor Judith Rodin's paper focuses on a gender-related aspect of eating—dieting and "feeling too fat." Her work
indicates that women, compared with men, spend more time and
energy in dieting and are more concerned with being fat whether or
not they actually are. She suggests that women respond to a cultural
imperative to be attractive; currently, to be attractive is to be thin.
Women's conceptions of ideal body weights have become increasingly less, yet actuarial statistics over the past 20 years have shown rising
average body weights in women under 30. Concern with weight has
led to an increase in the number women with eating disorders such as
bulimia and anorexia nervosa. Professor Rodin points out that

women are also "expanding, challenging, and discarding sex-role stereotypes on many frontiers" and raises the question whether these circumstances are related to the preoccupation with thinness.

In her paper she examines differential effects on women and men of cultural attitudes about obesity. Obesity carries a stigma even for children and is met with psychological, social, and economic punishment. Physical attractiveness in our society carries many rewards, more so for women than for men. Studies of physical attractiveness usually use pictures that show the full figure of the woman but only the face of the man. Society, according to Professor Rodin, has in the past also dictated that women alter their bodies to achieve "unnatural" attractiveness ideals, such as through the 19th-century use of corsets, and there has been an implicit relation between weight and attractiveness.

Biological factors of weight regulation are also discussed. Body weights deemed desirable by many women are described as biologically unrealistic from several standpoints, including hereditary factors, sex-linked hormones, developmental changes that lead to increased fat storage (puberty, pregnancy, and menopause), and disturbance of metabolic processes caused by repeated dieting. Besides these biological variables there is also the psychological dimension of feeling deprived, which often leads women to stop dieting and to overeat.

As stated previously, the ideal female figure has become increasingly thin. Professor Rodin suggests that the pursuit of thinness is a form of competition and achievement behavior. Happiness is associated with being thin; shame is associated with unsuccessful dieting attempts or failure to reach the perceived ideal, albeit unrealistic, degree of thinness. It is interesting that both sexes are misinformed about the degree of thinness the other sex finds attractive; females underestimate and males overestimate the body size desired by the other sex.

Professor Rodin concludes that "it is not vanity or conceit but shame and social pressure that lead to women's preoccupation with their appearance." This preoccupation has serious psychological and physical consequences; weight concerns and efforts to be thin may cause a large majority of women to be at risk of developing an eating disorder. She urges that individuals who study eating disorders as well as those interested in clinical interventions and in the psychology of women should be better informed about the importance of women's feelings about bodily appearance. Data from such work will help clarify a "profound and almost universal experience among women in current Western societies."

To reiterate, the topics of the Nebraska Symposium on Motivation over the past 32 years have reflected mainstream changes in psychological theory. The contents of this volume reflect an additional change, the new recognition given to the female gender. Psychology of women courses are now found on most campuses, and many new associations have been developed, such as Division 35 of the American Psychological Association, American Women in Psychology, and the Feminist Psychotherapy Institute, to deal with issues concerning women. Participants in this Symposium are always chosen for outstanding scholarship; for the first time in its history, all the speakers are women. (In the previous 31 years, there were 184 male and eight female participants.)

Grateful acknowledgment is made for help provided by the faculty of the University of Nebraska–Lincoln, particularly Professor Richard Dienstbier for his work as series editor. Special recognition is merited by Professor Natalie Porter for the excellent conversation hours she conducted with the speakers and audience after each session and to Professor Roberta Morris for her able participation in these discussions. Finally, many thanks to our graduate students, particularly the Friday Afternoon Group, for their support.

THEO B. SONDEREGGER
Professor of Psychology

Reciprocal Relations between Cognitive and Affective Development— With Implications for Sex Differences

Anne Anastasi

Fordham University

*I*n recent years psychologists have shown increasing interest in reintegrating those aspects of behavior traditionally classified as cognitive and noncognitive, or ability and personality. The linkages and interrelationships have been investigated from many angles (Clark & Fiske, 1982; Tomkins & Izard, 1965), and the research findings have implications for several areas of psychology. Within psychometrics and differential psychology, however, the separation between cognition and affect has tended to persist longer. Traditionally, abilities have been primarily the concern of psychometricians and educational psychologists, whereas feelings and motivation have been primarily the concern of social psychologists and personality theorists. Available testing instruments, moreover, typically deal with the assessment of either cognitive or affective characteristics.

It is my purpose in this chapter to examine how the relationship between cognitive and affective aspects of behavior can contribute to an understanding of individual differences. These relationships include both the effects of transient states on current behavior and the cumulative effects of more durable dispositions or traits on the development of the individual. It should also be recognized that the effects of cognitive and affective characteristics may be mutual and reciprocal rather than unidirectional. Either can influence the development of the other. *Affect* is used here as a broad term to cover all noncognitive characteristics, including feelings, moods, emotions, attitudes, and motives. *States* refer to temporary conditions; *traits* denote more durable dispositions or behavioral variables.

Effects of Transient States

Much of the research on the relations between affective states and cognitive behavior has been conducted by experimental psychologists. Some of this research, however, has implications for an understanding of individual differences in aptitude test performance and in the acquisition of knowledge. Several instruments have been developed for assessing temporary states, including anxiety, anger, depression, and hostility, among others (Curran & Cattell, 1976; Lubin, 1967; McNair, Lorr, & Droppleman, 1971; Spielberger, Gorsuch, & Lushene, 1970; Spielberger, Vagg, Barker, Donham, & Westberry, 1980; Zuckerman & Lubin, 1960–1967). These instruments have been used chiefly for clinical purposes, as in evaluating the outcome of therapeutic interventions. The experimentally oriented studies have generally relied on specially designed techniques rather than standardized inventories to ascertain the presence of feeling states. In many studies the affective state was experimentally induced, as for example, through hypnotic suggestion or through recalling or reading about happy or sad events (Bower, 1981).

Although several studies deal with more than one type of effect, their findings can be grouped into three major categories, covering the relation of affect to task performance, to learning, and to memory.

AFFECT AND TASK PERFORMANCE

In psychometrics, a well-known example of the influence of feeling states on task performance is provided by studies of *text anxiety* (Morris, Davis, & Hutchings, 1981; Sarason, 1980; Spielberger, Gonzales, & Fletcher, 1979; G. S. Tryon, 1980). Persons high in test anxiety tend to perceive evaluative situations as personally threatening. Factor analyses of the responses to self-report inventories have identified two major components of test anxiety, namely, emotionality and worry. The emotionality component comprises feelings and physiological reactions, such as tension and increasing heart rate. The worry or cognitive component includes negative self-oriented thoughts, such as expectation of doing poorly and concern about the consequences of failure. These thoughts draw attention away from the task-oriented behavior required by the test and thereby disrupt performance.

Research with schoolchildren and college students suggests that both school achievement and intelligence test scores are negatively correlated with measures of text anxiety. Several recent investigations have called into question the common stereotype of the test-anxious student who knows the subject matter but "freezes up" when taking a test (Culler & Holahan, 1980). Students who score high on a test anxiety scale obtain lower grade-point averages and tend to have poorer study habits than do those who score low on test anxiety. Moreover, treatment interventions to reduce test anxiety produce improvement in both test performance and course work, especially when the treatment is directed to the self-oriented, cognitive component. The best results are obtained from multiple treatment programs that include behavior therapy techniques to reduce emotionality and worry as well as training to improve study skills. It can be seen that the findings regarding test anxiety illustrate the reciprocal effects of cognitive and affective changes; they also suggest the operation of cumulative, long-term effects in both affective and cognitive development.

Although test anxiety has been extensively investigated because of its immediate practical implications, the effects of other feeling states on task performance have also received some attention. The testing literature provides many examples of the effect of pleasant and unpleasant feelings on the cognitive test performance of both children and adults (see Anastasi, 1982, pp. 38–41). In one early study, children's IQs on the Goodenough Draw-a-Man Test averaged significantly higher after writing a composition on "The Best Thing That Ever Happened to Me" than they did after writing a composition on "The Worst Thing That Ever Happened to Me" (McCarthy, 1944). Similar differences have been found with other tests and other populations of test takers. In several of these studies, the contrasting feeling states were induced by providing antecedent success experiences as one experimental condition and antecedent failure experiences as the other.

More recent research by experimental psychologists has explored the specific ways feeling states may influence task performance. There is evidence, for example, that relatively mild, pleasant feeling states, such as are likely to be aroused by minor events of everyday life, can lead to differences in problem-solving strategies (Isen,

Means, Patrick, & Nowicki, 1982). In one series of experiments, positive affects were induced by such small incidents as receiving a free sample (note pad, nail clipper), partaking of refreshments (juice and cookies), watching a funny movie, or being told one had successfully performed a simple task. In comparison with controls, the experimental subjects were more likely to follow simplified, speedy kinds of solutions. In some circumstances these procedures could result in either improved performance, through the use of more effective strategies, or impaired performance, through carelessness. In tasks providing immediate feedback, however, the experimental subjects were more often successful than the controls. They used more efficient strategies, were more responsive to feedback, and wasted less time than did the controls.

What these results show is that mild affective states *can* influence task performance. The specific effects, however, depend upon several moderator variables pertaining to the particular affect aroused, the nature of the task, the situational context, and the personal characteristics of the participants.

ROLE OF AFFECT IN LEARNING AND MEMORY

There is some evidence that depressed states retard learning. Clinical reports indicate that depressed patients are poor learners (Beck, 1970, 1974). According to one hypothesis, the effect of depression on learning may be similar to that of test anxiety insofar as the self-devaluative thoughts associated with depression compete with the processing of task-relevant information. The depressed mood interferes with the efficient use of active, effortful learning strategies such as clustering, mnemonic or elaborative devices, and rehearsal (Leight & Ellis, 1981). The result has been characterized as a sort of cognitive rigidity.

Similar effects of depression on learning and recall were demonstrated with normal college students, through the use of experimentally induced depressed states (Leight & Ellis, 1981). The materials to be learned consisted of letter groups, so chosen and presented as to maximize the opportunities for learners to introduce chunking strategies. In the depressed state, the students not only showed slower progress from trial to trial but also made less use of chunking than occurred in neutral or elated states. In a later series of experiments with meaningful verbal materials, several specific processes whereby depression may influence learning and memory were more fully explored (Ellis, Thomas, & Rodriguez, 1984).

Another investigation assessed individual differences in learning in relation to self-ratings of naturally occurring moderate-to-mild states of elation or depression (Hettena & Ballif, 1981). At the beginning of one of their regular class sessions, a total of 105 college students of both sexes rated their mood at the time by checking one of 10 descriptive statements on an elation-depression continuum. The statements actually used by the students ranged from "feeling very good and cheerful" (Mood 8) to "Spirits low and somewhat blue" (Mood 3). The students were then presented with six sentences, individually typed on cards, and were asked to rate each sentence on a 10-point scale of pleasantness-unpleasantness. The sentences had been chosen so that three were clearly pleasant and three clearly unpleasant. The students were next asked to study each sentence for 30 sec and were then told to write down by free recall as much as they could remember of each sentence.

Various statistical analyses of both individual records and extreme mood groups yielded the following major results: Mood correlated significantly with amount of material produced. The more elated subjects recalled more than the depressed subjects; they also gave more highly differentiated evaluations of the sentences. The more depressed subjects recalled less and tended to assign less differentiated, neutral ratings to the sentences.

It might be noted that the findings on the differentiation of ratings are corroborated by at least one other study (Messick, 1965) but are inconsistent with the findings of still other studies (Bower & Cohen, 1982). We could speculate that the conditions of this study encouraged the subjects to perceive the rating procedure as a task to be performed rather than as an expression of subjective feelings. Accordingly, the elated respondents were more alert and careful in making fine discriminations; the depressed respondents were less observant and more superficial in their behavior, thus yielding mean ratings closer to neutral for each sentence. Depressed respondents also tend to avoid risk taking and to be less confident about their choices (Isen et al., 1982), and this tendency may be reflected in the choice of neutral rather than extreme positions. Furthermore, the subjects in this study were asked to evaluate new material, presented at the time; their evaluations did not require the retrieval of material stored in long-term memory. Still another relevant feature of the study is that the sentences to be rated represented compact semantic units, which were internally fairly homogeneous and relatively unambiguous in pleasantness or unpleasantness. This feature would reduce the likelihood that the depressed subjects could focus their attention on unpleasant details and the elated subjects on pleasant details within any one sentence.

While these speculations may be of theoretical interest, the demonstrated effects of mood on learning and on quality of task performance are of primary concern for our present purpose. Perhaps it is the influence of mood on the participants' evaluation of the task as a whole that is most relevant. If, when given the task instructions, the elated subjects thought, "This is fun—it's like a game," and the depressed subjects thought, "So what—I could care less," these reactions could account for both the superior learning and the more discriminative ratings of the former.

MOOD CONGRUITY AND MEMORY

Some of the research on affect and memory has been concerned with mood congruity. Essentially, the findings indicate that similarity of mood, such as happy or sad, serves as a powerful cue in retrieving content from one's memory store.[1] This mood-congruity effect was especially well demonstrated in the extensive research conducted by Gordon Bower and his associates (Bower, 1981; Bower & Cohen, 1982). Using primarily hypnosis for the experimental induction of moods, these investigators found that when subjects were in happy or sad moods they were more likely to recall word lists learned when in similar moods. The mood induced at the recall stage also facilitated the recall of pleasant or unpleasant events in recent or more remote life experiences. It was further shown that such moods as happiness, sadness, or anger influenced judgment of familiar persons or objects and interpretation of ambiguous remarks; they affected the degree of optimism or pessimism in the prediction of life events; and they were reflected in such responses as free associations to neutral words and the imaginative content of TAT (Thematic Apperception Test) stories.

Although this research has certainly made a significant contribu-

---

1. Some evidence suggests, however, that this effect may not occur with content that was well learned and is readily accessible (see Leight & Ellis, 1981, pp. 263–264).

tion to our understanding of how memory works, it has less direct bearing on the understanding of individual differences in cognitive development. Unlike the studies cited in the preceding section, the research of Bower and his associates failed to reveal any overall effect of mood on learning or retention. The subjects did not perform better in one mood than in another. Several methodological differences may account for these inconsistent findings. Among them are the use of induced versus natural states (Hettena & Ballif, 1981) and learners' opportunity for introducing efficient or inefficient learning strategies (Leight & Ellis, 1981).

The relation between affect and cognitive performance represents a relatively new area of research, and we must recognize that there are still many unanswered questions and untested hypotheses. In general, there is suggestive evidence that temporary states may affect individual differences in task performance and in learning; but it would be unreasonable to expect major effects. For the latter, we need to look at more durable, long-term influences. It is also relevant to note that the well-established results on mood congruity and selective retrieval suggest a probable mechanism for cumulative effects. Whenever an individual fails in task performance, this experience will tend to revive earlier failure experiences, thereby reinforcing and perpetuating an unpleasant feeling state. A corresponding effect will occur with repeated success experiences. Thus a state that is experienced repeatedly and in a variety of contexts is well on the way to becoming a habitual disposition or enduring trait.

Long-Term Effects of Personality Traits

GLOBAL LONGITUDINAL STUDIES

We now turn from a consideration of the immediate effects of transitional states on *current performance* to a consideration of the cumulative effects of more enduring dispositions, or personality traits, on the *development of abilities*. Some data on these effects are provided by global longitudinal studies, which vary widely in duration and in the age levels investigated. One survey of early research with groups extending from preschool children to college students included both short-term longitudinal studies and concurrent correlations of personality test scores with intelligence test scores and with indexes of academic achievement (Dreger, 1968). Both approaches yielded a number of suggestive relationships between personality variables and intellectual performance, but causal effects are difficult to identify.

An unusually extensive body of longitudinal data has recently been analyzed by a group of researchers at the Institute of Human Development of the University of California in Berkeley (Eichorn, Clausen, Haan, Honzik, & Mussen, 1981). The data were originally collected in three well-known longitudinal studies initiated some fifty years ago at the Institute, for somewhat different purposes. Eventually, the three samples were merged and the data pertaining to development from adolescence to middle age were identified and submitted to sophisticated statistical analyses. IQ changes were investigated in relation to scores on the California Psychological Inventory (CPI) and to Q sorts by clinicians derived from case records, projective tests, and intensive interviews.

Some of the relationships found in the Berkeley study were quite complex, suggesting significant interactions with age and sex. For example, adolescents who were highly controlled, dependable, calm, and somewhat aloof from their peers were those who had the higher IQs in both adolescence and middle life; but the correlation between IQ and these personality variables disappeared when both sets of measures were obtained during the middle years. Several personality variables, however, yielded significant correlations both within and across age levels. Of the CPI scales, the following were significantly associated with IQ at middle age and with rises in IQ: Intellectual Efficiency, Achievement via Independence, Tolerance, and Responsibility. A rising IQ, as well as magnitude of IQ at both age levels, was also associated with a Q-sort factor labeled "Cognitively Invested." Some correlations between IQ at middle age and adolescent personality characteristics were actually higher than the correlations between IQ and the same personality variables measured at middle age, or higher than the cross-age correlations of the personality variables themselves.

Although most of the published studies focus on the effects of personality variables on intellectual changes, there is some evidence that the relation between personality and intellect is reciprocal. Not only do personality characteristics affect intellectual development, but intellectual level also affects personality development. Suggestive data in support of this relation are provided by Plant and Minium (1967) in a composite analysis of prior studies. Drawing upon the data gathered in five longitudinal investigations of college-bound young adults, the authors selected the upper and lower 25% of each sample in terms of intelligence test scores. These contrasted groups were then compared on various personality tests that had been administered to particular samples on two or more occasions. The personality tests included measures of attitudes, values, motivation, and interpersonal traits. The results of this analysis revealed a strong tendency for the high-aptitude groups to exhibit substantially more personality changes described as "psychologically positive" than did the low-aptitude groups. The high-aptitude students exhibited more change over time, and the changes were in the direction of the responses typical of college students in general.

In recent years there has been increasing interest in the study of affective factors in infant development. Several investigations have found substantial correlations between ratings of infant behavior on personality variables and subsequent cognitive development, as assessed by such instruments as the Bayley Scales of Infant Development and the Stanford-Binet (Birns & Golden, 1972; Matheny, Dolan, & Wilson, 1974; McCall, 1976; Yarrow & Pedersen, 1976). Infant behavior ratings were derived from various sources, including the Infant Behavior Record of the Bayley scale, videotaped laboratory observations, and parents' reports on early childhood temperament scales. In general, infants who exhibit positive affect, active interest, and responsiveness in a testing situation are likely to learn more and to advance faster in cognitive development as a result of their early experiences. They are also likely to respond favorably to later academic activities that involve interaction with adults in goal-oriented tasks. A further advantage stems from the influence such infant behavior exerts on the social behavior of adult caretakers, which will in turn enhance the child's opportunities for learning (Haviland, 1976; Wilson & Matheny, 1983).

STUDIES OF SELECTED PERSONALITY CONSTRUCTS

The longitudinal studies we have considered thus far were designed as global, exploratory investigations. Although personality constructs were employed in synthesizing the empirical findings, these constructs were typically developed in the course of the study, either by such statistical procedures as factor analysis or by clinical applications of personality theory to the interpretation of the data. The studies were not designed at the outset to test hypotheses about particular constructs. In the 1970s and 1980s the research became more highly focused. We now find a growing number of studies specifically planned around certain personality constructs, notably self-concepts, locus of control, and achievement motivation. Several of these studies include data bearing on the role of such constructs in intellectual development (Bloom, 1976; Uguroglu & Walberg, 1979).

Self-concepts and related self-evaluations. The construct of self-concept merges with certain related constructs designated as self-esteem (Coopersmith, 1967/1981a, 1981b; Rosenberg, 1963, 1965) and self-efficacy (Bandura, 1982; Zimmerman & Ringle, 1981). Moreover, self-concept itself is multifaceted (Jordan, 1981; Shavelson, Hubner, & Stanton, 1976; Uguroglu & Walberg, 1979; Wylie, 1979). Studies using global self-concepts may yield inconsistent results or fail to reveal significant correlations with other variables where a more narrowly defined construct, such as academic self-concept, will yield more consistent and significant results. This is especially true with those individuals or groups, such as certain cultural minorities, for whom academic achievement may not rank high in the personal value system. In such cases a high global self-concept, slanted by the respondent to reflect his or her own value system,[2] would not be expected to correlate significantly with academic achievement or intellectual functioning (Jordan, 1981).

In a meta-analysis of 40 published studies of school populations from the 1st to the 12th grade, Uguroglu and Walberg (1979) analyzed correlations between self-concept measures and indexes of cognitive achievement; the latter included standardized achievement tests, ability tests, and grades. The results showed an overall mean correlation of .41 between achievement and academic self-concept and a mean correlation of .29 between achievement and a general self-concept. It was also found that the correlations rose from the 1st to the 12th grade. Furthermore, the correlations tended to be higher with grades than with test scores, a finding that may reflect the contributions of motivational and attitudinal variables to teachers' evalua-

---

2. Some global self-concept instruments include descriptive statements sampling heterogeneous contexts, such as academic, social, emotional, and physical (Coopersmith, 1967/1981a, 1981b; Shavelson & Bolus, 1982). Others provide broad, content-general statements that respondents may interpret with reference to the most appropriate basis for themselves (Jordan, 1981; Rosenberg, 1963, 1965).

tions of student performance, as well as the cumulative effect of such variables on long-term achievement.

A limitation of most available studies is that only concurrent relations were investigated. This procedure makes it impossible to identify the direction of causal influence. A well-designed study that takes into account both the multifaceted nature of the self-concept and directionality of effect was conducted by Shavelson and Bolus (1982). Data were obtained from a total of 99 seventh- and eighth-grade students. The criterion of academic achievement was based on first- and second-semester grades in English, mathematics, and science. Self-report instruments were administered to provide measures of a global self-concept, measures of a general academic self-concept, and measures of subject-matter-specific self-concepts in English, mathematics, and science. All measures were obtained on two occasions, in February and June of the same year.

In their data analysis, Shavelson and Bolus followed essentially a cross-lagged design to assess the relative magnitude of effect in both directions, that is, effect of achievement on self-concept and effect of self-concept on achievement. By means of both correlational analysis and analysis of covariance structure (Bentler, 1980; Shavelson & Stuart, 1981), the authors demonstrated the causal predominance of self-concept over achievement. The models of cross-lagged causal paths that were tested provided an excellent fit to the empirical data, accounting for 97% or more of the covariation. At the same time, it was shown that academic achievement and academic self-concept, although correlated, are in fact separate constructs. In other words, a student's academic self-concept is not merely his or her recollection of past grades.

Locus of control and other aspects of causal attribution. The construct known as "locus of control" first came into prominence with the publication of a monograph by Rotter (1966). As originally defined, this construct refers to the extent to which an outcome is perceived as contingent upon one's own behavior or as the result of conditions beyond one's control. Locus of control can itself be recognized as one aspect of a broader concept of causal attribution, a concept that has received increasing attention from many investigators (see Antaki & Brewin, 1982; Lefcourt, 1982; Weiner, 1982).

To account for the diverse emotional and motivational reactions aroused by particular outcomes, three major dimensions of causal attribution have been proposed and corroborated by empirical data

(Abramson, Seligman, & Teasdale, 1978; Weiner, 1982). The first, *locus of control* in the narrower sense, characterizes the cause as internal (e.g., aptitude, effort, health) or external (e.g., task difficulty, help from others, luck). A second dimension, *stability*, differentiates between more enduring causes, such as aptitude, and more changeable or modifiable causes, such as health, mood, and effort, all of which are internal. A third dimension, *controllability*, differentiates between causes in terms of the degree to which the condition is under the individual's control. This dimension is illustrated by the difference between failure attributed to lack of effort and failure attributed to temporary illness, both of which are internal and modifiable causes. Another relevant consideration is the stringency of one's standard for self-evaluation: How high does the individual set the standard for judging his or her own success or failure? (Bandura, 1982).

It has also been hypothesized, with some supporting evidence, that when causal attribution leads to an attitude of helplessness and hopelessness, neither self-concept nor achievement motivation shows any relation to performance (Coleman, 1966; Vance, 1973). Thus what one believes about the environment may represent a threshold phenomenon for the differential effects of other personality variables.

It is obvious that causal attribution is a fertile area for exploring the influence of affect on cognitive development. Yet in contrast to the large number of studies reporting data on the relation of academic achievement to self-concepts, relatively few studies have investigated its relation to locus of control or other attributional dimensions. In the previously cited survey of 40 studies on elementary and high school students (Uguroglu & Walberg, 1979), there were only 13 correlations with locus of control,[3] in contrast to 206 with various types of self-concepts. The mean correlation between locus of control and academic achievement in these studies was .32.

A few studies have found that the individual's perception of causal attribution is significantly correlated not only with performance on intelligence and achievement tests but also with such achievement-related variables as task orientation, attentiveness, time spent doing homework, and time spent in intellectual free-play activities (Crandall, Katkowsky, & Crandall, 1965; Crandall, Katkowsky, & Preston,

3. A few used measures of field dependence, which is conceptually close to locus of control and was combined with the latter in this survey.

1962; Rotter, 1966; Walden & Ramey, 1983). Such findings are of particular interest in suggesting mechanisms whereby affect may influence cognitive development—a question I shall return to in a later section.

Achievement motivation. The important contribution of achievement motivation to individual differences in task performance has been widely recognized and investigated in many contexts. Achievement motivation has also played a prominent part in discussions of sex differences in aptitude and achievement (Fyans, 1980, sect. 5), as we shall see in a later section. And it has strong conceptual ties to both self-concept, on the one hand, and locus of control, on the other. Beginning with the early and quite broad definition of achievement need (n-Ach) by Murray (1938), this personality construct has undergone several decades of research, chiefly by McClelland and his associates (McClelland, 1961/1976; McClelland, Atkinson, Clark, & Lowell, 1953/1976) and later by Atkinson and his associates (Atkinson & Feather, 1966; Atkinson & Raynor, 1974). This research used primarily TAT-like fantasy measures to assess level of achievement motivation. Other investigators have explored the construct through a variety of self-report and self-descriptive instruments (see, e.g., Herrenkohl, 1972; Jackson, Ahmed, & Heapy, 1976).

As is true of so many trait constructs, there is a growing body of research indicating that achievement motivation is a multidimensional concept. Through factor analyses, as well as through multitrait-multimethod correlation matrices, as many as 10 discriminable factors have been identified. One well-designed study (Jackson et al., 1976) yielded six first-order, oblique factors (Status with Experts, Acquisitiveness, Achievement via Independence, Status with Peers, Competitiveness, and Concern with Excellence). Factor analysis of these factors yielded three second-order factors, designated Competitive Acquisitiveness, Status, and Excellence. An important implication of multidimensionality is that the various dimensions of achievement motivation may interact differently with such demographic variables as sex, age, academic level, socioeconomic status, and ethnic background (Herrenkohl, 1972).

It is noteworthy that in the research following the original TAT tradition, there has also been considerable evolution in the definition of the achievement motivation construct (Atkinson & Raynor, 1974, chap. 2). At the outset, achievement motivation was identified in rather general terms, as a desire to perform well in relation to some standard of excellence, although the notion of competitive striving was often included. Gradually this definition was expanded to encompass the resultant of two separate motives: the tendency to achieve success and the tendency to avoid failure, the latter being related to test anxiety. Still later came a recognition of so-called extrinsic motives, such as the tendency to seek approval or to comply with authority, as well as of the motivation provided by more distant goals that are anticipated when one perceives the present activity as instrumental to their attainment (Atkinson & Raynor, 1974, chaps. 7–10).

Data on the relation of cognitive development to achievement motivation—however defined and measured—are relatively meager. The previously cited survey of published studies on elementary and high school students reports 13 correlations with criteria of academic ability, having a mean value of .31. Some relevant data are reported by Atkinson and his co-workers (Atkinson, O'Malley, & Lens, 1976; Lens, Atkinson, & Yip, 1979) from a follow-up study of 6th-, 9th-, and 12th-grade boys and girls. In this study significant relations were found between cumulative high school grade-point average and an index of resultant achievement motivation obtained three or six years earlier. Resultant achievement motivation was defined as the difference between the tendency to seek success, as assessed from scores on TAT-like stories, and the tendency to avoid failure, as assessed from scores on a text-anxiety inventory. Atkinson's research on achievement motivation as a whole is particularly relevant to an understanding of the mechanisms whereby motivation may influence development, a question to which I shall now turn.

Etiological Mechanisms for Long-Term Effects

To find significant relations between affect and cognitive development—even through longitudinal studies and cross-lagged analyses—represents only a first step. It does not explain *how* noncognitive variables affect cognition. Through what mechanisms do attitudes, beliefs, and motives influence the development of one's abilities? In the effort to answer this questions, we can find many suggestive leads scattered through the literature on motivation, learning, and human performance. The contributions include both provocative theoretical analyses and some well-designed empirical investigations. The multiplicity of approaches and terminology, exhibiting varying degrees of overlap, almost defies classification. To facilitate communication, however, I have grouped a diversity of approaches into three major categories, which can be loosely labeled time-on-task, attention control, and environmental mastery.

TIME-ON-TASK

On the basis of some 25 years of research on achievement motivation, John Atkinson and his co-workers (Atkinson, 1974; Atkinson et al. 1976) formulated a comprehensive schema representing the inter-relationships of abilities, motivation, and environmental variables. A key concept in this schema is time-on-task, namely, the time the individual spends on a particular activity, such as studying or carrying out a job-related function. Motivation influences both the efficiency with which a task is performed and the time devoted to it relative to other activities. Level of performance results from the individual's relevant abilities and the efficiency with which he or she applies those abilities to the current task. The final achievement or product reflects the combined influence of level of performance and time spent at work.

Another major component of the Atkinson schema pertains to the lasting, cumulative effect of task performance on the individual's own cognitive and motivational development. This step represents a feedback loop to the individual's personality. Its influence should be manifested in the individual's future performance, both on tests and in real-life activities. The predictive value of the Atkinson schema was demonstrated with both computer simulations and empirical analyses of longitudinal data (Atkinson, 1974; Atkinson et al. 1976; Lens et al. 1979).

The role of time-on-task in relation to affective variables is likewise recognized by Bandura (1982), who writes, "Judgments of self-efficacy also determine how much effort people will expend and how long they will persist in the face of obstacles or aversive experiences" (p. 123). From still another angle, Bloom (1976, chap. 4) observes that affective characteristics influence the student's use of learning time, including overt attention to the task and amount of covert relevant thinking during the learning situation. Several indexes of both overt and covert time-on-task were found to correlate in the .50s and .60s with final achievement in college courses and with learning gains as measured by achievement tests. This finding has been repeatedly corroborated by several investigations with elementary and high school students, covering time spent in both school work and homework (Bennett, 1976; Berliner, 1979; Denham & Liberman, 1980, chaps. 2, 3; Keith, 1982; Lerner, 1981; Tang & Baumeister, 1984).

ATTENTION CONTROL

The control and regulation of attention plays an important part in intellectual development. What one attends to, how deeply attention is focused, and how long attention is sustained contribute to one's cognitive growth. The selectivity of attention leads to selective learning—and this selection will differ among persons exposed to the same immediate situation. Such selective learning, moreover, may influence the relative development of different aptitudes and the formation of varied trait patterns (Anastasi, 1970, 1983).

Research on the reciprocal relation between affect and attention suggests that the regulation of attention is related both to mood at the time and to individual differences in more stable personality traits (Hamilton, 1981). The cognitive, information-processing act in attention is accompanied by an affective continuum extending from absorption, concentration, and intrinsic task enjoyment to boredom, mind wandering, day dreaming, and distractibility.

Another area of relevant research is concerned with response styles, notably reflection-impulsivity (Messer, 1976). First described by Kagan and his associates (Kagan, Rosman, Day, Albert, & Phillips, 1964), reflection-impulsivity is usually measured by presenting drawings of familiar figures along with several facsimiles differing in one or more details. Impulsives are identified as those who respond quickly and make many errors, while the reflectives respond more slowly with fewer errors. Time and error scores are negatively correlated, the size of the correlations increasing with age. This negative correlation is not found among preschoolers, however, who appear not to have developed the strategy of delaying their response in order to scrutinize details. Such children also show no evidence of the motive to perform well on an assigned task, which may be an antecedent for reflective behavior.

The reflective style has been investigated in relation to many behavioral variables (Brodzinsky, 1982; Lee, Vaughn, & Kopp, 1983; Messer, 1976). Reflectives excel on several tests of memory and reasoning of the type used to assess intelligence. They tend to sustain attention longer on a task than do impulsives. They are better able to delay motor responses, and they exhibit more self-control than do impulsives in situations involving delay of gratification. There is also some evidence that impulsivity is associated with school failure, learning disabilities, and reading problems.

It should be noted that attention control is related to time-on-task, and especially to covert time-on-task. Basically, the several aspects of attention control serve to intensify the effect of time devoted to relevant activities and contribute more potently to aptitude development.

ENVIRONMENTAL MASTERY

A third type of mechanism whereby affect can influence cognitive development may be most succinctly described as the motivation for environmental mastery. Although applicable throughout the life span, this mechanism has been studied most thoroughly at the infant level, as well as in animal research (see, e.g., Woodworth, 1958, pp. 79–88). Different investigators have described the relevant behavior as stimulus seeking, sensation seeking, exploration, environmental manipulation, and spontaneous play. Each of these terms singles out some specific manifestation of the class of behaviors under consideration. Some writers have introduced the concepts of competence motivation (R. W. White, 1959, 1960) and mastery motivation (Yarrow et al., 1983), which focus on the individual's achieving control over his or her environment. Still others have been concerned with the limitations of traditional need-reduction theories of motivation, which consider basic organic drives such as hunger, thirst, and sex the ultimate sources of all motivation. These writers have argued, with considerable supporting evidence, that there is another major source of motivation variously described as outgoing motivation, intrinsic motivation, experience-producing motivation, and information-processing motivation (Harlow, 1950; Hayes, 1962; Hunt, 1965, 1969; Taylor, 1960; Woodworth, 1958).

There is an impressive accumulation of both empirical and theoretical literature pertaining to environmental-mastery motivation. For our purposes, we can describe environmental-mastery behavior as including the observation, exploration, manipulation, and control of one's environment. Such behavior begins with the infant's earliest efforts to gain information from his or her world through visual fixation of objects. Visual observation is soon combined with auditory and tactual exploration. There is evidence to suggest that such exploratory behavior is not a general, random response to stimulation but is a specific way of processing relevant information. The child's behavior tends to be appropriate to particular changes in object properties. In one experiment, for example, changes in the texture of stimulus objects evoked an *increase* in time spent in looking and fingering, together with a *decrease* in such behavior as pushing and throwing; changes in shape had the same effects while also evoking an increase in rotating the object and in transferring it from one hand to the other (Ruff, 1984).

Through manipulation, the child also discovers that he or she can affect the environment, as in dropping a block to see it fall and hear it hit the floor, or waving a bell to make it ring. Environmental mastery is later manifested in more complex problem-solving and goal-directed activities. It also expands to include effects on the behavior of caretakers or other associates. In older children and adults, it undoubtedly merges with the achievement drive, which, however, incorporates elements of competition, socially established performance standards, and the attainment of remote goals.

It is apparent that, by its very nature, the motive for environmental mastery should be a prime contributor to cognitive development. And there is increasing evidence in the experimental literature that it does so contribute. Let me cite two major investigations as examples. Burton White at Harvard directed an intensive longitudinal study of a small sample of children during the first six years of life (B. L. White, 1978). Repeated observations and testing revealed several suggestive relationships between early environmental-mastery behavior and later cognitive competence. Specifically, gaining information visually through "steady staring" at 12 to 15 months correlated .85 with Stanford-Binet IQ at 3 years and .70 with IQ on the Wechsler Preschool and Primary Scale of Intelligence (WPPSI) at 5 years. Seeking attention from an adult at 12 to 15 months correlated .61 with Stanford-Binet at age 3 and .60 with WPPSI at age 5.

Leon Yarrow and his associates at the National Institute of Child Health and Human Development report a well-designed study of mastery motivation during the first year of life (Yarrow et al., 1983, 1984). Data were collected at 6 and 12 months with a set of tasks designed to assess three aspects of mastery motivation:

1. effect production—manipulating objects to produce visual or auditory feedback;
2. practicing sensorimotor skills—removing objects from or inserting them into containers;
3. Problem solving—using detours or means-end relationships to obtain toys.

Time was recorded for several indicators of mastery behavior, including latency to involvement with materials, visual attention to materials, exploratory behavior, and persistence on task-related or goal-directed behavior. The Bayley Scales of Infant Development were also administered at 6 and 12 months in order to investigate concurrent and cross-age relations between mastery motivation and developmental competence. The results suggested that a child's motivation for mastery may be a better predictor of later competence than are earlier measures of competence. Another finding pertains to developmental transformations in the expression of mastery motivation from 6 to 12 months. There was a temporal progression in both the tasks that elicited this behavior and the kind of behavior elicited, such as visual regard, exploration, and persistence.

HEREDITY, ENVIRONMENT, AND THE QUESTION "HOW?"

Even before individual differences in aptitudes could be empirically assessed, the source of these differences in the individual's heredity and past environment was vigorously debated—and the debate continues. Some 25 years ago, I suggested that investigators may have been asking the wrong questions about heredity and environment and that a more fruitful approach might be to ask the question "How?" (Anastasi, 1958b). Rather than asking *which* differences are hereditary and which acquired, or *how much* of the variance is attributable to heredity and how much to environment, it would be better to investigate the modus operandi of hereditary and environmental influences in the development of individual differences. What is the chain of events whereby particular hereditary and environmental factors interact to produce the behavioral differences observed at any given stage of individual development?

Some investigators have proposed that the effect of genes on aptitudes may be mediated by affective or motivational factors (Dreger, 1968; Hayes, 1962; Scarr, 1981). That genes could *directly* determine

individual differences in, for example, verbal or mathematical aptitude seems unlikely in the light of current knowledge about the development of human behavior. What is needed is more information
about the many intervening steps in the etiological chain of events
from genes to behavior. The role of motivation may represent one
such step.

Although several investigators have acknowledged the contribution of motivation to intellectual development, its primary role in this
regard was most explicitly recognized by Hayes (1962), who wrote,
"Intelligence is acquired by learning, and inherited motivational
makeup influences the kind and amount of learning which occurs.
The hereditary basis of intelligence consists of drives, rather than
abilities as such" (p. 302). Hayes went on to discuss experience-
producing drives and cited evidence for genetically controlled motivational differences between strains from several species, whether
naturally occurring or produced by selective breeding.

An early example is provided by Searle's (1949) study of rats from
the maze-bright and maze-dull strains developed by R. C. Tryon
(1940). Searle's findings demonstrated that the two strains differed in
several emotional and motivational factors rather than in general ability. Further evidence is reported by Scott and Fuller (1951) from an
extensive project on learning and other behaviors of several breeds
and cross-breeds of dogs. The authors concluded that "differences in
performance are produced by differences in emotional, motivational,
and peripheral processes, and that genetically caused differences in
central processes may be either slight or non-existent" (p. 29). The
investigators also identified breed differences in physiological characteristics, which could in turn be related to the observed behavioral
differences.

More recently, Scarr (1981) also offered a motivationally oriented
theory of cognitive differences. On the basis of extensive research on
early childhood development, she proposed that "intellectual competence is best seen as the result of a motivationally determined history of learning" (p. 1160), and she stressed "the role of the genotype
in determining which environments actually *become* experiences"
(p. 1162) in an individual's learning history.

Data on the possible organic bases of affective behavior are more
difficult to obtain for humans than for other species. However, some
notable efforts have been made in this direction, particularly in regard to impulsivity, sensation seeking, and anxiety (Zuckerman,
1983). An example is provided by research on the biological correlates

of sensation seeking, recently reviewed by Zuckerman, Buchsbaum, and Murphy (1980). The studies surveyed dealt principally with a sensation-seeking scale designed for college students and other adult groups. Performance on this scale was investigated in relation to the orienting reflex (also observed in animals and infants) and in relation to biological variables, including average evoked potentials and certain endogenous biochemicals. The authors suggest that exploratory behavior may represent a balance between sensation seeking and fearfulness or anxiety.

It is apparent that an optimum level of sensation seeking is most conducive to intellectual pursuits, while either extreme tends to be associated with pathological conditions. Moreover, it seems likely that sensation seeking exhibits developmental transformations, as is true of other experience-producing drives (e.g., Eichorn et al., 1981; Hayes, 1962; McCall, 1976; Yarrow et al., 1983). Both the specific manifestations of these drives and their effects on cognitive development probably differ from one age level to another. In our efforts to trace the etiology of individual differences in aptitudes, we cannot expect simple answers. It should also be recognized that to identify an experience-producing drive as a source of cognitive development does not in itself demonstrate a genetic origin; nor can genetic origin be inferred from the establishment of a biological basis for the behavior under consideration. These findings merely advance the investigation of the etiological chain further toward primary gene effects.

Implications for Sex Differences

INTERACTION OF PHYSICAL AND ATTITUDINAL VARIABLES

Research on sex differences provides a particularly rich source of data on the role of attitudinal and motivational variables in the development of aptitude differences. In human societies, physical differences between females and males often interact with attitudinal variables in the individual's cognitive development. It has long been recognized, at least by some investigators, that hereditary physical differences between the sexes are likely to lead to sex differences in experiential and learning histories and may thereby contribute to sex differences in aptitudes. Some of these possible etiological mechanisms were proposed in early surveys of sex differences (Anastasi, 1958a, 1981; Scheinfeld, 1943; Seward, 1946).

One example is provided by the developmental acceleration of the female, a sex difference that begins before birth and extends to maturity. Not only do girls reach puberty earlier than boys, but throughout childhood they are also further advanced toward their own adult status in all physical traits, such as height, weight, and skeletal development. The developmental acceleration of girls in infancy has been offered as one hypothesis to account for their more rapid progress in the acquisition of language, which may give them a head start in verbal development as a whole. Female advantage in manual dexterity and in speed and control of fine movements may also arise initially from developmental acceleration. In general, delicate movements follow gross bodily movements in individual development. Hence girls should develop fine motor coordination at a younger age than boys. These initial, biologically determined sex differences may affect the acquisition of skills and interests, thereby setting in motion a progressive mechanism of differentiation between the sexes.

Another conspicuous set of biological sex differences pertains to general body size, muscular strength, and speed and coordination of gross bodily movements, in all of which males excel. Of course, here as in all other traits, we must not lose sight of the overlapping of distributions. But the mean sex differences in these physical characteristics are certainly conspicuous. Sex differences in gross motor coordination, for example, have been noted from infancy and tend to increase throughout childhood (Gesell et al., 1940). These physical differences may in turn influence the development of specialized interests and aptitudes. For instance, it is possible that boys' superior strength and better coordination encourage them to explore mechanical objects in their early environment and thereby stimulate development of spatial orientation and mechanical aptitudes. Moreover, girls' acceleration in verbal communication, considered together with boys' greater ability to move about and to manipulate objects, may provide a clue to subsequent sex differences in problem-solving approaches. From early childhood, girls may learn to meet problems through social communication, while boys may learn to meet problems by spatial exploration and independent action.

How do culturally transmitted attitudes enter into these etiological chains? The initial advantage enjoyed by each sex in early childhood may be perpetuated through sex-role stereotypes into school-age and adult activities, well beyond the point where the physical differences are themselves relevant to performance in reading, mechanics, and other traditionally sex-typed cognitive domains. Similar cultural perpetuation tends to occur with occupational roles. At one time most occupations required heavy manual labor. Gradually, work activities became more dependent upon symbolic, abstract, verbal, and interpersonal functions, with a minimum of direct physical activity. The development of computers and robotics has greatly accelerated this trend, reducing even further the need for physical labor on the part of the human operator. It is also noteworthy that sex differences in physical performance may themselves have been decreasing in recent decades as a result of changing life experiences. Relevant evidence can be found in an analysis of the records of Olympic athletes from 1934 to 1976 (Lips & Colwill, 1978, p. 148).

SOME RELEVANT MOTIVATIONAL DIFFERENCES

There is an extensive research literature on sex differences in achievement drive (Caplan, 1979; Stein & Bayley, 1973), self-confidence (Lenney, 1977), causal attribution of personal success and failure (Dweck & Bush, 1976; Dweck, Davidson, Nelson, & Enna, 1978; Nash, 1979), and other personality variables that have implications for cognitive growth. The results illustrate the hazards of simplistic interpretations. Whether men or women excel in the attitudes that are conducive to the development of particular aptitudes depends on other interacting variables. In achievement motivation, for example, both sexes strive for excellence and success in tasks that they perceive as appropriate to their sex roles. The desire for social approval—from one's peers, or from authority figures, or both—strengthens the expression of achievement drive in sex-appropriate activities by both sexes. Considerable attention has been given to so-called fear of success, or motive to avoid success, particularly among women (Horner, 1972; Spence, 1974). Actually, what is involved is fear of deviating from accepted sex-role standards and the adverse social consequences of such deviance. This reaction to nontraditional roles characterizes males as well as females (Nash, 1979, pp. 275–279).

Research results on self-confidence, causal attributions, and learned helplessness can also be best understood in the light of perceived sex-role appropriateness and social consequences. A frequently cited finding is that males are more likely to attribute success to their own ability and failure to unstable factors such as luck or effort, while the reverse occurs among females. Such attributions, either by the individual performer or by teachers or other evaluators, have obvious implications for the individual's future motivation in similar tasks. Sex differences in outcome attribution, however, are moderated by several concomitant variables, such as type of task, availability and nature of feedback, and (in the case of schoolchildren) whether feedback is provided by teachers or by age peers.

Research on creativity also provides some relevant data. In one investigation with college students (Harrington & Andersen, 1981), scores on several scales designed to assess creative self-concept correlated positively with masculinity scores for *both* sexes; the mean correlations were .55 for men and .52 for women. Correlations of creative self-concept with femininity scores were negative and much lower for both sexes; mean correlations were -.30 for men and -.06 for women. Essentially, these results indicated that the self-reported personality traits that significantly differentiate the more creative from the less creative persons in various fields resemble more closely the traits traditionally associated with men than the traits traditionally associated with women.

Sex differences in interests and in value systems have been investigated over many decades. Several of these differences are in areas that have obvious relevance to cognitive achievement and to the development of aptitudes. For example, in a major research project on mathematically talented adolescents (Fox, 1976; Fox, Tobin, & Brody, 1979), the participants took the Allport-Vernon-Lindzey Study of Values. On this instrument, the percentage of boys obtaining their highest score in the theoretical value was more than double the percentage of girls who did so. Most of the girls scored highest in the social value. The theoretical scale also differentiated the highly precocious boys from the less precocious boys in the group. The sex difference in the value system was proposed as one possible reason for the much smaller proportion of girls than boys who took advantage of the accelerated mathematics classes offered to the project participants.

APTITUDES IN RELATION TO MOTIVATIONAL VARIABLES

There is a small but growing number of studies on sex differences that analyzed the direct relation between motivational variables and aptitudes. In one of the earliest of these studies (Milton, 1957), total problem-solving scores correlated significantly with Terman-Miles masculinity scores; this relation was found not only in the combined sex groups but also within each sex. In other words, the women with the

Reciprocal Relations between Cognitive and Affective Development

more masculine scores on the Terman-Miles were better problem solvers than those with the more feminine scores; and the same relation held among the men.

Similar correlations with global masculinity-femininity scores have been reported for tests of spatial aptitudes. This cluster of aptitudes has been studied extensively in relation to biological, psychological, and cultural variables (McGee, 1979, 1982; Nash, 1979; Newcombe, 1982). At least two distinct spatial factors have been identified, commonly designated spatial visualization and spatial orientation. Training and experiential history may play an important role in the development of individual and group differences in spatial aptitudes (Berry, 1966; Connor, Serbin, & Schackman, 1977; MacArthur, 1967; Nash, 1979). Male superiority in spatial aptitudes has been found with considerable consistency, especially in adolescent and adult groups. The significance and magnitude of the sex difference, however, varies with the nature of the test, particularly as regards its factorial composition, dimensionality, and other process variables (Wattanawaha & Clements, 1982). The cognitive style known as field dependency has been shown to have a strong spatial-aptitude component. Several investigators report substantial positive correlation of masculinity scores on sex-role inventories with performance on spatial aptitude tests, as well as with field independence as measured by Embedded-Figure and Rod-and-Frame tests. Again this relation holds within each sex group, as well as in the combined groups (Nash, 1979; Vaught, 1965).

More recent studies on verbal and quantitative aptitudes, using more sophisticated methodology and more clearly defined constructs, have found similar relations. For instance, in an investigation of schoolchildren from the 2nd to the 12th grade, reading and arithmetic scores on standardized achievement batteries proved to be more a function of the child's perception of these subjects as sex-appropriate or sex-inappropriate than of the child's own sex, individual preference for masculine or feminine sex role, or personal liking or disliking for reading or arithmetic (Dwyer, 1974). In another study (Fitzpatrick, 1978), the achievement of bright 10th-grade girls in mathematics, as assessed by both grades and standardized tests, was significantly related to the students' attitudes toward various aspects of the female role. Those girls showing a more liberal orientation on the women's role scale performed better in mathematics than did those with a more traditional orientation.

Recent surveys of the research on sex differences in reading among schoolchildren suggest that, although more than one hypothesis may be needed to account for these differences, perceived sex-appropriateness of reading appears to be one of the most promising explanations (Bank, Biddle, & Good, 1980; Nash, 1979). Cross-cultural investigations also tend to support this hypothesis. Studies in England and Germany, for example, did not reveal the sex difference in reading performance found among American schoolchildren, and this finding was consistent with sex-role perceptions across these cultures (Nash, 1979).

Sex differences in mathematical aptitudes have received particular attention by researchers. Lynn Fox and her co-workers (Fox, Brody, & Tobin, 1980; Fox, Tobin, & Brody, 1979) have written extensively on the sources of sex differences in math performance, drawing in part on a long-term project with mathematically precocious youth. Sex differences in math aptitude tests are greatly reduced when math course-taking is controlled. But approaching the problem from another direction, we find that males and females with the same initial tested ability in math function differently with regard to subsequent course selection, course attrition, and acceleration. Although some of these course-taking differences result from external pressures, personal choice significantly affects the decisions. Conspicuous sex differences in math interests and attitudes, as well as performance, begin to appear by the seventh grade.

Research by other investigators sheds some further light on these findings. A longitudinal study of over 1,000 schoolchildren in Grades 1 to 3 (Entwisle & Baker, 1983) demonstrated that girls developed lower performance expectations for math than did boys, even though in the first three grades there were no significant overall sex differences in either arithmetic marks or standardized achievement tests in arithmetic. Cross-age analyses of data for individuals supported the hypothesis that parental expectations regarding math achievement influence children's own expectations and that both influence their marks. Another longitudinal study was concerned with changes from Grades 8 to 11, as assessed by a set of specially chosen ability and attitudinal measures (Sherman, 1980). The results again demonstrated sex differences in attitudes toward math and the effect of such attitudes on subsequent math achievement. For example, the more a girl stereotyped math as a male domain in Grade 8, the lower was her math problem-solving score in Grade 11 and the lower was her reported confidence in learning math in Grade 11.

In closing this chapter, and particularly this section on implications for sex differences, there is one more point I want to emphasize. In many cultures today, the social climate and the expectations regarding sex roles have been changing conspicuously. Insofar as attitudes about sex-appropriateness of performance domains alter, we would expect sex differences in aptitudes to show corresponding changes (Anastasi, 1981). Current societal restructurings regarding the position of men and women thus provide one more natural quasi-experiment to investigate the etiology of human behavior—one more opportunity to try and learn *how* the individual differences come about.

REFERENCES

Abramson, L. Y., Seligman, M. E. P., & Teasdale, J. D. (1978). Learned helplessness in humans: Critique and reformulation. *Journal of Abnormal Psychology, 87,* 49–74.
Anastasi, A. (1958a). *Differential psychology* (3rd ed.). New York: Macmillan.
Anastasi, A. (1958b). Heredity, environment, and the question "How?" *Psychological Review, 65,* 197–208.
Anastasi, A. (1970). On the formation of psychological traits. *American Psychologist, 25,* 899–910.
Anastasi, A. (1981). Sex differences: Historical perspectives and methodological implications. *Developmental Review, 1,* 187–206.
Anastasi, A. (1982). *Psychological testing* (5th ed.). New York: Macmillan.
Anastasi, A. (1983). Evolving trait concepts. *American Psychologist, 38,* 175–184.
Antaki, C., & Brewin, C. (Eds.). (1982). *Attributions and psychological change: Applications of attributional theories to clinical and educational practice.* New York: Academic Press.
Atkinson, J. W. (1974). Motivational determinants of intellective performance and cumulative achievement. In J. W. Atkinson & J. O. Raynor, (Eds.), *Motivation and achievement* (pp. 389–410). Washington, DC: Winston.
Atkinson, J. W., & Feather, N. T. (Eds.). (1966). *A theory of achievement motivation.* New York: Wiley.
Atkinson, J. W., O'Malley, P. M., & Lens, W. (1976). Motivation and ability: Interactive psychological determinants of intellective performance, educational achievement, and each other. In W. H. Sewell, R. M. Hauser, & D. L. Featherman (Eds.), *Schooling and achievement in American society* (pp. 29–60). New York: Academic Press.
Atkinson, J. W., & Raynor, J. O. (Eds.). (1974). *Motivation and achievement.* Washington, DC: Winston.

Bandura, A. (1982). Self-efficacy mechanism in human agency. *American Psychologist, 37,* 122–147.

Bank, B. J., Biddle, B. J., & Good, T. L. (1980). Sex roles, classroom instruction, and reading achievement. *Journal of Educational Psychology, 72,* 119–132.

Beck, A. T. (1970). *Depression: Causes and treatment.* Philadelphia: University of Pennsylvania Press.

Beck, A. T. (1974). The development of depression: A cognitive model. In R. J. Friedman & M. M. Katz (Eds.), *The psychology of depression: Contemporary theory and research* (pp. 3–27). Washington, DC: Winston.

Bennett, N. (1976). *Teaching styles and pupil progress.* Cambridge, MA: Harvard University Press.

Bentler, P. M. (1980). Multivariate analysis with latent variables: Causal modeling. *Annual Review of Psychology, 31,* 419–456.

Berliner, D. C. (1979). Tempus educare. In P. L. Peterson & H. J. Walberg (Eds.), *Research on teaching: Concepts, findings, and implications* (pp. 120–135). Berkeley, CA: McCutchan.

Berry, J. W. (1966). Temne and Eskimo. *International Journal of Psychology, 1,* 207–229.

Birns, B., & Golden, M. (1972). Prediction of intellectual performance at 3 years from infant test and personality measures. *Merrill-Palmer Quarterly, 18,* 53–58.

Bloom, B. S. (1976). *Human characteristics and school learning.* New York: McGraw-Hill.

Bower, G. H. (1981). Mood and memory. *American Psychologist, 36,* 129–148.

Bower, G. H., & Cohen, P. R. (1982). Emotional influences in memory and thinking: Data and theory. In M. S. Clark & S. T. Fiske (Eds.), *Affect and cognition: The Seventeenth Annual Carnegie Symposium on Cognition* (pp. 291–331). Hillsdale, NJ: Lawrence Erlbaum Associates.

Brodzinsky, D. M. (1982). Relationship between cognitive style and cognitive development: A 2-year longitudinal study. *Developmental Psychology, 18,* 617–626.

Caplan, P. J. (1979). Beyond the box score: A boundary condition for sex differences in aggression and achievement striving. In B. A. Maher (Ed.), *Progress in experimental personality research* (Vol. 9, pp. 41–87). New York: Academic Press.

Clark, M. S., & Fiske, S. T. (Eds.). (1982). *Affect and cognition: The Seventeenth Annual Carnegie Symposium on Cognition.* Hillsdale, NJ: Lawrence Erlbaum Associates.

Coleman, J. S., et al. (1966). *Equality of educational opportunity.* Washington, DC: U.S. Government Printing Office.

Connor, J. M., Serbin, L. A., & Schackman, M. (1977). Sex differences in children's response to training on a visual-spatial test. *Developmental Psychology, 13,* 293–294.

Coopersmith, S. (1981a). *The antecedents of self-esteem*. Palo Alto, CA: Consulting Psychologists Press. (Original work published 1967.)

Coopersmith, S. (1981b). *Self-Esteem Inventories*. Palo Alto, CA: Consulting Psychologists Press.

Crandall, V. C., Katkowsky, W., & Crandall, V. J. (1965). Children's beliefs in their own control of reinforcement in intellectual-academic achievement situations. *Child Development, 36*, 91–109.

Crandall, V. J., Katkowsky, W., & Preston, A. (1962). Motivational and ability determinants of young children's intellectual achievement behaviors. *Child Development, 33*, 643–661.

Culler, R. E., & Holahan, C. J. (1980). Test anxiety and academic performance: The effects of study-related behavior. *Journal of Educational Psychology, 72*, 16–20.

Curran, J. P., & Cattell, R. B. (1976). *Eight State Questionnaire (8 SQ)*. Champaign, IL: Institute for Personality and Ability Testing.

Denham, C., & Liberman, A. (Eds.). (1980). *Time to learn*. Washington, DC: National Institute of Education.

Dreger, R. M. (1968). General temperament and personality factors related to intellectual performance. *Journal of Genetic Psychology, 113*, 275–293.

Dweck, C. S., & Bush, E. S. (1976). Sex differences in learned helplessness: I. Differential debilitation with peer and adult evaluators. *Developmental Psychology, 12*, 147–156.

Dweck, C. S., Davidson, W., Nelson, S., & Enna, B. (1978). Sex differences in learned helplessness: II. The contingencies of evaluative feedback in the classroom and III. An experimental analysis. *Developmental Psychology, 14*, 268–276.

Dwyer, C. A. (1974). Influence of children's sex role standards on reading and arithmetic achievement. *Journal of Educational Psychology, 66*, 811–816.

Eichorn, D. H., Clausen, J. A., Haan, N., Honzik, M P., & Mussen, P. H. (Eds.). (1981). *Present and past in middle life*. New York: Academic Press.

Ellis, H. C., Thomas, R. L., & Rodriguez, I. A. (1984). Emotional mood states and memory: Elaborative encoding, semantic processing, and cognitive effort. *Journal of Experimental Psychology: Learning, Memory, and Cognition, 10*, 470–482.

Entwisle, D. R., & Baker, D. P. (1983). Gender and young children's performance in arithmetic. *Developmental Psychology, 19*, 200–209.

Fitzpatrick, J. L. (1978). Academic underachievement, other-direction, and attitudes toward women's roles in bright adolescent females. *Journal of Educational Psychology, 70*, 645–650.

Fox, L. H. (1976). The values of gifted youth. In D. P. Keating (Ed.), *Intellectual talent: Research and development* (pp. 273–284). Baltimore, MD: Johns Hopkins University Press.

Fox, L. H., Brody, L., & Tobin, D. (Eds.). (1980). *Women and the mathematical mystique*. Baltimore, MD: Johns Hopkins University Press.

Fox, L. H., Tobin, D., & Brody, L. (1979). Sex role socialization and achievement in mathematics. In M. A. Wittig & A. C. Petersen (Eds.), *Sex-related differences in cognitive functioning: Developmental issues* (pp. 303–325). New York: Academic Press.

Fyans, L. J., Jr. (Ed.). (1980). *Achievement motivation: Recent trends in theory and research.* New York: Plenum.

Gesell, A., et al. (1940). *The first five years of life.* New York: Harper.

Hamilton, J. A. (1981). Attention, personality, and the self-regulation of mood: Absorbing interest and boredom. In B. A. Maher & W. B. Maher (Eds.), *Progress in experimental personality research* (Vol. 10, pp. 281–315). New York: Academic Press.

Harlow, H. F. (1950). Learning and satiation of response to intrinsically motivated complex puzzle performance by monkeys. *Journal of Comparative and Physiological Psychology, 43,* 289–294.

Harrington, D. M., & Andersen, S. M. (1981). Creativity, masculinity, femininity, and three models of psychological androgeny. *Journal of Personality and Social Psychology, 41,* 744–757.

Haviland, J. (1976). Looking smart: The relationship between affect and intelligence in infancy. In M. Lewis (Ed.), *Origins of intelligence* (pp. 353–377). New York: Plenum.

Hayes, K. J. (1962). Genes, drives, and intellect. *Psychological Reports, 10,* 299–342.

Herrenkohl, R. C. (1972). Factor-analytic and criterion study of achievement orientation. *Journal of Educational Psychology, 63,* 314–326.

Hettena, C. M., & Ballif, B. L. (1981). Effects of mood on learning. *Journal of Educational Psychology, 73,* 505–508.

Horner, M. S. (1972). The motive to avoid success and changing aspirations of college women. In J. M. Bardwick (Ed.), *Readings on the psychology of women* (pp. 62–67). New York: Harper & Row.

Hunt, J. McV. (1965). Intrinsic motivation and its role in psychological development. In D. Levine (Ed.), *Nebraska Symposium on Motivation* (Vol. 13, pp. 189–282). Lincoln: University of Nebraska Press.

Hunt, J. McV. (1969). The epigenesis of intrinsic motivation and the fostering of early cognitive development. In J. McV. Hunt, *The challenge of incompetence and poverty* (pp. 94–111). Urbana: University of Illinois Press.

Isen, A. M., Means, B., Patrick, R., & Nowicki, G. (1982). Some factors influencing decision-making strategy and risk taking. In M. S. Clark & S. T. Fiske (Eds.), *Affect and cognition: The Seventeenth Annual Carnegie Symposium on Cognition* (pp. 243–261). Hillsdale, NJ: Lawrence Erlbaum Associates.

Jackson, D. N., Ahmed, S. A., & Heapy, N. A. (1976). Is achievement a unitary construct? *Journal of Research in Personality, 10,* 1–21.

Jordan, T. J. (1981). Self-concepts, motivation, and academic achievement of black adolescents. *Journal of Educational Psychology, 73,* 509–517.

Kagan, J., Rosman, B. L., Day, D., Albert, J., & Phillips, W. (1964). Information processing in the child: Significance of analytic and reflective attitudes. *Psychological Monographs, 78* (1, Whole No. 578).

Keith, T. Z. (1982). Time spent on homework and high school grades: A large-sample path analysis. *Journal of Educational Psychology, 74,* 248–253.

Lee, M., Vaughn, B. E., & Kopp, C. B. (1983). Role of self-control in the performance of very young children on a delayed-response memory-for-location task. *Journal of Developmental Psychology, 19,* 40–44.

Lefcourt, H. M. (1982). *Locus of control: Current trends in theory and research.* (2nd ed.). Hillsdale, NJ: Lawrence Erlbaum Associates.

Leight, K. A., & Ellis, H. C. (1981). Emotional mood states, strategies, and state-dependency in memory. *Journal of Verbal Learning and Verbal Behavior, 20,* 251–266.

Lenney, E. (1977). Women's self-confidence in achievement settings. *Psychological Bulletin, 84,* 1–13.

Lens, W., Atkinson, J. W., & Yip, A. G. (1979). *Academic achievement in high school related to "intelligence" and motivation as measured in sixth, ninth, and twelfth grade boys and girls.* Unpublished manuscript, University of Michigan, Ann Arbor.

Lerner, B. (1981). The minimum competence testing movement: Social, scientific, and legal implications. *American Psychologist, 36,* 1057–1066.

Lips, H. M., & Colwill, N. L. (1978). *The psychology of sex differences.* Englewood Cliffs, NJ: Prentice-Hall.

Lubin, B. (1967). *Depression Adjective Check List.* San Diego, CA: Educational and Industrial Testing Service.

MacArthur, R. (1967). Sex differences in field dependence for the Eskimo: Replication of Berry's findings. *International Journal of Psychology, 2,* 139–140.

Matheny, A. P., Dolan, A. B., & Wilson, R. S. (1974). Bayley's Infant Behavior Record: Relations between behaviors and mental test scores. *Developmental Psychology, 10,* 696–702.

McCall, R. B. (1976). Toward an epigenetic conception of mental development in the first three years of life. In M. Lewis (Ed.), *Origins of intelligence* (pp. 97–122). New York: Plenum.

McCarthy, D. (1944). A study of the reliability of the Goodenough drawing test of intelligence. *Journal of Psychology, 18,* 201–216.

McClelland, D. C. (1976). *The achieving society.* New York: Irvington. (Original work published 1961.)

McClelland, D. C., Atkinson, J. W., Clark, R. A., & Lowell, L. (1976). *The achievement motive.* New York: Irvington. (Original work published 1953.)

McGee, M. G. (1979). Human spatial abilities: Psychometric studies and environmental, genetic, hormonal, and neurological influences. *Psychological Bulletin, 86,* 889–918.

McGee, M. G. (1982). Spatial abilities: The influence of genetic factors. In

M. Potegal (Ed.), *Spatial abilities: Development and physiological foundations* (pp. 199–222). New York: Academic Press.

McNair, D. M., Lorr, M., & Droppleman, L. F. (1971). *Profile of Mood States (POMS)*. San Diego, CA: Educational and Industrial Testing Service.

Messer, S. B. (1976). Reflection-impulsivity: A review. *Psychological Bulletin, 83*, 1026–1052.

Messick, S. (1965). The impact of negative affect on cognition and personality. In S. S. Tomkins & C. E. Izard (Eds.), *Affect, cognition, and personality* (pp. 98–128). New York: Springer-Verlag.

Milton, G. A. (1957). The effects of sex-role identification upon problem-solving skills. *Journal of Abnormal and Social Psychology, 55*, 208–212.

Morris, L. W., Davis, M. A., & Hutchings, C. H. (1981). Cognitive and emotional components of anxiety: Literature review and a revised worry-emotionality scale. *Journal of Educational Psycholo y, 73*, 541–555.

Murray, H. A. (1938). *Explorations in personality*. New York: Oxford University Press.

Nash, S.C. (1979). Sex role as a mediator of intellectual functioning. In M. A. Wittig & A. C. Petersen (Eds.), *Sex-related differences in cognitive functioning: Developmental issues* (pp. 263–302). New York: Academic Press.

Newcombe, N. (1982). Sex-related differences in spatial ability: Problems and gaps in current approaches. In M. Potegal (Ed.), *Spatial abilities: Development and physiological foundations* (pp. 223–250). New York: Academic Press.

Plant, W. T., & Minium, E. W. (1967). Differential personality development in young adults of markedly different aptitude levels. *Journal of Educational Psychology, 58*, 141–152.

Rosenberg, M. (1963). The association between self-esteem and anxiety. *Psychiatric Research, 1*, 135–152.

Rosenberg, M. (1965). *Society and the adolescent self-image*. Princeton, NJ: Princeton University Press.

Rotter, J. B. (1966). Generalized expectancies for internal versus external control of reinforcement. *Psychological Monographs, 80* (1, Whole No. 609).

Ruff, H. A. (1984). Infants' manipulative exploration of objects: Effects of age and object characteristics. *Developmental Psychology, 20*, 9–20.

Sarason, I. G. (Ed.). (1980). *Test anxiety: Theory, research, and applications*. Hillsdale, NJ: Lawrence Erlbaum Associates.

Scarr, S. (1981). Testing for children: Assessment and the many determinants of intellectual competence. *American Psychologist, 36*, 1159–1166.

Scheinfeld, A. (1943). *Women and men*. New York: Harcourt, Brace.

Scott, J. P., & Fuller, J. L. (1951). Research on genetics and social behavior at the Roscoe B. Jackson Memorial Laboratory, 1946–1951—A progress report. *Journal of Heredity, 42*, 191–197.

Searle, L. V. (1949). The organization of hereditary maze-brightness and maze-dullness. *Genetic Psychology Monographs, 39*, 279–325.

Seward, G. H. (1946). *Sex and the social order*. New York: McGraw-Hill.

Shavelson, R. J., & Bolus, R. (1982). Self-concept: The interplay of theory and methods. *Journal of Educational Psychology, 74*, 3–17.

Shavelson, R. J., Hubner, J. J., & Stanton, J. C. (1976). Self-concept: Validation of construct interpretations. *Review of Educational Research, 46*, 407–441.

Shavelson, R. J., & Stuart, K. R. (1981). Application of causal modeling to the validation of self-concept interpretations of test scores. In M. D. Lynch, A. A. Norem-Hebeisen, & K. J. Gergen (Eds.), *Self-concept: Advances in theory and research* (pp. 223–235). Cambridge, MA: Ballinger.

Sherman, J. (1980). Mathematics, spatial visualization, and related factors: Changes in girls and boys, Grades 8–11. *Journal of Educational Psychology, 72*, 476–482.

Spence, J. T. (1974). Thematic apperception and attitudes toward achievement in women: A new look at the motive to avoid success and a new method of measurement. *Journal of Consulting and Clinical Psychology, 42*, 427–437.

Spielberger, C. D., Gonzales, H. P., & Fletcher, T. (1979). Test anxiety reduction, learning strategies, and academic performance. In H. F. O'Neil, Jr., and C. D. Spielberger (Eds.), *Cognitive and affective learning strategies* (pp. 111–131). New York: Academic Press.

Spielberger, C. D., Gorsuch, R. L., & Lushene, R. E. (1970). *STAI manual for the State-Trait Anxiety Inventory*. Palo Alto, CA: Consulting Psychologists Press.

Spielberger, C. D., Vagg, P. R., Barker, L. R., Donham, G. W., & Westberry, L. G. (1980). The factor structure of the State-Trait Anxiety Inventory. In I. G. Sarason & C. D. Spielberger (Eds.), *Stress and anxiety* (Vol. 7, pp. 95–109). New York: Hemisphere.

Stein, A. H., & Bayley, M. M. (1973). The socialization of achievement orientation in females. *Psychological Bulletin, 80*, 345–366.

Tang, T. Li-P., & Baumeister, R. F. (1984). Effects of personal values, perceived surveillance, and task labels on task preference: The ideology of turning play into work. *Journal of Applied Psychology, 69*, 99–105.

Taylor, D. W. (1960). Toward an information-processing theory of motivation. In M. R. Jones (Ed.), *Nebraska Symposium on Motivation* (Vol. 8, pp. 51–78). Lincoln: University of Nebraska Press.

Tomkins, S. S., & Izard, C. E. (Eds.). (1965). *Affect, cognition, and personality*. New York: Springer-Verlag.

Tryon, G. S. (1980). The measurement and treatment of test anxiety. *Review of Educational Research, 50*, 343–372.

Tryon, R. C. (1940). Genetic differences in maze-learning ability in rats. *Yearbook of the National Society for the Study of Education, 39*, Part 1, 111–119.

Uguroglu, M. E., & Walberg, H. J. (1979). Motivation and achievement: A quantitative synthesis. *American Educational Research Journal, 16*, 375–389.

Vance, E. T. (1973). Social disability. *American Psychologist, 28,* 498–512.

Vaught, G. M. (1965). The relationship of role identification and ego strength to sex differences in the Rod-and-Frame Test. *Journal of Personality, 33,* 271–283.

Walden, T. A., & Ramey, C. T. (1983). Locus of control and academic achievement: Results from a preschool intervention program. *Journal of Educational Psychology, 75,* 347–358.

Wattanawaha, N., & Clements, M. A. (1982). Qualitative aspects of sex-related differences in performance on pencil-and-paper spatial questions, Grades 7–9. *Journal of Educational Psychology, 74,* 878–887.

Weiner, B. (1982). The emotional consequences of causal attributions. In M. S. Clark & S. T. Fiske (Eds.), *Affect and cognition: The Seventeenth Annual Carnegie Symposium on Cognition* (pp. 135–209). Hillsdale, NJ: Lawrence Erlbaum Associates.

White, B. L. (1978). *Experience and environment: Major influences on the development of the young child* (Vol. 2). Englewood Cliffs, NJ: Prentice-Hall.

White, R. W. (1959). Motivation reconsidered: The concept of competence. *Psychological Review, 66,* 297–333.

White, R. W. (1960). Competence and the psychological stages of development. In M. R. Jones (Ed.), *Nebraska Symposium on Motivation* (Vol. 8, pp. 97–141). Lincoln: University of Nebraska Press.

Wilson, R. S., & Matheny, A. P., Jr. (1983). Assessment of temperament in infant twins. *Developmental Psychology, 19,* 172–183.

Woodworth, R. S. (1958). *Dynamics of behavior.* New York: Holt, Rinehart and Winston.

Wylie, R. C. (1979). *The self-concept: Vol. 2. Theory and research on selected topics.* Lincoln: University of Nebraska Press.

Yarrow, L. J., Macturk, R. H., Vietze, P. M., McCarthy, M. E., Klein, R. P., & McQuiston, S. (1984). Developmental course of parental stimulation and its relationship to mastery motivation during infancy. *Developmental Psychology, 20,* 492–503.

Yarrow, L. J., McQuiston, S., MacTurk, R. H., McCarthy, M. E., Klein, R. P., & Vietze, P. M. (1983). Assessment of mastery motivation during the first year of life: Contemporaneous and cross-age relationships. *Developmental Psychology, 19,* 159–171.

Yarrow, L. J., & Pedersen, F. A. (1976). The interplay between cognition and motivation in infancy. In M. Lewis (Ed.), *Origins of intelligence* (pp. 379–399). New York: Plenum.

Zimmerman, B. J., & Ringle, J. (1981). Effects of model persistence and statements of confidence on children's self-efficacy and problem solving. *Journal of Educational Psychology, 73,* 485–493.

Zuckerman, M. (Ed.). (1983). *Biological bases of sensation seeking, impulsivity, and anxiety.* Hillsdale, NJ: Lawrence Erlbaum Associates.

Reciprocal Relations between Cognitive and Affective Development

Zuckerman, M., Buchsbaum, M. S., & Murphy, D. L. (1980). Sensation seeking and its biological correlates. *Psychological Bulletin, 88*, 187–214.

Zuckerman, M., & Lubin, B. (1960–1967). *Multiple Affect Adjective Check List.* San Diego, CA: Educational and Industrial Testing Service.

Gender Differences:
A Biosocial Perspective

Anke A. Ehrhardt

Columbia University and New York
State Psychiatric Institute

Introduction

*T*his paper focuses on gender-related behavior, a field in which evidence is accumulating that both prenatal and postnatal influences have significant effects. Of all prenatal factors to consider, sex hormones are of particular interest for the development of gender. Our knowledge about the effects of sex hormones on the central nervous system has rapidly advanced over the last two decades, making it imperative for behavioral scientists to be familiar with some of the basic principles of neuroendocrinology.

From studies on children exposed to abnormal levels of sex hormones at birth we have learned about some of the possible hormone-behavior relations that may operate within the normal population. However, any potential influence of sex hormones needs to be integrated into an interactive model that takes both constitutional and social-environmental factors into account.

Hormones and Environment: An Interactional Approach

The study of gender-related behavior has to take a multifactorial approach. Our awareness of both biological and psychosocial factors in the analysis of behavior can be considered progress; however, we

A modified version of parts of this paper is included in A. A. Ehrhardt, The psychobiology of gender, in A. S. Rossi (Ed.), *Gender and the life course* (Hawthorne, NY: Aldine Publishing Co., 1985).

are too often tied to searching for the one most important factor to explain a specific behavior unit. The model which is most often applied is the main-effect model. The main-effect model for the study of gender postulates that there is *one* factor, be it hormonal or social-environmental, that most typically determines or predominantly influences behavioral outcome. Accordingly, a defect in the constitution, an abnormality in the prenatal or postnatal hormonal make-up, produces a specific gender identity or disorder, irrespective of the individual's social environment. Or, alternatively, a pathogenic environment will produce a disorder in gender behavior, no matter what the individual's genes, hormones, or sex organs are (Sameroff & Chandler, 1975). The main-effect model has the advantage of being simple, practical for the researcher, and conclusive. However, there are many cases that do not fit a one-factor model.

An alternative approach to the study of gender-related behavior is the dynamic interactional model. This is an interactional model that is not *static* and does not assume that behavior can be explained by any combination of two factors which are fixed rather than dynamic but takes into account that all factors are active participants and interact with each other and are therefore to be thought of as pliable modifiers. It is important to note that such a model does not assume greater directionality in development, that is, a greater etiologic importance of one particular factor. Thus, the constants in development are not hormonal traits on one side and the environmental reaction to these traits on the other, but instead a transactional process in which both sets of factors participate as equal partners.

An interactional approach to gender-related behavior has not been popular in the past. Explanations of gender-related behavior have been heavily influenced by whichever factors, social-environmental or biologic, were in vogue at a particular time. Admittedly, it is tempting to think in dichotomous terms rather than of an interactive model that integrates the relative roles of constitutional and environmental factors. This is in part due to the fact that a dynamic interactional model requires a more complex approach, presenting the investigator with the difficulty of determining the point at which all the important factors necessary to explain a particular behavior have been assessed. To add to the complexity, it is conceivable that between individuals a specific behavior unit may be determined by different chains of events with different sets of factors having more or less importance. This is of course not to imply that there are endless possibilities in the process of behavior development. It seems probable that we will be able to identify common sequences of interactions responsible for shared or typical behavior patterns.

PRINCIPLES OF MAMMALIAN DIFFERENTIATION

Among the many constitutional variables to consider in the area of gender-related behavior, sex hormones are of particular importance. Over the last 20 to 30 years there have been rapid advances in behavioral endocrinology (see review by Beach, 1981). The research on mammalian sexual differentiation is the most exciting area relating to the study of human gender-related behavior. The emerging evidence is based predominantly on the study of rats, mice, guinea pigs, and nonhuman primates.

The methodology for studying the interaction of hormones and behavior as it relates to mammalian sexual differentiation has become highly sophisticated. There has been an increase in the number of species studied, the type of behavioral patterns investigated has become more inclusive and varied, the number of hormones analyzed has increased markedly, and particularly impressive is the greater accuracy of the biochemical techniques used for measuring and controlling endocrine variables. In the modern era of neuroendocrinology, our knowledge has been advanced far beyond the mere fact that hormonal effects have to be mediated via the central nervous system. Recently, structural sex differences in the brain have been demonstrated, steroid receptor cells identified, and the pathways of behaviorally significant hormones described (see review by McEwen, 1983).

The original so-called "central hypothesis" focused on the prominent role of androgens and particularly of testosterone as the most potent of all androgens. It was found that the presence of testosterone during a critical time of development is crucial for male sexual differentiation, while female sexual differentiation ensues in the absence of androgens. This principle was established in the study of normal animals and by experimental hormonal modification of male and female animals. For instance, if you deprive a genetic male of androgen by castration or by treatment with an antagonist to testostrone, a so-called antiandrogen, the development of the reproductive tract goes along female lines. Or conversely, if you provide a female fetus with androgen by injection during the critical time of differentiation, the genitals will become masculinized. Behavior differentiation has been demonstrated as being controlled by the same principle in several subhuman species. The behaviors that have been measured in nonhuman mammals include both sexual behavior and nonreproductive behavior, such as aggressive play fighting, activity, maze learning, sensitivity to taste and pain, and other sex-dimorphic behavior traits. Different sets of behavior could be modified differentially, so that different types of change were distinguished as "defeminization" and "masculinization." The terms were defined by Beach et al. (1972) thus: "*Masculinization* of the female refers to the induction of anatomical, physiological or behavioral characteristics or traits which normally are well developed in males but lacking or poorly developed in females. *Defeminization* signifies partial or complete inhibition of traits normally well developed in females but absent or weakly developed in males."

The importance of distinguishing between so-called masculinization and defeminization became clear when it was found that hormones could modify different behavior sets, that is, so-called masculine behavior sets could be augmented in females by the exposure to androgens without canceling out behavior patterns typical for females, and vice versa.

The central hypothesis of organization also implies a *critical time phase* during which sex hormones can alter CNS differentiation during development. In lower mammals, this phase has been established as prenatal/neonatal, and in nonhuman primates is limited to the prenatal developmental time.

More recently, we have gained knowledge of how testosterone exerts its influence on the brain. We now know that testosterone affects the developing brain in the rat through two pathways. One is by being transformed to estrogen and binding to specific estrogen receptors, a process called aromatization; the other is by so-called 5-alpha-reductase, which is reduction of testosterone to nonaromatizible androgens that bind to different androgen receptors (McEwen, 1983).

We have also learned that different behaviors are influenced by different actions on the brain and that the various sex hormones can antagonize each other; for instance, progesterone can act as an anti-androgen if injected at certain times in development and at certain doses.

Whereas the role of the sex hormones during prenatal/neonatal times has been described as organizational (which means they permanently influence CNS differentiation), sex hormones during adulthood have been labeled as activational, suggesting that they can activate behavior that has been preorganized during development. Sex hormones in adulthood have a facilitatory effect on sex-related responses. In other words, for example, in the rat, androgen is needed for the expression of male behavior, which will occur if there is normal output of testosterone from the animal's testes or if the rat is castrated in adulthood and injected with androgen. However, this effect will occur only if the male fetus and neonate was not deprived of androgen at the critical time of CNS differentiation. The hormonal effect in adulthood has, therefore, been termed temporary and reversible in contrast to the permanent and developmental action of the same hormone during fetal differentiation.

The important principle of the interactional or reciprocal relationship between hormones and environment encompasses the fact that environmental conditions can affect hormonal levels, for instance, the fact that testosterone decreases if a male monkey loses a dominant position in a hierarchy of social relations, or that research on human behavior suggests that stress, physical or psychological, lowers testosterone values temporarily, or the well-known observation that women's menstrual cycles are affected by travel, nutrition, and even by living conditions with other females in a dormitory situation (McClintock, 1971).

What do we know about the application of these principles to the study of human gender-related behavior? We certainly know that one cannot generalize from one species to another; rats and monkeys, for example, differ in some important ways from each other. The question is rather whether one should include any of these established principles of hormones and behavior in nonhuman mammals as researchable hypotheses for the study of human gender-related behavior. I would suggest that one has to pay attention to hormonal variables in order to explain important developmental sequences—provided, of course, that one does not generalize from animal behavior but puts the observation to vigorous tests for human behavior, and provided that one is not seduced by a main-effect model but applies transactional thinking, and provided one uses the sophisticated methods developed by the behavioral endocrinologists for measuring hormones in animal behavior. We must focus on clearly defined behavior units rather than global and complex units—and we must never forget that biological markers are as modifiable as learned behavior.

Examples from several areas of psychoendocrine research will illustrate a biosocial perspective.

Gender Identity

Gender identity is a crucial aspect of a person's development. The definitions of gender identity vary; most of them imply a person's sense of belonging to one sex or the other, male or female. Until about 30 years ago, scientists and clinicians did not use the term "gender," but spoke of sex. Sex was determined by biology, and at that time biology meant structure of gonads, testicular or ovarian. If a person's sex was in doubt, as in babies born with ambiguous genitalia, an exploratory laporotomy and a histologic examination decided whether the sex of rearing was to be male or female. The underlying assumption was, of course, that the gonads represented the *true* sex and also determined a person's feelings of identity. In 1945, Albert Ellis published a review article based on 84 cases of hermaphrodites, pointing out that the sex role in such cases "accords primarily not with his or her internal or external somatic characteristics, but rather with his or her masculine or feminine upbringing" (Ellis, 1945). The breakthrough, however, came in 1955 when John Money in two articles (Money, Hampson, & Hampson, 1955a,b) formulated a new theory of the determinants of sex, using for the first time the term "gender role/identity." The introduction of "gender role" and "gender identity" as new terms was critical because it meant having a term that was not bound to biologic sex and a term that included other than sexual behaviors as it had to do with masculinity and femininity. But the most important scientific advance of the theory proposed was that sex was determined by a number of variables, including psychologic and social sex, rather than one.

The theory of John Money and his colleagues that the determination of sex depends on a number of variables like links in a chain was pioneering and may be considered a major contribution to our knowledge of psychosexual differentiation. It led to a fundamental change in the traditional policy regarding the sex of rearing of intersex babies. Money and the Hampsons added a new criterion for sex assignment, namely, the prognosis of sexual functioning of the individual. They justified this by formulating a new theory of gender development on the basis of their unique and rich case material. Their theory held that the best "prognosticator" of gender identity is the sex of assignment and rearing. They also added another dimension in their model, namely, a concept of critical time during which aspects of gender identity get formed—typically the age of 2½ years—and made comparison to the process of imprinting. Money and the Hampsons had observed gender change at later points in development but warned that it carried an increased risk of psychopathology for the individual. Ambiguity of gender identity had been observed by them and was identified as a sequela of ambiguity in rearing. Therefore, clinicians were advised to minimize such ambiguities by rapid decision making, by counseling the parents, and by surgically correcting the appearance of the external genitalia in accordance with the assigned sex. Under the leadership of Money and his medical collaborators and with the weight of a prestigious institution like The Johns Hopkins Hospital behind it, sex of assignment on the basis of future social and sexual functioning became an adopted policy on a worldwide basis.

The model of gender identity development continued to be a useful one even when prenatal sex hormones and their effects on gender-related behavior came under study. On the basis of their findings, researchers in the field generally agreed that variations of prenatal sex hormones may affect temperament and predispose it to a certain pattern of sex-dimorphic behavior but did not appear to have a major influence on the formation of gender identity (Money & Ehrhardt, 1972).

Recently the discussion of gender identity formation was rekindled when a newly diagnosed syndrome of male pseudohermaphroditism was described for a group of people in the Dominican Republic. It was of particular interest that the majority of these individuals changed their gender assignment from female to male at puberty. Although the phenomenon is of interest, the conclusion of Imperator McGinley, Peterson, Gautier, and Sturla (1979) that it suggests that testosterone has more effect in determining male gender identity than does the sex of rearing has been met with criticism and skepticism from several researchers (Ehrhardt, 1985; Meyer-Bahlburg, 1982; Rubin, Reinisch, & Haskett, 1981). The discussion that ensued about the development of gender identity often resembles a regression into the outdated thinking in terms of biology versus social environment or innate versus learned, rather than following an interactive model that takes into consideration the very specific endocrine variables and cultural conditions as they appear to affect the behavior of the particular patient population in the Dominican Republic.

Sex Differences of Behavior

The second area exemplifying the importance of a biosocial approach is the study of sex differences in behavior. An important fact that is too often overlooked is that there are many more similarities than differences between boys and girls and women and men. The measurement of masculine and feminine behavior almost always reveals a distribution that is represented by vastly overlapping curves rather than being totally dichotomous. Therefore, "masculine" or "feminine" behavior means that the behavior is more typical for boys or girls rather than exclusively male or female.

ROUGH-AND-TUMBLE PLAY

Among the many behavior patterns in which girls and boys differ in our society, there are some which are more suitable than others for the study of the interaction between sex hormones and learning. Aggressive outdoor play behavior has been shown to be a consistent sex difference between boys and girls on a long-term basis (Maccoby and Jacklin, 1974). This behavior pattern also has a relatively well-defined analogue in other primates, such as the rhesus monkey, who display a pattern of rough-and-tumble play that is sex-dimorphic (Goy, 1978). And it has been shown in animal experiments that the expression of rough play behavior can be influenced by the manipulation of prenatal sex hormones (Goy & Resko, 1972).

One approach to the complicated undertaking of teasing apart the contribution of genetic, hormonal, and social-environmental factors in the development of gender-related behavior is to assess the behavior of human beings who are known to have a hormonal abnormality. The findings on such abnormal groups may point to hormone-behavior relations that also operate in the expression of behavior variation within and between groups of normal boys and girls. Such a research strategy, of course, represents an extreme-group approach that may highlight a hormonal effect that normally affects behavior in much more subtle ways. Therefore, it has to be seen as a first step and as hypothesis rendering rather than as conclusive or generalizable to the normal situation.

Taking this extreme-group approach, the behavior of girls and boys in whom prenatal androgen levels were disturbed (i.e., in whom there was excess prenatal androgen due to an endocrine syndrome called congenital adrenal hyperplasia or due to maternal intake of androgenic pregnancy drugs, or lack of androgen in XY individuals due to androgen insensitivity or lowered androgen due to the counteraction of exogeneously administered steroids such as progesterone and estrogens) was assessed in a number of different studies and compared to various control groups (see reviews by Ehrhardt & Meyer-Bahlburg, 1981; Money & Ehrhardt, 1972).

The sex-dimorphic behavior patterns that were assessed in this type of research went beyond physically energetic play behavior and varied from study to study. The methodology applied included most often detailed interviews with children and their parents, sometimes teacher ratings, questionnaires, and, rarely, direct observational measurement. I will use rough-and-tumble play behavior as an example for a biosocial perspective. Without attempting to give a comprehensive review, I will draw on some of the existing evidence.

The picture that has emerged from the research on females and males with unusual prenatal hormonal histories suggest that high levels of prenatal androgens are correlated with high levels of physically active outdoor play behavior in childhood. Girls with a history of prenatal androgenization were typically long-term tomboys, frequently involved in physically active play and sports behavior, and preferred boys to girls as playmates. The tomboyish behavior pattern in these girls with a history of abnormally high levels of prenatal androgens is, of course, dependent on many factors, some prenatal and some postnatal. The existing studies attempted to control carefully for powerful postnatal variables and it was concluded that although rearing factors clearly contributed to the behavior development, they did not entirely explain it. If one applies interactional thinking to the interpretation of the behavior differences between prenatally androgenized girls and normal controls, one may consider that variations of sex hormones before birth predispose the central nervous sytem to physically energetic outdoor play behavior. However, this conclusion does not mean that the behavior is mechanistically predetermined by sex hormones. A predisposition possibly related to prenatal androgens simply means a greater likelihood of developing a certain behavior pattern. Whether and how the behavior will be expressed depends on the socialization process after birth. Girls who have a predisposition to physically active play behavior may frequently join boys rather than girls in active outdoor play. They also are more likely to be called tomboys. However, this will occur only if they grow up in a family and a large societal context that permits and encourages this type of behavior for girls. If, on the other hand, the environment imposes a greater degree of sex stereotyping and explicitly discourages physically active play behavior in girls, the original predisposition may not be expressed at all or may lead to maladjustment and unhappiness.

The same biosocial perspective applies to the interpretation of sex differences in the normal population. Boys and girls are known to differ in their levels of prenatal androgens and a male fetus is exposed to much higher levels of testosterone secreted by his own testes from the first trimester of pregnancy on (Abramovich, Herriot, & Stott, 1983). It is an established fact that this difference in androgens is responsible for the sex-dimorphic differentiation of the external sex organs into penis and scrotum or clitoris and vagina. On the basis of evidence from animal experiments, it seems plausible that the higher androgen levels may also affect the brain and predispose boys to exhibit more readily aggressive, physically active play behavior.

However, the extent of the behavior difference between girls and boys depends on the degree of gender-specific reinforcement. Traditionally, Western society has reinforced rough-and-tumble play in boys and doll play and infant care in girls. The socialization process has widened the gap between girls and boys and has misled us into believing that the differences are greater than they actually are. Over the last decade, girls have been given more opportunities to become involved in school athletics and after only a very short time the gap between men and women is narrowing in some areas of sports.

Not only is it important to see sex differences as the end result of the complex interplay of various factors, it is also crucial that we not go beyond the boundaries of our information. As an example, if boys show a stronger propensity toward physically active play behavior than girls show, one should not extrapolate and conclude that girls are more passive and dependent, have less initiative and less leadership behavior, and generally are less assertive. Being reinforced for physically active play behavior and strongly encouraged to compete in sports may foster important characteristics of assertiveness, the ability to win and to lose, leadership, and dominance. If adult men and women traditionally differ in those aspects of behavior, the reason is not a simple hormonal factor, but a complex chain of events possibly starting with a sex hormone difference before birth that may affect a very specific and limited behavior unit, for example, the threshold for the expression of physically energetic play behavior. Therefore, it is imperative that we be always cognizent of the particular societal context of behavior in which sex differences occur. Otherwise, we may erroneously attribute more power to hormonal and other constitutional factors than to societal and historical aspects.

Whereas girls with unusually high levels of androgen typically demonstrate a high degree of physically active outdoor play behavior and often a pronounced degree of tomboyism, the evidence of the opposite effect is much more scanty and inconsistent. This is in part due to the fact that the available clinical syndromes of either androgen insensitivity or exogeneously lowered androgen (by pregnancy drugs given to the mothers) are not as appropriate as those which have been studied for the effects of increased androgen before birth.

The human clinical syndrome that mostly approximates the antithesis of fetal androgenization of the genetic female is the syndrome of androgen insensitivity in an XY individual. In the complete form of the syndrome, the tissue of the body is totally androgen insensitive and therefore sexual differentiation of the external genitalia ensues along female lines. Sex of rearing is female. Gender-related behavior has been systematically assessed in adult women with this condition (Ehrhardt, Epstein, & Money, 1968). Their recalled childhood play behavior was stereotypically female with no special pattern of long-term tomboyism. While this fits the hypothesis of a relationship between low androgen and a predisposition to less physically energetic outdoor play behavior, observations on prepubertal girls with this syndrome in comparison with appropriate controls have not yet been done.

We also still lack a systematic assessment of sex-dimorphic behavior in boys with lowered androgen exposure in utero, that is, males with a prenatal defect in testosterone production or synthesis, compared with the behavior of appropriate control groups. The sex organs of such boys are usually masculinized enough for the sex of rearing to be male. The penis may be small, with or without undescended testes. The choice of this clinical syndrome for the study of any prenatal hormonal effect is, of course, complicated by the appearance of the external sex organs, which typically require multiple surgical procedures. The correction of the genital defect is usually not completed until well into the middle childhood years of such a boy and may never be perfect. Therefore, the situation is quite different from the syndrome of fetal androgenization in genetic females. Their genitals are also affected at birth (enlargement of clitoris and sometimes fusion of the labia), but are usually corrected within the first few weeks or months of life. This makes it possible to preselect a sample of girls who were exposed to high levels of androgen before birth but whose genitals were corrected shortly after birth so that their appearance was comparable to that of other girls (Ehrhardt, Epstein, & Money, 1968).

Other clinical entities chosen for the study of lowered prenatal androgens are those of children whose mothers were treated with pregnancy drugs that may counteract androgens, that is, progestogens and estrogens. The use of sex hormones in the treatment of problem pregnancies was first introduced in the 1940s after it had become known that the successful initiation as well as maintenance of pregnancy depended to a large extent on hormones produced by the mother as well as by the fetal-placental unit. High-risk pregnancies such as those threatened by spontaneous abortion, premature birth, stillbirth, or congenital abnormalities often in conjunction with pathologic states of the pregnant mother, such as diabetes or toxemia of pregnancy, were thought to be linked to deficiencies of hormone production, and supplementation seemed to be the logical approach to treatment.

Although animal experiments have demonstrated that certain progestogens (a term that includes both naturally occurring and synthetic progestational agents) and estrogens counteract androgens, the effect is complicated because it depends on the type of drug and dosage, whether the effect is anti-androgenic or the opposite. Since androgen is secreted by both male and female fetuses (albeit to a much lesser degree in females by the adrenals), the potentially anti-androgenic effects of pregnancy drugs were tested in studies on both boys and girls. The evidence from this type of research is based on only a few studies that are only partly comparable because they typically vary in age of subjects tested, pregnancy complications of the mothers, and type and dosage of drugs administered. One also has to keep in mind that the potential anti-androgenic influence of these progestogens alone or in combination with estrogens is much more speculative than the androgenic action, because the children's sex organs are typically normal. While this is an advantage in terms of a less confounding effect of the appearance of the sex organs at birth than in the high-androgen syndromes, it also means that it is entirely inferential whether the development of the fetus was indeed affected by the exogenously administered sex steroids or not.

According to the theory that high levels of prenatal androgens predispose to high physical-energy expenditure in outdoor play behavior, one would expect the opposite effect in those children whose mothers were treated with pregnancy drugs containing progestogens alone or in combination with estrogens. And indeed, progesterone exposure in boys correlated negatively with physically active play behavior and also negatively with tomboyism in girls (Zussman, Zussman, & Dalton, 1977). In a separate study, progestogens and estrogens in combination were found to be negatively correlated with athletic coordination in boys (Yalom, Green, & Fisk, 1973). The findings of both studies are problematic, however, since the mothers' pregnancy conditions (toxemia and diabetes, respectively) were not optimally matched in the control groups.

In a third study, the potential effect of progesterone alone and in combination with various estrogens was studied under conditions of less severe pregnancy complications in the experimental group and in comparison with more appropriate control groups (Ehrhardt, Grisanti, & Meyer-Bahlburg, 1977; Meyer-Bahlburg, Feldman, & Ince, 1984; Ehrhardt, Meyer-Bahlburg, Grisanti, & Ehrhardt, 1977; Meyer-Bahlburg, Feldman, Ehrhardt, & Cohen, 1984). The evidence that emerged from this study was not consistent across all samples. Boys whose mothers were treated with progestinic drugs alone (medroxyprogesterone acetate) were not different from normal controls in respect to rough-and-tumble play, but those who were exposed to various combinations of progestogens and estrogens described themselves as less athletically able than the controls (borderline significant). The maternal reports of those boys did not differ in either sample. The mothers of girls who were exposed to exogenous progestogens (medroxyprogesterone acetate) described their daughters as significantly less physically active in outdoor play and as less athletically able than the mothers of the controls did. The same was true for mothers of the combination group regarding athletic ability but not for unstructured physically active play behavior. The reports of the girls themselves did not differ significantly from those of their controls. Although all differences that were found regarding this aspect of childhood development supported the hypothesis, the differences were not dramatic and may, at best, point to very subtle effects of a prenatal hormone factor.

NURTURANCE AND PARENTING

The extreme-group approach of assessing the gender-related behavior of children with either too high or too low androgen exposure has pointed to other differences of less interest in terms of core sex differences that are consistent cross-culturally and across species. An exception is perhaps the findings on nurturance behavior, in particular the expression of parenting (interest in babies and infant care) and its childhood rehearsals (doll play and babysitting). Whether prenatal hormones differentially affect a predisposition to nurturance in females and males is currently under debate. If a hormonal factor is involved, it has to be seen as a threshold effect that may predispose women to an increased readiness to respond with nurturance to the young. As it has aggressive play behavior in males, Western society has strongly reinforced caregiving and nurturance in women, and boys and men have traditionally not been well prepared for sharing in adult parenting roles.

The evidence, based on the study of unusual conditions, for a prenatal sex hormonal effect has suggested that girls with exposure to high levels of prenatal androgens are less interested in doll play and babysitting in childhood and in having children and caring for infants in adulthood (Ehrhardt, 1973; Ehrhardt & Baker, 1974; Money & Ehrhardt, 1972). The opposite effect has been suggested for XY women with the syndrome of androgen insensitivity (Money, Ehrhardt, & Masica, 1968). Girls who were exposed to progesterone drugs alone or in combination with estrogens either did not differ from controls in doll play and interest in infants or showed mild effects toward increased nurturance (Ehrhardt, Meyer-Bahlburg, Feldman, & Ince, 1984; Zussman et al., 1977). Genetic males with unusually low androgen levels who were raised as boys have either not been comprehensively studied for their interest in doll play and parenting or were found not to differ from normal controls (see review by Ehrhardt & Meyer-Bahlburg, 1981). So far, the evidence for a prenatal hormonal effect on nurturance is at best fragmentary. The studies on the effects of pregnancy drugs containing progesterone alone or in combination with estrogen is hampered by small sample sizes and differences in pregnancy conditions, drug dosage, and timing of exposure. The behavior differences observed in such studies suggest a very mild effect toward increased nurturance in girls and no effect in boys. Earlier research on girls who were exposed to high levels of prenatal androgens suggested stronger effects in the direction of masculinization, that is, behavior more typical for boys, with less interest in doll play and infant care. Whether this behavior pattern is independent of the increased physical energy expenditure in outdoor play is not clear because both behavior clusters typically occurred together.

FEMALES WITH PRENATAL EXPOSURE TO DIETHYLSTILBESTROL: A NEW STUDY

Most studies of the effects of pregnancy drugs on sex-dimorphic behavior have involved those containing progestogens alone or in combination with estrogens (see review by Meyer-Bahlburg & Ehrhardt, 1980). Estrogens alone were usually not administered, except in the case of the synthetic estrogen diethylstilbestrol (DES). This drug is of particular interest from several different viewpoints. Most important, after being heralded as beneficial for the prevention and correction of pregnancy complications and after having been widely prescribed to women during the 1940s, 1950s, and 1960s, prenatal exposure to DES was found to be associated with a highly increased risk of the develoment of a rare form of cancer, clear-cell carcinoma of the vagina or cervix, in the daughters (Herbst, Ulfelder, & Poskanzer, 1971). After this discovery, several large-scale studies were initiated to assess thoroughly the potential health implications for affected mothers, daughters, and sons. Fortunately, the most tragic implication of cancer in the daughters was rare (0.14 to 1.4 per 1,000 through age 24). However, other abnormalities of the reproductive system emerged. One-third of DES daughters developed vaginal epithelial changes, the malignant potential of which is unclear (Noller et al., 1981). Other complications include menstrual irregularities and pregnancy problems (Barnes et al., 1980; Bibbo et al., 1977). More recently, it has documented that DES sons are affected also; about a third show a variety of genitourinary disorders (e.g., hypoplastic testes), while the effects of DES exposure on infertility and neoplasia are unclear (Gill, Schumacher, Hubby, & Blough, 1981).

Apart from the visible and obvious health implications, DES is also of interest for its potential effect on the prenatal differentiation of the central nervous system. In animal experimental research, DES has been shown to have a paradoxical effect of masculinizing some aspects of behavior in female rats and guinea pigs and of demasculinizing the sexual behavior of male rats (Hines, Alsum, Gorski, & Goy, 1982; Hines, Dohler, & Gorski, 1982; Monroe & Silva, 1982). This paradoxical effect of DES in lower mammals has been explained by the fact that the nonsteroidal DES does not bind to alphafeto-protein, which typically prevents other estrogens that circulate in the feto-placental unit from reaching the brain and therefore from becoming biologically inactive (Plapinger & McEwen, 1978). DES, therefore, can have effects on the brain receptor level similar to those of androgens that are converted to estrogens. One would expect, therefore, that the behavior in genetic female animals exposed to DES would show greater similarity to that of males than to that of DES-unexposed controls. In genetic males, estrogen administration has the opposite effect, presumably because of a competitive action and therefore suppression of the fetal testosterone production and release.

Over the last three years, my colleague Heino F. L. Meyer-Bahlburg and I have been involved in a study of young women and men in their late teens and twenties who were exposed to prenatal DES treatment. A study of any potential effects of prenatal DES on postnatal gender-related behavior needs, of course, to take special care in the matching of appropriate control groups for some of the postnatal complications, particularly in the case of young women for the cancer threat.

The design of our project employed several groups of females and males with different control groups, some matched on health conditions, others on family status (i.e., unexposed siblings). We also included only young women and men whose prenatal DES exposure was documented by medical chart to correct for errors in memory and to be able to estimate dosage and duration of drug exposure.

The behavioral measures included assessments of many different aspects of mental health, life style, and also gender-related behavior. The preliminary analysis is based on the first sample of N = 30 young women with DES exposure compared with a control group of N = 30 women who had had an abnormal Pap smear and thereby also an indication of abnormalities of the reproductive organs and potential cancer risk. The two groups were comparable in age and social class and were both recruited through the same gynecological office. Regarding the hypothesis concerning gender-related behavior, we postulated that DES females would differ in the direction of being less feminine or more masculine than their controls. In terms of physical energy expenditure and nurturance, this would mean an increased tendency to physically energetic play behavior and a decreased expression of nurturance toward infants. So far, our results indicate partial support for our hypothesis: DES females showed less parenting rehearsal in childhood, that is, less doll play, less maternal role playing, less interest in infants, judging from self and mothers' reports. They also showed less interest in getting married in childhood rehearsal play and were less inclined actually to get married and to attempt pregnancy and childbirth in adulthood. There was no difference between the two groups in physically energetic play behavior. In fact, according to mothers only, DES females were less frequently involved in rough-and-tumble play during childhood (Ehrhardt et al., 1984). Analogous data on the male samples are not available yet.

The findings so far suggest that young women who were exposed to prenatal DES show less interest in parenting behavior. Before one concludes that the prenatal hormonal factors have a role in this behavior difference, one, of course, has to consider and assess many postnatal factors that may have augmented and influenced or entirely explain this finding. For instance, being aware of reproductive difficulties in adulthood may have led to less interest in becoming a parent. This would not solely explain the childhood data, since on the average DES females were informed of their prenatal exposure to DES only in their late teens or early twenties. But the recall of childhood play behavior may have been selectively biased toward less interest in parenting. It is also possible that the family rearing style, specifically the encouragement of doll play and infant care, differed in the two groups. We have attempted to apply transactional thinking and to include as part of our design the assessment of environmental factors of this kind. We also will have a separate comparison between DES females and their unaffected sisters to further control for family style. In any event, these findings are another example of how important a biosocial approach is and how one has to carefully conceptualize, assess, and analyze the different factors that may be important in the development of a specific behavior pattern.

Conclusion

The study of gender-related behavior has been hampered in the past by the narrowly defined main-effect model that posits biology versus learning. Instead, a biosocial perspective that includes constitutional as well as environmental factors needs to be applied if we want to make progress in our understanding of complex phenomena such as gender identity development and other aspects of gender-related behavior. Studies of females and males with a history of abnormal sex hormones before birth have pointed to important factors that may influence the expression of behavior differences within and between gender. The future study of gender-related behavior will be greatly enhanced by following an interactional model.

REFERENCES

Abramovich, D. R., Herriot, R., & Stott, J. (1983). Dihydrostestosterone levels at midpregnancy and term: A comparison with testosterone concentrations. *British Journal of Obstetrics and Gynaecology, 90,* 232–234.

Barnes, A. B., Colton, T., Gundersen, J., Noller, K. L., Tilley, B. C., Strama, T., Townsend, D. E., Hatab, P., & O'Brien, P. C. (1980). Fertility and outcome of pregnancy in women exposed in utero to diethylstilbestrol. *New England Journal of Medicine, 302,* 609–613.

Beach, F. A. (1981). Historical origins of modern research on hormones and behavior. *Hormones and Behavior, 15,* 325–376.

Beach, F. A., Kuehn, R. E., Sprague, R. H., & Anisko, J. J. (1972). Coital behavior in dogs—XI. Effects of androgenic stimulation during development on masculine mating responses in females. *Hormones and Behavior, 3,* 143–168.

Bibbo, M., Gill, W. B., Azizi, F., Blough, R., Fang, V. S., Rosenfield, R. L., Schumacher, G. F. B., Sleeper, K., Sonek, M. G., & Wied, G. L. (1977). Follow-up study of male and female offspring of DES-exposed mothers. *Obstetrics and Gynecology, 49,* 1–8.

Ehrhardt, A. A. (1973). Maternalism in fetal hormonal and related syndromes. In J. Zubin & J. Money (Eds.), *Contemporary sexual behavior: Critical issues in the 1970's.* Baltimore: Johns Hopkins Press.

Ehrhardt, A. A. (1985). The psychobiology of gender. In A. S. Rossi (Ed.), *Gender and the life course.* Hawthorne, NY: Aldine Publishing Co.

Ehrhardt, A. A., & Baker, S. W. (1974). Fetal androgen, human CNS differentiation and behavior sex differences. In R. C. Friedman, R. M. Richart, & R. L. Vande Wiele (Eds.), *Sex differences in behavior* (pp. 53–76). New York: Wiley & Sons.

Ehrhardt, A. A., Epstein, R., & Money, J. (1968). Fetal androgens and female gender identity in the early-treated andrenogenital syndrome. *Johns Hopkins Medical Journal, 122,* 160–167.

Ehrhardt, A. A., Grisanti, G. C., & Meyer-Bahlburg, H. F. L. (1977). Prenatal exposure to medroxyprogesterone acetate (MPA) in girls. *Psychoneuroendocrinology, 2,* 391–398.

Ehrhardt, A. A., & Meyer-Bahlburg, H. F. L. (1981). The effects of prenatal hormones on gender identity, sex-dimorphic behavior, sexual orientation and cognition. *Science, 211,* 1312–1318.

Ehrhardt, A. A., Meyer-Bahlburg, H. F. L., Feldman, J. F., & Ince, S. E. (1984). Sex-dimorphic behavior in childhood subsequent to prenatal exposure to exogenous progestogens and estrogens. *Archives of Sexual Behavior, 13,* 457–477.

Ehrhardt, A. A., Meyer-Bahlburg, H. F. L., Rosen, L., Feldman, J. F., Veridiano, N. P., Elkin, E. J., & McEwen, B. (1984, October). Gender-related behavior development in females following prenatal exposure to diethylstilbestrol (DES). Abstract for Annual Meeting of the American Academy of Child Psychiatry, Toronto, Canada.

Ellis, A. (1945). The sexual psychology of human hermaphrodites. *Psychosomatic Medicine, 7,* 108–125.

Gill, W. B., Schumacher, G. F. B., Hubby, M. M., & Blough, R. R. (1981). Male genital tract changes in humans following intrauterine exposure to diethylstilbestrol. In A. L. Herbst & H. A. Bern (Eds.), *Developmental effects of diethylstilbestrol in pregnancy* (pp. 103–119). New York: Thieme-Stratton.

Goy, R. W. (1978). Development of play and mounting behavior in female rhesus monkeys virilized prenatally with esters of testosterone or dihydrotestosterone. In D. J. Chivers & J. Herberts (Eds.), *Recent advances in primatology* (Vol. 1). New York: Academic Press.

Goy, R. W., & Resko, J. A. (1972). Gonadal hormones and behavior of normal and pseudohermaphroditic nonhuman female primates. In E. B. Astwood (Ed.), *Recent progress in hormone research* (pp. 707–733). New York: Academic Press.

Herbst, A. L., Ulfelder, H., & Poskanzer, D. C. (1971). Andenocarcinoma of the vagina: Association of maternal stilbestrol therapy with tumor appearance in young women. *New England Journal of Medicine, 284,* 878–881.

Hines, M., Alsum, P., Gorski, R. A., & Goy, R. W. (1982). Prenatal exposure to estrogen masculinizes and defeminizes behavior in the guinea pig. *Abstracts, Society for Neuroscience, 8,* 196.

Hines, M., Dohler, K. D., & Gorski, R. A. (1982, June). Rough play in female rats following pre- and postnatal treatment with diethylstilbestrol or testosterone. 14th Conference on Reproductive Behavior, East Lansing, Michigan, *Abstracts,* p. 66.

Imperato McGinley, J., Peterson, R. E., Gautier, T., & Sturla, E. (1979). Androgens and the evolution of male-gender identity among male pseudohermaphrodites with 5 α-reductase deficiency. *New England Journal of Medicine, 300,* 1233–1237.

McClintock, M. K. (1971). Menstrual synchrony and suppression. *Nature, 229,* 244–245.

Maccoby, E. E., & Jacklin, C. N. (1974). *The psychology of sex differences.* Stanford: Stanford University Press.

McEwen, B. S. (1983). Gonadal steroidal influences in brain development and sexual differentiation. In R. O. Greep (Ed.), *Reproductive physiology IV, International review of physiology* (Vol. 27, pp. 99–145). Baltimore: University Park Press.

Meyer-Bahlburg, H. F. L. Hormones and psychosexual differentiation: Implications for the management of intersexuality, homosexuality, and transsexuality. *Clinics in Endocrinology and Metabolism, 11,* 681–701.

Meyer-Bahlburg, H. F. L., & Ehrhardt, A. A. (1980). Sex hormone administration during pregnancy: Behavioral sequelae in the offspring. In D. D. Youngs & A. A. Ehrhardt (Eds.), *Psychosomatic obstetrics and gynecology* (pp. 3–17). New York: Appleton Century-Crofts.

Meyer-Bahlburg, H. F. L., Feldman, J. F., Ehrhardt, A. A., & Cohen, P. (1984). Effects of prenatal hormones exposure versus pregnancy complications on sex-dimorphic behavior. *Archives of Sexual Behavior, 13,* 479–495.

Meyer-Bahlburg, H. F. L., Grisanti, G. C., & Ehrhardt, A. A. (1977). Prenatal effects of sex hormones on human male behavior: Medroxyprogesterone acetate (MPA). *Psychoneuroendocrinology, 2,* 283–290.

Money, J., & Ehrhardt, A. A. (1972). *Man and woman, boy and girl.* Baltimore: Johns Hopkins Press.

Money, J., Ehrhardt, A. A., & Masica, D. N. (1968). Fetal feminization induced by androgen insensitivity in the testicular feminizing syndrome: Effect on marriage and maternalism. *Johns Hopkins Medical Journal, 123,* 105–114.

Money, J., Hampson, J. G., & Hampson, J. L. (1955a). An examination of some basic sexual concepts: The evidence of human hermaphroditism. *Bulletin of the Johns Hopkins Hospital, 97,* 301–319.

Money, J., Hampson, J. G., & Hampson, J. L. (1955b). Hermaphroditism: Recommendations concerning assignment of sex, change of sex, and psychologic management. *Bulletin of the Johns Hopkins Hospital, 97,* 284–300.

Monroe, J. A., & Silva, D. A. (1982, August). Effects of neonatal diethylstilbestrol (DES) on adult male rats' sexual behavior. Paper presented at the 90th Annual Convention of the American Psychological Association, Washington, DC.

Noller, K. L., Townsend, D. E. & Kaufman, R. H. Genital findings, colposcopic evaluation, and current management of the diethylstilbestrol-exposed female. In A. L. Herbst & H. A. Bern (Eds.), *Developmental effects of diethylstilbestrol (DES) in pregnancy* (pp. 81–102). New York: Thieme-Stratton, Inc., 1981.

Plapinger, L., & McEwen, B. S. (1978). Gonadal steroid–brain interactions in sexual differentiation. In J. B. Hutchinson (Ed.), *Biological determinants of sexual behaviour* (pp. 135–140). New York: John Wiley & Sons.

Rubin, R. T., Reinisch, J. M., & Haskett, R. F. (1981). Postnatal gonadal steroid effects on human behavior. *Science, 211,* 1318–1324.

Sameroff, A. J., & Chandler, M. J. (1975). Reproductive risk and the continuum of caretaking causality. In F. D. Horowitz (Ed., *Review of child development research* (Vol. 4, pp. 187–244). Chicago: University of Chicago Press.

Yalom, I. D., Green, R., & Fisk, N. (1973). Prenatal exposure to female hormones. *Archives of General Psychiatry, 28,* 554–561.

Zussman, J. U., Zussman, P. P., & Dalton, K. (1977, August). Effects of prenatal progesterone on adolescent cognitive and social development. Paper presented at the 3rd Annual Meeting of the International Academy of Sex Research, Bloomington, Indiana.

Gender Identity and Its Implications for the Concepts of Masculinity and Femininity

Janet T. Spence

University of Texas at Austin

Introduction

*P*erhaps stimulated by recent societal concern with changing sex roles or by my own raised consciousness, I have become impressed with how frequently the words "masculinity" and "femininity" or "masculine" and "feminine" are currently found in newspapers and magazines and other popular media, often in descriptions of individuals.

In attending to the appearance of these terms, my intent has not been to conduct an informal word count to determine whether they are approaching star status in frequency of usage in the English language. Rather I have become interested in how the adjectives masculine and feminine, and even more the nouns masculinity and femininity, are used. What are their meanings? What information are the writers or speakers trying to convey? And what do members of the audience make of them? When one asks such questions aloud, as I have occasionally done, the usual reaction, even from professional colleagues, is a look of surprise or irritation that suggests these queries are so perversely obtuse and the answers so self-evident that they merit no reply beyond "What do you mean, what do I mean?" But my puzzlement is genuine, and if one takes such questions seriously it becomes apparent that, more often than not, satisfactory answers are not easily formulated.

DEFINITIONAL UNCERTAINTIES

Ordinarily we can find the meaning of words by consulting a dictionary. However, in this case a search through standard works primarily shows how little enlightment their definitions provide. A typical example is the *Random House Dictionary* (1969) I happen to have on my desk. Feminine is defined as "1. pertaining to a woman or girl: *feminine beauty; feminine dress;* 2. like a woman: weak; gentle. 3. effeminate, womanish. 4. belonging to the female sex, female." Unlike most dictionaries, the Random House gives femininity a separate entry, but the definition is not particularly helpful, the first meaning being "the quality of being feminine; womanliness," and the second "women collectively." Masculine is given a definition parallel to that for feminine, but, reverting to common practice, masculinity appears only at the end of the entry for masculine, remaining undefined and merely described as a noun.

These definitions indicate that one meaning of masculine and feminine is identification of an observable object, event, or quality as gender related—that is, as a psychologist would describe it, the words are labels for those properties of persons, objects, or behaviors that the descriptive or prescriptive stereotypes of a given culture consider associated with or more characteristic of one sex than the other. It is clear from the context in which they appear that masculine and feminine are frequently used in this purely empirical sense, and what is concretely implied can usually be inferred by anyone familiar with the speaker's or writer's culture. Thus if one reads in the fashion section of the *New York Times* that this year's style in women's clothes is more feminine than last year's, it is a good bet that the tailored look is out and frills and soft lines are in. It should be understood, of course, that what is considered masculine or feminine at one time and place may be oppositely classified at others or may even be gender neutral. For example, in this but not all countries, skirts are worn exclusively by women, and in times past, but not now, pants were worn exclusively by men.

Often, however, these adjectives are not linked to specific objects, qualities, or behaviors but, particularly when a person is being described, are used abstractly or globally, as in "Mary is very feminine" or "John isn't particularly masculine." Typically such characterizations are not amplified further, and in the absence of explanation they seem to imply the presence (or lack) of either some totality of gender-related qualities or some underlying essence of maleness or femaleness that can be inferred from observable qualities. When used as nouns, these terms even more exclusively appear to denote a fundamental essence, especially when they refer to one's own or another's sense of masculinity or femininity, as in "She's very secure in her femininity." The definition of femininity I quoted above, "the quality of being feminine: womanliness" is thus right on target.

To return to my earlier questions, What is this essence or basic sense of masculinity or femininity? When someone describes an individual as masculine or feminine, what concrete information, if any, does the speaker intend to convey? What inferences can the listener legitimately make about the person's characteristics? The difficulty in answering the latter question is particularly acute when the only specific data offered are counterstereotypic. Two examples from my growing collection illustrate such mixed messages. In a newspaper article about a prominent woman television reporter, the writer first described her subject's assertive, forceful style of interviewing and then went on to say that, nevertheless, she was highly feminine. Other than reassuring the reader that this personage, despite her "masculine" interview behavior, is not in other respects particularly deviant and is therefore an acceptable if not likable human being, what was the writer trying to say? What, as readers, do we now know about her that we did not know before? Can we safely assume that she likes to cook and sew, loves children, is kind and sweet, is bored by football, and so on down the whole catalog of socially desirable attributes that women are expected to display—except, of course, for her on-the-job assertiveness? The writer did not find it necessary to enlighten her audience, immediately going on to describe her subject's career. Lest I be accused of making too much of a single casual statement, I should add that the article's headline read "[Ms. X] Highly Feminine."

Another recent article in my local newspaper featured a young high-school student, male, who was an excellent chef and did much of the cooking for his family. It was the latter, apparently, that made the young man remarkable enough to be worth an article; there is nothing untoward about males working for pay as cooks or chefs, but preparing family meals takes on a significantly different meaning. Before launching into a description of his culinary accomplishments, the writer stated that the young man was perfectly masculine. Again, what do we know about him—except perhaps that in appearance and other conspicuous qualities the writer did not find him visibly effeminate? In both instances we are told that an individual deviates from her or his gender stereotype in some notable way yet remains feminine or masculine. What then are masculinity and femininity? If one can violate normative expectations in one major domain yet remain a masculine man or feminine woman, how are these essences to be inferred or diagnosed?

In our own research (Spence & Sawin, 1984) we attempted to find answers to these questions by asking middle-aged, middle-class men and women to specify what constitutes masculinity or femininity in themselves and in others. Although often articulate on other topics, these men and women often stammered, said they didn't know, or demanded what the interviewer meant by these terms. When they did give substantive replies, they produced answers that were sparse, exquisitely banal, and variable in content. Many indicated that they were aware of gender stereotypes but frequently denied their relevance to real manliness or womanliness. Yet later in the interview some of these same men and women used these terms unselfconsciously to describe themselves or others, though usually without indicating what aspects of appearance, behavior, or psychological makeup led to this characterization.

Despite the absence of contextual cues to give some hint about their meanings, despite the inability of lexicographers as well as ordinary people to supply satisfactory definitions in their abstract senses, writers and speakers continue to use the words masculinity and femininity, seemingly secure in the knowledge that they are meaningful, a confidence that appears to be shared by their unquestioning audience. Masculinity and femininity, it appears, are amorphous concepts, rich in their conotations but left undefined and unanalyzed.

Although masculinity and femininity and related constructs such as sex-role identification are pivotal in many theories of the psychologies of males and females, psychologists have rarely done any better than the community at large in offering definitions or conceptual analyses of these terms. We use them glibly, jumping back and forth between empirical usage (i.e., as labels for specific gender-differentiating qualities or objects) and abstract conceptual use with no particular referents, without even noticing the transition. Few have seemed to notice, let alone care, that the meaning of these concepts has been left unspecified. Since psychologists are ordinarily sensitive to such matters, this omission is itself a puzzle that requires explanation.

Gender Identity and Concepts of Masculinity and Femininity

CONCEPTUAL UNCERTAINTIES

Beginning with the Terman-Miles tests of a half-century ago, psychologists have presumed to devise self-report questionnaires to measure masculinity and femininity, even in the absence of an explicit definition of these abstractions or of a conceptual framework to guide test construction. Constantinople (1973) was among the first to call attention to this peculiarity in her frequently cited but underappreciated 1973 article, "Masculinity-Femininity: An Exception to the Famous Dictum?" in which she considered conventional tests yielding a single masculinity-femininity score for each respondent. In most instances, she noted, items were drawn from pools created for other purposes on the basis of their capacity to distinguish between the sexes.

The absence of criteria by which items were selected for these masculinity-femininity tests, save the pragmatic one that males and females differed in their responses to them, does not imply that masculinity and femininity have been regarded by test developers and users as purely empirical notions, unrelated to any theoretical assumptions about the nature of gender-differentiating phenomena. Rather, these assumptions have been left unstated, which has had the unintended side effect of relieving test developers of the responsibility of determining their validity and has encouraged test users to accept as self-evident the utility of the construct the instruments purport to measure.

After analyzing the theoretical propositions underlying the construction of major masculinity-femininity tests and finding them wanting, Constantinople (1973) concluded that the concepts of masculinity and femininity were among the muddiest in all of psychology. At later points I will describe these theoretical assumptions and consider briefly the empirical evidence relevant to them. For the moment I will note only that despite the enormous attention the masculinity and femininity concepts have attracted in the decade since the publication of Constantinople's article, little progress has been made toward clarification. If anything, the introduction of the hypothesis that masculinity and femininity are independent dimensions, as a rival of the bipolar hypothesis on which traditional masculinity-femininity measures are predicated, has further roiled the waters. This is especially so because most of those who have explicitly espoused this two-factor theory have, without apparent awareness, simultaneously hung on to the older bipolar conceptualization of masculinity-femininity under the guise of such concepts as sex-role orientation or sex-role identification (Spence, 1984). Stirring up the waters still further, a growing number of investigators (e.g., Coffman & Levy, 1972; Deaux, 1982; Orlofsky, 1981), including my colleagues and myself (e.g., Spence & Helmreich, 1978; Spence, 1984) have adopted positions suggesting that both the single-factor and two-factor models of masculinity and femininity, as currently conceived, have little validity.

The confusions and controversies that have arisen in recent years, many of them centering on the Bem Sex Role Inventory (BSRI; Bem, 1974), the Personal Attributes Questionnaire (PAQ; Spence, Helmreich, & Stapp, 1974, 1975), and similar instruments used to measure the separate masculinity and femininity constructs, have led some commentators (e.g., Beere, 1983) to suggest in exasperation that the terms masculinity and femininity be expunged from our scientific vocabulary. Those whose aspirations for society are to wipe out or minimize sex-role and other gender-related distinctions may find this suggestion particularly appealing.

CHAPTER PREVIEW

Whether a society in which gender distinctions are reduced to those necessitated by anatomy ever will or ever could come about is difficult to predict. However, it is unarguable that at present, as in earlier times, gender is one of the earliest and most central components of the self-concept and serves as an organizing principle through which many experiences and perceptions of self and others are filtered.

In this presentation I will contend that masculinity and femininity or such related terms as manliness or womanliness are highly meaningful and personally significant concepts to most individuals and that attempts to dismiss them as useless are premature. At the same time, I will argue that conventional theories about masculinity and femininity, whether conceived as end points of a single bipolar continuum or as independent continua, are founded on assumptions whose implications the empirical evidence refutes, thus demanding a fresh theoretical approach. After reviewing these assumptions and the relevant evidence, I will outline an alternative theory of self-concepts of masculinity and femininity linked to the relatively neglected concept of gender identity, as opposed to the more familiar concept of sex-role identity.

This formulation, I mention in advance, is a dichotomous one, conceiving of masculinity and femininity as separate but basically incompatible, paralleling the dimorphism of biological sex. In this limited sense it is similar to traditional bipolar models and to the dualistic formulations of such theorists as Carl Jung, Erik Erikson, and David Bakan, in which masculinity and femininity or male and female principles are conceived as antinomies. This proposition may come as a surprise to those who have accepted our Personal Attributes Questionnaire (PAQ; Spence et al., 1974; Spence & Helmreich, 1978) as well as the highly similar Bem Sex Role Inventory (BSRI; Bem, 1974) as measures of self-concepts of masculinity and femininity and have regarded demonstrations of the statistical independence of scores on the so-called masculinity and femininity scales of these instruments as definitive evidence that masculinity and femininity are orthogonal dimensions.

These empirical results obtained with the BSRI and PAQ I regard as quite genuine, rather than as attributable to some kind of methodological artifact, as one defender of a conventional bipolar formulation has attempted to argue (Baumrind, 1982). It is the interpretation of these instruments as measures of masculinity and femininity that I dispute. After a shaky conceptual start in the initial pair of articles (Spence et al., 1974, 1975) introducing the PAQ, in which we identified the scales as measures of masculinity and femininity, my colleagues and I (e.g., Spence & Helmreich, 1978) retreated from this position. More specifically, we have come to reject the proposition that scores on these instruments, which are largely or wholly confined to items describing limited classes of socially desirable gender-differentiating personality traits, can be used to make inferences about individuals' perceptions of their masculinity and femininity or their sex-role orientation. According to our current views, which an increasing number of investigators are beginning to share (e.g., Feather & Said, 1983; Major, Carnevale, & Deaux, 1981; Mills & Tyrrell, 1983; Nettles & Loevinger, 1983; Orlofsky, 1981; Tellegen & Lubinski, 1983), the PAQ and BSRI measure only what their manifest content indicates, namely two constellations of personality characteristics. From this perspective the terms masculine and feminine can legitimately be used in conjunction with the two major scales on these instruments only in the empirical sense—that is, as identifying the fact that, both stereotypically and in self-report, the items on one scale are more characteristic of females and the items on the other scale are more characteristic of males, at least in samples from the

United States. The same argument can be made about all other extant tests of masculinity-femininity or masculinity and femininity: the labels can be defended only to the extent that they are being used in their empirical senses. As might be inferred from these statements, I am suggesting that to date no valid technique has been devised to assess masculinity and femininity as global theoretical concepts, primarily because previous efforts have been based on erroneous premises.

Before moving on to describe these premises, I should emphasize once more the critical distinction between empirical and theoretical usages of masculine and feminine and other gender-related terms. In the former instance these terms are merely nominal labels for observable qualities or events that are more closely associated with members of one gender than the other in a given culture, whereas in the latter instance the terms refer to hypothetical properties of the individual that must be inferred rather than directly observed. Unless otherwise specified, my future references to the terms masculine and feminine or masculinity and femininity will be in their general, conceptual sense.

Prior Theoretical Conceptions

SINGLE-FACTOR MODELS

Masculinity-femininity. Until the mid-1970s, the dominant theoretical conception of masculinity and femininity represented what can be identified as a single-factor model (Spence, 1984). The major features of this model are illustrated by traditional self-report tests of masculinity-femininity in which the response to each item is scored as masculine or feminine and item scores are then totaled for each individual to reveal where the person falls on a hypothetical masculinity-femininity continuum. As I noted earlier, the items on these tests were not initially devised or selected according to some theoretical conception but came from sources conveniently at hand; the criterion for item inclusion was the capacity of an item to distinguish between men and women as groups, and, in the case of the MMPI M-F scale, between heterosexuals and homosexuals as well (Constantinople, 1973). In most instruments item content is heterogeneous, covering a number of domains. Further, there is wide variability in content among these masculinity-femininity tests.

The usefulness of these approaches rests on the validity of several interrelated assumptions: (a) The abstract, hypothetical qualities of masculinity and femininity form a single bipolar dimension, with most males falling toward the masculine extreme and most females falling toward the feminine extreme. (b) All the concrete attributes, attitudes, and behaviors that normatively are more characteristic of males than females in a given culture are reliable indicators of masculinity, and their absence is a reliable indicator of femininity; conversely, the presence and absence of characteristics associated with females are indicators of femininity or masculinity, respectively. Thus standing on these discrete indicators can collectively be used to place an individual on the masculinity-femininity continuum. (c) It follows that in statistical terms, the various classes of gender-differentiating qualities and behaviors are substantially correlated within each sex and, in their totality, contribute to a single bipolar factor as revealed by factor analyses.

The same series of assumptions also underlies a number of other techniques used to measure the hypothetical masculinity-femininity dimension. For example, common techniques used with children are the IT test and more direct methods of assessing sex-typed toy preferences, such as asking children to rate their like or dislike of various playthings or observing their choices when they are presented with an array of sex-typed toys, from dump trucks to tea sets. No theoretical reasons have ever been offered for using toy preferences to detect children's degree of masculinity or femininity; it seems safe to infer that one type of gender-differentiating characteristic has been regarded as being as diagnostic as any other, toy preference being chosen simply because of ease of measurement.

If the single-factor assumption is correct, any given gender-differentiating characteristic is in principle as satisfactory as any other as an indicator of masculinity-femininity, making unimportant the way a subset of items is selected from the population of potential items. In empirical content, items could equally well be randomly drawn from the entire universe, be a nonrepresentative sample selected from several domains, or be drawn exclusively from one specific domain, such as personality traits, recreational interests, or, for children, toy preferences.

Sex-role Identification. The concept of sex-role identification is predicated on the same bipolar, unidimensional assumptions as the concept of masculinity-femininity. But it is richer and more dynamic in its implications and could be said to incorporate the more static masculinity-femininity construct.

Sex-role identification theories, whose origins may be traced back to Freud's classic theory, are designed to identify the processes by which children at each developmental stage acquire the characteristics, attitudes, values, and behaviors that their society specifies as appropriate for their gender and that ultimately lead them to assume the roles and responsibilities assigned to men and to women and to develop the skills necessary to discharge their roles effectively. Although varying in their details, sex-role identification theories have in common the proposition that in the course of normal development, young children come to identify with or attempt to model themselves after their own sex or particular members of it, such as their same-sex parent. This identification process leads children to internalize their society's masculine or feminine role standards and related expectations and to strive throughout life to meet these standards as well as to evaluate others' behavior according to its gender appropriateness. These theories imply that the various characteristics and behaviors defined as appropriate for each gender at any given developmental period are simultaneously acquired and continue to be developed and maintained by means of a common set of factors associated with the identification process. This in turn suggests that gender-differentiating phenomena are implicitly assumed to be unifactorial in structure.

The expression "sex-role orientation" has crept into the literature in recent years, frequently as a description of what the PAQ and BSRI purportedly measure. The term seems to be interchangeable with either the sex-role identification or the more purely descriptive masculinity-femininity construct. In either case bipolarity is being implied, masculine role orientation versus feminine role orientation.

A note on the term sex role. Before moving from single-factor conceptualizations of gender phenomena to a discussion of two-factor ones, I will digress briefly to comment on the term sex role itself. The construct of role, as employed by anthropologists, sociologists, and social psychologists, refers to a position an individual occupies in an organized social structure, the responsibilities and privileges associated with that position, and the rules of conduct governing interactions between individuals in this and other positions. The different sets of roles assigned to males and to females are collectively identified as sex roles.

A practice that has become common in psychology is to give the sex-role label to all sex differences of a psychological nature (save, in most instances, differences in cognitive abilities), whether or not they involve role preferences, attitudes, or adoptions (Angrist, 1969). This custom is unfortunate in several respects. First, it introduces terminological awkwardness and confusion, for example, when one tries to explain that some measures given the sex-role label actually tap sex-role attitudes or behaviors but that other measures with the same label tap gender-differentiating qualities (such as personality traits) that are not roles. Second, the practice encourages the assumption or takes for granted the validity of the hypothesis that all gender-related properties are so tightly associated that it is legitimate to make inferences about sex-role attitudes, preferences, or behaviors from measures of other types of gender-differentiating characteristics. However, if the single-factor, bipolar conception turns out to be valid, it does little real harm to identify as sex-roles both role and nonrole phenomena, since everything is correlated with everything else. On the other hand, if it turns out that there is little correlation between most classes of gender-differentiating phenomena, as the data increasingly suggest, identifying all gender-related attributes and behaviors as sex roles is pernicious, encouraging the belief that one has literally measured or can accurately predict sex-role attitudes, preferences, or behaviors when one has not or cannot. Further, as Hill and Lynch (1983) have observed, the practice has caused genuine sex-role phenomena to be relatively neglected as topics of research.

TWO-FACTOR MODEL

Numerous investigators have interpreted the rationale undergirding the constructon of conventional masculinity-femininity tests as necessarily implying that masculine and feminine qualities (in their empirical sense) *cannot* coexist in the same individual. Whether this is a legitimate conclusion depends on what theoretical interpretation one elects to give to scores that fall in the center of the possible range. Such scores are far from unknown and, at least in some individuals of both sexes, represent a positive endorsement of an approximately equal number of masculine and feminine alternatives. If taken literally, these data, which have been available for decades, indicate that male-associated and female-associated characteristics can and often do occur in the same individual.

Be that as it may, a conviction was abroad that single-factor theories of masculinity-femininity necessarily presumed that a conjunction of both masculine and feminine traits, interests, and behaviors is impossible. If this were true, it would dash any hopes of achieving the kind of gender-free society that Bem (1974, 1978) and others have advocated—that is, a society in which the roles, privileges, and responsibilities now differentially assigned according to sex are assumed by both men and women. In such a society both sexes would also be expected to develop the desirable qualities that are now stereotypically associated with men or with women so that both sexes could effectively discharge their broadened sets of role responsibilities. Thus, in order to advance this ideological vision, it became necessary to argue that both masculine and feminine qualities can coexist.

In her 1974 article in which she introduced the BSRI, Bem presented a theory that, upon analysis, rests on two claims. First, that gender-related attributes and behaviors can be divided into two statistically independent classes, masculine and feminine. Since they are independent, masculine and feminine qualities can thus occur in the same individual. Second, that masculine and feminine self-images, or the global properties of masculinity or femininity, are also independent, with the appearance, or at least the self-reports, of specific gender-differentiating qualities being indicators of the strength of each of these hypothetical dimensions.

To investigate these hypotheses, Bem constructed a self-report measure in which items were classified as masculine or feminine and assigned to separate scales. Although called a sex-role inventory, the items on the so-called masculinity scale primarily referred to desirable self-assertive, self-oriented personality traits, and those on the so-called femininity scale primarily referred to desirable nurturant, interpersonally oriented traits. The data Bem (1974) reported confirmed her expectations, showing that although men scored higher on the masculinity scale and women on the femininity scale, there were minimal correlations between the two scales within each sex. Shortly thereafter my colleagues and I (Spence et al., 1974, 1975) published data from the independently derived but empirically similar Personal Attributes Questionnaire that also showed the two scales to be essentially orthogonal.

These findings led Bem and a large number of other investigators to reject the bipolar conception of masculinity and femininity out of hand and, at least seemingly, to accept the rival proposition that the theoretical concepts of masculinity and femininity constitute independent continua. On one level this formulation is a radical departure from the traditional bipolar view and, judging from the torrent of articles that the appearance of the BSRI and PAQ has generated, has been widely regarded as such. On another level it varies only in a relatively minor way from the bipolar, unifactorial model. Although gender-differentiating phenomena are now presumed to fall into two classes, masculine and feminine, the remaining assumptions of the unidimensional model are retained. That is, the attributes, attitudes, and behaviors within each class are assumed to contribute to a single factor, masculinity or femininity. This, of course, implies that all types of masculine or feminine qualities are presumed to be reliable diagnostic indicators of the masculinity or femininity concepts.

It should be noted that identifying scores on scales measuring narrow classes of male- and female-associated traits as measures of the global concepts of masculinity and femininity is a theoretical inference, involving assumptions that must be empirically validated rather than accepted a priori. In the absence of confirming evidence, all that could legitimately be claimed from the psychometric data obtained with the BSRI and PAQ is that self-reports of two specific constellations of gender-related traits are uncorrelated.

A side commentary on self-assertive and expressive traits. Soon after introducing the original version of the PAQ, my colleagues and I came to the conclusion that both single-factor and two-factor models were deficient. We also shortened the instrument, restricting the items to those tapping agentic, self-assertive traits and expressive, interpersonally oriented traits (Spence & Helmreich, 1978). This decision was in part pragmatic—based on our conviction that scales that are homogeneous in character have greater utility—but was largely dictated by theoretical considerations. A number of theoretical approaches to the psychologies of men and women directly or indirectly implicate these trait dimensions as cardinal distinctions between men and women and link them to the maintenance if not the initial emergence of sex-role systems in which men are assigned primary responsibility for their society's political and economic institutions and women primary responsibility for nurturing children and caring for the family dwelling. Popular justifications of traditional sex-role systems also place heavy reliance on these purported differences in the psychological makeup of men and women. In developing and using the shortened PAQ in our subsequent research, our immediate goals were to explore the implications of these theories by determining the extent to which gender differences in these trait dimensions could be observed in various groups, the factors that contributed to their emergence, and their relation to a number of other characteristics and behaviors.

PSEUDOACCEPTANCE OF THE TWO-FACTOR MODEL

The almost ritualistic statement that one finds these days in articles and textbooks devoting space to sex roles and the concepts of masculinity and femininity is that, whereas it was once believed that masculinity and femininity were bipolar, it has been established that they are separate and independent. Although there are holdouts (e.g., Baumrind, 1982), it appears that in the opinion of the majority, the two-factor theory has won a decisive victory over the one-factor model. The victory, however, is more apparent than real. To take an important example, a careful reading of Bem's publications (e.g., 1974, 1977, 1981) suggests that, although nominally promoting the notion that masculinity and femininity are independent and that the BSRI measures this pair of constructs, her theoretical speculations and empirical tests of them using the BSRI have typically been based on *unidimensional* concepts related to sex typing. In this theory a single continuum is implied, a continuum in which those who are strongly sex typed in their self-images and role identification (i.e., masculine men and feminine women) are assigned to one extreme; at the other extreme are those who are not sex typed, identifying with neither the masculine nor the feminine role. This sex-typing notion has recently been melded into Bem's (1981) theory of gender schemata in which individuals are described as ranging from the highly schematic to the aschematic. In both instances a single continuum is specified, running from zero (aschematic or not sex typed) to some high value.

By way of contrast, Bem's unidimensional gender schema, at least as presented in her publications to date, can be compared with the gender schema theory of Markus and her colleagues (e.g., Markus, Crane, Bernstein, & Siladi, 1982), which is genuinely based on a two-factor conceptualization of masculinity and femininity. Thus Markus et al. postulate that there are two gender schemata, one masculine and one feminine, the strength of individuals' tendency to employ each of these schemata being assessed by their scores on the masculinity scale and on the femininity scale of the BSRI. In addition to proposing that there are two gender schemata rather than only one, Markus et al. (1982) make what I (Spence, 1984) have elsewhere called gender-parallel predictions. That is, the theory specifies that in both men and women masculinity scores are positively related to the use of masculine schemata and femininity scores are related to the use of feminine schemata. Bem's unidimensional theory, on the other hand, employs a mirror-image model. That is, sex-typed men, defined as those with high scores on the masculinity scale and low scores on the femininity scale, and sex-typed women, defined as those with the reverse pattern of scores, can be classified together, despite the radical difference in their patterns of BSRI scores. Thus, according to the Bem's theory, it is sex typing, not BSRI scores per se, that produces the greatest use of gender schema in both men and women.

The type of two-factor theory advanced by Markus, however, is relatively rare. Most investigators using the BSRI and PAQ have committed themselves to unidimensional constructs, even though obstensibly postulating that masculinity and femininity are independent.

There are two critical differences between earlier theories that incorporated a bipolar, single-factor model of masculinity-femininity or sex-role identification and the later unidimensional theories of Bem and her followers. First, whereas it was once popularly assumed that gender-congruent sex typing was necessary for psychological well-being and effective functioning, Bem (1974) and others have proposed that men and women who are not sex typed have an advantage over sex-typed individuals. Second, it has been made explicit that it is possible for an individual to exhibit both masculine and feminine attributes and behaviors. Earlier theories tended to remain silent on this point or to imply the contrary.

As I hinted earlier, I infer that at least initially Bem wanted to claim that individuals who have identified themselves with neither the masculine nor the feminine role and therefore have no need to limit themselves by adopting only the qualities and behaviors stereotypically associated with their sex almost automatically develop and display both sets of qualities, but for reasons that are unrelated to gender. And it is the non-sex-typed or non-role-identified individual possessing both the qualities we now call masculine and the qualities we now call feminine who is the model member of a gender-free society. Results obtained with the BSRI did indeed indicate that one could be both masculine and feminine in the empirical sense, at least in the personality traits tapped by this instrument. However, these findings were not merely interpreted as revealing the essential independence of sets of gender-differentiating self-assertive and interpersonally oriented qualities but also the independence of self-images of masculinity and femininity. It is this linkage that ties Bem's theory to a two-factor model.

Having demonstrated that self-assertive and nurturant traits were independent, Bem then essentially reverted to a unidimensional model, simultaneously retaining the BSRI, with its two independent scales, as a measure of individual differences in degree of sex typing or, more recently, gender schematization.

Many of the confusions and controversies that have arisen in the recent literature stem from trying to force two theoretically incompatible models into one and tying both to a single instrument, the BSRI or PAQ. (For a more detailed analysis, see Spence, 1984). One illustration of the problems that have been so generated is the uncertainty about the score combinations on the so-called masculinity and femininity scales of these instruments that represent lack of sex typing. At various times and places, candidates suggested by Bem and by others have been individuals with equal scores on both scales, only those with relatively high scores on both scales, only those with relatively low scores on both scales, or even every score combination other than those representing conventional sex typing. The difficulties a unidimensional theory encounters in specifying who is less sex typed or gender aschematic than whom on the BSRI or PAQ become even more apparent when one compares the problems of this theory with the straightforward, trouble-free predictions generated by the gender schema theory of Markus and her colleagues (1982), which is based on the two-factor model of masculinity and femininity.

MULTIFACTOR MODEL

The way to resolve the inherent contradictions in much of the current theorizing about masculinity and femininity in which work with the BSRI and other two-scale instruments is often embedded is not, however, to embrace wholeheartedly the two-factor model. The relevant empirical evidence provides no better support for this conceptualization of the masculinity and femininity constructs than for one-factor theories of masculinity-femininity or sex-role identification.

Unidimensional models, you recall, imply that the heterogeneous

collection of personal and behavioral variables that distinguish between the genders contribute statistically to a single factor so that in
devising instruments to measure the underlying dimension one may
sample this array as one pleases. The theory that proposes that masculinity and femininity are independent implies, instead, that factor
analyses should reveal two orthogonal factors, with items describing
attributes and actions more characteristic of males belonging to one
and those more characteristic of females belonging to the other.
However, studies reporting correlations between various bipolar
masculinity-femininity tests or the results of factor analyses involving both individual masculinity-femininity measures of heterogeneous content and pooled items drawn from several measures do not
suggest the presence of only one or even two factors. (For a detailed
review of these data, see Constantinople, 1973.) Instead, they unambiguously indicate that the classes of traits, attributes, values, interests, preferences, and behaviors that differentiate the genders are
multifactorial, with varying degrees of relation among factors. Later
research that has included the BSRI and PAQ among its self-report
measures (e.g., Bem, 1974; Major et al., 1981; Orlofsky, 1981; Spence
& Helmreich, 1978; Wakefield, Sasek, Friedman, & Bowden, 1976)
substantiate these conclusions.

By and large, items that are relatively homogeneous in content
tend to cling together. When one looks at content categories, one
sometimes finds that the items can be assigned to separate masculine
and feminine clusters that are relatively independent statistically.
The socially desirable self-assertive traits and nurturant, interpersonally oriented traits found on the PAQ and BSRI are one example, each
cluster contributing to a single factor that is orthogonal to the other
(Helmreich, Spence, & Wilhelm, 1981). In other instances bipolarity has been found. The results of self-ratings on the adjectives "masculine" and "feminine," items found on the BSRI masculinity and
femininity scales, respectively, provide an example of particular
theoretical interest. In a factor analysis of the BSRI, Pedhazur and
Tetenbaum (1979) demonstrated that in both sexes responses to this
pair of items were strongly correlated in a negative direction and contributed to a separate two-item bipolar factor that was minimally related to other BSRI factors. Further, these investigators reported that
although there was some variability in scores on this two-item factor
within each sex, there was almost no overlap between score distributions for the two sexes, almost all of the men falling toward the masculine pole and almost all women toward the feminine pole. Other

investigators (e.g., Edwards & Spence, 1983; Major et al., 1981; Storms, 1980) have also reported substantial negative correlations between self-ratings on the adjectives masculine and feminine and relatively small correlations with the personality trait items on the PAQ or BSRI.

Investigations that have related the PAQ and BSRI to more behaviorally oriented measures indicate that these instruments are relatively successful in predicting behaviors that might reasonably be expected to be influenced by self-assertive and interpersonally oriented characteristics per se (e.g., Spence & Helmreich, 1980). However, when the dependent measures involve sex-role behaviors and preferences that could not be expected to be influenced by these constellations of traits, significant relationships with BSRI or PAQ scores often fail to emerge. The journals are littered with dozens of BSRI and PAQ studies testing hypotheses derived from the assumption that these instruments measure the abstract concepts of masculinity and femininity or sex-role identification that failed to be confirmed. Some statistically significant relationships have been reported, but typically the effects are small, accounting for only a miniscule portion of the variance and not always being replicable (e.g., Bem & Lenney, 1976; Helmreich, Spence, & Holahan, 1979).

The data thus suggest that gender-differentiating self-assertive and nurturant characteristics do not provide a special understanding of sex-role and other gender-relevant phenomena, despite the pivotal role they have been assigned by a number of theorists. Nor do they support the assumption that the PAQ and BSRI are useful not merely as personality measures but also as measures of such broad concepts as masculinity and femininity or sex-role identification. This conclusion does not state that relations betwen sex-typed behaviors and the BSRI or PAQ that cannot reasonably be attributed to self-assertive and interpersonally oriented traits never have been or never will be found. Rather it suggests that these relations are not frequent enough, consistent enough, or large enough to justify using these personality questionnaires as measures of such abstract constructs as masculinity and femininity, sex typing, gender schematization, sex-role orientation, and so forth.

Implications. The intent of these remarks is not to criticize the BSRI and PAQ per se but rather to question the validity of the concepts that many have presumed they measure. The theoretical validity of conventional masculinity-femininity tests can also be disputed. That is, the evidence indicating that the diverse collection of observable, normatively expected distinctions between males and females are multifactorial discredits current theories of masculinity and femininity, be they of the one- or two-factor variety. The fundamental logical error that seems to have been made is to assume that an aggregation of statistical facts distinguishing between two groups of individuals, in this instance men and women, can automatically be combined to arrive at portraits of the typical member of each group. This procedure is warranted, however, only if the items on the list of distinguishing characteristics are shown to be highly correlated within each group. The data unambiguously indicate that this is not the case. Instead it appears that few men and women exhibit all or even most of the qualities and behaviors "typical" of their gender or expected of them by societal stereotypes. Most men and women exhibit a fair number of gender-congruent characteristics, but the particular assortment varies widely from one man or woman to the next.

This conclusion suggests, in turn, that extant theories of sex-role development are vastly oversimplified. Most of these theories imply that at each developmental period, gender-related qualities, attitudes, and behaviors emerge and are sustained as a total package, as it were, attributable to a common, monolithic set of processes. If they are to be useful, our theories will have to be elaborated to take into account the fact that even among men and women who are perceived as normal representatives of their gender there is heterogeneity in the patterns of role-associated qualities and behaviors they exhibit. Further, a multiplicity of variables contributes to the etiology of sex-typed characteristics that vary not only from one type of characteristic to another but also from one man or woman to another. The available evidence also suggests that these variables are not necessarily associated with the gender-related expectations of parents and peers or with general societal sex-role standards (e.g., Baumrind, 1982; Spence & Helmreich, 1978).

TWO APPROACHES TO MASCULINITY AND FEMININITY

Once one concedes that specific gender-related phenomena are multidimensional, what is to be done with the concepts of masculinity and femininity? The answer depends on the sense in which these constructs are being used. Some investigators may wish to refer only to the structure of observable gender-differentiating qualities. In this instance masculinity-femininity is the label given to the bipolar property that, according to one set of the theories, underlies the single statistical factor to which all these qualities purportedly contribute. In parallel fashion, masculinity and femininity identify the pair of properties that, according to a second set of theories, underlie the two statistical factors to which these qualities can be assigned. When they are used in this sense, the data suggest that the global concepts of masculinity-femininity or masculinity and femininity should be abandoned as without scientific validity. The same conclusion can be drawn about such concepts as sex-role orientation that have been linked to similar assumptions about the relations among gender-differentiating characteristics.

When laypersons speak of their own or another's masculinity or femininity, they quite obviously have something bipolar in mind. Masculinity and femininity, we can infer, are assumed to be qualitatively different and basically incompatible, almost all men being perceived and perceiving themselves as to some degree masculine rather than feminine and almost all women being perceived and perceiving themselves as feminine rather than masculine. It could be that people, acting as naive scientists, have adopted the same single-factor, bipolar conception of masculinity-femininity implicitly adopted by most psychologists. However, this seems to me unlikely, primarily on impressionistic grounds, although there are scraps of relevant objective evidence to support my suspicion. For example, recall that self-ratings on the adjectives masculine and feminine are substantially correlated in a negative direction. These self-ratings, however, have relatively little relation to the two orthogonal clusters of personality traits on the BSRI and PAQ. Also suggestive is a recent study by Deaux and Lewis (1983) of the components of gender stereotypes. Although subjects tended to perceive positive correlations between the occurrence of some categories of gender-related phenomena, significant relationships did not uniformly occur, and when they did they were typically small in magnitude. It has also been found that gender stereotypes are not monolithic. Clifton, McGrath, and Wicks (1976), for example, reported that different constellations of characteristics are associated with adult females identified as clubwomen, housewives, career women, and so forth.

The data then, suggest that most men and women have not adopted an implicit theory about the unidimensional structure of gender-differentiating phenomena. Their personal senses of masculinity or femininity appear to be phenomenologically real, even though their meanings remain unarticulated, and to be relatively independent of any given class of masculine or feminine attributes and behaviors.

I suspect that most psychologists have employed these unanalyzed and undefined abstractions in the same way as those in the community at large, which may account both for psychologists' seeming lack of interest in defining them and for the persistence of bipolar views even among those who apparently believe they have adopted a two-factor theory. However, a priori acceptance of the masculinity and femininity concepts as self-evidently real has had the unfortunate consequence of leading us to devise measures of these constructs based on unstated theoretical assumptions and to cling to these measures in the face of an impressive array of empirical data that refute the assumptions that provide their rationale.

The argument that current conceptualizations of masculinity and femininity are inadequate but that nonetheless the constructs of masculinity and femininity are psychologically meaningful is neither satisfying nor sufficient. In the remainder of this chapter I will attempt to discern and explicate the meanings of these constructs.

Masculinity, Femininity, and Gender Identity

SELF-CONCEPTS OF MASCULINITY AND FEMININITY

Almost all men and women appear to have a firm sense of their own masculinity or femininity, a sense that is a central component of their self-identity and that it is important to preserve. In labeling this elemental aspect of self, people use various terms—such as masculinity or femininity, manliness or womanliness, or being a real man or real woman. In subsequent discussion, however, I will refer only to masculinity and femininity.

Gender identity. The basic proposition I will advance is that these senses of masculinity or femininity can be described by appealing to the concept of gender identity. Following such theorists as Green (1974), Money and Ehrhardt (1972), and Stoller (1968), I define gender identity as a fundamental existential sense of one's maleness or femaleness, an acceptance of one's gender on a psychological level that, with rare exceptions, parallels and complements awareness and acceptance of one's biological sex.

The foundations of gender identity, according to Money and Ehrhardt (1972) and others, are laid down very early in life. The first question people typically ask on hearing about the birth of a baby is "Is it a boy or a girl?" with the child's sex being impressed upon the child and others from this time forward. It is therefore not surprising that by two and a half years of age almost all children are consistently able to identify themselves as boy or girl and attach considerable importance to being correctly identified by others. Gender identity is thus fairly well established even before the child is mature enough to recognize the anatomical differences between the sexes or to understand the phenomenon of gender constancy, an accomplishment most children do not achieve until they are four or five (e.g., Martin & Halverson, 1983; Slaby & Fry, 1975; Bussey & Bandura, 1983). Gender identity, as defined above, is thus a primitive, unarticulated concept of self, initially laid down at an essentially preverbal stage of development and maintained at an unverbalized level. As such, a person's sense of masculinity or femininity is ineffable—incapable of being put into words. The apparent inability even of verbally sophisticated adults to specify what they mean, despite their willingness to speak of their personal sense of masculinity or femininity, is thus intrinsic to these self-concepts.

Otherwise normal children occasionally exhibit severe disturbances in gender identity. As described in the *Diagnostic and Statistical Manual of Mental Disorders* (DSM III; American Psychiatric Association, 1980),

> The essential features [of disorders of gender identity] are a persistent feeling of discomfort and inappropriateness in a child about his or her anatomic sex and the desire to be, or insistence that he or she is, of the other sex. In addition, there is a persistent repudiation of the individual's own anatomic attributes. This is not merely the rejection of stereotypical sex role behavior as, for example, in "tomboyishness" in girls or "sissyish" behavior in boys, but rather a profound disturbance of the normal sense of maleness or femaleness. (p. 264)

Other overt manifestations include a marked preference for other-sex playmates, cross-sex dressing, and a desire to engage only in those activities stereotypically associated with the other sex. Another group recognized in DSM III as having gender identity problems consists of transsexuals, adults who may or may not have exhibited overt signs of gender identity disturbance in childhood but who report that they have always felt that they were members of one sex trapped in the body of the other.

But such disturbances are rare, gender identity being achieved by almost all physiologically normal children at an early age, seemingly automatically, and maintained throughout life. It may be for this reason that, aside from those concerned with childhood psychopathology, few psychologists have paid attention to the gender identity construct, as defined above, focusing instead on the concept of sex- (or gender-) *role* identity.

Gender identity versus sex-role identity. Both constructs could be retained, gender identity being regarded as a forerunner of sex-role identity although not inevitably leading to its development. Indeed, Bem (1978) has adopted a position of this sort. Although she advocates restructuring society so that there are no role distinctions between men and women and hence no sex-role identification, she has conceded that the development of at least a mild sense of gender identity is probably inevitable and even desirable. I am suggesting, however, not only that the sex-role identification concept lacks validity, at least in its current form, but that an elaboration of the functions of gender identity yields a theoretical account that provides a better fit to the available data.

Gender identity and the development of gender-related qualities. As I outlined earlier, the data suggest that very few men and women correspond to our society's prescriptive and descriptive stereotypes in all significant respects and that most are diverse in the sets of characteristics they do exhibit. Yet most men and women are recognizable members of their genders, socially acceptable in their eyes and the eyes of others. Within broad limits, there is more social tolerance for deviations from gender stereotypes than psychologists' theories have typically acknowledged—increasingly so, perhaps, in recent decades in which our sex-role attitudes have become more permissive. (See Ehrhardt, this volume.)

Children are exposed to multiple exemplars of males and females: parents and other significant adults, siblings, and peers, to say nothing of characters encountered in books, on television, and through other media. Even among those of the same age and sex, these individuals not only differ in their own qualities and in their role-related values but also may not be consistent in the behaviors they display and those they advocate. Fathers vary, for example, not only in their athletic ability and active participation in sports but also in the degree to which they associate these activities with masculinity or the male role. Whether or not they themselves are athletic, some fathers may demand that their sons take part in sports and discourage their daughters from doing so, whereas others may encourage both their sons and daughters and still others may be permissive or even indifferent about their children's athletic activities. Similarly, mothers who by choice have paid employment outside the home may love cooking and other domestic tasks, whereas those who elect not to work may avoid these duties whenever they can. Or housewives may be assertive and aggressive in their personal characteristics yet insist that they and their children be deferent to their husbands as head of the household. Others who serve as children's models and teachers show the same kind of diversity.

Nonetheless, as the literature attests (e.g., Kuhn, Nash, & Brucken, 1978; Marcus & Overton, 1978), children absorb at a remarkably early age many of the gender stereotypes of their culture, often in exaggerated form. They may insist, for example, that all physicians are men and all nurses are women, even when they have been personally exposed to exceptions. Or, even in the face of egalitarian parents striving to give their children a nonsexist upbringing, they may be adamant about wearing the "right" kinds of clothes for their sex, playing only with gender-appropriate toys, or otherwise clinging to concrete and obvious signs of their maleness or femaleness. But with greater experience and cognitive sophistication, these stereotypes become more aligned with reality and absolutist standards tend to relax.

Young children's desire to adopt the conspicuous qualities associated with their own sex and age and their tendency to emulate same-sex models (e.g., Blakemore, LaRue, & Olejnik, 1979; Bussey & Bandura, 1983; Perry & Bussey, 1979) very probably represent their attempt to confirm and define their emerging sense of self-identity in general and their gender identity in particular, as well as an effort to win the approval of others and avoid their disapproval. With time, however, the role of gender identity in guiding the acquisition of gender-congruent attributes and behaviors becomes minimized. Gender identity may make same-sex models more salient, but to the extent that the individual is motivated to develop and display particular gender-related characteristics *because* they are gender-appropriate, other factors such as sex-role attitudes increasingly take over this guiding function. Like all other attributes, attitudes, and behaviors, the particular constellation of gender-related characteristics a child initially acquires and continues to develop throughout life—or conversely those characteristics he or she fails to develop—depends on the interaction of a complex set of external and internal factors that include the child's own abilities and temperament. Except for those sex-typed characteristics that are highly valued and consistently exhibited by others of the same sex (Bussey & Perry, 1982; Perry & Bussey, 1979), or cross-typed characteristics that elicit strong disapprobation among almost all members of a given culture, heterogeneity rather than uniformity is therefore likely to be the rule.

To reiterate what I suggested above, once gender identity is well established, its etiological contribution becomes less potent and more indirect. Instead, it becomes the function of gender-congruent characteristics, however they are developed, to preserve and protect people's gender identity or sense of masculinity or femininity. As long as individuals perceive themselves as having enough of these characteristics, their masculinity or femininity is taken for granted and is seldom a subject of conscious concern or reflection. Thus in the interview study (Spence & Sawin, 1984) I mentioned earlier, to which I will continue to refer, a number of men and women, when questioned about their senses of masculinity or femininity, told us such things as "It's something I've never had to think about," "I've never had a problem with masculinity," or "I'm a woman and always have been."

What constitutes an adequate amount of gender-relevant qualities for a given individual is determined by a complex calculus operating below the level of conscious awareness. The elements entering into these calculations vary across individual men and women and, within individuals, shift with age and changes in role responsibilities and other life circumstances. The variables most likely to be entered into the equation with positive values are gender-congruent characteristics and role behaviors that the person perceives himself or herself as displaying, with valued attributes being given special weight. Unless the individual highly prizes them, desirable gender-congruent attributes the person does not possess are likely to be regarded as unimportant and hence excluded from the calculations rather than being entered with negative values. Similarly, the individual's gender-incongruent qualities are likely to be discounted, particularly when the person considers them desirable for their own sake, these qualities being interpreted as properly belonging to people in general and not, as stereotype would have it, only to members of the other sex. In short, people strive to keep their sense of masculinity or femininity intact, using those gender-appropriate behaviors and characteristics they happen to possess to confirm their gender identity and attempting to dismiss other aspects of their makeup as unimportant.

Most men and women appear to be secure in their gender identity most of the time. However, new developmental tasks may create stresses that cause individuals to doubt their masculinity or femininity and struggle to reaffirm it. Adolescents, for example, are especially likely to question their masculinity or femininity until they prove to themselves their sexual adequacy or their attractiveness to the opposite sex. This period is often particularly troublesome for adolescents who begin to recognize that their sexual preferences are for members of their own sex, particularly those who have accepted the belief that homosexuality is immoral or a form of mental illness. Homosexuals' histories, however, seldom include signs of disturbances in gender identity in childhood, and rarely do homosexuals change their identity upon discovering or admitting their sexual orientation. Further, many regain their equanimity, especially in this increasingly tolerant era, by disparaging the importance of sexual preference and using other aspects of themselves to revalidate their sense of masculinity or femininity. The feeling of many heterosexuals that gay men and lesbians cannot be real men or women reflects the weight that heterosexuals place on sexual orientation in assessing their own and others' masculinity or femininity but not the value assigned to this aspect of self by homosexuals who have managed to make peace with themselves.

Unfortunate life events can also trigger self-doubts. Women are especially vulnerable to such happenings as the loss of a spouse or problems in finding one, the inability to conceive or bear children, or damage to their physical attractiveness. Aside from their fear about sexual potency, men's strong identification with the role of worker and family provider can make the loss of a job or inability to find adequately compensated work a particularly powerful threat to their feelings of masculinity. They may try to reduce these feelings of inadequacy by compensatory activity. For example, unemployed men who abuse their wives or sit in bars all day drinking with buddies may not only be expressing their anxieties and frustrations but also be attempting to restore their confidence in their masculinity. Assuming that the precipitating circumstances persist, more constructive, long-term solutions involve reassessment—attributing the threatening events to sources outside the self, minimizing their significance for masculinity or femininity, and assigning greater weight to those positive features of self one has retained. To put the matter abstractly, in the face of change individuals tend to rearrange their internal calculus so that the sum is maintained or restored to the threshold level that allows the person to validate his or her gender identity.

The tenor of my remarks is that whereas many men and women experience self-doubts from time to time and some are even chronically insecure about their masculinity or femininity, what is problematic is lack of confidence in one's adequacy, not uncertainty and ambivalence about the congruence of one's gender identity with one's biological sex. Fearing that one is inadequate as a man or woman is not the same as suspecting that psychologically one is more like the other sex. Obviously there are dramatic exceptions, such as transsexuals, but these are extremely rare.

The contention that almost all individuals are certain at least about the direction of their gender identity may be an exaggeration. However, the all-too-common practice of interpreting the appearance of a few conspicuous counterstereotypic qualities or, especially for women, the expression of personal discontent with the strictures imposed by conventional sex-role expectations as indicators of ambivalence or uncertainty about one's gender identity or as a desire to identify with the other sex have made me leery. I am particularly uncomfortable when these disturbances in gender identity are said to exist at some deep, unconscious level, ignoring individuals' conscious self-images or the host of ways they resemble other members of their gender.

Interpretations of this sort, which imply a psychopathological condition in need of therapeutic intervention, are less prevalent now than in less liberated times, but they still persist. (DSM III sets stringent standards for the diagnosis of disorders of gender identity, as illustrated by the criteria I quoted earlier.) Until our models of masculinity and femininity acknowledge the multidimensional nature of gender phenomena, until better diagnostic instruments have been devised, and until information is accumulated that will allow us to come to reasonable, data-based conclusions, I am reluctant to con-

cede that there are a great many men and women who at some unconscious level are uncertain about or have rejected their masculinity or
femininity.

Implications for social change. One implication of this theoretical
position is that societal attitudes about what is appropriate for one or
both genders can change, often quite rapidly, without creating
threats to individuals' personal sense of masculinity or femininity. Or
perhaps it is more accurate to say that because these senses are relatively invulnerable and not necessarily tied to any specific attribute
or behavior, rapid social change is possible. For example, before
World War II relatively few women elected to work except from economic necessity, and most men were reluctant to let their wives work
because they believed it reflected negatively on their capacity to fulfill
their role as family provider. But during the war manpower shortages
made it necessary for more women to join the labor force, often in jobs
that had been done almost exclusively by men; overnight, Rosie the
Riveter became a patriotic figure. Women experienced this wartime
need for their services not as a loss in femininity but as a redefinition,
even if a temporary one, of the significance of doing men's work. A
second example may be found in the "hippy era" when a number of
rebellious young men began to sport long hair. They were not trying
to imitate women or to change their gender identity; they adopted
this among other behaviors as a visible, nose-tweaking symbol of
their rejection of mainstream values and life-styles. As the shock
value wore off and it became apparent that long hair was not a signal
of effeminacy, the fashion spread and ultimately became socially
acceptable.

Masculinity and femininity as dimensionalized concepts. Self-
ratings on the adjectives masculine and feminine are substantially
but far from perfectly correlated in a negative direction. Further, it has
been shown (e.g., Pedhazur & Tetenbaum, 1979) that although
men's and women's distributions are widely separated, there is
variability within each sex in scores on a two-item scale made of this
pair of adjectives. This variability, of course, would be expected from
the imperfect correlations between the two items.

These self-ratings probably have two components. The first is the
individual's report of his or her sense of gender identity. This judgment, I have suggested, tends to be all or none, such that if one is
masculine one is not feminine and vice versa. This component tends

to drive the self-ratings of the two sexes toward opposite poles. The second component is made up of a calculus different from the one individuals use to assess their gender identity as masculine or feminine, being more related to their overall assessment of their actual qualities than to their phenemenological sense of maleness or femaleness. That is, the question How masculine and/or how feminine are you? tends to lead people to sum up their specific qualities that stereotypically are associated with males and with females, these sums then being entered into their ratings. The equations people use in these calculations are to some degree idiosyncratic, not everyone entering the same qualities or giving various qualities equal weights. Nonetheless individuals appear to be responsive to the empirical as well as the existential meanings of masculine and feminine.

Data from our interview study support these speculations. Most men and women expressed confidence in their sense of masculinity or femininity and picked a fairly high number when asked to rate themselves numerically on a 10-point unipolar scale (of masculinity for men and femininity for women). Yet it was not uncommon for respondents to volunteer specific ways they were unmasculine or unfeminine.

EVALUATION OF MASCULINITY AND FEMININITY IN OTHERS

The same two elements also appear in processing information about others, but to different degrees depending on the particular judgment being made. When statements are made about others' security or insecurity in their masculinity or femininity, an inference seems to have been made about those persons' feelings of self-confidence in their gender identity. In other instances, particularly when the description includes a reference to the degree to which someone is masculine or feminine, it seems likely that an estimate of the total set of gender-relevant qualities the person exhibits has been added to the assessment process.

Evidence supporting these conjectures can be found in a study by Major et al. (1981) in which subjects rated protocols of (bogus) male and female stimulus persons (SPs) on the adjectives masculine and feminine. Subjects were given data on the SPs' scores on the PAQ such that among the male and the female SPs all four combinations of relatively high and relatively low scores on the self-assertiveness and expressiveness scales were represented. Recall that the trait items on the PAQ were all selected because they had been demonstrated to be related to descriptive stereotype ratings. Thus these personality profiles could be expected to be related to ratings on masculinity and femininity, independent of the SPs' gender. This was found to be the case: SPs in the two groups with high self-assertiveness scores were rated as more masculine than the two low-scoring groups, and similarly, SPs in the two groups with high expressiveness scores were rated as more feminine than the two low-scoring groups. At the same time it was found that, within each PAQ group, ratings of male SPs were markedly higher on the adjective masculine and lower on the adjective feminine than those of female SPs and, further, that these ratings were substantially correlated in a negative direction. The subjects' ratings, then, appeared to be driven by two components: masculinity and femininity as bipolar opposites (gender identity), the former belonging to men and the latter to women, and specific gender-related attributes, in this instance self-assertive and expressive attributes. These two classes of gender-related characteristics, subjects seemed to appreciate, can vary independently, despite gender identity.

Turning to the operation of these assessment processes in real life, even in casual first encounters people tend automatically to scan those they meet and to classify them in various ways. Almost all of us feel impelled, if nothing else, to identify another's sex and are likely to make a conscious search for additional information if the initial set of cues does not permit an unambiguous judgment. Given sufficient time and inclination, people tend to go beyond this simple male/female classification to make a rapid assessment of gender-related qualities that allows a decision about the person's acceptability as a representative member of his or her gender. As additional information becomes available, these initial judgments tend to become more refined, reflecting decisions about the degree to which another person is masculine or feminine.

When the first interaction with another individual is brief, judgments are heavily influenced by the person's physical characteristics, dress, and mannerisms. With further and more extensive encounters, other data become available and enter into these calculations, either reinforcing one's initial impressions or modifying them. For example, the masculinity of a slightly built man whose voice and body movements seem effeminate may be suspect, especially to those who regard these characteristics as signs of homosexuality. However, if it is later observed that the man is forceful and assertive in his dealings with others and it becomes known that he is happily married and the father of five, his physical attributes and mannerisms are likely to be heavily discounted, the ultimate assessment being that he is fairly masculine. A number of other types of factors are also likely to influence these calculations of masculinity or femininity, such as the age and role of the person being assessed, and situational factors that affect the degree to which gender is salient in the interactions.

There is also variability among individuals in the equations they employ; people enter different quantities or assign them different weights even when given access to the same information. Such factors as implicit theories about gender phenomena, values, sex-role attitudes and personal preferences, and the degree to which gender is personally salient are all influential.

There is also an interesting and probably bidirectional relationship between liking and masculinity and femininity. Masculine men and feminine women, that is, those who exhibit a number of desirable gender-congruent attributes (even though they may deviate from the stereotype in significant ways), are liked more than those who are judged unmasculine or unfeminine (e.g., Kristal, Sanders, Spence, & Helmreich, 1975). However, it also seems probable that a man or woman who is liked for qualities unrelated to gender is regarded as more masculine or more feminine than a person who is less admirable.

A question answered. In opening this chapter I asked what people meant when they described others as masculine or feminine—what information they intended to convey. The answer I have just proposed is that they are offering a summative assessment, arrived at in idiosyncratic ways. Although a group of observers, given access to the same data, reach their decision through various routes, there is nonetheless likely to be some degree of agreement about any given individual. However, those who are not privy to these data and have to rely solely on another's description of a particular individual as, for example, highly masculine or not very feminine, have not been provided with much specific information. That is, these global characterizations do not permit inferences about particular attributes or behavioral patterns the person does or does not exhibit. The feeling that one understands what is being concretely conveyed is thus largely illusory.

In principle, however, it is possible to determine the observable characteristics that have entered into these calculations and discover how they are combined. It might be valuable to study the processes by which people arrive at their decisions, as some (e.g., Major et al., 1981) are already doing. Self-report instruments could also be devised whose items have been selected to be representative of the various of classes of attributes and behaviors considered important to survey, and in the manner of conventional masculinity-femininity tests, a single score could be obtained for each respondent that would allow people to be roughly ordered with respect to the degree to which they are masculine or feminine in the totality of their gender-related attributes. Whether it would be particularly useful to put this much effort into developing a measure that would yield only a gross characterization is quite another matter.

Summary and Concluding Statement

In this chapter, I have suggested that although the terms masculine and feminine and masculinity and femininity have rarely been defined, they appear to have two types of meaning both for psychologists and for the community at large. First, masculine and feminine have an empirical meaning, being used as labels to identify specific objects, events, or qualities that in a given culture are perceived as more closely associated with males or with females. Second, these adjectives and, even more exclusively the nouns masculinity and femininity, are used as theoretical constructs that refer to a fundamental property or aspect of the individual's self-concept that is not directly observable. Masculinity and femininity in this second sense are conceived as bipolar opposites, almost all men having a firm sense of their psychological masculinity and almost all women having a similar sense of their femininity.

The implicit assumptions on which conventional theories of masculinity-femininity are predicated imply that all gender-related phenomena contribute to a bipolar femininity-masculinity factor so that assessment of an individual's masculine and feminine qualities (in the empirical sense of these terms) can be used to infer his or her position on the hypothetical masculinity-femininity continuum. Constructs such as sex-role identification and sex-role orientation are based on the same assumptions. More recently it as been proposed that masculine and feminine qualities and their accompanying self-images of masculinity and femininity constitute instead two separate, statistically independent dimensions. However, most investigators nominally advancing this two-factor model and tying the measurement of masculinity and femininity to instruments containing separate scales of masculine and feminine attributes have in fact employed unidimensional bipolar models, based on such concepts as sex-role identification, sex typing, or gender schema.

The empirical data, however, support neither the one-factor nor the two-factor model of gender-differentiating phenomena, suggesting instead that they are multidimensional. To the extent that the concepts of masculinity-femininity (and other similar unidimensional constructs) or of masculinity and femininity are intended to represent the structure of gender-relevant characteristics, these constructs lack validity.

I proposed, however, that masculinity and femininity, as they refer to an individual's self-concept, be retained and reconceptualized as gender identity: a basic phenomenological sense of one's maleness or femaleness that parallels awareness and acceptance of one's biological sex and is established early in life. Although gender identity plays some etiological role in the development of specific sex-typed characteristics and behaviors in the young child, other sets of factors take over this function once gender identity is firmly established. The result is considerable diversity within each sex in the particular constellations of gender-congruent and gender-incongruent characteristics and behaviors that individuals exhibit. Yet gender identity remains intact; people utilize the gender-appropriate characteristics they do possess to protect and validate their sense of masculinity or femininity. Stressful life events or the development of incongruent attributes may threaten a person's self-confidence in his or her gender identity but do not change its direction. Security in one's sense of masculinity or femininity can be restored by discounting the significance of these events or attributes for maleness or femaleness.

In reacting to others, people also appear to employ bipolar conceptions of masculinity and femininity, but in describing the degree to which another person is masculine or feminine, they seem to be giving estimates of the totality of gender-related qualities that person possesses, based on available information. Thus, in practice, judgments of masculinity and femininity in the sense of gender identity and in the sense of concrete gender-differentiating qualities are often interwined.

In conclusion, individuals can doubtless be roughly ordered from high to low in the degree to which they exhibit the full range of characteristics stereotypically associated with their gender, in the conventionality of their sex-role attitudes, in the salience of gender considerations in their reactions to themselves and to others, and in their tendency to employ gender schemata in processing information about the self or others. The multifactorial model of gender-related phenomena implies that an individual's standings on each of these dimensions must be independently assessed rather than measured by any specific collection of gender-related characteristics one pleases or by any all-purpose instrument. Unless appropriate techniques are used to measure these various properties, useful tests of their theoretical implications for other attributes and behaviors cannot be conducted.

REFERENCES

American Psychiatric Association. (1980). *Diagnostic and statistical manual of mental disorders* (3rd ed.). Washington, DC: Author.

Angrist, S. A. (1969). The study of sex-roles. *Journal of Social Issues, 15,* 215– 232.

Baumrind, D. (1982). Are androgynous individuals more effective persons and parents? *Child Development, 53,* 76–80.

Beere, C. A. (1983). Instruments and measures in a changing, diverse society. In B. L. Richardson and J. Wirenberg (Eds.), *Sex role research: Measuring social change.* New York: Praeger.

Bem, S. L. (1974). The measurement of psychological androgyny. *Journal of Consulting and Clinical Psychology, 42,* 155–162.

Bem, S. L. (1977). On the utility of alternate procedures for assessing psychological androgyny. *Journal of Consulting and Clinical Psychology, 45,* 196– 205.

Bem, S. L. (1978). Beyond androgyny: Some presumptuous prescriptions for a liberated sexual identity. In J. A. Sherman and F. L. Denmark (Eds.), *The psychology of women: Future directions in research.* New York: Psychological Dimensions.

Bem, S. L. (1981). Gender schema theory: A cognitive account of sex typing. *Psychological Review, 88,* 369–371.

Bem, S. L. & Lenney, E. (1976). Sex-typing and the avoidance of cross-sex behavior. *Journal of Personality and Social Psychology, 33,* 48–54.

Blakemore, J. E. O., LaRue, A. A., & Olejnik, A. B. (1979). Sex-appropriate toy preference and the ability to conceptualize toys as sex-role related. *Developmental Psychology, 15*, 339–340.

Bussey, K., & Bandura, A. (1983). Influence of gender constancy and social power on sex-linked modeling. Manuscript submitted for publication.

Bussey, K., & Perry, D.G. (1982). Same-sex imitation: The avoidance of cross-sex models or the acceptance of same-sex models? *Sex Roles, 8*, 773–784.

Clifton, A. K., McGrath, D., & Wicks, B. (1976). Stereotypes of women: A single category? *Sex Roles, 2*, 135–148.

Coffman, R., & Levy, B. I. (1972). The dimensions implicit in psychological masculinity-femininity. *Educational and Psychological Measurement, 32*, 975–985.

Constantinople, A. (1973). Masculinity-femininity: An exception to the famous dictum? *Psychological Bulletin, 80*, 389–407.

Deaux, K. (1982). From individual differences to social categories: Analysis of a decade's research on gender. Presidential address, Midwestern Psychological Association, Minneapolis, May, 1982.

Deaux, K., & Lewis, L. L. (1983). Components of gender stereotypes. Manuscript submitted for publication.

Edwards, V., & Spence, J. T. (1983). Gender schemata and gender-differentiating traits: A test of three hypotheses. In preparation.

Feather, N. T., & Said, J. A. (1983). Preference for occupations in relation to masculinity, femininity, and gender. *British Journal of Social Psychology, 22*, 113–127.

Green, R. (1974). *Sexual identity conflict in children and adults.* New York: Basic Books.

Helmreich, R. L., Spence, J. T., & Holahan, C. K. (1979). Psychological androgyny and sex-role flexibility: A test of two hypotheses. *Journal of Personality and Social Psychology, 37*, 1631–1644.

Helmreich, R. L., Spence, J. T., & Wilhelm, J. A. (1981). A psychometric analysis of the Personal Attributes Questionnaire. *Sex Roles, 7*, 1097–1108.

Hill, J. P., & Lynch, M. E. (1983). The intensification of gender-related role expectations during early adolescence. In J. Brooks-Gunn and A. C. Petersen (Eds.), *Girls at puberty: Biological and psychosocial perspectives.* New York: Plenum.

Kristal, J., Sanders, D., Spence, J. T., & Helmreich, R. (1975). Inferences about the femininity of competent women and their implications for likability. *Sex roles, 1*, 33–40.

Kuhn, D., Nash, S. C., & Brucken, L. (1978). Sex role concepts of two- and three-year olds. *Child Development, 49*, 445–451.

Major, B., Carnevale, P. J. D., & Deaux, K. (1981). A different perspective on androgyny: Evaluations of masculine and feminine personality characteristics. *Journal of Personality and Social Psychology, 41,* 988–1001.

Marcus, D. E., & Overton, W. F. (1978). The development of cognitive gender constancy and sex role preferences. *Child Development, 49,* 434–444.

Markus, H., Crane, M., Bernstein, S., & Siladi, M. (1982). Self-schemas and gender. *Journal of Personality and Social Psychology, 42,* 38–50.

Martin, C. L., & Halverson, C. F., Jr. (1983). Gender constancy: A methodological and theoretical analysis. *Sex Roles, 9,* 775–790.

Mills, C. J., & Tyrrell, D. J. (1983). Sex-stereotypic encoding and release from proactive inhibition. *Journal of Personality and Social Psychology, 45,* 772–781.

Money, J., & Ehrhardt, A. E. (1972). *Man and woman, boy and girl.* Baltimore: Johns Hopkins University Press.

Nettles, E. J., & Loevinger, J. (1983). Sex role expectations and ego level in relation to problem marriages. *Journal of Personality and Social Psychology, 45,* 676–687.

Orlofsky, J. L. (1981). Relationship between sex role attitudes and personality traits and the Sex Role Behavior Scale-1: A new measure of masculine and feminine role behaviors and interests. *Journal of Personality and Social Psychology, 40,* 927–940.

Pedhazur, E. J., & Tetenbaum, T. J. (1979). Bem Sex Role Inventory: A theoretical and methodological critique. *Journal of Personality and Social Psychology, 37,* 996–1016.

Perry, D. G., & Bussey, K. (1979). The social learning theory of sex differences: Imitation is alive and well. *Journal of Personality and Social Psychology, 37,* 1699–1712.

Slaby, R. G., & Frey, K. S. (1975). Development of gender constancy and selective attention to same-sex models. *Child Development, 46,* 849–856.

Spence, J. T. (1984). Masculinity, femininity, and gender-related traits: A conceptual analysis and critique of current research. In B. A. Maher (Ed.), *Progress in experimental research* (Vol. 13). New York: Academic Press.

Spence, J. T., & Helmreich, R. L. (1978). *Masculinity and femininity: Their psychological dimensions, correlates, and antecedents.* Austin: University of Texas Press.

Spence, J. T., & Helmreich, R. L. (1980). Masculine instrumentality and feminine expressiveness: Their relationships with sex role attitudes and behaviors. *Psychology of Women Quarterly, 5,* 147–163.

Spence, J. T., Helmreich, R., & Stapp, J. (1974). The Personal Attributes Questionnaire: A measure of sex-role stereotypes and masculinity-femininity. *JSAS Catalog of Selected Documents in Psychology, 4*, 43–44, MS 617.

Spence, J. T., Helmreich, R., & Stapp, J. (1975). Ratings of self and peers on sex-role attributes and their relation to self-esteem and conceptions of masculinity and femininity. *Journal of Personality and Social Psychology, 32*, 29–39.

Spence, J. T., & Sawin, L. L. (1984). Images of masculinity and femininity: A reconceptualization. In V. O'Leary, R. Unger, & B. Wallston (Eds.), *Sex, gender and social psychology*. Hillsdale, NJ: Lawrence Erlbaum Associates.

Stoller, R. (1968). *Sex and gender: On the development of masculinity and femininity*. New York: Science House.

Storms, M. (1980). Theories of sex-role identity. *Journal of Personality and Social Psychology, 38*, 783–792.

Taylor, M. C., & Hall, J. A. (1982). Psychological androgyny: A review and reformulation of theories, methods, and conclusions. *Psychological Bulletin, 92*, 347–366.

Tellegen, A., & Lubinski, D. (1983). Some methodological comments on labels, traits, interaction, and types in the study of "femininity" and "masculinity": Reply to Spence. *Journal of Personality and Social Psychology, 44*, 447–455.

Wakefield, J. A., Jr., Sasek, J., Friedman, A. F., & Bowden, J. D. (1976). Androgyny and other measures of masculinity-femininity. *Journal of Consulting and Clinical Psychology, 44*, 766–660.

Sex Differences in Achievement Patterns[1]

Jacquelynne Eccles
University of Michigan

Sex differences in achievement patterns have long interested social scientists. Many theories have been proposed to explain these presumed differences, often without solid evidence that they do in fact exist (see Frieze, Parsons, Johnson, Ruble, & Zellman, 1978, and Maccoby & Jacklin, 1974, for full discussion). Lest I succumb to the same temptation, I have set out three goals for this chapter: (1) To review these differences in a specific subset of achievement behaviors; (2) to summarize a comprehensive theory explaining these differences; and (3) to present the results of a longitudinal study designed to evaluate this theory.

Sex Differences in Achievement Patterns

Achievement has been operationalized in many ways. In laboratory studies it is often defined in terms of task choice, persistence in the face of failure, task performance, speed of performance, and scores on tests of motivation, anxiety, cognitive style, achievement, and aptitude. Field researchers and sociologists have defined it in terms of grades in school, scores on standardized tests of achievement and aptitude, course-enrollment patterns, activity choices, performance in competitive activities such as sports or spelling bees, persistence in

1. The research reported here was supported by grants from the National Institutes of Education, Mental Health, and Child Health and Development. Grateful acknowledgment goes to all my colleagues who have worked with me on the project described in this chapter. Special thanks go to Susan Goff-Timmer, Carol Kaczala, Judith Meece, and Carol Midgley, without whose collaboration the ideas and the work reported here might never have come to be.

the classroom or on the job, motivational style, occupational choice, income, and career advancement. Since sex differences occur on only some of these variables, we need to be specific about the achievement behaviors of interest when we discuss sex differences. Furthermore, we must avoid assuming that the sex differences on these various measures are determined by similar factors. Individual differences on these various indexes of achievement are shaped by different processes. Similar variations should exist for sex differences. Consequently, we should not expect simple explanations for sex differences in achievement patterns; many processes will be involved, and the relative importance of these processes will vary depending on the particular achievement behavior chosen for study.

My discussion is limited to a set of achievement behaviors that either reflect real-life achievement choices or are linked to these choices. These include scores on standardized tests of academic achievement and aptitude, grades in school courses, course-enrollment patterns, persistence on laboratory tasks, persistence on or single-minded devotion to occupational achievement activities, and college major and occupational choices.

TEST SCORES AND SCHOOL GRADES

Sex differences on tests of quantitative and verbal skills emerge with some regularity among adolescents and older subjects (see Eccles [Parsons], 1984; Hyde, 1981). For example, at 13 and 17, girls scored better than boys did on the National Assessment Tests of reading, literature, art, and music; in contrast, boys scored better than girls on the science and math tests (Grant & Eiden, 1982). The math and science differences (but not the verbal differences) also show up regularly on the Scholastic Achievement Tests administered nationally by the Educational Testing Service (1980). The quantitative differences (but again not the verbal differences) appear to emerge earlier among gifted populations (Benbow & Stanley, 1980, 1983). It is important to note, however, that even the math and science differences do not emerge with great consistency during the elementary school years. Furthermore, these differences are not very large (accounting for less than 4% of the variance; Hyde, 1981), are not found universally even in advanced high school populations, and are not evident in course grades at any level including college (see Eccles, [Parsons], 1984).

PERSISTENCE

There is a widespread belief in psychology that girls are less persistent in the face of failure on laboratory tasks than boys (see Eccles
Parsons, 1983, Eccles [Parsons], Adler, & Meece, 1984). V. C. Crandall and E. Crandall (personal communication, 1983) and I have reviewed the developmental literature related to this hypothesis and
find no consistent support for it. Although the nature of girls' responses to failure is affected by the sex and age of the evaluator
(Dweck & Bush, 1976), girls' behavioral responses in terms of persistence and accuracy following failure on laboratory tasks are, by and
large, similar to those of boys (e.g. Beck, 1977–1978; Crandall, 1969;
Diener & Dweck, 1978; Dweck, 1975; Dweck & Reppucci, 1973; Eccles, 1983; Eccles Parsons, 1983; Eccles (Parsons), Adler, & Meece,
1984; Nicholls, 1975; Rholes, Blackwell, Jordan, & Walters, 1980; and
Veroff, 1969). This is not to say that there are no gender effects on the
behavioral measures used in these studies. Indeed, under some conditions boys and girls respond differently to both performance feedback and task manipulations. But in my opinion there is little evidence that girls are more likely than boys to give up after academic
failures or to exhibit what might be labeled a learned helplessness
response to challenge or failure.

But what about persistence in everyday achievement settings? It is
difficult to define and measure persistence in these achievement settings primarily because it is difficult to define real-life achievement. It
is even more difficult to assess sex differences in persistence in everyday achievement activities, primarily because males and females engage in different types of achievement activities. Consequently, it is
also difficult to select a criterion activity without biasing the results in
favor of males or females, depending on the activity chosen. For example, defining persistence in terms of occupational status and comparing males and females on this variable clearly biases our conclusion in favor of males. But while acknowledging this value bias, it is
still instructive to compare males and females on a set of variables
assumed to be indicators of achievement persistence by the culture at
large. You are forewarned, however, that these indicators do favor
males in part because they represent typical male achievement activities.

One such indicator is advancement through the educational system toward higher degrees. While males and females receive approx-

imately equal numbers of bachelor's degrees, the number of males going on to obtain advanced degrees, even in traditionally female-stereotyped fields, exceeds the number of females. Furthermore, this discrepancy increases with the level of the degree being considered (National Center for Educational Statistics, 1980).

Another such indicator is advancement through the occupational system toward ever higher levels of responsibility and authority. Females are less likely than males to climb these achievement ladders; and when they do, they typically climb at a slower rate than males even in traditional female-stereotyped fields such as education (Frieze et al., 1978; Vetter, 1981). Although institutional barriers undoubtedly contribute to the sex difference on this indicator, psychological factors are also important (see Eccles & Hoffman, in press).

One final indicator of persistence is single-minded devotion to one's occupational role. This indicator can be assessed in a variety of ways, including the number of hours one puts into one's work, willingness to ask one's family to make sacrifices for one's career advancement, and concern over one's work to the exclusion of other concerns. Although we lack extensive data on these or similar variables, several studies suggest that males, on the average, exceed females on each (e.g., Baruch, Barnett, & Rivers, 1983; Bryson, Bryson, & Johnson, 1978; Eccles & Hoffman, in press; Goff-Timmer, Eccles, & O'Brien, 1984; Maines, 1983; Parsons & Goff, 1980).

COURSE AND OCCUPATIONAL CHOICE

Perhaps the most marked sex differences in achievement behavior are associated with the achievement activities males and females engage in. From early childhood, boys and girls select different achievement activities whenever they are given the choice (Huston, 1983). Although there have been some recent changes, these differences remain dramatic; boys still play football and baseball whereas girls do gymnastics and cheerleading. When they get to high school and have some choice about their courses, males and females still make predominantly sex-stereotyped selections (National Center for Educational Statistics, 1980), especially on career or vocationally relevant courses. This pattern holds up in college and in the occupational world (Eccles & Hoffman, in press) and may be one important cause of the persistence of sex differences in adult earnings.

SUMMARY

Although there are no consistent sex differences for course grades and indexes of persistence on laboratory tasks, there are small but consistent differences on tests of mathematical reasoning and scientific knowledge favoring males among older children, adolescents, and adults. The differences on tests of language skills and on tests of knowledge in literature, music, and art are less consistent but favor females when found. Finally, fairly consistent differences emerge on indicators of persistence and single-minded pursuit of high levels of adult occupational achievement, achievement-related activity choices in childhood and adulthood, high school course-enrollment patterns, college majors, and occupational choice.

Although very important, institutional barriers and discrimination are not entirely responsible for these differences. There is ample evidence that psychological factors are also important. And in fact many psychological explanations have been proposed to account for sex differences in achievement patterns. For example, the underrepresentation of females in the professions has been attributed to low self-confidence (Barnett & Baruch, 1978; Crandall, 1969; Nicholls, 1975; Parsons, Ruble, Hodges, & Small, 1976), fear of success (Horner, 1972), fear of loss of femininity (Tangri, 1972), nonconscious sex-role ideology (Lipman-Blumen & Tickameyer, 1972), differential values and orientation (Parsons & Goff, 1980; Stein & Bailey, 1973; Tittle, 1981), and low independence (Hoffman 1972; Stein & Bailey, 1973). Reviewing and evaluating each of these theories is beyond the scope of this chapter (see Frieze et al., 1978; Parsons & Goff, 1980; and Eccles Parsons, 1983, for recent reviews). But it is clear that a more comprehensive, integrative theory is necessary if we are to advance our understanding of these complex phenomena. My colleagues and I have proposed such a model (see Eccles (Parsons), Adler, Futterman, Goff, Kaczala, Meece, & Midgley, 1983). It is summarized in the next section.

A Model of Achievement Choices

Over the past several years my colleagues and I have been interested in the motivational factors influencing long-range achievement goals such as career or occupational choice, major selection in college, and the integration of work and family roles. Our interest in this area initially grew out of our concern over the underrepresentation of women in professional careers. Like many of our contemporaries, we set out to explain why bright, capable women were not achieving at the same levels as their male peers. We tried to identify the factors constraining women's efforts to attain these nontraditional, high-level achievement goals.

But troubled by the assumption that choosing a nontraditional career reflects maturity and enlightenment whereas choosing a traditional career reflects immaturity and sex-role rigidity, we have redirected our focus. This assumption inevitably leads the researcher to ask, "Why aren't women more like men?" A more appropriate, and less biased, question is, "Why do men and women make the choices they do?" To answer this latter question, we returned to basic motivational models and decided to treat long-range, life-defining achievement choices as analogous to task choices. Given this perspective, we have developed an expectancy/value model of achievement choice based on the expectancy × value models of Lewin (1938) and Atkinson (1964). This model, depicted in Figure 1, links achievement choices to expectancies for success and to the importance or value an individual attaches to the available achievement options. It also specifies the relation of these constructs to cultural norms, experience, aptitude, and a set of personal beliefs and attitudes associated with achievement activities. The model is built on the assumption that it is not reality itself (i.e., past successes and failures) that most directly influences choices, but rather one's interpretation of reality. The influence of reality on achievement beliefs, outcomes, and future goals is assumed to be mediated by causal attributional patterns, by the input of primary socializers, by one's needs and values, by one's self-schemata, and by one's perceptions of the various choices themselves. Each of these factors is assumed to contribute both to the expectations one holds for future success at the options available and to the subjective value one attaches to these options. Expectations and subjective value, in turn, are assumed to influence achievement-related behaviors, including the decision to engage in particular activities, the intensity of effort expended, and one's actual performance.

The model assumes that achievement decisions, such as the decision to enroll in an advanced mathematics class or to major in education rather than engineering, are made in the context of a variety of choices. Furthermore, it assumes that these choices, whether made

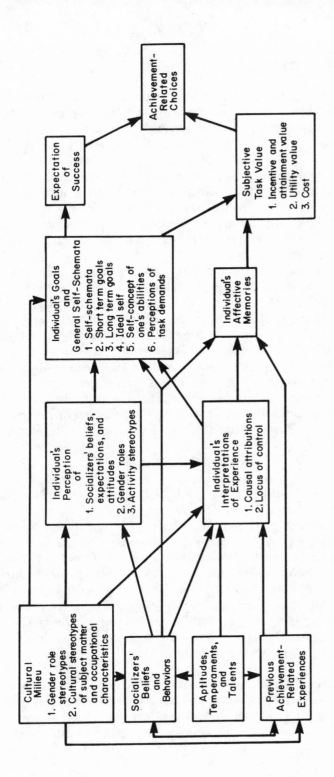

FIGURE 1. General model of achievement choices.

consciously or nonconsciously, are guided by one's expectations for success at the various options, by such core personal values as achievement needs, competency needs, and gender-role schemata, by more utilitarian values such as the importance of a particular course for one's future goals, and by the potential cost of investing time in one activity rather than another. Thus, if a female likes math but feels the effort it will take to do well is not worthwhile because it decreases the time she will have available for some other preferred activity, she will be less likely to continue taking math than the female who both likes math and thinks her efforts at mastering it are worthwhile and important.

Because expectancies and the variables linked to self-concept have received so much attention, I will not discuss them further here (see Eccles (Parsons) et al., 1983, for a more complete discussion). Suffice it to say that expectations, confidence in one's ability to succeed, and personal efficacy are critical mediators of achievement behaviors. Their role as mediators of sex differences in achievement behaviors is less clear (see Eccles (Parsons), et al., 1984, for more discussion). Since the role of values as mediators both of general achievement behaviors and of sex differences in achievement choices has received less attention, and since I believe it is one primary mediator of sex-differentiated achievement choices, I will discuss values in more detail here.

VALUES AS MEDIATORS OF ACHIEVEMENT CHOICES

Like others (e.g., Crandall, 1969; Crandall, Katkovsky, & Preston, 1962; Raynor, 1974; Spenner & Featherman, 1978; Stein & Bailey, 1973), we assume that task value is a quality of the task that contributes to the increasing or declining probability that an individual will select it. We have defined this quality in terms of three components: the utility value of the task in promoting the achievement of one's long-range goals; the incentive value of engaging in the task in terms of more immediate rewards and pleasure one gets from the activity; and the cost of engaging in the activity.

Incentive and attainment values. Incentive value can be conceptualized in several ways, two of which are of particular interest to me. On the one hand, incentive value can be conceptualized in terms of the immediate rewards, intrinsic or extrinsic, that performing a task will provide. For example, playing tennis could be intrinsically rewarding because it makes one feel healthy, or extrinsically rewarding because one is paid for the performance.

Incentive value can also be conceptualized in terms of the needs and personal values an activity fulfills. As they grow up, people develop an image of who and what they are. This image is made up of many component parts, including conceptions of one's personality and capabilities, long-range goals and plans, schemata regarding the proper roles of men and women, instrumental and terminal values (Rokeach, 1973), motivational sets, self-schemata, and social scripts regarding proper behavior in a variety of situations. Some parts of an individual's image are central or critical to his or her self-definition and should exert the most influence on behavior (see also Markus, 1980). For example, if being a good athlete is a central part of one's self-image, then one should work at continuing to be a good athlete. Since personal needs and values are part of one's self-image, the degree of influence wielded by these values and needs should also be determined by their centrality to an individual's self-definition (see also Parsons & Goff, 1980). Consequently, personal needs and values should operate in ways that both reduce the probability of engaging in those activities or roles perceived as inconsistent with one's central values and increase the probability of engaging in roles or activities perceived as consistent with one's definition of self.

But what links personal needs, values, and self-schemata to task selection? We believe people perceive tasks in terms of certain characteristics that can be related to needs, values, and self-schemata. For example, a difficult task requiring great effort for mastery may be perceived as an achievement task; if it also involves pitting one's performance against others', it may be perceived as a competitive task. Other tasks may be perceived in terms of nurturance, power, asthetic pleasure, and so on. The decision to engage in one of these tasks may require one to demonstrate or exercise the characteristics associated with the task. Whether this requirement is seen as an opportunity or a burden will depend on the individual's needs, motives, self-schemata, and personal values and his or her desire to demonstrate these characteristics to both the self and others. Essentially, I am arguing (1) that individuals seek to confirm their possession of those characteristics central to their self-images, and (2) that various tasks provide the opportunity to do exactly this. If one values the characteristics assumed to be inherent in a task, one will regard task involvement as an opportunity to confirm one's self-image and will be more likely to engage in the task than someone who does not value the characteristics associated with the task. For example, tennis should be especially attractive (have high incentive value) to someone who values competitive, athletic competence, precisely because playing tennis provides the opportunity to demonstrate athletic competence to both the self and others.

This analysis implies that the incentive value of any particular task will be influenced by three sets of beliefs. First, it will depend on the individual's perception of the characteristics of the task or, more specifically, on the needs and characteristics he or she believes the task will fulfill or demonstrate. Second, it will depend on the individual's own hierarchy of values, needs, motives, and self-schemata. And finally, it will depend on the extent to which the individual believes that participating in the task will fulfill his or her central needs or affirm his or her self image.

We have labeled this third belief attainment value. And since gender-role socialization influences both the development of one's self-schemata and personal values as well as our stereotypes of the characteristics associated with various achievement activities, gender-role socialization will affect the attainment value each individual attaches to various achievement options.

Perceived cost. The value of a task will also depend on a set of beliefs that can best be characterized as the cost of participating in the activity. This cost is influenced by many factors, such as anticipated anxiety, anticipated negative responses from one's peers, friends, parents, colleagues, or neighbors, fear of failure, and the negative affective memories one has associated with similar activities in the past. Gender-role socialization can influence each of these negative affective variables (see Eccles [Parsons], 1984, for a full discussion).

The cost of any given activity or life-defining achievement choice can also be conceptualized in terms of the loss of time and energy for other activities and life-defining roles. People have limited time and energy, so they cannot do everything they would like. They must choose among activities. To the extent that one loses time for Activity B by engaging in Activity A, and to the extent that Activity B is high in one's hierarchy of importance, then the subjective cost of engaging in A increases. Alternatively, even if the attainment value of A is high, the value of engaging in A will be reduced to the extent that the attainment value of B is higher and to the extent that engaging in A jeopardizes the probability of successfully engaging in B.

GENDER-ROLES AND TASK VALUE

The implications of this analysis for our understanding of sex differences in achievement choices are clear. Since socialization shapes individuals' goals and values, men and women undoubtedly acquire different values and goals through the process of gender-role socialization. In terms of task value, gender differences in value structure can manifest themselves in several ways. For one, gender-role socialization can create a gender-differentiated hierarchy of core personal values (such as their terminal and instrumental values; Rokeach, 1973). Consequently, tasks embodying various characteristics should have different attainment values for men and women. For example, men may be more likely to engage in athletic activities because they place more importance on demonstrating their athletic competence than do women. Differences in career choice may reflect similar processes. For example, Dunteman, Wisenbaker, and Taylor (1978) found that being thing-oriented rather than person-oriented predicted becoming a math or science major. Similarly, Fox and Denham (1974) found that mathematically talented children are relatively low on social value and high on theoretical, political, and economic values. In both of these studies, the females were less likely to hold the math- and science-related values than were males. Not surprisingly, then, the females were also less likely to aspire to math- and science-related careers than the males in both studies.

Alternatively, the structure of men's and women's hierarchies of values might differ. If so, then women ought to rank order the importance of various activities differently than men do. For example, if women see the parenting role as more important than a professional career role while men rate these roles as equally important, then women should be more likely than men to resolve life's decisions in favor of the parenting role. This differential would be especially marked if women see the career options not only as of lower importance but also as detrimental to the successful completion of their parenting goals.

Similarly, men and women could differ in the density of their goals and values. As noted earlier, men seem more likely than women to exhibit a single-minded devotion to one particular goal. In contrast, women seem more likely than men to be involved in several activities simultaneously. This difference could reflect differing density patterns for the hierarchy of goals and personal values. That is, women may place high attainment value on several goals and activities, while men may differentiate more among the options open to them. If this is true, then the cost of engaging in their primary goal in terms of other important goals will be less for men than for women.

Finally, a gender-differentiated hierarchy of task values could result from gender differences in people's perceptions of various tasks and in the very definition of success and failure on these tasks (see also Frieze, Frances, & Hanusa, 1983). One of the primary characteristics of gender roles is that they define the activities that are central to one's occupancy of the role. In essence, gender roles define what one should do with one's life in order to be successful in that role. To the extent that one holds success in one's gender role as a central component of one's identity, then activities that fulfill this role will have high value and activities that detract from one's successful fulfillment of this role will have lower, and perhaps even negative, subjective value. If staying home with one's children and being psychologically available to them most of the time is a central component of one's gender-role schema, then involvement in a demanding, high-level career will have reduced value because it conflicts with a more central component of one's identity.

Adherence to one's gender role may be so central to an individual that merely knowing, even at a subconscious level, that a particular activity is stereotypically part of the opposite gender's role will be sufficient to prevent further consideration of engaging in that activity. Consequently, gender-role schemata (beliefs regarding the composition of both male and female gender roles) can effectively limit the range of options one even considers as well as affecting the subjective value one attaches to the various options considered.

Gender roles can also influence one's very definition of successful performance of activities considered central to one's identity. Consequently, men and women may differ in their conceptualization of the requirements for successful task participation and completion. If so, then men and women should approach and structure their task involvement differently. The parenting role provides an excellent example of this process. If males define success in the parenting role as an extension of their occupational role, they may respond to parenthood with increased commitment to their career goals and with emphasis on encouraging competitive drive in their children. In contrast, if women define success in the parenting role as a high level of involvement in their children's lives, they may respond to parenthood with decreased commitment to their career goals.

Differences in approach to various careers can be interpreted similarly. For example, it is a common finding that academic women publish less than academic men. One possible explanation relies on the reasoning outlined here. Females may define the faculty role equally in terms of teaching, service, and publications; in contrast, males may define the faculty role more in terms of research and publications. If so, then male and female faculty members should approach their professional role quite differently, and as a consequence females should have weaker publication records than men.

SUMMARY

In summary, the model depicted in Figure 1 builds on the theoretical base of expectancy/value models of task choice. In addition, by elaborating on the construct of value, it has provided a link between expectancy/value models and the growing literature on the self.

What distinguishes this model from other models of achievement behavior is its attention to the issue of *choice*. Whether done consciously or not, people make choices among a variety of activities all the time. For example, they decide whether to work hard at school or just to get by; they decide which intellectual skills to develop or whether to develop any at all; they decide how much time to spend doing homework; they decide whether to take difficult courses or to spend their extra time with their friends; and they decide which occupations to prepare themselves for. We have tried to address the issue of choice directly and to develop a model that allows us to predict the type of choices being made. Furthermore, we have tried to specify the kinds of socialization experiences that shape individual differences on the mediators of these choices, especially in the academic achievement domain (see Eccles (Parsons) et al., 1983).

Furthermore, because we have focused on choice rather than avoidance, we believe this model provides a more positive perspective on women's achievement behavior than is common in some popular psychological explanations for sex differences in achievement patterns. Beginning with the work associated with need achievement and continuing to current work in attribution theory, a variety of scholars have considered the origin of sex differences in achievement. Many of these scholars have looked for the origin either in motivational differences or in expectancy/attributional differences. For example, in the fifties and sixties, several studies focused on sex differences in need achievement. In 1966 Horner introduced the concept of fear of success and suggested that sex differences in achievement reflected high levels of fear of success in women.

In the early seventies, Weiner and his colleagues (see Weiner, 1972) introduced an attributional model of achievement motivation and paved the way for a new set of hypotheses regarding sex differences in achievement, a set focusing on cognitive-mediational variables. Within this new framework, sex differences in achievement have been attributed variously to differences in expectations, self-confidence, causal attribution patterns, and learned helplessness. So, for example, it has been argued that women have lower expectations for success, are less confident in their achievement-related abilities, are more likely to attribute their failure to lack of ability, are less likely to attribute their success to ability, and are more likely to exhibit a learned helplessness response to failure. Furthermore, it has been argued that these differences mediate the sex differences we observe in achievement patterns.

There are several problems with this body of work. First, because they assumed a deficit model of female achievement, researchers have focused their attention on the question "How are women different from men?" rather than "What influences men's and women's achievement behavior?" Second, the assumption that the differences uncovered in most studies actually mediate sex differences in achievement behavior has rarely been tested. Instead, many studies simply demonstrate a statistically significant difference between males and females and conclude that this difference accounts for sex differences in achievement behavior. Third, and most important, the deficit perspective has limited the range of variables studied. Researchers have focused most of their attention on variables linked to self-confidence and expectancies, since high self-confidence is one of those "good" things that facilitates men's competitive achievement.

The dominance of this deficit perspective in sex-difference research has been especially marked in the past decade. Our model provides a very different perspective. By assigning a central role to the construct of subjective task value, we have offered an alternative explanation for sex differences in achievement patterns. This alternative explanation puts male and female achievement choices on a more equal footing. Our model makes salient the hypothesis that differences in male and female achievement patterns result from the fact that males and females have different but equally important and valuable goals for their lives. This view differs markedly from explanations that attribute sex differences in achievement patterns to females' lack of confidence, low expectations, or debilitating attributional biases. Instead of characterizing females as deficient males, our perspective, outlined in more detail in Parsons and Goff (1980) and Eccles (Parsons) (1984), legitimizes females' choices as valuable on their own terms rather than as a reflection or distortion of male choices and male values. Gilligan (1982) has made a similar point regarding males' and females' moral judgments.

But how well does this model do in generating important research questions and in explaining sex differences in achievement choices? To answer this question, we have studied the origin of sex differences in a "real-life" achievement activity—enrollment in advanced high-school mathematics. Some major components of this research program are described in the next section.

Sex Differences in Course-Enrollment Patterns

As I noted earlier, two areas of cognitive functioning reveal fairly consistent patterns of sex differences (see Eccles Parsons, 1984; Wittig & Petersen, 1979). Girls typically perform better than boys on verbal tasks, whereas boys perform better than girls on quantitative tasks. Sex differences in high school course enrollment, college majors, and adult careers reflect a similar pattern. For example, among the B.A. degrees awarded in 1978, women received only 6% of those awarded in engineering, 23% in architecture, 26% in computer and informational science, 22% in physical science, and 41% in mathematics. In contrast, 57% of B.A.s in letters, 73% of B.A.s in education, 76% of B.A.s in foreign languages, and 88% of B.A.s in library science went to women (National Center for Educational Statistics, 1979, 1980). Clearly, these sex differences are larger than one would expect based on the achievement test score differences alone. This is especially true for the math-related achievement domains. For example, in 1978 37% of the pool of first-year students eligible to major in engineering were women.[2] In contrast, only 13% of those actually planning to major in

2. We estimated the proportion of women eligible to enter these fields by calculating the number of women scoring above 500 on the math SAT (Educational Testing Service, 1979); 500 is approximately the mean score on the math SAT of students expressing an interest in majoring in math or the physical sciences. Hyde (1981), using a different method of estimating the available pool of female potential scientists and engineers, arrived at a comparable figure of 37%.

engineering were women, and only 6% of the bachelor's degrees in engineering in 1978 went to women. Similar though less dramatic results characterize the population planning to major in the physical sciences. Clearly, the proportion of female participation in quantitative fields is much lower than the available pool would predict.[3]

Sex Differences in Math Participation: Recent Explanations

Recent attention has focused on the origin of this underrepresentation of females in math-related fields. While some researchers still argue that this difference primarily reflects biologically based gender differences, the magnitude of the occupational differences outlined above casts doubt on this perspective (see Meece, Parsons, Kaczala, Goff, & Futterman, 1982, and Eccles [Parsons], 1984, for reviews). Attitudinal and motivational factors clearly play a substantial role in shaping this sex-differentiated achievement pattern. Research has yielded four basic explanations for this problem:

1. Males outperform females on spatial problem-solving tasks and on other mathematics aptitude measures. Consequently, they are more able to continue in math (Aiken, 1976; Wittig & Pedersen, 1979).

2. Males receive more encouragement than females from parents, teachers, and counselors to enroll in advanced mathematics courses or to pursue math-oriented careers (Casserly, 1980; Fox, Tobin, & Brody, 1979; Luchins & Luchins, 1980; Parsons, Adler, & Kaczala, 1982; Parsons, Kaczala, & Meece, 1982).

3. Mathematics is commonly perceived as a male achievement domain. Consequently, because of its potential conflict with their gender-role identity, females are more likely to avoid mathematics (Fen-

---

3. This underrepresentation of females in math and science is very costly both for females and for society at large. In almost all occupational fields, females can expect to earn less than their male peers. But the mean income for both males and females is particularly low in nonscientific, female-dominated occupations. Both males and females earn more in math-related occupations than in nonscientific occupations. In addition, among recent graduates, females are most likely to earn salaries commensurate with those of their male peers in scientific and technical fields (Grant & Eiden, 1982). Also, society is in need of as many mathematically trained and scientifically literate college graduates as it can get to fill jobs in a wide range of industries and service professions.

nema & Sherman, 1977; Nash, 1979; Sherman & Fennema, 1977; Stein & Smithells, 1969).

4. Males perceive themselves as more competent and report greater confidence in learning mathematics than females (Eccles Parsons, 1984; Fennema & Sherman, 1977; Fox et al., 1979).

The research traditions associated with each of these explanations have provided insights into the mechanisms contributing to students' math achievement behaviors. However, because researchers have approached this area of study from a variety of theoretical perspectives, each has tended to focus on a limited subset of possible causes. What has been missing is a comprehensive, theoretical framework that acknowledges the complex interplay of these many factors, takes into account the sociocultural context in which course-enrollment decisions take place, and provides a more comprehensive approach to the problem. Our model provides such a comprehensive approach.

EMPIRICAL TEST: OVERVIEW

To test the utility of our model for explaining sex differences in math participation, we conducted a large-scale cross-sectional/longitudinal study of the ontogeny of students' achievement beliefs, attitudes, and behaviors. Given our conceptualization of math participation as a task choice construct, we felt it was important to include measures of the students' attitudes toward at least one other subject area. The decision not to take math might seem very logical in the face of evidence that a student really likes another subject better. Since English is the other major achievement domain that evidences consistent sex differences, we assessed students' attitudes toward English as well as toward math. We also assessed the students' achievement plans and outcomes in both math and English.

We began our study with a cross section of 300 students in Grades 6–9, their parents, and their math teachers. One year later, 94% of these same students were retested. During the second year, an additional control group of 329 students in Grades 5–12 was recruited. We used this sample to assess test-retest effects and to rule out the possibility that our longitudinal findings reflected the effect of unique historical events rather than more general developmental change. These analyses indicated that test-retest effects were minimal and the changes in the students' attitudes from Year 1 to Year 2 did not reflect the effect of unique historical events. Based on these results and on the fact that we had modified our questionnaire slightly from Year 1 to Year 2, the control and Year 2 samples were merged, making a total Year 2 sample of 668 children. The cross-sectional data presented here are based on this expanded Year 2 sample.

Data were collected in several forms: student record data, a student questionnaire, a parent questionnaire, a teacher questionnaire, and classroom observations. Information taken from each student's school record included final grades in mathematics and English for the four years (1975–1979) before the study, the two years of the study, and each year following the study until the students graduated from high school. Any standardized achievement test scores in the student's file were also recorded. Thus we have comprehensive data on each of our students' participation and achievement in both math and English throughout their secondary school careers. Only a small portion of these data are summarized in this chapter. I will focus primarily on the student questionnaire data that are most directly related to the issue of sex differences in math and English achievement patterns. The parent and classroom observational data have been reported elsewhere (see Parsons, Adler, & Kaczala, 1982; Parsons, Kaczala, & Meece, 1982).

According to our model, general beliefs influence task-specific beliefs, which in turn influence achievement behaviors. To operationalize this model, we created variables to coincide with each of these three levels of the psychological variables. Given our concern with sex differences, we were especially interested the following general beliefs: gender-role schemata, stereotyping of math as a male domain, and perceptions of encouragement to continue taking math by parents, teachers, and peers. We developed measures of these general beliefs and of the following specific beliefs: expectancy of success, perceived ability, perceived task difficulty, perceived amount of effort necessary to succeed, perceived importance of the subject, perceived cost of success, perceived worth of the effort necessary to succeed, perceived utility value of the subject, and reasons one would take advanced-level math courses. For achievement outcome measures, we asked the students whether they planned to continue taking math and English and, if so, how much; we asked their proposed college major and their career goals; we collected their grades in their math and English courses; and we recorded their actual course-enrollment patterns.

The attitudinal variables were factor analyzed using the maximum likelihood factor analytic procedure developed by Joreskog and Sorbom (1978). Three identical factors emerged for both the math and the English items: Self-Concept of Ability, Perceived Task Difficulty, and Subjective Task Value. The Self-Concept factor included all items tapping perceived ability, perceived performance, and expectations for success in current and future courses. The Task Difficulty factor included items tapping perceived task difficulty, perceived effort needed to do well, and estimates of actual level of effort. The Subjective Task Value factor included all items related to perceived utility value, enjoyment of the subject, and perceived importance of doing well. Confirmatory factor analysis supported the reliability of this factor structure. The data reported in this chapter concern these three factors and focus on the relation of these specific beliefs to achievement choice patterns. All effects reported are significant at the $p < .05$ level or better.

FIRST-ORDER EFFECTS

Relatively few sex differences merged, but those that did formed a fairly consistent pattern. Across both years, boys, compared with girls, rated their math ability higher, felt they had to exert less effort to do well in math, and held higher expectancies for future successes in math, even though there were no sex differences on any of the objective measures of math performance. In addition, boys in Year 1 rated both their current math courses and advanced math courses as easier than did the girls; boys in Year 2 had higher expectancies for success in current (as well as future) math courses; and boys in Year 2 rated math as more useful than the girls. Finally, both boys and girls rated math as more useful for males than for females.[4] Thus, to the extent that there are sex differences on these self- and task-perception variables, boys had a more positive view both of themselves as math learners and of math itself.

These differences are even more dramatic when one compares the students' attitudes toward both math and English from a developmental perspective. To assess developmental differences we looked at both the age effects within the cross-sectional sample and the

4. However, male students endorsed this stereotype to a much greater extent than female students.

ABILITY

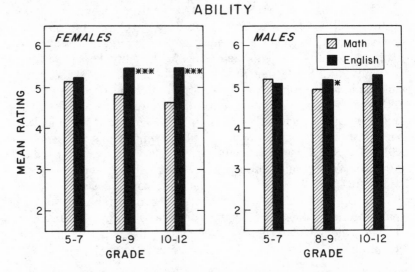

FIGURE 2. Grade × sex × content area effects: Self-Concept of Ability (* *p* <.05, ***
p <.001).

PERCEIVED TASK DIFFICULTY

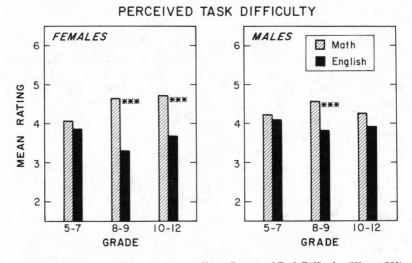

FIGURE 3. Grade × sex × content area effects: Perceived Task Difficulty (*** *p* <.001).

Sex Differences in Achievement Patterns

SUBJECTIVE TASK VALUE

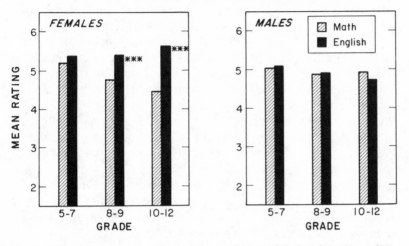

FIGURE 4. Grade × sex × content area effects: Subjective Task Value (*** $p < .001$).

test-retest effects in the longitudinal sample. Comparable developmental conclusions emerged in both sets of analyses. In general, the females became more positive toward English and more negative toward math as they grew older. In contrast, boys attitudes toward both subjects remained fairly stable over time and across grade levels. These effects are best illustrated with the three major attitudinal factors. First, consider Self-Concept of Ability. As is apparent from Figure 2, female students' estimates of their math ability declined linearly with age. Two additional comparisons are important. By 8th grade the females rated their English ability higher than their math ability, and by 10th grade they rated their math ability lower than the boys rated theirs. Neither of these effects are present in the earlier grades. Comparable effects emerge for Perceived Task Difficulty (see Figure 3), and for Subjective Task Value (see Figure 4). The sex differences are especially marked for Subjective Task Value. By 10th grade the females rated English as more valuable than math. Furthermore, they rated math as less valuable and English as more valuable than did the males.

These changes in the females' attitudes toward both math and English are especially interesting given the nature of our sample. First of all, we have no indication that there is a measurable difference in the math performance between the males and females in this sample on either their course grades or their scores on standardized achievement tests. Second, the male and female students also had comparable test scores on standardized achievement tests in English at each grade level. Third, the female students earned higher grades than the male students in their English courses beginning at about the 8th grade. Fourth, when one compares the students' standardized test scores across years, the older females in this sample had higher scores than the younger females. Consequently, the older female students, if anything, had higher math ability, on the average, than the younger female students. They also scored higher on tests of English ability than did the younger female students. Thus, despite the fact that the female population became more select in terms of both English and math achievement scores with advancing grade level, and despite the fact that there were no apparent sex differences on math performance measures, the attitudes of the female students toward math declined with age whereas their grades did not. In contrast, both their attitudes and their actual performance in English increased with age.

Given our perspective that choice is the critical mediator of achievement differences, these results certainly lead to the prediction that female students will elect less math than English and male students will continue to take courses in both subject areas. This is, in fact, what has happened in this sample. The females were less likely to take 12th grade advanced math course than the males, but their English enrollment patterns did not differ. There were no sex differences in math enrollment before the 12th grade.

The analyses described thus far suggest several important sex differences in students' attitudes. Females in general have a more negative attitude than boys toward math learning and toward themselves as math learners. Furthermore, females also have a more negative view of math than of English. These differences certainly could mediate sex differences in achievement patterns, but the mere existence of these differences does not support their importance as variables mediating sex differences in achievement patterns. The critical question is whether these differences, in fact, make a difference. To answer this, we ran a series of correlational and multivariate regression analyses. Several important results emerged.

RELATIONAL ANALYSES

First we ran a series of analyses relating our gender-role constructs to student attitudes. Several researchers have suggested that the stereotype of math as a male domain inhibits female participation in math. To evaluate this hypothesis and its many variations, we correlated the students' rating of the usefulness of advanced math for both males and females, their perception of math as being more useful to males, their gender stereotyping of math ability, and their ratings of themselves on a simplified version of the Personal Attributes Questionnaire (PAQ; Spence, Helmreich, & Stapp, 1975) with the other student measures. Femininity (or more appropriately Expressivity) as measured by the PAQ was not related to either student attitudes or their achievement patterns. Masculinity (or Instrumentality), however, was related positively to measures of both expectancy and Self-Concept of Math Ability for both males and females.

Several investigators (e.g., Nash, 1979) have suggested that it is the interaction of gender-role identity with gender stereotypes regarding the nature of the task that influences students' attitudes toward a subject. We used multivariate contingency tables to assess the effect of personality type on math attitudes and achievement and to test whether gender-role identity, as measured by a personality inventory, interacts with gender-role stereotypes of math in influencing students' attitudes toward math. Gender-role classification had no significant influence on any of the student attitude or achievement measures, either as a main effect or in interaction with the gender-role stereotyping of math as a masculine domain. Gender-role stereotyping of math did, however, influence Subjective Task Value. The extent to which a female judged math to be useful for women did not relate to its subjective value for her. Instead, it was the perceived usefulness of math for males that predicted positively math's subjective value for both males and females. One might conclude from these data that the stereotype of math as a male domain has a positive effect for everyone and ought to be encouraged; but results from other studies suggest that this conclusion is oversimplified. Instead, what it suggests is that perceiving math as more useful for males than for females does not necessarily have a negative consequence for girls, perhaps especially when the stereotype reflects an awareness of the high-status jobs that are both male dominated and math related. We need to know the subjective meaning of these stereotypes for the individual before we can predict their effect on Subjective Task Value. In this case it may be the status of the job rather than its male domination that elevates the perceived usefulness of advanced math courses for these high-ability boys and girls.

We next assessed the relations of the student attitudinal variables to achievement plans, performance, and actual enrollment patterns. As predicted, for both males and females, Self-Concept of Ability and Subjective Task Value correlated positively with students' plans to continue taking math and English, with the students' grades in both math and English one year later, and with the students' actual course-enrollment decisions in math measured one to three years later (see Table 1). These results provide initial support for the predicted influence of attitudinal variables on achievement behaviors. But these attitudinal variables are intercorrelated and are correlated with past grades. Before we can understand the effect of attitudes on achievement, we need to answer two additional ques-

Table 1

Correlations Between Attitudes and Achievement Outcomes for Math and English

Variable	1	2	3	4	5	6
1 Past Performance	—	.50**	.30**	-.10	.14	.25**
2 Grade Year 1	.44**	—	.36**	-.19*	.11	.23**
3 Self-Concept of Ability	.35**	.27**	—	-.49**	.50**	.46**
4 Perceived Task Demands	-.15	-.05	-.54**	—	-.09	-.21**
5 Subjective Task Value	.12	.16	.59**	-.13	—	.60**
6 Plans to Continue Taking Subject	.17*	.16	.35**	-.04	.44**	—
7 Course Enrollment: Grade 12, math only	.39**	.42**	.17	.15	.36**	.17

Note: Correlations are based on Year 2 data base. Results for English items are in upper triangle; results for math items are in lower triangle.

* $p < .05$.

** $p < .01$.

Table 2
Stepwise Multiple Regression: Predictors of Subjective Educational Plans

	English			Math	
Step	Multiple R^2	Predictor	Step	Multiple R^2	Predictor
1	.51	Subjective Value of English	1	.22	Subjective Value of math
2	.54	Self-Concept of English Ability	2	.29	Self-Concept of Math Ability
			3	.33	Subjective Value of English

tions: Which of these attitudes are most critical? and Are any of the attitudes as critical as past performance in shaping subsequent achievement behaviors? To answer these questions we used stepwise multiple regression procedures. Subjective Value of Math, Subjective Value of English, Self-Concept of Math Ability, and Self-Concept of English Ability were regressed on Subjective English Educational Plans and on Subjective Math Educational Plans in two stepwise (hierarchical) regression analyses. In both analyses, Subjective Task Value emerged as the most powerful predictor of educational plans (see Table 2). These results suggest that Subjective Task Value is the attitude that mediates sex differences in achievement choice patterns.

To test for the hypothesized mediating role of Subjective Task Value in explaining actual sex differences in achievement choices, we tested for sex differences in course-enrollment patterns for mathematics. We were unable to run a comparable test for English because English is required for all three years of high school in the school districts we sampled. Since there was a significant sex difference in course enrollment in the 12th grade, we were able to test the mediating role of task value on course enrollment in math. These results, depicted in Figure 5, are consistent with the hypothesis that sex difference in math course enrollment are mediated by the sex

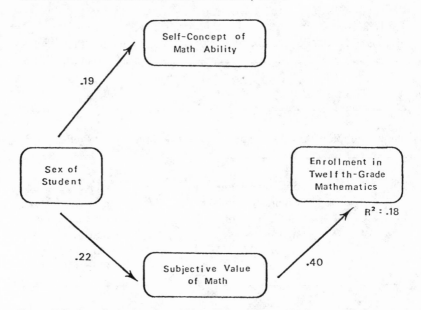

FIGURE 5. Path analysis of math variables. (Columnwise multiple repression equation procedures were used to estimate the path coefficients. The standardized path coefficients, which are regression coefficients, reflect the relative predictive power of each variable. All paths are significant at the $p < .05$ level or better.)

difference in Subjective Task Value, not by the sex difference in Self-Concept of Math Ability.

Thus, as predicted, Subjective Task Value emerged as the most powerful predictor of students' Subjective Educational Plans. Furthermore, the significant sex × age × subject area interaction yielded results consistent with the developmental predictions of our model. High school females had a more positive attitude toward English and a less positive attitude toward math than did the junior high school females, especially in terms of Subjective Task Value. Projecting these developmental patterns into the late adolescent years should produce a marked sex difference in attitudes toward the value of math and English and in actual course enrollment decisions, and in fact this happened; the females were more likely to drop math before high school graduation than were the males. Finally, our data suggest that it is Subjective Task Value rather than Self-Concept of Math Ability that mediates this sex difference in course-enrollment patterns.

EMPIRICAL TEST: MALES VERSUS FEMALES

The data discussed thus far were drawn from the entire sample, based on the assumption that comparable relations would hold for both males and females. The zero-order correlations calculated for each sex separately support this assumption for the variables we have discussed thus far (see Table 1), but this is not the case for the correlations of these attitudes with past performance. A very important sex difference emerged when we compared the correlations of students' attitudes with their past grades and with a composite score reflecting their relative position within their grade level on their course grades and standardized achievement test scores. These results are illustrated in Figure 6. The males' attitudes, across the board, were more directly related to their performance history than were females' attitudes. This is true for both math and English. Furthermore, it is especially interesting to note, given the importance of Subjective Task Value, that the value females placed on both math and English was unrelated to their history of performance in either subject.

These results suggest that different factors influence the achievement decisions of males and females. To test this hypothesis directly, we ran stepwise regressions separately for males and females.

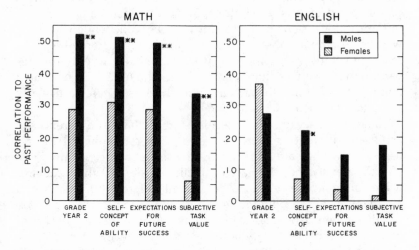

FIGURE 6. Correlations of beliefs and performance with past performance (sex effects, * $p < .05$, ** $p < .01$).

Table 3
Stepwise Regressions: Math Enrollment

			Female		
Step	R^2	Variable		Partial R	Significance
0	.18	Past Performance		.43	.0005
1	.25	Subjective Task Value		.37	.004

Since past performance is such an important predictor of course enrollment for both males and females, we entered it at the first step. This procedure allows us to assess whether attitudinal variables have any independent influence on achievement patterns beyond what they share with past performance. The results are illustrated in Table 3. As expected, past performance emerged as a strong predictor of course enrollment for both males and females. However, it was a stronger predictor for males; and for males, attitudes made little independent contribution to their course-enrollment decisions. In contrast, Subjective Task Value is an important independent predictor for females. Independent of how well or how poorly they were doing in math, women who enjoy math and think it is important were more likely to enroll in advanced math courses than were women who either did not enjoy math or did not think that advanced math courses were particularly important or useful.

Taken as a package, these results suggest that sex differences in achievement choice patterns are a function primarily of two processes. First, they are a function of the sex difference in Subjective Task Value; second, they are a function of the fact that academic achievement values seem to be shaped differently in males and females. Males' enrollment decisions appear to be influenced primarily by their performance history. In contrast, females' decisions appear to be influenced by both their performance history and the value they attach to the subject. This discrepancy, however, probably reflects the fact that the value the males attached to both math

Table 3 *continued*

		Male		
Step	R^2	Variable	Partial R	Significance
0	.26	Past Performance	.51	.0004

and English was related to their performance history in the subject. Consequently, the value they attached to the subject did not emerge as a strong independent predictor of course choice for the males. In contrast, the value females attached to academic subjects was more independent of their performance history. Consequently, for females value could, and did, enter into the regression equation as a significant independent predictor of their enrollment decisions.

These results raise two important questions: (1) What factors influence the value individuals attach to various achievement options? and (2) Why does the effect of performance history on Subjective Task Value differ for males and females? We are now exploring the variables that shape the value males and females attach to various achievement activities in an effort to broaden our understanding of the ontogeny of sex differences in achievement choice patterns. We are focusing on two sets of variables. The first set relates to the effect of gender-role stereotyping on beliefs and attitudes. We now believe that gender roles influence achievement patterns primarily through their effect on the value individuals attach to the many achievement options available to them. To test this hypothesis, we are evaluating the relation between gender-role salience, gender-role stereotypes of various activities, and achievement beliefs and choices.

The second set of variables we are exploring relates to the socialization of achievement values. Parental beliefs and attitudes appear to be particularly important. Parents, more than teachers, have sex-differentiated perceptions of their children's math aptitude, despite the similarity in the actual performance of their sons and daughters. Parents also believe that advanced math is more important for boys than for girls. Finally, our initial work suggests that parents' beliefs regarding their children's math aptitude are stronger predictors of the students' attitudes toward math than are indicators of the students' actual performance in math (see Parsons, Adler, & Kaczala, 1982).

Conclusion

In this chapter I have summarized a comprehensive model explaining achievement choices, have applied this model to the question of sex differences in achievement choices, and have summarized the results of a developmental study of sex differences in achievement choices generated by this model. The model differs from other explanations of sex differences in achievement behavior primarily in its focus on choice and its stress on the importance of task value as a critical mediator of sex differences in patterns of achievement choices. The results reported support this perspective. Sex differences in the decision to enroll in 12th-grade advanced math courses were mediated by the sex differences in the perceived value of advanced math courses. Furthermore, subjective task value was the most influential attitudinal variable in the course decisions of both boys and girls. However, since the subjective value of math was related positively to performance history in math for boys, enrollment in 12th-grade math was predicted primarily by performance history. Subjective task value played a larger predictive role in girls' enrollment decisions.

We find these results encouraging for two reasons. First, we believe they suggest a more positive view of women's achievement motivation than is inherent in other theories. Many popular explanations of sex differences in achievement choices are based on deficit models of female achievement orientation. For example, sex differences in achievement patterns have been attributed to females' learned helplessness, low self-concepts, low-expectancy attributional patterns, and fear of success. Each of these theories suggests that females are deficient in some critical component of achievement motivation. They imply that if only females had as much of this component as males they would make the same achievement choices as males. While we did find some sex differences that might be interpreted as reflecting these types of deficits, we found little support for the suggestion that females' achievement patterns were being driven by these variables to any greater extent than were males' achievement patterns. Instead, our data suggest that sex differences in achievement choices reflect these differences: (a) Females and males attach different subjective task values to various achievement options (in this case math and English courses); (b) females weight the subjective value of the activity more heavily in their achievement decisions than males; and (c) the value females attach to various achievement activities is influenced by different factors than is the value males attach to the same activities.

Second, we find these results encouraging because they highlight the importance of modifiable factors in both male and female achievement patterns. Studies of intervention programs (see Eccles & Hoffman, in press) clearly demonstrate that the value students attach to various school subjects can be modified with appropriate role models, information, and career guidance. Further, studies of effective teachers (e.g., Casserly, 1980) also demonstrate that students' achievement values and goals are affected by their classroom experiences. Despite these findings, junior and senior high school students receive little career guidance and little active encouragement to develop their talents to the fullest and to consider the full range of occupational choices available to them. Our results suggest that boys and girls make different achievement decisions because they attach different values to course options. This difference may well result from the stereotypes boys and girls hold of math-related occupations (see Boswell, 1979; Eccles Parsons, 1984) and from the fact that girls seem to be ignoring information about their own talents and skills in deriving the values they attach to various achievement activities. Both of these potential mediating systems can be influenced by better career guidance and by the active involvement of teachers and parents in helping young women identify their talents and consider occupations that take advantage of these talents.

REFERENCES

Aiken, L. (1976). Update on attitudes and other affective variables in learning mathematics. *Review of Educational Research, 46*, 293–311.

Atkinson, J. W. (1964). *An introduction to motivation.* Princeton, NJ: Van Nostrand.

Barnett, R. C., & Baruch, G. K. (1978). *The competent woman.* New York: Irvington Publishers.

Baruch, G., Barnett, R., & Rivers, C. (1983). *Lifeprints.* New York: McGraw-Hill.

Beck, J. A. L. (1977–1978). Locus of control, task expectancies, and children's performance following failure. *Journal of Educational Psychology, 71*, 207–210.

Benbow, C. P., & Stanley, J. C. (1980). Sex differences in mathematical ability: Fact or artifact? *Science, 210*, 1262–1264.

Benbow, C. P., & Stanley, J. C. (1983). Sex differences in mathematical reasoning ability: More facts. *Science, 222*, 1029–31.

Boswell, S. (1979). *Nice girls don't study mathematics: The perspective from elementary school.* Paper presented at the annual meeting of the American Educational Research Association, San Francisco.

Bryson, R., Bryson, J. B., & Johnson, M. F. (1978). Family size, satisfaction, and productivity in dual-career couples. *Psychology of Women Quarterly, 3*, 67–77.

Casserly, P. (1980). *An assessment of factors affecting female participation in advanced placement programs in mathematics, chemistry, and physics.* Report to the National Science Foundation. In L. H. Fox, L. Brody, & D. Tobin (Eds.), *Women and the mathematical mystique.* Baltimore: Johns Hopkins University Press. (Original publication 1975).

Crandall, V. C. (1969). Sex differences in expectancy of intellectual and academic reinforcement. In C. P. Smith (Ed.), *Achievement-related behaviors in children.* New York: Russell Sage Foundation.

Crandall, V. J., Katkovsky, W., & Preston, A. (1962). Motivational and ability determinants of young children's intellectual achievement behaviors. *Child Development, 33*, 643–661.

Diener, C., & Dweck, C. S. (1978). An analysis of learned helplessness: Continuous change in performance, strategy, and achievement cognitions following failure. *Journal of Personality and Social Psychology, 36*, 451–462.

Dunteman, G. H., Wisenbaker, J., & Taylor M. E. (1978). *Race and sex differences in college science program participation.* Report to the National Science Foundation. North Carolina: Research Triangle Park.

Dweck, C. S. (1975). The role of expectations and attributions in the alleviation of learned helplessness. *Journal of Personality and Social Psychology, 31*, 674–685.

Dweck, C. S., & Bush, E. (1976). Sex differences in learned helplessness: I. Differential debilitation with peer and adult evaluations. *Developmental Psychology, 12,* 147–156.

Dweck, C. S., & Reppucci, N. D. (1973). Learned helplessness and reinforcement responsibility in children. *Journal of Personality and Social Psychology, 25,* 109–116.

Eccles, J. (1983). The development of attributions, self and task perceptions, expectations, and persistence. Unpublished manuscript, University of Michigan.

Eccles, J., & Hoffman, L. W. (In press). Sex roles, socialization, and occupational behavior. In H. W. Stevenson & A. E. Siegel (Eds.), *Research in child development and social policy* (Vol. 1). Chicago: University of Chicago Press.

Eccles Parsons, J. (1983). Attributional processes as mediators of sex differences in achievement. *Journal of Educational Equity and Leadership, 3,* 19–27.

Eccles (Parsons), J. (1984). Sex differences in mathematics participation. In M. Steinkamp & M. Maehr (Eds.), *Women in science.* Greenwich, CT: JAI Press.

Eccles (Parsons), J., Adler, T. F., Futterman, R., Goff, S. B., Kaczala, C. M., Meece, J. L., & Midgley, C. (1983). Expectations, values and academic behaviors. In J. T. Spence (Ed.), *Achievement and achievement motivation.* San Francisco: W. H. Freeman.

Eccles (Parsons), J., Adler, T., & Meece, J. L. (1984). Sex differences in achievement: A test of alternate theories. *Journal of Personality and Social Psychology, 46,* 26–43.

Educational Testing Service. (1980). *National college-bound seniors, 1979.* Princeton, NJ: College Entrance Examination Board.

Fennema, E., & Sherman, J. (1977). Sex-related differences in mathematics achievement, spatial visualization and affective factors. *American Educational Research Journal, 14,* 51–71.

Fox, L. H., & Denham, S. A. (1974). Values and career interests of mathematically and scientifically precocious youth. In J. C. Stanley, D. P. Keating, & L. H. Fox (Eds.), *Mathematical talent: Discovery, description, and development.* Baltimore: Johns Hopkins University Press.

Fox, L. H., Tobin, D., & Brody, L. (1979). Sex-role socialization and achievement in mathematics. In M. A. Wittig & A. C. Petersen (Eds.), *Sex-related difference in cognitive functioning: Developmental issues.* New York: Academic Press.

Frieze, I. H., Francis, W. D., & Hanusa, B. H. (1983). Defining success in classroom settings. In J. M. Levine & M. C. Wang (Eds.), *Teacher and student perceptions: Implications for learning.* Hillsdale, NJ: Lawrence Erlbaum Associates.

Frieze, I. H., Parsons, J. E., Johnson, P., Ruble, D. N., & Zellman, G. (1978). *Women and sex roles: A social psychological perspective.* New York: Norton.

Gilligan, C. (1982). *In a different voice.* Cambridge, MA: Harvard University Press.

Goff-Timmer, S., Eccles, J., & O'Brien, K. (1984). How children use time. In F. T. Juster & F. Stafford (Eds.), *Time, goods, and well-being.* Ann Arbor, MI: Institute for Social Research Press.

Grant, W. F., & Eiden, L. J. (1982). *Digest of educational statistics.* Washington, DC: National Center for Educational Statistics, United States Department of Education.

Hoffman, L. W. (1972). Early childhood experiences and women's achievement motives. *Journal of Social Issues, 28,* 129–156.

Horner, M. (1972). Toward an understanding of achievement-related conflicts in women. *Journal of Social Issues, 28,* 157–175.

Huston, A. C. (1983). Sex-typing. In P. Mussen & E. M. Hetherington (Eds.), *Handbook of child psychology,* (Vol. 4). New York: John Wiley.

Hyde, J. S. (1981). How large are cognitive gender differences? A meta-analysis. *American Psychologist, 36,* 892–901.

Joreskog, K. G., & Sorbom, D. (1978). *EFAP: Exploratory Factor Analysis Program: User's guide.* Chicago: National Educational Resources.

Lewin, K. (1938). *The conceptual representation and the measurement of psychological forces.* Durham, NC: Duke University Press.

Lipman-Blumen, J., & Tickameyer, A. R. (1975). Sex roles in transition: A ten year perspective. *Annual Review of Sociology, 1,* 297–337.

Luchins, E. H., & Luchins, A. S. (1980). Female mathematics: A contemporary appraisal. In L. H. Fox, L. Brody, & D. Tobin (Eds.), *Women and the mathematical mystique.* Baltimore: Johns Hopkins University Press.

Maccoby, E. E., & Jacklin, C. N. (1974). *Psychology of sex differences.* Stanford, CA: Stanford University Press.

Maines, D. R. (1983). *A theory of informal barriers for women in mathematics.* Paper presented at the annual meeting of the American Educational Research Association, Montreal.

Markus, H. (1980). The self in thought and memory. In D. M. Wegner & R. R. Vallacher (Eds.), *The self in social psychology.* New York: Oxford University Press.

Meece, J. L., Eccles (Parsons), J., Kaczala, C. M., Goff, S. B., & Futterman, R. (1982). Sex differences in math achievement: Toward a model of academic choice. *Psychological Bulletin, 91,* 324–348.

Nash, S. C. (1979). Sex role as a mediator of intellectual functioning. In M. A. Wittig & A. C. Petersen (Eds.), *Sex-related differences in cognitive functioning: Developmental issues.* New York: Academic Press.

National Center for Educational Statistics. (1979, 19 September). Proportion of degrees awarded to women. Reported in *Chronicle of Higher Education.*

National Center for Educational Statistics. (1980, 28 January). Degrees awarded in 1978. Reported in *Chronicle of Higher Education.*

Nicholls, J. G. (1975). Causal attributions and other achievement-related cognitions: Effects of task outcomes, attainment value, and sex. *Journal of Personality and Social Psychology, 31,* 379–389.

Parsons, J. E., Adler, T. F., & Kaczala, C. M. (1982). Socialization of achievement attitudes and beliefs: Parental influences. *Child Development, 53,* 310–321.

Parsons, J. E., & Goff, S. G. (1980). Achievement motivation: A dual modality. In L. J. Fyans (Ed.), *Recent trends in achievement motivation: Theory and research.* Englewood Cliffs, NJ: Plenum.

Parsons, J. E., Kaczala, C., & Meece, J. (1982). Socialization of achievement attitudes and beliefs: Classroom influences. *Child Development, 53,* 322–339.

Parsons, J. E., Ruble, D. N., Hodges, K. L., & Small, A. W. (1976). Cognitive-developmental factors in emerging sex differences in achievement-related expectancies. *Journal of Social Issues, 32,* 47–61.

Raynor, J. O. (1974). Future orientation in the study of achievement motivation. In J. W. Atkinson & J. O. Raynor (Eds.), *Motivation and achievement.* Washington, DC: Winston Press.

Rholes, W. S., Blackwell, J., Jordan, C., & Walters, C. (1980). A developmental study of learned helplessness. *Developmental Psychology, 16,* 616–624.

Rokeach, M. (1973). *The nature of human values.* New York: Free Press.

Sells, L. W. (1980). The mathematical filter and the education of women and minorities. In L. H. Fox, L. Brody, & D. Tobin (Eds)., *Women and the mathematical mystique.* Baltimore: Johns Hopkins University Press.

Sherman, J., & Fennema, E. (1977). The study of mathematics by high school girls and boys: Related variables. *American Educational Research Journal, 14,* 159–168.

Spence, J. T., Helmreich, R. L., & Stapp, J. (1975). Ratings of self and peers on sex-role attributes and their relation to self-esteem and conception of masculinity and femininity. *Journal of Personality and Social Psychology, 32,* 29–39.

Spenner, K., & Featherman, D. L. (1978). Achievement ambitions. *Annual Review of Sociology, 4,* 373–420.

Stein, A. H., & Bailey, M. M. (1973). The socialization of achievement orientation in females. *Psychological Bulletin, 80,* 345–366.

Stein, A. H., & Smithells, T. (1969). Age and sex differences in children's sex-role standards about achievement. *Developmental Psychology, 1,* 252–259.

Tangri, S. S. (1972). Determinants of occupational role innovation among college women. *Journal of Social Issues, 28,* 195–207.

Tittle, C. K. (1981). *Careers and family: Sex roles and adolescent life plans.* Beverly Hills, CA: Sage.

Veroff, J. (1969). Social comparison and the development of achievement motivation. In C. P. Smith (Ed.), *Achievement-related motives in children.* New York: Russell Sage Foundation.

Vetter, B. M. (1981). Women scientists and engineers: Trends in participation. *Science, 214,* 1313–1321.

Weiner, B. (1972). *Theories of motivation: From mechanism to cognition.* Chicago: Markham.

Wittig, M. A., & Petersen, A. C. (Eds.). (1979). *Sex-related differences in cognitive functioning: Developmental issues.* New York: Academic Press.

Sex as an Attributional Fact

Virginia E. O'Leary

American Psychological Association

Ranald D. Hansen

Oakland University

*T*he existence of sex biases favoring men has been amply documented both across centuries and across cultures (cf. Broverman, Vogel, Broverman, Clarkson, & Rosenkrantz, 1972; Fernberger, 1948; McKee & Sherrifs, 1959; Steinman & Fox, 1966; Rosaldo & Lamphere, 1974). More important, sex biases have been found to differentially affect the outcomes women and men achieve in a variety of laboratory settings (cf. Deaux & Emswiller, 1974; Feldman-Summers & Kiesler, 1974; Heilman & Guzzo, 1978; Kahn, O'Leary, Kruelwitz, & Lamm, 1980; Rosen & Jerdee, 1974a,b; Unger, 1979), in the economic marketplace (cf. Brown, 1979; Kanter, 1977; O'Leary, 1974; Terborg, 1977), and in clinical practice (Abramowitz & Dokecki, 1977).

As Unger (1979) has observed, the results obtained in a number of studies using no stimulus materials other than the words "female" and "male" or names such as "Anne" and "John" indicate that sex plays an important role in determining the criteria for mental health (Broverman, Broverman, Clarkson, Rosenkrantz, & Vogel, 1970), the evaluation of the artistic merit of paintings (Pheterson, Kiesler, & Goldberg, 1971), and the qualifications of student applicants for a study-abroad program. Rapidly accumulating empirical evidence published during the past decade clearly suggests that the behavioral similarities between women and men are substantially greater than the differences (cf. Deaux, 1976; Eagly, 1978; Maccoby & Jacklin, 1974; O'Leary, 1977; Unger, 1979). Yet the belief in sex differences persists and is evinced by the predilection of perceivers (both men and women) to differentially attribute traits, behavioral characteristics, and even causes for identical performance as a function of the sex of the performer (Wallston & O'Leary, 1981).

Grady (1979) has suggested that there are two loci of sex differences: *subject sex differences*, or differences that are within the individual perceiver of behavior, and *stimulus sex differences*, or differences that arise in response to the sex of the person perceived. The fact that in many of the studies cited above the patterns of judgments about women and men are similar for female and male subjects argues against sex-linked bias as a function of sex of subject (O'Leary & Donoghue, 1978) and suggests instead that a more potent source of bias lies in the sex of the stimulus person. Until the cognitive and perceptual mechanisms that serve to maintain these biases are understood, change in the societal status of women cannot reasonably be anticipated.

One area of research that has potential value in understanding the persistence of the belief in sex differences focuses on people's explanations for why other people behave as they do. Grounded mainly in attributional research and theorizing, this approach argues that our understanding and prediction of how people react to events around them is enhanced by knowing their explanations for these events (Heider, 1958; Green & Mitchell, 1979). Three aspects of explanation have been the focus of this body of literature (cf. Kelley & Michela, 1980). First (cf. Kelley, 1967; 1972a,b), theoretical models have been organized around perceived *locus of cause*. The assumption underlying these models and the associated research is that the dimensionalization of naive causes into forces within the behaver versus forces in the behaver's environment is pivotal to understanding perceivers' explanations of and reactions to social behavior. Second, a number of theoretical models and a good deal of research have centered on perceivers' translation of a person's behavior into *traits*. The aim of this work is to specify the conditions under which perceivers ascribe traits to an actor based on available information about the actor and the actor's environment (cf. Jones & McGillis, 1976). Finally, a great deal of activity has revolved around the development of an attribution theory of *performance*. This line of work, tracing its roots to Heider (1958) and Weiner (1972), draws heavily on the first two domains described above. The central tenet of this approach is that perceivers' evaluation of achievement is mediated by their understanding of the causes for a given performance and the contingent diagnostic value of the performance for evaluating the performer's skill or motivation or both.

Taken together, these three areas of concern form the bulk of current attribution literature. They have in common the assumption that behavior acquires meaning at an interpretive level where behaviors are related—perceptually or cognitively—to causal forces. They assert that the same behavior may acquire different meaning at this more "embedded" level (Heider, 1958). We shall take the position in this chapter that behavior can acquire different meaning and significance at this more embedded level of understanding as a function of the behaver's sex. That is, the same behavior performed by women and by men does not necessarily have the same meaning for the perceiver. On the one hand, this can be seen as a "smart" process whereby the perceiver is knowingly motivated to rationalize women's and men's identical behaviors toward some sociopolitical or economic goal. On the other hand, perceived sex differences can be construed as attributional facts, largely "mindless" (cf. Langer & Imber, 1979), making the sociopolitical and economic goal of sexual equity more difficult to attain. In either case, attribution theory is a structure within which we can approach an understanding of the persistence of beliefs in sex differences.

Locus of Cause

Heider (1958) argued that perceivers establish cause for an event by identifying a plausible antecedent factor with which the effect covaries. Both Heider and Kelley (1967) claimed that perceivers can detect a simple covariation of a cause with an effect and on the basis of the covariation attribute the effect to the cause. They both also allowed for perceivers' capacity to deal with multiple plausible causes. Heider referred to this state of affairs as ambiguous mediation (we shall return to this notion shortly). Kelley (1967; 1972a,b) presented instances in which the perceiver was faced with multiple plausible causes and described the perceivers' naive covariation solutions to these more complex causal dilemmas.

Covariation has been identified as the primary commonsense rule under which perceivers operate to establish cause for an effect. But attribution theory extends the analysis of causal perception beyond this specification of commonsense rules. First, attribution theorists have taken a stab at developing a schematic processing view of causal cognition (Hansen, in press; Kelley, 1972b). Second attribution theorists have come to accept the position that the full causal implications of perceivers' explanations for events must be understood at a deeper or more embedded level of meaning (Ronis, Hansen, & O'Leary, 1983; Weiner, 1979; Weiner, Nirenberg, & Goldstein, 1976; Weiner, Russell, & Lerman, 1979; Wimer & Kelley, 1982). A primary dimension of meaning embodied in all attribution theories is the location of the cause in the person or in the environment.

SIMPLE COVARIATION MATRIXES

Most basic to attribution theory is perceivers' capacity to interpret the presence or absence of an effect as a function of the presence of causal forces (Heider, 1958; Kelley, 1972a,b). Perceivers attribute an effect to a cause present when the effect is present and absent when the effect is absent. Further, perceivers are seen as having the ability to interpret the covariation of an effect with at least two causal forces, each having multiple levels (Kelley, 1967). Thus, perceivers can reasonably make causal sense out of the covariation patterns captured in the matrixes shown in Figure 1 (Hansen & Lowe, 1976; McArthur, 1972, 1976).

In the left matrix the effect (evaluation of motion pictures) is seen as covarying with stimuli (movies) and not with persons (viewers). Any given person's evaluation of any given movie can be attributed to the movie. Any one target person's evaluation of any given movie predicts all persons' evaluation of that movie but not the target person's evaluation of any other movie. In the right matrix the effect is seen as covarying with persons but not with stimuli. Any given person's evaluation of any given movie can be attributed to the person. Any one person's evaluation of a target movie predicts that person's evaluation of any other movie but not other persons' evaluation of the target movie. In the center matrix the effect is seen as covarying with both persons and stimuli. Any given person's evaluation of any given movie should be attributed to both the person and the movie. Any given target person's evaluation of any given target movie predicts neither other people's evaluation of the target movie nor the target person's evaluation of other movies. But how likely are perceivers to detect these various patterns of covariation? Kelley (1967, 1972b) claimed that perceivers faced with multiple plausible causes attempt to gather complete information in order to make confident attributions. Short of gathering complete information, Kelley (1972a) allows for perceivers to make attributions, but with much less confidence.

PERSONS

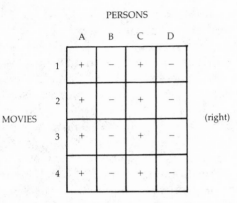

MOVIES   (right)

PERSONS

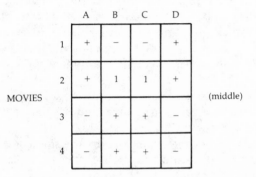

MOVIES   (middle)

PERSONS

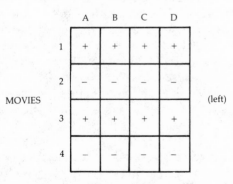

MOVIES   (left)

FIGURE 1. Matrices illustrating covariation of behavior effect with person (right), stimuli (left) and both (middle)

Obviously the perceiver, having acquired all matrix entries, could plausibly interpret the causal patterns in each. However, Heider (1958) and others (cf. Hansen, 1980; Jones & Davis, 1965) have suggested that perceivers typically do not attempt to obtain complete information. These theorists contend that perceivers operate under a principle of sufficient cause. That is, once a cause-effect covariation has been established on the basis of partial information, perceivers make a causal attribution without seeking more information. Orvis, Cunningham, and Kelley (1975) made a similar point. In their research they constrained some subjects to one category of information and requested an attribution. Subjects given column 1 of the left matrix in Figure 1 made a stimulus attribution; those given row 1 of the right matrix made a personal attribution. Although these data do not argue that perceivers cease searching once they establish a simple covariation, they do indicate that perceivers can base attributions on partial information. It also should be noted that attributions based on partial information did not seem to be made with any less confidence than those based on complete information. This is of particular interest in situations such as that diagramed in the center matrix of Figure 1.

If, as some suggest (Hansen, 1980; McArthur, 1972), perceivers seek information in a given pattern, they may be more or less likely to detect a given covariation. For example, a perceiver who searches information within persons and across stimuli (acquiring one column of a Figure 1 matrix) and who stops upon accumulating covariation evidence would come to the same causal conclusion given the patterns in the left and the center matrixes. A perceiver who searches information within stimulus and across persons (acquiring one row of a Figure 1 matrix) and who ceases to search upon detecting a covariation might mistake the covariation pattern in the center matrix for that in the right matrix. In short, multiply caused effects could be interpreted differently as a function of the perceivers' search for evidence of sufficient cause. Alternatively, a covariation may be less likely to be detected by some search strategies than by others. The issue then becomes whether perceivers' search patterns can be theoretically specified. Hansen (1980, in press) has argued that this is the case, suggesting that perceivers' search for covariation information is directed by their naive guesses as to the most likely source of covariation. That is, perceivers tend to view effects as a result of simple rather than complex covariation. Given the availability of multiple causes, perceivers tend to identify one as the most likely cause and then seek covariation evidence supporting their guess. An issue of interest, then, is the nature and basis of perceivers' speculation about the cause of behavior.

SEX-DETERMINED CAUSAL GUESSES

We wish to advance the hypothesis that sex of the behaver is one basis for naively locating the cause for behavior in the person or in the person's environment. To test this, subjects (Hansen & O'Leary, 1983) were asked to make attributions for a man's or a woman's behavior. Behaviors were either emotions or achievements. Women's behavior was attributed to stimulus cause significantly less often than men's and to personal cause significantly more often than men's. Subjects made these attributions with no information beyond the person's name and a behavior statement. The stimulus was not described and the behavior was not elaborated. It seemed likely, therefore, that these attributional divergences seen as a function of performer sex represented perceivers' naive guesses about the most potent causal force acting on men's and women's behavior. In terms of our previous discussion, women's behavior may be seen as covarying more with perceived attributes of women and men's may be seen as covarying more with properties of stimuli. We conducted two experiments to explore this covariation hypothesis.

In these experiments perceivers were given behavioral data that should have been ambiguous with regard to causal source. They were given an effect that could logically be seen as covarying with either or both of two causal forces: one in actors and one in stimuli in the actors' environments. Conceptually these perceivers were given the entries on the diagonal of the middle matrix in Figure 1. After learning that each of a number of actors—each interacting with a different stimulus—behaved differently, subjects were asked to explain the behavioral variance. That is, they were asked to solve for covariation: Was the effect covarying with persons (right matrix), stimuli (left matrix), or both (middle matrix)? Attribution theorists have agreed, more or less, on perceivers' probable solution.

Theoretically perceivers should have applied the *discounting* principle (Kelley, 1972a) to arrive at a solution. This principle states that an effect occurring in the presence of multiple causes is attributed less to any one factor than if the effect occurs in the presence of one factor alone. The effect is discounted as an instance of a clear covariation with any one of the multiple factors. However, there is reason to suspect that perceivers do not discount in the theoretically specified manner in all instances (cf. Enzle, Hansen, & Lowe, 1975; Hansen & Hall, 1983). As we have already noted, a number of theorists contend that perceivers seek only cause sufficient to explain an event rather than a complete accounting of the influence of all available forces. Finding that one cause is sufficient to explain a pattern of effects, perceivers may not be concerned with the discounting of this cause that should result from the presence of a second cause. Based on our research indicating that women's behavior was attributed less to stimulus and more to personal cause than men's behavior, we anticipated different solutions to the ambiguous covariation problems as a function of performer sex. We expected ambiguous covariation of behavior with personal and stimulus forces to be interpreted as a simple person-effect covariation when actors were women and as a simple stimulus-effect covariation when actors were men. We did not anticipate discounting effects in either case. Simply, given a matrix diagonal that could be perceived as any of the three illustrated in Figure 1, perceivers will construe women's behavior in terms of a covariation with persons (Figure 1, right) and men's behavior in terms of a covariation with stimuli (Figure 1, left). Covariation with both persons and stimuli (Figure 1, middle) was not expected to prevail, even though theoretically it should.

Experiment 1. In one experiment (Hansen & O'Leary, 1983) we gave equal numbers of women and men one-sentence descriptions of behaviors ambiguously covarying with persons and stimuli. The actors were either women or men, and the behaviors occurred in response to emotion-eliciting stimuli (movies) or achievement-eliciting stimuli (tasks). The descriptions were written to represent the ambiguous covariation illustrated by the entries on the diagonals of the matrixes in Figure 1: (1) "Twelve (women/men) each viewed a different movie; some laughed while watching the movie they saw and others did not." (2) "Twelve (women/men) each played a different game; some won and received prizes and others did not win." Subjects were asked to estimate the extent to which the described effect covaried with "differences among the people (women/men)" and with "differences among the stimuli (movies/games)." They indicated their estimates on separate 11-point scales anchored at 0 ("not at all") and at 10 ("to a very great extent")

Table 1
Perceived Covariation of Behavior with Persons and Stimuli in Two Experiments

	Women		Men	
Experiment	Persons	Stimuli	Persons	Stimuli
1	7.02_a	3.52_b	4.41_b	7.08_a
2	4.83_a	3.60_b	3.61_b	4.82_a

Note: Row means not sharing a common subscript differ significantly ($p <$ .05). In both experiments, higher numbers indicated greater perceived covariation.

following each factor. It was made clear that these were indepen- dent ratings and that responses need not be correlated. That is, subjects were made to feel comfortable identifying the effect as a simple covariation with one factor or discounting both factors as the covarying factor. The results of this experiment can be seen in Table 1 (top row). As we expected, subjects did not discount. The effect was not interpreted as an instance of ambiguous covariation with two causal factors. Women's behavior was seen as covarying with persons. Men's behavior was seen as covarying with stimuli.

Experiment 2. We presented subjects with a conceptual replication of the ambiguous covariation problem using visual rather than paper-and-pencil stimulus materials in a second experiment (O'Le- ary & Hansen, unpublished). An equal number of women and men viewed videotapes of people rating products in a "consumer marketing survey." These videotapes had been carefully con- structed using male and female undergraduates as actors. The actors followed carefully constructed scripts of ratings and nonver- bal behavior. Subjects saw each of six actors rate different products. Each actor gave his or her product a different rating. Camera angles had been selected to make the actor and the stimulus (product) equally prominent in the visual field (cf. Taylor & Fiske, 1978). After viewing the videotape, subjects indicated the extent to which the effect (different ratings) covaried with persons or with stimuli. They did this on two 7-point scales labeled at 0 ("not at all") and at 6 ("to a

Table 2
Effect of Sex and Role Congruence of Stimulus on Perceived Covariation

Covariation	Women Actors		Men Actors	
	Stimuli Role Congruent	Stimuli Role Incongruent	Stimuli Role Congruent	Stimuli Role Incongruent
Persons	4.06_b	5.58_c	2.81_a	4.39_b
Stimuli	3.94_{ab}	3.25_a	5.38_c	4.27_b

Note: Means not sharing a subscript differ significantly ($p < .05$). Higher numbers indicate greater perceived covariation of effect with causal factor.

very great extent"). Again it was made clear that covariation assigned to persons need not correlate with that assigned to stimuli: They could feel free to discount. As indicated in Table 1 (bottom row), the pattern of these data paralleled that of the first experiment. Women's behavior was seen as covarying more with persons than with stimuli. Men's behavior was seen as covarying more with stimuli than with persons. The effects obtained in the second experiment, however, were not nearly as robust as those of the first.

In part this was due to the nature of the stimuli used in the experiment. The traditional paradigm used to explore the effects of sex on causal attributions has shown that sex of performer interacts with sex-defined behavior, roles, and behavioral domains (Deaux & Emswiller, 1974; Taynor & Deaux, 1975; Unger, 1979). Experiment 2 was no exception to this basic finding. Half of the subjects observed actors rating products congruent with traditional sex-linked expectancies, and half viewed actors rating products incongruent with traditional sex-linked experiences. Subjects viewed men or women rating various brands of either diapers or shaving cream. Pilot testing had indicated that (a) men's perceived greater experience with shaving cream than with diapers equaled women's perceived greater experience with diapers than with shaving cream, and (b) perceived variance in shaving cream equaled that in diapers. Any differences in perceived covariation of products with ratings could be accounted for only in terms of the sex of the raters and the link of the products to the female or male role. The significant interaction of actor sex and role congruence of product obtained in the experiment is obvious in Table 2. These results are interpretable within the framework of an attributional approach to expertise (Kelley, 1967). Increasing familiarity should result in a perceived greater capacity of the person to mediate accurately the qualities of a stimulus falling within the familiar domain. Thus, covariation of ratings of products familiar to raters should tend to be seen in terms of product variance. The tendency to view men's behavior as covarying with stimulus variance should be accentuated for male-role-congruent stimuli and attenuated for male-role-incongruent stimuli. The tendency to perceive women's behavior as covarying with variance in persons should be accentuated for female-role incongruent stimuli and attenuated for female-role-congruent stimuli. This described the pattern of effects observed.

SEX-DETERMINED INFORMATION SEARCH

We begin our discussion of information search, which we see as a most critical determinant of causal attributions, with an assertion. *Perceivers infer the causal role of an actor's dispositions in producing behavior by coming to know, or assuming, the provocative power of stimulus properties.* Behavior consistent with the known or assumed provocative properties of a stimulus is attributed to those properties. Behavior inconsistent with the known or assumed provocative properties of a stimulus is attributed to the actor's dispositions. If the provocative properties of a stimulus are not known or cannot be assumed by the perceiver, information connoting those properties will be sought.

Researchers have noted that perceivers often come to "know" the properties of a stimulus from their own experience (their own behavior in its presence, if you wish). This self-based (Hansen & Donoghue, 1977; Hansen & Stonner, 1978) or egocentric consensus (Heider, 1958; Ross, 1977) has been shown to be very persuasive to the perceiver. It seems to derive its power from perceivers' assumption that their own behavior is an unambiguous mediation of stimulus properties. Researchers also have found that perceivers often assume the properties of stimuli and then ignore these properties when explaining behavior. Referred to as the fundamental attribution error (Ross, 1977), perceivers' tendency to ignore the stimulus when making causal sense of behavior probably reflects their assumption of stimulus provocation and the view that stimulus properties are a necessary but not sufficient explanation of behavior. This can be described as a perceptual context effect (cf. Jones & Nisbett, 1972; Taylor & Fiske, 1978) or as the perceivers' discrimination between conditions necessary for a behavior to occur and the causes, given these conditions, necessary and sufficient to explain a particular behavior (Einhorn & Hogarth, 1982). In these instances the perceiver would be expected to seek information connoting stimulus properties. For example, perceivers who had tasted a beverage did not seek or use information on others' reactions to the drink when explaining its consumption by a specific target actor (Hansen & Donoghue, 1977; Nisbett, Borgida, Crandall, & Reed, 1976). They "knew" the drink did not taste good, and this knowledge provided a benchmark against which others' evaluations could be judged. Those perceivers who had not tasted the beverage, however, sought and used information on the power of the stimulus to provoke a particular evaluation.

Information search for purposes of making an attribution has been described by Kelley (1967; 1972b). He organized this search into three information dimensions. One of these dimensions—consensus—was a search of multiple persons' behavior in the presence of the stimulus. If most people react similarly to a stimulus, the perceiver infers the power of the stimulus to provoke that response. Ice cream enjoyed by most people is judged a good product. Note that it is the absence of a covariation of behavior with people that is informative of stimulus properties. The second dimension—distinctiveness—was a search of the target actor's behavior in the presence of multiple stimuli. If the person reacts similarly to many stimuli, the perceiver infers a propensity of the actor to behave in a certain way. A person who enjoys most ice cream is seen as an ice cream lover. His or her enjoyment of a particular ice cream, therefore, does not necessarily connote goodness of the product. Again, note that the absence of covariation—in this case, behavior with stimuli—is informative. The final dimension—consistency—was a search of the target actor's behavior in the presence of the target stimulus in many circumstances. If the person reacts similarly to the stimulus across many situations, the cause—be it in the person, the stimulus, or both—is seen as stable. The absence of covariation of behavior with circumstance is informative of stability. We shall have more to say about the special case of stability in the next two sections.

The question remains of which information dimension would have the highest information value. We argue that for the perceiver who knows or assumes the provocative properties of the stimulus, distinctiveness information would be of greatest value. However, for the perceiver who does not know or does not assume the properties of the stimulus, consensus information would be of greatest value. We therefore predicted a sex-determined information search. To the extent that perceivers view men's behavior as unambiguously mediating stimulus properties, they should be less interested in acquiring consensus information and more interested in acquiring distinctiveness information. To the extent that perceivers view women's behavior as ambiguously mediating stimulus properties, they should be more interested in consensus. These predictions were based on the proposition (Hansen, 1980; McArthur, 1972) that consensus information directly connotes the power of a stimulus to provoke a behavior. Our position here is close to a paradox. We maintain that the primary determinant of attributional inference is the perceived properties of a stimulus. We argue that consensus information most directly connotes these stimulus properties. But we also contend that perceivers often may not seek consensus information and are particularly unlikely to do so when making attributions for men's behavior. We reconcile these hypotheses by noting that the stimulus-caused component can be seen as a context effect—perhaps schematic— and that perceivers are unlikely to seek consensus unless there is reason to assume that the actor's behavior is not attributable to the stimulus. Our data indicated that this state of affairs is more probable when perceivers are faced with a woman's behavior than with a man's.

Experiment 3. This experiment has been reported elsewhere (Hansen & O'Leary, 1983), so we will not elaborate here. Subjects read descriptions of a male or a female engaging in a stereotypically masculine or feminine behavior (Broverman et al., 1972). In one replication of the experiment the actor was described as behaving in a risky (masculine) or cautious (feminine) way. In the other the actor was described as behaving in a meek, acquiescent, and compliant way (feminine) or in a forceful, profane, and noncompliant way (masculine). After reading the descriptions, subjects were asked to indicate their interest in acquiring consensus (how others behaved in response to the same stimulus), distinctiveness (how this person behaved in response to other stimuli), and consistency information (how this person behaved in response to this stimulus at other times).

The results were not completely anticipated. Congruence of behavior with sex role did not have the predicted effects. In fact, the only effect obtained was on perceivers' interest in discovering whether an actor's behavior was consistent when she or he acted out of role as opposed to in role. Perceivers were more interested in acquiring consistency information when the actor's behavior was not congruent with sex role. We will return to this finding later in the chapter when we discuss the implications of consistency for trait inferences.

In both replications, subjects were more interested in acquiring consensus information when explaining a woman's behavior than a man's. They were no more interested in distinctiveness when explaining a man's behavior than a woman's. We might note, however, that perceivers' interest in distinctiveness information was greater than their interest in consensus in every condition. This more or less fit our predictions. We are tempted to conclude that perceivers must seek more information to explain a woman's behavior than a man's because they must first discover something about the stimulus— something they are willing to infer from the man's behavior.

Experiment 4. This experiment is a companion study to the second experiment. Subjects were shown a videotape of either a male or a female actor rating a product pretested as being judged more familiar to women's experience (diapers) or men's experience (shaving cream). They saw and heard the actor rate the product as average. The subjects were asked to estimate the actor's rating of 10 other products of the same type. That is, they were asked to generate distinctiveness information. We based our predictions of these distributions on two premises. First, Kelley (1967) suggested that expertise can be defined in terms of the person's capacity to mediate differences among stimuli. To the extent that experience is seen as expertise, estimated variance in a woman's rating of diapers and a man's rating of shaving cream should exceed that in a women's ratings of shaving cream and a man's ratings of diapers. Second, we have argued that men's behavior is seen as a less ambiguous mediation of stimulus properties than is women's behavior. To the extent that sampled stimuli are varied—pretesting indicated that both product categories are seen as equally varied—estimated variance in a man's ratings of products should exceed that in a woman's ratings.

The subjects also were shown a videotape of 10 other "participants" in the rating experiment. They saw each of these others but did not hear or see their ratings of the same product rated by the actor. Subjects were asked to predict the ratings of these 10 other people. One third of the subjects saw a sample of 10 men, one third saw a sample of 10 women, and one third saw a sample of 5 women and 5 men. Our predictions for these consensus distributions were based on the same two premises as our distinctiveness predictions. First, to the extent that experience counts toward expertise, across-rater variance should be judged as lower for familiar than for unfamiliar products. Second, to the extent that men's behavior is seen as more linked to stimulus properties than women's, variance in men's behavior toward the same stimulus should be estimated as lower than variance in women's behavior.

Some of the results were a surprise. The analysis of the variance in consensus distributions failed to show any effects due to products. We had expected this to interact with the sex composition of the sample for which the distributions had been generated. Experience did not count with regard to expected consensus, but sex of the sample did. Standard deviations of distributions generated for male raters ($M = .933$) were significantly lower—$F(2,166) = 2.99$, $p <.005$—than those of distributions generated for mixed-sex ($M = 1.395$) or female raters ($M = 1.433$). Men were seen as behaving more similarly than women in all rating conditions. This was the effect anticipated by our contention that men's behavior is seen as more reflective of the stimulus than is women's.

The absence of product effects in consensus distributions was not paralleled in the distinctiveness distributions (see Table 3). A man's ratings of familiar products were estimated to evidence greater variance than his ratings of unfamiliar products. A woman's ratings of familiar and unfamiliar products were estimated to evince about the same variance. With regard to sensitivity to stimulus properties, experience counts toward expertise for a man but not for a woman.

Subjects in this experiment were also asked to indicate their interest in acquiring consensus information from the people they saw but did not hear and distinctiveness information about the actor's ratings of other products in the same category. As in the first experiment reported in this section, no effects were evident on perceivers' desire to obtain distinctiveness information. But just as

Table 3

Effects of Actor Sex and Familiarity with Stimulus on Estimated Variance in Actor's Behavior Toward Multiple Stimuli

	Actor Sex	
Familiarity	Male	Female
High	1.547_a	1.328_{ab}
Low	1.105_b	1.379_{ab}

Note: Means not sharing a common subscript differ significantly ($p < .05$).

Table 4
Effects of Actor Sex and Sample Sex on Rated Interest in Acquiring Consensus Information from the Sample

Actor	Sample Composition		
	Male	Female	Mixed Sex
Female	7.52_c	5.04_a	7.13^b
Male	6.02_{ab}	6.08_{ab}	5.65_a

Note: Means not sharing a common subscript differ significantly ($p < .05$).

in the last experiment, perceivers' overall interest in acquiring distinctiveness information was higher than their interest in acquiring consensus information. Subjects' ratings of their interest in consensus can be seen in Table 4. These findings were as predicted from our contention that (a) perceivers have a primary interest in establishing the properties of a stimulus and (b) stimulus properties are perceived as unambiguously mediated by men's behavior but not by women's. Perceivers were more interested in acquiring consensus information when attempting to explain a woman's behavior than a man's, but only if the sample from which the consensus information was derived allowed for access to men's behavior.

SEX-DETERMINED ATTRIBUTIONS

The research reported to this point clearly led us to anticipate perceivers' greater stimulus attributions for men's behavior than for women's. In Experiments 1 and 2, men's behavior more than women's was described as covarying with stimulus properties. In Experiments 3 and 4, variance estimated in men's behavior toward a target stimulus was lower than that estimated in women's behavior. This also was implied by perceivers' consensus preferences in both of the last two experiments, given acceptance of our proposition that perceivers' primary focus is on definition of stimulus properties. The picture regarding personal attributions was not as clear as that for stimulus attributions. The results of Experiments 1 and 2 indicated that perceivers are more likely to construe variance in women's behavior than

Table 5
Effects of Actor Sex on Personal and Stimulus Attributions in Three Experiments

Attribution	Experiment 1		Experiment 2		Experiment 3	
	Male	Female	Male	Female	Male	Female
Person	5.81	6.73	4.97	6.51[a]	6.33	6.36
Stimulus	7.51[b]	6.37	6.05[b]	5.03	7.01[b]	5.41

[a]Personal attributions for women's behavior significantly exceed those for men's in this experiment.
[b]Stimulus attributions for men's behavior significantly exceed those for women's in this experiment.

men's behavior in terms of covariation with persons. In Experiments 3 and 4, however, variance estimated to be introduced by persons was no more for a woman's behavior than for a man's. Similarly, perceivers were not less interested in acquiring distinctiveness information for a man than for a woman. The findings of the second two experiments, with the exception of the actor-sex interaction with product, implied that personal attributions for a man's behavior and for a woman's would be about equal. We entered this third research series with these two hypotheses in mind.

Experiments 5 through 7. Three experiments were conducted as companion studies to Experiments 3 and 4. In the first two experiments, subjects made attributions for a man's or woman's behavior that was stereotypically masculine or feminine (risky or cautious in Experiment 5 and noncompliant or compliant in Experiment 6). In Experiment 7 subjects made attributions for a man's or woman's rating of a familiar or an unfamiliar product. The stimulus materials were described in the previous section of this chapter and elsewhere (cf. Hansen & O'Leary, 1983). In all three experiments, personal and stimulus attributions were made on separate 11-point (0–10) scales. Subjects were not required to correlate their attributions. Interestingly, the effect of actor sex on attributions was not substantially influenced by other factors in any of the experiments. The effect of actor sex on attributions can be seen in Table 5. In each experiment, as predicted, a man's behavior was more strongly attributed to the stimulus than was a woman's. In only one of the three experiments were personal attributions for a woman's behavior significantly stronger than those for a man's behavior. The trend, however, was marginal in one other experiment. These results on personal attributions were not conclusive. It appears that a divergence in personal attributions for women's and men's behavior may be situationally bound. No such disclaimer, however, is needed when describing the effect of sex on stimulus attributions. In all experiments, men's behavior was perceived as more clearly mediating stimulus properties than was women's behavior.

THE BARGAIN-BASEMENT EFFECT

Our interpretation of the effects described in these seven experiments is based on acceptance of a principle of cognitive economy

(Hansen, 1980). That is, perceivers seek to make attributions with the least information that will allow a confident inference, using the least complex cognitive processing strategy. We proposed that the most economical process is one in which the perceiver attempts to establish the properties of the stimulus in the actor's environment. Attribution research has convinced us that the provocative properties of stimuli are often assumed, known by virtue of the perceiver's prior experience with stimuli in the same or similar categories, or automatically processed prior to conscious attributional inferencing. In any case, once the provocative power of a stimulus has been established, the contribution of the actor's dispositions or propensities can be inferred by applying covariation principles (i.e., discounting, augmentation, compensatory causes, etc.).

The data obtained in these seven experiments indicated to us that sex of the actor, in part, may determine the most economical inference strategy. Consistently, perceivers seem to find the behavior of men to be a more compelling mediation of stimulus properties than the behavior of women. This led us to anticipate finding two phenomena. First, perceivers require little or no additional information to establish stimulus properties in a male actor's environment. Second, perceivers require additional information to establish stimulus properties in a female actor's environment. The information used, in the absence of an assumption of knowledge of these properties, is consensus information. The consensus information most sought is behavior of another person that is thought to unambiguously mediate stimulus properties. Such concensus information can be derived from the behavior of men. Put simply, male behavior is the *benchmark* for establishing the behavior provoked by a stimulus against which others' behavior can be compared. Men's behavior is sought both because it is seen as mediating stimulus properties and because it is more economical to process: the bargain-basement effect.

We do not contend that causal attributions for women's and men's behavior will necessarily be divergent. We have shown divergent attributions in instances when perceivers have no opportunity to gather, search, or process causal information. And we would expect these divergences when perceivers are operating in an impoverished information environment or are constrained to schematic processing (cf. Bargh, 1983). However, given the opportunity and the inclination to collect and process causal information, the attributions made for women's and men's behavior may be similar. Attribution researchers have shown that perceivers given access to distinctiveness, consensus, and consistency information will use it logically to arrive at an attribution regardless of the actor's sex. We merely suggest that this is a rather unusual occurrence outside the laboratory. In that more noisy domain, we argue that a man's behavior is judged as mediating stimulus properties until proved otherwise and a woman's behavior is judged as not mediating stimulus properties until proved otherwise. Given our view of the attribution process and the primacy of establishing stimulus properties, the probability of perceivers' discovering that a man's behavior was not stimulus caused seems lower than the probability of their discovering that a woman's behavior was. In commonsense terms, a woman's behavior will be seen as stimulus-provoked if her behavior is the same as a man's. If her behavior toward a stimulus is different from his, her behavior will tend to be attributed to her dispositions and his will continue to be attributed to the stimulus: the male benchmark.

Disposition and Traits

A major attribution theory—correspondent inference theory (Jones & Davis, 1965; Jones & McGillis, 1976)—attempts to describe the conditions under which perceivers infer an actor's traits from behavior. Much of this theory describes a process whereby perceivers isolate a consequence of the actor's behavior as the effect the actor was intending to produce by engaging in the behavior. This effect intended by behavior forms the basis for perceivers' inference about traits in the actor. We are not interested here in this "noncommon" effects analysis. We accept that perceivers focus on or isolate some particular effect as the basis for their trait inferences. We are interested in defining the *information value* of this effect for the perceiver inferring an actor's traits. Correspondent inference theory specifies that a behavior and its effect are informative of an actor's traits to the extent that they inform the perceiver of a level of trait or disposition in the actor departing from the level anticipated by the perceiver. In short, a behavior having a low perceived prior probability will be informative. Jones and McGillis (1976) cast this in light of Kelley's (1967) attribution theory. They entered distinctiveness, consensus, and consistency as prior probability variables and implied that these variables are informative of the cause of the behavior and the intent of the actor. Cause and intent were critical determinants of correspondence inference (the extent to which the actor's traits are described by the effects

produced by the actor's behavior). We wish to redefine trait inferences within the framework we have developed here.

*Trait inferences derive from the perception that (a) the actor intended some-
thing by behaving and (b) the cause of this intent was not accounted for by the
provocative power of stimulus properties.* Intent is the actor's apparent
desire to act on some or all of the properties of a stimulus: for example,
a desire to possess, change, or eliminate a property. A correspondent
trait inference, therefore, results from the perception of intent, identification of a stimulus property the actor intended to affect, and the
conclusion that the stimulus property was not sufficient to provoke
the intentional behavior. Again, here we are not interested in the
second of these three inferences. We will deal only with the perception of intent and causal attribution. Of primary interest is the influence of distinctiveness, consensus, and consistency information
on perceived intent, causal attributions, and consequently on trait
inferences.

INTENT

Jones and Davis (1965) as well as Jones and McGillis (1976) argued that
behaviors and effects with high prior probability are seen as intended.
Most discussion on the point has focused on consensus-based
probability. Jones and Davis referred to consensus as social desirability. Socially desirable effects were those seen by the perceiver as likely
to be produced (or desired) by most people. Jones and McGillis refined this notion to category-based expectancies. Consensus defined
by the behavior of most people became consensus defined by the
behavior of members of a category to which the actor was assigned by
the perceiver (e.g., female or male). Nevertheless, the concept remained the same across these formulations of the theory: High consensus yields an inference of intent. The reader might feel some discomfort regarding this hypothesis given the statement of information
value above. We indeed did state that the information value of behavior for trait inference is defined as the inverse of prior probability.
High consensus behavior, then, would not be informative of an
actor's traits. This is not a contradiction, as we will explain when deal-
ing with causal attribution and trait inferences.

Distinctiveness and particularly consistency are theoretically predicted to be perceived as diagnostic of intent. Jones and his associates
noted that effects constantly sought are seen as intended. That is, low

distinctiveness and high consistency lead to inferences of intent. The greater in number and the more varied the stimuli toward which an actor directs similar behaviors, the more likely the perceiver is to infer intent. The greater in number and the more varied the circumstances in which an actor directs the same behavior toward a target stimulus, the more likely the perceiver is to infer intent. Of these three categories, consistency should be the most potent. We might note, for example, that any act involving choice implies some level of intent. Consistent choice yields a more confident intent inference.

Experiment 8. An experiment was conducted to test the influence of distinctiveness, consensus, and consistency on intent inferences (Hansen & Hall, 1983). We anticipated that perceivers generally assume that behavior is intentional (cf. de Charms, 1968). Thus we expected a relatively high level of perceived intent. Further, this reasoning led us to expect that in the absence of causal information perceivers will assume information levels consistent with intentionality. Perceivers would tend to assume low distinctiveness unless given high, high consistency unless given low, and high consensus unless given low. The experiment was designed, therefore, as a $3 \times 3 \times 3$ factorial with three levels (high, low, absent) each of distinctiveness, consensus, and consistency. Each subject in the experiment was exposed to all levels in the factorial. A different behavior in a different domain was used for each exposure. Behaviors were counterbalanced across subjects with regard to the factorial cells. Each behavior was described as producing one effect. The valence of the effect (positive or negative) was counterbalanced across subjects. (Person X held person Y's place in line at the supermarket; Y was happy to discover this upon returning. Or Person X did not hold person Y's place in line at the supermarket; Y was unhappy to discover this upon returning.) After each behavioral description were one, two, or three pieces of causal information according to condition. In one instance—absent, absent, absent—no information was included. The information statements were manipulated in the traditional fashion (cf. Orvis et al., 1975). After reading each behavior and the information, subjects indicated the extent to which the actor intended to produce the effect described. (Did X intend to make Y happy?) Throughout the experiment, persons were designated by symbols rather than by name to avoid the—obviously—anticipated sex of actor and target effects.

The results were more or less as anticipated. The only factor to produce a significant main effect was consistency. This was congruent with our prediction that consistency would have the most potent influence on intent inferences. The analysis also detected two significant two-way interactions. The first was less interesting than the second. It indicated that consensus interacted with distinctiveness. It did indicate that, in the absence of distinctiveness, no consensus yielded the same high level of intent inference as did high consensus, with low consensus yielding a lower level of intent. Likewise, in the absence of consensus, low distinctiveness and no distinctiveness produced high levels of inferred intent as opposed to the lower levels in high-distinctiveness conditions. The interaction was produced by the offsetting effects of consensus and distinctiveness when both were available. The other interaction—distinctiveness × consistency—was more interesting. Generally, consistency information overpowered distinctiveness information. Having no consistency information led to the same high level of trait inference as having high consistency in all conditions except high distinctiveness. Having low consistency information produced lower levels of intent than did high or no consistency except in high-distinctivenes conditions. High distinctiveness had sufficient power to overcome the effect of high consistency or the assumption of high consistency when it was not provided. This finding aside, the results did support the prediction that consistency would have the most potent effect on intent inferences. The results indicated that intent was perceived with greater confidence when perceivers had high consistency, high consensus, and low distinctiveness information.

Causal Attributions. The position we take with regard to causal attributions should be obvious from our presentation above. We anticipate that perceivers, unless they know or assume the provocative power of a stimulus, will base stimulus attributions on consensus information. High consensus should be most persuasive of stimulus cause. Low distinctiveness and low consistency, but particularly low distinctiveness (Hansen, 1980), should be persuasive of personal cause. We should note at this point that consensus has what seem to be conflicting implications for personal cause and intent consensus. Low consensus, on the other hand, should theoretically yield higher levels of personal cause than should high consensus. We do not see these as conflicting hypotheses. Rather, we contend that intent and cause represent the inferential outcomes of two different processes, both of which constitute the antecedent conditions of trait inference. We would, however, maintain that consensus information would not be a particularly potent factor in trait inferences because of these conflicting implications for traits.

TRAIT INFERENCES

As we stated at the outset of this section, we hypothesize trait inferences as the result of the perceiver's determining that an actor intended to produce an effect by performing a behavior and that the cause of the behavior was not attributable to the provocative power of the stimulus. This yields a view of the trait inference process as represented in Figure 2 (Hansen & Hall, 1983). Based on available or assumed information, the perceiver determines whether the effect of the behavior was intended and whether the behavior was attributable to the stimulus. If the answer to the first is yes and the answer to the second is no, the perceiver makes a confident inference of a trait in the person corresponding to the intent to produce the effect. Based on our research, we argue that this is most likely to occur when the perceiver possesses high consistency information—implying intent but not discounting personal cause—and low consensus information—having a weak effect on intent inference but a strong discounting effect on stimulus cause. We also contend that perceivers, to the extent that they do not seek causal information, are likely to assume that the behavior was intentional and personally caused. As a result, trait inferences from behavior are seen as relatively frequent (we will have more to say about the influence of the behaver's sex on this phenomenon).

Experiment 9. An experiment was conducted to test the view of the trait inference process illustrated by Figure 2 (Hansen & Hall, 1983). Subjects were given a short description of a behavior and one effect of the behavior. In addition, accompanying each behavior statement was information that (a) the person intended to produce the effect, the person did not intend to produce the effect, or the person's intention was unknown, and (b) the behavior was personally caused, the behavior was caused by the stimulus, or the cause was not known. After reading the description and the information appropriate to the 3 × 3 condition assignment, subjects were asked to indicate the prob-

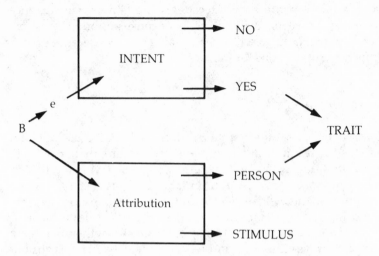

FIGURE 2. Model of trait inference process (after Hanson & Hall, 1983)

ability that the person possessed a trait corresponding to the produced effect (e.g., What is the probability that the adult has a disposition to enjoy making children smile?). As in Experiment 8, the behaviors associated with each of the nine within-subject conditions as well as the valence of the effect and behavior (e.g., Adult criticizes the child, making the child cry/Adult compliments the child, making the child smile) were counterbalances across subjects.

The results of the experiment were about as anticipated by the model. Main effects were produced by both provided attribution and provided intent statements. These main effects were elucidated by an interaction of the two factors. The highest level of intent inference was obtained in the condition where subjects learned both that the actor had intended to produce the effect and that the behavior was personally caused (estimated probability of the actor's possessing a trait correspondent to the effect, $M = 65.7\%$). The lowest level of intent inference was obtained where subjects learned both that the actor had not intended to produce the effect and that the behavior was stimulus caused (estimated probability of the actor's possessing a trait correspondent to the effect, $M = 35.6\%$). The influence of intent on trait inference was slightly greater than that of attribution. The results of this experiment strongly supported the view of the model illustrated in the figure.

Sex-Determined Trait Inferences

The influence of performer sex on trait inferences was not clear to us on either a theoretical or an empirical basis. The results of our investigations had yielded a slight tendency for attributors to see women's behavior as more personally caused than men's. However, this trend was mixed and inconsistent. One possible basis for predicting an actor-six effect on intent inferences—interest in consistency and distinctiveness information—argued against the effect. Perceivers were no more interested in either consistency or distinctiveness when evaluating a woman's behavior than a man's. These findings did not lend themselves to a clear empirically based prediction of an actor-sex effect. But the findings related to consensus might have offered some support. Perceivers did show greater interest in consensus when evaluating a woman's behavior than a man's. These findings provided an empirical indication of a sex difference. Theoretically, however, these effects would not be expected to dramatically affect trait inferences. As we have noted, the effects of consensus on intent and on cause inferences tend to offset each other. The greater assumed consensus for men's behavior would imply greater perceived intent but also stimulus cause. The male intended to act on the stimulus. The lesser assumed consensus for women's behavior would imply personal cause but also unintentional effects. The low efficacy of consensus on trait inferences—which we contend is a result of divergent implications for cause and intent—has been amply documented in the attribution literature (cf. Nisbett & Ross, 1980).

Of some potential interest was the finding that perceivers were more interested in consistency information when an actor's behavior was sex-role incongruent that when it was congruent. While this did not necessarily argue for stronger trait inferences in congruent than incongruent instances, we took this as a working hypothesis. Sex role is consensus or category-based information, and correspondent inference theory would anticipate an effect on trait correspondence. (Note that Jones and Davis defined correspondence as greater confidence in the actor's possession of a trait whereas Jones and McGillis defined it in terms of the perceiver's judgment that the actor possesses a level of trait discrepant with that of the category.) We have maintained that consensus information has little power to influence trait inferences. However, the data obtained in Experiment 3 indicated that perceivers may have been questioning the consistency of the person's role-inconsistent behavior. Because we see consistency as a critical determinant of trait inference, such questioning could be shown in a weakening of trait inferences in role-inconsistent conditions.

Experiment 10. We conducted an experiment in which subjects watched a videotape of a woman or a man engaging in one of two stereotypically masculine behaviors or one of two stereotypically feminine behaviors. The scripts used by the actors were elaborations of the behavior descriptions used in Experiment 3 (compliant/noncompliant and risky/cautious). Four professional actors—two women and two men—performed each sequence and were seen equally often by the subjects. At the conclusion of the videotape presentation, subjects were asked to estimate the probability that the person shown had a trait corresponding to his or her behavior (e.g., compliant). They also were asked to rate the apparent gender of the person on a bipolar scale (masculine/feminine). The results of the experiment were not encouraging for the hypothesis. For the most part, actors' behavior was judged diagnostic of their traits. Regardless of sex, actors behaving in a noncompliant fashion were judged noncompliant. Those behaving compliantly were judged compliant. Those engaging in a risky behavior were seen as daring and those engaging in cautious behavior were seen as cautious. Sex role had no substantial effects. The bipolar ratings of gender showed only actor-sex effects. Men were masculine and women were feminine no matter what they did. There was a trend for women acting in a masculine fashion to be judged less feminine than women acting in a feminine fashion, but this trend was not substantial. Thus these data indicated that sex becomes gender.

The findings of this experiment substantially replicated the research conducted by others (Locksley, Borgida, Brekke, & Hepburn, 1980) showing no influence of sex-role congruence of behavior on trait inferences and indicating that consensus has little effect on trait inferences (Nisbett & Ross, 1980). The absence of any substantial influence of sex-role congruence of behavior on perceived gender of the actor was of great potential interest. On the one hand, these data suggested that behavioral performance can be taken by the perceiver as a priori evidence of personal disposition (cf. Jones & Nisbett, 1972). On the other hand, congruence of behavior with sex role had no apparent effect on perceived gender; sex of actor became gender. This appears more encouraging in terms of stereotype deterioration than it probably is in fact. Darley and Gross (1983) showed that perceivers watching the performance of an actor including behaviors consistent with the stereotype of the category into which the actor had been placed and behavior inconsistent with the stereotype selectively used (or attended to) information consistent with the stereotype. Given an array of conflicting behavioral information—behaviors both congruent and incongruent with sex-role stereotypes—we would anticipate a demonstration of the robust nature of sex-role stereotypes. Indeed, this is even suggested in the pattern of performance evaluations given by teachers (subjects) for the female student (actor) in the Darley and Gross research. In spite of the appearance of the data obtained in Experiment 10, we contend that sex becomes gender and that gender defines the selective use of behavior so as to have the effect of maintaining sex-role stereotypes.

The theoretical framework we have developed and the research we have conducted *do not* lead us to conclude that perceivers are more likely to infer traits from the behavior of one sex or the other. Men's behavior and women's behavior are seen as equally indicative of their traits. Our research also could lead us to conclude that men are seen as masculine and women as feminine regardless of their behavior. However, two considerations preclude our taking this step. First, we have sampled only a small domain of sex-typed behaviors and have provided perceivers with no information about consistency or distinctiveness. We presume that in some domains sex-role-inconsistent behavior will reflect on the gender of the performer. We also presume that providing information that the person is consistently engaging in sex-role-inconsistent behavior would reflect on the gender of the performer. Second, the social cognition literature (cf. Bargh, 1983) indicates that perceivers are likely to be very attentive to unexpected behaviors when they have the time to process the information. In our research, perceivers were presented with behavior sequences that were short and fairly rapid. In such circumstances of rapid information flow perceivers may have been automatically processing information, which would decrease the probability that they would detect and process inconsistent information. In summary, we can conclude that we have reason to believe that perceivers are no more likely to infer a woman's than a man's traits from behavior. We have some reason to believe, however, that the traits inferred from their similar behaviors (e.g., masculine/feminine) will be different.

Performance and Achievement

In a study of the effect of performer sex on organizational decision making, Murphy (1977) found that both student-subjects and executives were much more likely to provide advancement opportunities (pay increments and promotions) to men than to women. The most striking discrepancy was obtained in promotion selection. The male was promoted in 11 of 22 cases; the female was never selected. The results of research conducted to examine differential causal explanations for success and failure using Weiner's (1972) taxonomy for determinants of achievement behavior have often been used to explain this type of discrepancy. Male and female perceivers generally agree that a man's successful performance on a task is caused by ability and a woman's equally successful performance is attributed to luck or effort or both (Deaux & Emswiller, 1974; Mednick & Weissman, 1975). It seems reasonable to expect that sex differences in the perceived causes of success will provide different reactions to it.

Heilman and Guzzo (1978) asked female and male MBA students to make recommendations regarding the appropriateness of various personnel actions taken on successful male and female employees. Four different causes for the hypothetical employees' success were described (ability, effort, task ease, and luck). When success was presented as due to ability or to effort, pay raises were viewed as an equally appropriate reward. However, promotion was deemed appropriate when success was presented as due to ability but not to effort. Promotion was strongly favored for those possessing high ability.

Attribution theorists (Heider, 1958; Weiner, 1979; Weiner et al., 1971; Weiner et al., 1979; Wimer & Kelley, 1982) contend that the consequences of perceivers' explanations of success and failure for performance evaluation must be analyzed in terms of their underlying meaning (Ronis, Hansen, & O'Leary, 1983). Weiner et al. (1971), for example, argued that the locus (internal/external) and stability (stable/unstable) of the perceived causes for performance mediate perceivers' expectations of future performance, affect, and evaluation of current outcomes. Within Weiner's framework, ability and effort are categorized as internal determinants of outcome. Most organizational rewards are designed, in part, to recognize personal accomplishments. Often ability has been categorized as stable and effort as unstable. Stability has been shown to be related to expectations of future performance (Ronis, Hansen, & O'Leary, 1983). To the extent that ability connotes personal and stable cause and effort con-notes unstable cause, promotion—linked to future performance ex-pectations— should be seen as more appropriate when success has been attributed to stable than to unstable personal cause. Men, whose success is more likely than women's to be seen as resulting from their skill, are more likely to garner promotions.

This is the traditional attributional analysis of this type of phe-nomenon, and so far it seems parallel to the observed differential organizational status of women and men. But two findings cast a shadow on this analysis. First, women received 40% less pay than men holding similar positions in organizations (U.S. Department of Labor, 1978). Given the analysis above, this implies that men's suc-cess is more strongly attributed to effort than women's. Yet most peo-ple looking at the available attribution literature would contend that just the opposite holds. Second, some attribution research has indi-cated that effort, not ability, should be the primary mediator of all organizational rewards (Green & Mitchell, 1979). We take the posi-tion that these conflicting findings can be reconciled within a model of performance evaluation that focuses on the meaning of effort.

THE MEANING OF EFFORT

Our theoretical approach to understanding the meaning of effort has been illustrated in Figure 3 (after O'Leary & Hansen, 1983). The per-ceived relations among these variables as prescribed by the model have been entered as signs. The direction of the relations designates

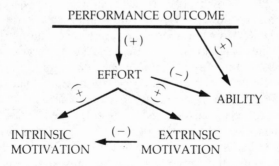

FIGURE 3. Inference model of performance evaluation (after O'Leary & Hansen, 1983).

the inferential embedding of the variables. For example, ability is inferred from performance outcome and effort. It therefore is more embedded than either outcome or effort. Again, the signs of the relations describe the effect of increasing levels of the less embedded variable on the more embedded variable. For example, increasing levels of effort inversely result in decreasing levels of inferred ability.

Ability and effort both are seen as facilitating performance. Increases in performance level should result in a perceived increase in ability or effort or both. Attribution logic—discounting—suggests that both would increase (Kelley, 1972a). Because both ability and effort facilitate performance, they logically compensate one another with regard to performance (Kelley, 1972b). That is, if two individuals achieve the same performance level, the person exerting less effort to attain that level will be seen as possessing greater ability (cf. Anderson & Butzin, 1974). As indicated in the model, we propose that ability is more embedded than effort and therefore less likely to be directly known. As a result we maintain that perceivers often attempt to infer ability by anchoring their inference in performance level and adjusting for effort. We conducted an experiment to demonstrate this compensatory relationship.

Experiment 11. Subjects were provided with information about the performance of participants on a task (sex of actor was undefined). The quality of performance was described as being low, below average, above average, or high relative to a standard comparison group. Embedded in the description of each performer were statements regarding the performer's level of effort, which was said to have been low, below average, above average, or high. After reading the description of the person's performance, subjects were asked to infer the person's level of ability. They indicated their responses on 21-point scales, with lower numbers indicating lower ability. The results have been illustrated in Figure 4. Both the main effect due to performance level and that due to effort level were significant. As can be seen in the figure, the compensatory relationship of ability and effort was obtained at each performance level. Increased effort to attain a given performance level resulted in lower inferred levels of ability.

Effort has meaning for the perceiver because it allows for the adjustment of ability levels. It also has meaning because it may connote underlying motivation. Attribution research indicates that effort generally is perceived as being under the intentional control of the individual (Weiner et al., 1979; Weiner, 1979). Heider (1958) con-

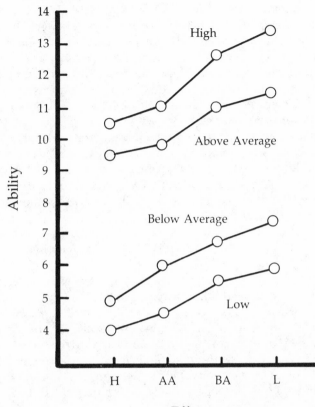

Effort

FIGURE 4. Impact of effort level and performance level on inferred levels of ability

tended that performers receive more praise for success and more condemnation for failure produced by controllable causes than by uncontrollable ones. Does effort, then, necessarily yield praise in the form of rewards (e.g., pay raises and promotion) when seen as a factor contributing to success? We contend not, for two reasons. First, as already noted, effort can be entered in a compensatory relationship to ability. If high effort is viewed as compensating for low ability, performance rewards—particularly promotion (Heilman & Guzzo, 1978)—will not be forthcoming. Second, the meaning of effort is determined in part by its perceived derivation from internal or external loci that are either stable or unstable.

We have proposed that intent inferences can best be conceptualized as independent of or parallel to causal inferences. Thus, although effort is seen as intended to produce some effect, the intention can be seen as caused by different factors. The locus and stability of these causes theoretically can alter the implications of effort for performance evaluation. This issue has been widely addressed by those studying intrinsic motivation (Deci, 1975). This work has focused on the perceived locus of motivating forces. Intrinsic motivation for the most part has been dealt with as a perceived residual force, much in the way we have described ability inferences. That is, intrinsic motivation is described as being inferred from levels of effort adjusted for levels of extrinsic motivating forces. Intrinsic motivation is compensatory to extrinsic motivation with regard to effort. Extrinsic motivating forces are construed as a multiplicative function of reinforcement level and the contingency of reinforcement on success.

Extrinsic forces = Rein level (p(Rein/Success) − p(Rein/Failure)

There are multiple implications of taking this view of effort as caused by factors that differ with regard to locus and stability (Elig & Frieze, 1979; Meyer, 1980; Ostrove, 1978; Ronis et al., 1983; Weiner et al., 1979; Wimer & Kelley, 1982). Most obviously, it implies that increased levels of effort may not be seen as diagnostic of lower levels of ability when this compensatory inference can be discounted by higher levels of extrinsic motivating forces (e.g., pay differentials). Beyond this, however, a performance attributed to effort would be expected to form a basis for perceivers' expectations of future performance only if (a) effort was perceived as internally caused, or (b) effort was perceived as externally caused, with future performance to occur in the same environment, and (c) the cause was perceived as stable. With this in mind, it is apparent that performance evaluation and the consequent allocation of rewards (e.g., pay raises and promotion) are contingent on the meaning of effort.

   1. Effort seen as intended by the performer to influence a stimulus property (i.e., to obtain a reward) and caused by the provocative power of the stimulus (i.e., factors within the performer are not necessary to explain the level of effort) (a) will tend to discount a compensatory inference of lower ability and (b) will be seen as persisting only if the effect (reward) is obtained.

   2. Effort seen as intended but not sufficiently explained by the provocative power of the stimulus (personal factors are necessary to explain the level of effort) will (a) tend to result in a compensatory infer-

ence of compensatory lower ability or (b) be more likely to be seen as resulting from intrinsic motivating factors and persisting if the intended effect (reward) is not obtained, or both.

These propositions are consistent with our position on cause and trait inferences. Upon seeing a behavior the perceiver tends to establish whether it can be accounted for by the provocative power of the stimulus. If so, the perceiver can infer that the behavior will persist only as long as the stimulus retains provocative power. Of course the provocative power of a monetary reward for performance diminishes and must be increased to maintain stable performance. If the behavior cannot be explained in terms of the stimulus, the perceiver seeks an additional cause. We have focused on two: low ability and intrinsic motivation. The perceiver using these causes to account for performance is not as likely to reward it. Low ability is not worthy of promotion. High intrinsic motivation connotes stable performance regardless of stimulus provocation. Monetary reward in this case might be judged a waste of a valuable and limited resource.

SEX-DETERMINED PERFORMANCE EVALUATION

We have argued that ability is inferred from performance as adjusted by level of effort. Attribution research exploring perceivers' explanations for the performance of women and men has indicated that men's performance is seen as more diagnostic of their abilities— more strongly attributed to their abilities—than is women's (Cash, Gillen, & Burns, 1977; Deaux & Emswiller, 1974; Deaux & Taynor, 1973; Etaugh & Brown, 1975; Feather & Simon, 1975; Feldman-Summers & Kiesler, 1974; Haccoun & Stacy, 1980). Because effort is perceived as compensatory to ability with regard to performance, this generally accepted finding implies two hypotheses. First, for any given level of performance a woman's effort should be perceived as exceeding that of an equally achieving man. Second, because men's perceived level of ability is adjusted less for effort than women's, increasing levels of performance should have a greater influence on men's perceived ability level than on women's. We conducted three studies to test these hypotheses.

Experiments 12 and 13. These experiments have been described elsewhere (O'Leary & Hansen, 1983) so we will not elaborate on them here. In both, subjects were given descriptions of a task and the performance level (low, below average, above average, high) of either a man or a woman. The task and the measure of performance were precisely specified so that subjects could not infer that one person's "above average" performance was different from that of another or judge the task as easier in one case than another. At the conclusion of one experiment, subjects were asked to predict the ability level of the person whose performance has been described. At the conclusion of the other experiment, subjects were asked to predict the effort level of the performer. They made their predictions on the same scales in both experiments. The results of each experiment supported the hypothesis tested. In the first experiment a woman's effort was estimated as significantly greater than a man's at every level of performance. In the second experiment, sex of performer interacted with performance level. The effect of increasing performance level on men's ability was much greater than that evinced on women's ability. Thus women were assumed to be trying harder, and performance level was judged more diagnostic of men's behavior than of women's. However, a full test of the second hypothesis required yet one more experiment in which both performance level and effort level were known and perceivers were required to infer ability levels.

Experiment 14. Subjects in this experiment were given the same description of a task as those in Experiments 11–13. As in the other experiments, the task described presumably allowed for precise specifications of effort, ability, and performance levels. In this experiment, however, only two levels (high and low) of performance and effort were used. The experiment was a 2 (performance level) × 2 (effort level) × 2 (performer sex) within-subjects factorial. Order of condition presentation was randomized across subjects. The significant three-way interaction evinced by perceivers' estimates of the performers' ability levels is illustrated in Figure 5. The interaction supported the hypothesis. It can be seen that effort was viewed as compensatory to ability at both performance levels for performers of both sexes. However, it also can be seen that the influence of performance level was more substantial on men's perceived ability level than on women's. Performance outcome was seen as more diagnostic of men's ability than of women's. This seems to offer a hint about why men may be more likely than equally achieving women to obtain a promotion that Heilman and Guzzo's (1978) research indicates is mediated by ability. *Although trying seems to hurt both women and men, success helps men more than women.*

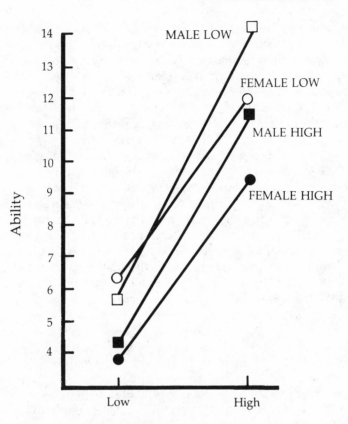

FIGURE 5. Impact of performance level, effort level, and performer sex in inferred levels of ability

To explain the lower remuneration of women than men for their (apparently) greater perceived efforts, we must speculate about the perceived causes of women's and men's efforts. Our position at this point should be fairly obvious: Men's effort is seen as more extrinsically caused than is women's. That is, men's effort is more likely to be seen as intended to produce an effect on the stimulus (obtain the reward). Because women's effort is not perceived as sufficiently explained by the provocative power (reinforcement) of the stimulus, perceivers are likely to seek other, personal, causes to explain women's effort. As we noted previously, one of these causes is intrinsic motivation. We predict that women's behavior is likely to be perceived as more intrinsically motivated than men's. Having made such a bold assertion—and we have no data to directly support us in this contention—we must say something about the possible origins of such a sex-determined divergence.

A number of researchers have reported data indicating that women may behave "as if" they were more intrinsically motivated than their male counterparts (Callahan-Levy & Messe, 1979; Kahn et al., 1980; Major & McFarlin, 1982; Major & Vanderslice, 1982). In one study (Major & McFarlin, 1982) women who were paid the same amount as men for working on a task worked longer than the men. In the other studies, women who expended the same effort as men on a task paid themselves less. A glance at our performance model should leave no doubt about how this might be interpreted by a perceiver. To the extent that perceivers' understanding of effort reflects this behavioral reality, women will be seen as less extrinsically motivated and more intrinsically motivated than men. Although not of particular concern here, it should be noted that at least two explanations are available for the behavioral differences reported in these experiments. Kahn et al. (1980) have argued that women and men value different outcomes. Men were described as more motivated to maximize their—publicly obtained—organizational gains. Women were described as more motivated by interpersonal gains. Others have argued for a different explanation. They have suggested that women and men use comparison with same-sex others to generate reward expectations (Chesler & Goodman, 1976; Major & Deaux, 1982). Because women are paid less, women's use of women as comparison others would result in lower reward expectations and hence in the behavioral self-fulfilling prophecy of rendering more effort for equal reward or equal effort for less reward. In any case, the "fact" of women's trying harder than men is not of concern here. We contend that women are perceived as trying harder even if they do not. Further, because men's effort is more likely than women's to be seen as intended to affect the environment (obtain a reward), trying hurts women but may help men. Thus we agree with Green and Mitchell (1979) in their contention that effort is pivotal in the performance-evaluation process. But we also argue that the meaning of effort is sex determined. Women's effort is perceived as intrinsically motivated and as compensating for lower ability. Men's effort is perceived as extrinsically motivated and not necessarily as compensatory to their ability. We can summarize our findings and speculations about sex-determined performance evaluation in this conclusion: *Trying hurts women more than men; success helps men more than women.*

The Attributional Images of Women and Men

We began with a number of questions and few answers. We have attempted some answers and asked many new questions. We set ourselves the goal of creating an attributional framework within which the persistence of beliefs in sex differences could be understood. We have created this framework and suggested how the attributional images of women and men could maintain the illusion of sex differences where few exist. We have asserted that perceivers understand behavior in terms of the power that a stimulus in the environment has to provoke it. We have argued that men's behavior is more likely than women's to be seen as reflecting stimulus properties. This logically led us to conclude that men's behavior is perceived as a benchmark of stimulus properties against which the behavior of women can be measured. That is, a woman's behavior will be seen as attributable to a stimulus in her environment only to the extent that her behavior is the same as that of a man reacting to the same stimulus. We extended this argument by suggesting that men's behavior is more likely than women's to be seen as intended to produce an effect on the stimulus, and then we explored the implications of this argument for performance evaluation. We have hypothesized and demonstrated that women's and men's identical behavior can acquire different meanings for perceivers at the attributional level.

Our research and theory as well as recent advances in social cognition research (cf. Wyer & Srull, in press) lead us to believe that the fundamental tendency to attribute men's behavior more than women's to stimulus properties may be the result of an "automatic" or a "mindless" cognitive process. Hansen (in press) recently has argued that attributions of behavior often are the result of automatic schematic processing of information. This is consistent with the view that initial encoding of behavior is accomplished through the use of "scripts" (Schank & Abelson, 1977) or "event schemas" (Taynor & Fiske, 1981). These scripts or event schemas are described as being organized episodically and incorporating causal linkages among script elements (cf. Schank, 1975). Thus, attention directed to behavior may result in causally associated elements also becoming salient. This schematic association may well come to conscious processing as an "attributional fact," without awareness of the automatic processing having resulted in their mutual salience. As such, these attributional facts would approach verisimilitude. If this is the case, they would be relatively difficult to challenge. In the complexity of our attribution models it is obvious that we do not contend that all attribution processing is automatic. Rather, we argue that automatic processing is more likely to make the stimulus a more salient component in perceivers' conscious processing of men's behavior than of women's.

It is important to note that we refer to these sex-determined attributional phenomena as attributional facts. For the perceiver, the distinction between actual and perceived—automatically processed—facts is blurry or nonexistent. To challenge these facts, in one sense, is to challenge perceivers' social reality. Many cognitive mechanisms, some of which we have described here, are available to take up the challenge. Although the attribution perspective we have developed here may allow us to approach understanding the persistence of beliefs in sex differences, it does not offer a magic bullet to shatter those beliefs.

REFERENCES

Abramowitz, C. V., & Dokecki, P. R. (1977). The politics of clinical judgment: Early empirical returns. *Psychological Bulletin, 84*, 460–476.
Abramson, P. R., Seligman, M. E. P., & Teasdale, J. (1978). Learned helplessness in humans: Critique and reformulation. *Journal of Abnormal Psychology, 87*, 49–74.
Anderson, N. H., & Butzin, C. A. (1974). Performance-motivation and ability: An integration-theoretical analysis. *Journal of Personality and Social Psychology, 30*(5), 598–604.
Bargh, J. A. (1983). Automatic and conscious processing of social information. In R. S. Wyer & T. K. Scrull (Eds.), *The handbook of social cognition*. Hillsdale, NJ: Erlbaum.
Birdwhistle, R. L. (1970). *Kinesis and content*. Philadelphia: University of Pennsylvania Press.
Broverman, I., Vogel, S. R., Broverman, D., Clarkson, F. E., & Rosenkrantz, P. S. (1972). Sex role stereotypes: A current appraisal. *Social Issues, 28*, 59–78.
Broverman, S. K., Broverman, D. M., Clarkson, F. E., Rosenkrantz, P. S., &

Vogel, S. R. (1970). Sex-role stereotypes and clinical judgments of mental health. *Journal of Consulting and Clinical Psychology, 34,* 1–7.

Brown, S. H. (1979). Male versus female leaders: A comparison of empirical studies. *Sex Roles, 5,* 595–612.

Callahan-Levy, C. M., & Messe, L. A. (1979). Sex differences in the allocation of pay. *Journal of Personality and Social Psychology, 37,* 433–446.

Cash, T. F., Gillen, B., & Burns, D. S. (1977). Sexism and beautyism in personnel consultant decision making. *Journal of Applied Psychology, 62,* 301–310.

de Charms, R. (1968). *Personal causation.* New York: Academic Press.

Chesler, P., & Goodman, E. J. (1976). *Women, money, and power.* New York: Morrow.

Darley, J. M., & Gross, P. H. (1983). A hypothesis-confirming bias in labeling effects. *Journal of Personality and Social Psychology, 44,* 20–33.

Deaux, K. (1976). Sex and the attribution process. In J. H. Harvey, W. J. Ickes, & R. F. Kidd (Eds.), *New directions in attribution research* (Vol. 1). New York: Wiley.

Deaux, K., & Emswiller, T. (1974). Explanations of successful performance on sex-linked tasks: What's skill for the male is luck for the female. *Journal of Personality and Social Psychology, 29,* 80–85.

Deaux, K., & Taynor, J. (1973). Evaluation of male and female ability: Bias works two ways. *Psychological Reports, 32,* 261–262a.

Deci, E. L. (1975). *Intrinsic motivation.* New York: Plenum.

Eagly, A. H. (1978). Sex differences in influenceability. *Psychological Bulletin, 85,* 86–116.

Einhorn, H. J., & Hogarth, H. M. (1982). Behavioral decision theory: Processes of judgment and choice. Annual Review of Psychology, 32, 53–58.

Elig, T. W., & Frieze, I. H. (1979). Measuring causal attributions for success and failure. *Journal of Personality and Social Psychology, 37,* 621–634.

Etaugh, C., & Brown, B. (1975). Perceiving the causes of success and failure of male and female performers. *Developmental Psychology, 11,* 103.

Feather, N. T., & Simon, J. G. (1975). Reactions to male and female success and failure in sex-linked occupations: Impressions of personality, causal attribution and perceived likelihood of difference consequences. *Journal of Personality and Social Psychology, 31,* 20–31.

Feldman-Summers, S., & Kiesler, S. B. (1974). Those who are number two try harder: The effect of sex on attributions of causality. *Journal of Personality and Social Psychology, 30,* 846–855.

Fernberger, S. W. (1948). Persistence of stereotypes concerning sex differences. *Journal of Abnormal and Social Psychology, 43,* 97–101.

Grady, K. E. (1975). Androgyny reconsidered. Paper presented at the meeting of the Eastern Psychological Association, New York City.

Green, S. G., & Mitchell, T. R. (1979). Attributional processes of leaders in leader-member interactions. *Organizational Behavior and Human Performance, 23,* 429–458.

Haccoun, D. M., & Stacy, S. (1980). Perceptions of male and female success or failure in relation to spouse encouragement and sex-association of occupation. *Sex Roles, 6,* 819–831.

Hansen, R. D. (1980). Common sense attribution. *Journal of Personality and Social Psychology, 39*(6), 996–1009.

Hansen, R. D. (in press). Cognitive economy and commonsense attribution processing. In J. H. Harvey & G. Weary (Eds.), *Attribution in contemporary psychology.* New York: Academic Press.

Hansen, R. D., & Donoghue, J. M. (1977). The power of consensus: Information derived from one's own and others' behavior. *Journal of Personality and Social Psychology, 35,* 294–302.

Hansen, R. D., & Hall, C. A. (1983). *Discounting and augmenting causal forces: The winner takes almost all.* Unpublished manuscript, Yale University.

Hansen, R. D., & Lowe, C. A. (1976). Distinctiveness and consensus: The influence of behavioral information on actors' and observers' attributions. *Journal of Personality and Social Psychology, 34*(3), 425–433.

Hansen, R. D., & O'Leary, V. E. (1983). Actresses and actors: The effects of sex on causal attributions. *Basic and Applied Social Psychology, 4*(3), 209–230.

Hansen, R. D., & Ronis, D. L. (1982). *Search patterns in answer to performance evaluation queries: Different questions, different information?* Unpublished manuscript, Oakland University/University of Michigan.

Hansen, R. D., & Stonner, D. M. (1978). Attributes and attributions: Inferring stimulus properties, actors' dispositions, and cause. *Journal of Personality and Social Psychology, 36,* 657–667.

Heider, F. (1958). *The psychology of interpersonal relations.* New York: Wiley.

Heilman, M. E., & Guzzo, R. A. (1978). The perceived cause of work success as a mediator of sex discrimination in organizations. *Organizational Behavior and Human Performance, 21*(3), 346–357.

Jones, E. E., & Davis, K. E. (1965). From acts to dispositions: The attribution process in person perception. In L. Berkowitz (Ed.), *Advances in experimental social psychology* (Vol. 2). New York: Academic Press.

Jones, E. E., & McGillis, D. (1976). Correspondent inferences and the attribution cube: A comparative reappraisal. In J. H. Harvey, W. J. Ickes, & R. F. Kidd (Eds.), *New directions in attribution research* (Vol. 1). Hillsdale, NJ: Erlbaum.

Jones, E. E., & Nisbett, R. E. (1972). The actor and the observer: Divergent perceptions of the causes of behavior. In E. E. Jones et al. (Eds.), *Attribution: Perceiving the causes of behavior.* Morristown, NJ: General Learning Press.

Kahn, A. S., O'Leary, V. E., Kruelwitz, J. E., and Lamm, H. (1980). Equity and equality: Male and female means to a just end. *Basic and Applied Social Psychology*, *1*(2) 173–197.

Kanter, R. M. (1977). *Men and women of the corporation*. New York: Basic Books.

Kelley, H. H. (1967). Attribution theory in social psychology. In D. Levine (Ed.), *Nebraska symposium on motivation*. Lincoln: University of Nebraska Press.

Kelley, H. H. (1972a). Attribution in social interaction. In E. E. Jones, D. E. Kanouse, H. H. Kelley, R. E. Nisbett, S. Valins, & B. Weiner (Eds.), *Attribution: Perceiving the cause of behavior*. Morristown, NJ: General Learning Press.

Kelley, H. H. (1972b). Causal schema and the attribution process. In E. E. Jones, D. E. Kanouse, H. H. Kelley, R. E. Nisbett, S. Valins, & B. Weiner (Eds.), *Attribution: Perceiving the cause of behavior*. Morristown, NJ: General Learning Press.

Kelley, H. H., & Michela, J. K. (1980). Attribution theory and research. *Annual Review of Psychology*, *31*, 457–499.

Langer, E. J., & Imber, L. G. (1979). When practice makes imperfect: Debilitating effects of overlearning. *Journal of Personality and Social Psychology*, *37*, 2014–2024.

Locksley, A., Borgida, E., Brekke, N., & Hepburn, C. (1980). Sex stereotypes and social judgment. *Journal of Personality and Social Psychology*, *39*, 821–831.

Maccoby, E. E., & Jacklin, C. N. (1974). *The psychology of sex differences*. Stanford: Stanford University Press.

Major, B., & Deaux, K. (1982). Individual differences in justice behavior. In J. Greenberg & R. L. Cohen (Eds.), *Equity and justice in social behavior*. New York: Academic Press.

Major, B., & McFarlin, D. (1982). *Impression management and gender differences in perceptions of fair performance for pay*. Unpublished manuscript, State University of New York at Buffalo.

Major, B., & Vanderslice, V. (1982). *Effects of pay expected on pay received: The self-confirming nature of initial expectations*. Unpublished manuscript, State University of New York at Buffalo.

McArthur, L. Z. (1972). The how and what of why: Some determinants and consequences of causal attributions. *Journal of Personality and Social Psychology*, *22*, 171–193.

McArthur, L. Z. (1976). The lesser influence of consensus and distinctiveness information on causal attributions: A test of the person-thing hypothesis. *Journal of Personality and Social Psychology*, *26*, 1–18.

McKee, J. P., & Sheriffs, A. C. (1959). Men's and women's beliefs, ideals, and self concepts. *American Journal of Sociology*, *65*, 356–363.

Mednick, M., & Weissman, H. J. (1975). The psychology of women — selected topics. *Annual Review of Psychology*, *26*, 1–18.

Meyer, J. P. (1980). Causal attributions for success and failure: A multivariate investigation of dimensionality, formation and consequences. *Journal of Personality and Social Psychology, 38*(5), 704–718.

Murphy-Berman, V. (1976). Effects of success and failure on perceptions of gender identity. *Sex Roles, 2*, 367–374.

Nisbett, R. E.; Borgida, E., Crandall, R., & Reed, J. (1976). Popular induction: Information is not always informative. In J. Carroll and J. Payne (Eds.), *Cognition and social behavior.* Hillsdade, NJ: Erlbaum.

Nisbett, R., & Ross, L. (1980. *Human inference: Strategies and shortcomings of social judgment.* Englewood Cliffs, NJ: Prentice-Hall.

O'Leary, V. E. (1974). Some attitudinal barriers to occupational aspirations in women. *Psychology Bulletin, 81*, 11, 809–816.

O'Leary, V. E. (1977). *Toward understanding women.* Monterey, CA: Brooks / Cole.

O'Leary, V. E., & Donoghue, J. M. (1978). Latitudes of masculinity: Reactions to sexual deviance in men. *Journal of Social Issues, 34*, 17–28.

O'Leary, V. E., & Hansen, R. D. (1983). Trying hurts women, helps men: The meaning of effort. In H. J. Bernardin (Ed.), *Women in the workforce.* New York: Lexington.

Orvis, D., Cunningham, J. E., & Kelley, H. H. (1975). A closer examination of causal inferences: The role of consensus, distinctiveness, and consistency information. *Journal of Personality and Social Psychology, 32*, 605–616.

Ostrove, N. (1978). Expectations for success on effort-determined tasks as a function of incentive and performance feedback. *Journal of Personality and Social Psychology, 36*, 909–916.

Pheterson, G. I., Kiesler, S. B., & Goldberg, P. A. (1971). Evaluation of the performance of women as a function of their sex, achievement, and personal history. *Journal of Personality and Social Psychology, 19*, 114–118.

Ronis, D. L., Hansen, R. H., & O'Leary, V. E. (1983). The stability of meaning: A test of the validity of Weiner's taxonomy. *Journal of Personality and Social Psychology, 44*, 702–711.

Rosaldo, M. Z., & Lamphere, L. (1974). *Women, culture and society.* Stanford: Stanford University Press.

Rosen, B., & Jerdee, T. H. (1974a). Influence of sex-role stereotypes on personnel decisions. *Journal of Applied Psychology, 59*, 9–14.

Rosen, B., & Jerdee, T. H. (1974b). Perceived sex differences in managerially relevant characteristics. *Sex Roles, 4*, 837–844.

Ross, L. O. (1977). The intuitive psychologist and his shortcomings: Distortions in the attribution process. In L. Berkowitz (Ed.), *Advances in experimental social psychology* (Vol. 10). New York: Academic Press.

Schank, R. C. (1975). *Conceptual information processing.* Amsterdam: North-Holland.

Schank, R. C., & Abelson, R. (1977). *Scripts, plans, goals and understanding: An inquiry into human knowledge structures.* Hillsdale, NJ: Erlbaum.

Steinmann, A., & Fox, D. J. (1966). Male-female perceptions of the female role in the United States. *Journal of Psychology, 64,* 265–276.

Taylor, S., & Fiske, S. (1978). Salience, attention and attribution: Top of the head phenomena. In L. Berkowitz (Ed.), *Advances in experimental social psychology* (Vol. 11). New York: Academic Press.

Taylor, S., & Fiske, S. (1981). Getting inside the head: Methodologies for process analogies in attribution and social cognition. In J. H. Harvey, W. Ickes, & R. F. Kidd (Eds.), *New directions in attribution research* (Vol. 3). Hillsdale, NJ: Erlbaum.

Taynor, J., & Deaux, K. (1975). Equity and perceived sex differences: Role behavior as defined by the task, the mode, and the actor. *Journal of Personality and Social Psychology, 32,* 381–390.

Terborg, J. R. (1977). Women in management: A research review. *Journal of Applied Psychology, 62,* 647–664.

Unger, R. K. (1979). *Female and male.* New York: Harper and Row.

U.S. Department of Labor, Women's Bureau. (1978). *1978 handbook on women workers.* Washington, DC: U.S. Government Printing Office.

Wallston, B. S., & O'Leary, V. E. (1981). Sex makes a difference: Differential perceptions of women and men. *Review of Personality and Social Psychology, 2,* 9–41.

Weiner, B. (1972). *Achievement motivation and attribution theory.* Morristown NJ: General Learning Press.

Weiner, B. (1979). A theory of motivation for some classroom experiences. *Journal of Educational Psychology, 71,* 3–25.

Weiner, B., Frieze, I. H., Kukla, A., Reed, L., Rest, S., & Rosenbaum, R. M. (1971). *Perceiving the causes of success and failure.* Morristown, NJ: General Learning Press.

Weiner, B., Nirenberg, R., & Goldstein, M. (1976). Social learning (locus of control) interpretations of expectancy of success. *Journal of Personality and Social Psychology, 44,* 52–68.

Weiner, B., Russell, D., & Lerman, D. (1979). The cognitive-emotive process in achievement-related contexts. *Journal of Personality and Social Psychology, 37*(7), 1211–1220.

Wimer, S., & Kelley, H. H. (1982). An investigation of the dimensions of causal attribution. *Journal of personality and Social Psychology, 43,* 1142–1162.

Wyer, R. S., & Srull, T. K. (in press). *Handbook of social cognition.* Hillsdale, NJ: Erlbaum.

Androgyny and Gender Schema Theory: A Conceptual and Empirical Integration

Sandra Lipsitz Bem

Cornell University

*A*s a feminist and a psychologist, I have long wrestled with one central question: How does the culture transform male and female infants into masculine and feminine adults? How does it create the many gender differences in behavior, motivation, and self-concept that transcend the dictates of biology?

Although this question has no single or simple answer, I shall focus in this chapter on what I see as the most psychologically interesting source of gender differentiation and what has also been the central concern of my own research, namely, the psychology of the individual as it pertains to gender. That is, I shall focus on the thoughts and feelings about gender that individuals carry around in their heads and on how these influence the way they perceive, evaluate, and regulate not only their own behavior but the behavior of others. Before proceeding to that topic, however, I should like to make a few general comments about two other important sources of gender differentiation, biology and the contemporary environment.

First, biology. Although the question remains open as to which gender differences derive even in part from biology, here I should like to emphasize that it is the interaction of biology with culture—and not biology alone—that determines how similar or different males and females actually are. Another way to say this is that whereas the sex-differentiated aspects of human biology are relatively constant, the cultural context varies a great deal, sometimes exaggerating the influence of biology, sometimes counteracting it, and sometimes—

in a more neutral fashion—simply letting the influence of biology shine through without either exaggerating or counteracting it.

I said a moment ago that I am a feminist. For the record, I should say this does not mean I do not think there are any biologically based sex differences in behavior. Likewise, it also does not mean I think we should try to manipulate the culture so as to eliminate whatever biologically based sex differences there are. It does mean, however, that insofar as possible, we should let the distribution of activities and roles across males and females reflect nothing but biology. That is, we should try to arrange our social institutions so that they do not themselves diminish the full range of individual differences that would otherwise exist within each sex. If, under those conditions, it turns out that more men than women become engineers or that more women than men decide to stay at home with their children, I shall live happily with those sex differences as well as with any others that emerge. But I am willing to bet that the sex differences that emerge under those conditions will not be nearly as large or as diverse as the ones that currently exist in our society.

Let me shift now to the here-and-now environment. It is clear that there are many ways the contemporary environment affects males and females differentially. For example, there are institutional practices that explicitly treat males and females differently, such as the greater availability of athletic training for males and of parental leave for females. Similarly, there are institutional practices that have the effect of treating males and females differently even though the practices themselves are not explicitly based on sex, such as giving bonus points to veterans on civil service examinations, setting age requirements on admissions to graduate and professional schools, and the fact that the school day and the work day do not coincide. And finally, there are normative expectations that distinguish between males and females, such as the fact that women but not men are asked to bake cookies for bake sales and are called home from work when their children get sick at school.

Although many if not most of these contemporary practices probably derive historically from a time when the sex-differentiated aspects of human biology were more pertinent to the demands of daily living than they are now and thereby dictated a sex-based division of labor, nevertheless these practices now establish an environment that is sufficient to create and maintain many gender differences without any contribution from biology. Whatever gender differences the contemporary environment can produce, of course, it can also take away. Accordingly, if the many gender-differentiated practices that abound in our culture were ever to be eliminated, then males and females could finally begin to be as *similar* as their biology allows.

Not all gender differences are maintained solely by external forces, of course, for individuals bring to the situation preferences, skills, personality attributes, behaviors, and self-concepts that they acquired during childhood and that are consistent with their culture's definitions of masculinity and femininity. Accordingly, I turn now to a discussion of sex typing, the psychological process whereby male and female children become "masculine" and "feminine."

Sex Typing

As every parent, teacher, and developmental psychologist knows, male and female children become "masculine" and "feminine" at a very early age. By the time they are four or five, for example, girls and boys have typically come to prefer activities defined by the culture as appropriate for their sex and also to prefer same-sex peers. The acquisition of sex-appropriate preferences, skills, personality attributes, behaviors, and self-concepts is typically referred to within psychology as the process of sex typing.

The universality and importance of this process is reflected in the prominence it has received in psychological theories of development, which seek to elucidate how the developing child comes to match the template defined as sex appropriate by his or her culture. Three major theories of sex typing have been especially influential: psychoanalytic theory (Bronfenbrenner, 1960; Freud, 1959a, 1959b), social learning theory (Mischel, 1970), and cognitive-developmental theory (Kohlberg, 1966). More recently, I have introduced a fourth theory of sex typing into the psychological literature—gender schema theory (Bem, 1981b). To provide a background for the conceptual issues that gave rise to gender schema theory, I will begin with a discussion of the three theories of sex typing that have been dominant within psychology to date.

PSYCHOANALYTIC THEORY

The first psychologist to ask how male and female are transmuted into masculine and feminine was Freud. Accordingly, in the past virtually every major sourcebook in developmental psychology began its discussion of sex typing with a review of psychoanalytic theory (e.g., Mussen, 1969).

Psychoanalytic theory emphasizes the child's identification with the same-sex parent as the primary mechanism whereby children become sex typed, an identification that results from the child's discovery of genital sex differences, from the penis envy and castration anxiety that this discovery produces in females and males respectively, and from the successful resolution of the Oedipus conflict. Although a number of feminist scholars have found it fruitful in recent years to work within a psychoanalytic framework (e.g., Chodorow, 1978; Rubin, 1975), the theory's "anatomy is destiny" view has been associated historically with very conservative conclusions regarding the inevitability of sex typing.

Of the three dominant theories of sex typing, psychoanalytic theory is almost certainly the best known outside the discipline of psychology, although it is no longer especially popular among research psychologists. In part this is because the theory is difficult to test empirically. An even more important reason, however, is that the empirical evidence simply does not justify emphasizing either the child's discovery of genital sex differences in particular (Kohlberg, 1966; McConaghy, 1979) or the child's identification with his or her same-sex parent (Maccoby & Jacklin, 1974) as a crucial determinant of sex typing.

SOCIAL LEARNING THEORY

In contrast to psychoanalytic theory, social learning theory emphasizes the rewards and punishments that children receive for sex-appropriate and sex-inappropriate behaviors, as well as the vicarious learning that observation and modeling provide. Social learning theory thus locates the source of sex typing in the sex-differentiated practices of the socializing community.

Perhaps the major virtue of social learning theory for psychologists is that it applies to the development of psychological femaleness and maleness the very same general principles of learning that are already known to account for the development of a multitude of other behaviors. Thus, as far as the formal theory is concerned, gender does not demand special consideration; that is, no special psychological mechanisms or processes must be postulated to explain how children become sex typed beyond those already used to explain how children learn other socialized behaviors.

The theory's generality also constitutes the basis of its appeal to feminist psychologists in particular. If there is nothing special about gender, then the phenomenon of sex typing itself is neither inevitable nor unmodifiable. Children become sex typed because sex happens to be the basis of differential socialization in their culture. In principle, however, any category could be made the basis for differential socialization.

Although social learning theory can account for the young child's acquiring a number of particular behaviors that are stereotyped by the culture as sex appropriate, it treats the child more as a passive recipient of environmental forces than as an active agent striving to organize and thereby comprehend the social world. This view of the relatively passive child is inconsistent with the common observation that children themselves frequently construct and enforce their own version of society's gender rules. It is also inconsistent with the fact that the flexibility with which children interpret society's gender rules varies predictably with age. In one study, for example, 73% of the 4 year olds and 80% of the 9 year olds believed—quite flexibly— that there should be no sexual restrictions on one's choice of occupation. Between those ages, however, children held more rigid opinions, with the middle children being the least flexible of all. Thus, only 33% of the 5 year olds, 10% of the 6 year olds, 11% of the 7 year olds, and 44% of the 8 year olds believed there should be no sexual restrictions on one's choice of occupation (Damon, 1977).

This particular developmental pattern is not unique to the child's interpretation of gender rules. Even in a domain as far removed from gender as syntax, children first learn certain correct grammatical forms through reinforcement and modeling. As they get a bit older, however, they begin to construct their own grammatical rules on the basis of what they hear spoken around them, and only later still can they allow for exceptions to those rules. Thus only the youngest and the oldest children say "ran"; children in between say "runned" (Cazden, 1968; Clark & Clark, 1977). What all of this implies, of course, is that the child is passive in neither domain. Rather, she or he is actively constructing rules to organize—and thereby to comprehend—the vast array of information in her or his world.

COGNITIVE-DEVELOPMENTAL THEORY

Unlike social learning theory, cognitive-developmental theory focuses almost exclusively on the child as the primary agent of his or her own sex-role socialization, a focus reflecting the theory's basic assumption that sex typing follows naturally and inevitably from universal principles of cognitive development. As children work actively to comprehend their social world, they inevitably "label themselves—call it alpha—and determine that there are alphas and betas in the environment. Given the cognitive-motivational properties of the self, . . . the child moves toward other alphas and away from betas. That is, it is the child who realizes what gender he or she is, and in what behaviors he or she should engage" (Lewis & Brooks-Gunn, 1979). In essence, then, cognitive-developmental theory postulates that, because of the child's need for cognitive consistency, self-categorization as female or male motivates her or him to value whatever is seen as similar to the self in gender. This gender-based value system, in turn, motivates the child to engage in gender-congruent activities, to strive for gender-congruent attributes, and to prefer gender-congruent peers. "Basic self-categorizations determine basic valuings. Once the boy has stably identified himself as male, he then values positively those objects and acts consistent with his gender identity" (Kohlberg, 1966).

The cognitive-developmental account of sex typing has been so influential since its introduction into the literature in 1966 that many psychologists now seem to accept almost as a given that the young child will spontaneously develop both a gender-based self-concept and a gender-based value system even in the absence of external pressure to behave in a sex-stereotyped manner. Despite its popularity, however, the theory fails to explicate why sex has primacy over other potential categories of the self such as race, religion, or even eye color. Interestingly, the formal theory itself does not dictate that any particular category should have such primacy. Moreover, most cognitive-developmental theorists do not explicitly ponder the "why sex" question, nor do they even raise the possibility that other categories could fit the general theory just as well. To the extent that cognitive-developmental psychologists address this question at all, they seem to emphasize the perceptual salience to the child of the observable differenes between the sexes, particularly biologically produced differences such as size and strength (e.g., Kohlberg, 1966; Lewis & Brooks-Gunn, 1979; Ullian, 1981).

The implicit assumption here that sex differences are naturally and inevitably more perceptually salient to children than other differences may not have cross-cultural validity. Although it may be true that our culture does not construct any distinctions between people that we perceive to be as compelling as sex, other cultures do construct such distinctions, for example, distinctions between those who are high caste and those who are low caste, between those who are inhabited by spirits and those who are not, between those who are divine and those who are mortal, between those who are wet and those who are dry, or between those who are open and those who are closed (e.g., Meigs, 1976; Moore, 1976). Given such cross-cultural diversity, it is ironic that a theory emphasizing the child's active striving to comprehend the social world should not be more open to the possibility that some distinction other than sex might be more perceptually salient in another cultural context. What appears to have happened is that the universality and inevitability that the theory claims for the child's cognitive processes have been implicitly and gratuitously transferred to one of the many substantive domains upon which those processes operate: the domain of gender.

This is not to say, of course, that cognitive-developmental theory is necessarily wrong in its implicit assumption that all children have a built-in readiness to organize their perceptions of the social world on the basis of sex. Perhaps evolution has given sex a biologically based priority over many other categories. The important point, however, is that the question of whether and why sex has cognitive primacy is extratheoretical for cognitive-developmental theory. To understand why children become *sex* typed rather than, say, race or caste typed, we still need a theory that explicitly addresses the question of how and why children come to utilize sex in particular as a cognitive organizing principle.

Gender Schema Theory

Gender schema theory (Bem, 1981b, 1983) contains features of both the cognitive-developmental and the social learning accounts of sex typing. In particular, gender schema theory proposes that sex typing derives in large measure from gender-schematic processing, from a generalized readiness on the part of the child to encode and to organize information—including information about the self—according to the culture's definitions of maleness and femaleness. Like cognitive-developmental theory, then, gender schema theory proposes that sex typing is mediated by the child's own cognitive processing. However, gender schema theory further proposes that gender-schematic processing is itself derived from the sex-differentiated practices of the social community. Thus, like social learning theory, gender schema theory assumes that sex typing is a learned phenomenon and hence that it is neither inevitable nor unmodifiable.

In this chapter I shall first consider in some detail what gender-schematic processing is and how it produces gender differences. I shall then review the empirical evidence that links gender-schematic processing to sex typing. Finally, I shall explore the conditions that produce gender-schematic processing in the first place, thereby providing an explicit account of why sex comes to have cognitive primacy over other social categories. (For two other conceptualizations of sex typing that also utilize the concept of a cognitive schema, see Markus, Crane, Bernstein, & Siladi, 1982; and Martin & Halverson, 1981.)

GENDER-SCHEMATIC PROCESSING

Gender schema theory begins with the observation that the developing child invariably learns his or her society's cultural definitions of femaleness and maleness. In most societies, these definitions comprise a diverse and sprawling network of sex-linked associations encompassing not only those features directly related to female and male persons, such as anatomy, reproductive function, division of labor, and personality attributes, but also features more remotely or metaphorically related to sex, such as the angularity or roundedness of an abstract shape and the periodicity of the moon. Indeed, no other dichotomy in human experience appears to have as many entities linked to it as does the distinction between female and male.

But there is more. Gender schema theory proposes that, in addition to learning such content-specific information about gender, the child also learns to invoke this heterogeneous network of sex-related associations in order to evaluate and assimilate new information. The child, in short, learns to encode and organize information in terms of an evolving gender schema.

A schema is a cognitive structure, a network of associations that organizes and guides an individual's perception. A schema functions as an anticipatory structure, a readiness to search for and assimilate incoming information in schema-relevant terms. Schematic information processing is thus highly selective and enables the individual to impose structure and meaning onto a vast array of incoming stimuli. More specifically, schematic information processing entails a readiness to sort information into categories on the basis of some particular dimension, despite the existence of other dimensions that could serve equally well in this regard. Gender-schematic processing in particular thus involves spontaneously sorting persons, attributes, and behaviors into masculine and feminine categories or "equivalence classes" regardless of their differences on a variety of dimensions unrelated to gender—for example, spontaneously placing items like "tender" and "nightingale" into a feminine category and items like "assertive" and eagle" into a masculine category. Like schema theories generally (Neisser, 1976; Taylor & Crocker, 1981), gender schema theory thus construes perception as a constructive process in which it is the interaction between incoming information and an individual's preexisting schema that determines what is perceived.

What gender schema theory proposes, then, is that the phenomenon of sex typing derives in part from gender-schematic processing, from an individual's generalized readiness to process information on the basis of the sex-linked associations that constitute the gender schema. Specifically, the theory proposes that sex typing results in part from the assimilation of the self-concept itself to the gender schema. As children learn the contents of their society's gender schema, they learn which attributes are to be linked with their own sex and hence with themselves. This does not simply entail learning the defined relationship between each sex and each dimension or attribute—that boys are to be strong and girls weak, for example—but involves the deeper lesson that the dimensions themselves are differentially applicable to the two sexes. Thus the strong-weak dimension itself is absent from the schema to be applied to girls just as the dimension of nurturance is implicitly omitted from the schema to be applied to boys. Adults in the child's world rarely notice or remark upon how strong a little girl is becoming or how nurturant a little boy is becoming, despite their readiness to note precisely these attributes in the "appropriate" sex. The child learns to apply this same schematic selectivity to the self, to choose from among the many possible dimensions of human personality only that subset defined as applicable to his or her own sex and thereby eligible for organizing the diverse contents of the self-concept. Thus do children's self-concepts become sex typed, and thus do the two sexes become, in their own eyes, not only different in degree, but different in kind.

Simultaneously, the child also learns to evaluate his or her adequacy as a person according to the gender schema, to match his or her preferences, attitudes, behaviors, and personal attributes against the prototypes stored within it. The gender schema becomes a prescriptive standard or guide (cf. Kagan, 1964), and self-esteem becomes its hostage. Here, then, enters an internalized motivational factor that prompts an individual to regulate his or her behavior so that it conforms to cultural definitions of femaleness and maleness.

From the perspective of gender schema theory, then, males and females behave differently from one another on the average because, as individuals, they have each come to perceive, evaluate, and regulate both their own behavior and the behavior of others in accordance with cultural definitions of gender appropriateness. Thus do cultural myths become self-fulfilling prophecies, and thus, according to gender schema theory, do many gender differences emerge.

It is important to note that gender schema theory is a theory of process, not content. Because sex-typed individuals are seen as processing information and regulating their behavior according to whatever definitions of femininity and masculinity their culture happens to provide, it is the process of dividing the world into feminine and masculine categories—and not the content of the categories—that is central to the theory. If the culture has arbitrarily clustered a multidimensional hodgepodge of heterogeneous attributes into a category it calls "masculinity" or "femininity," then that hodgepodge is what the sex-typed individual will take as the standard for his or her behavior. Accordingly, sex-typed individuals are seen to differ from other individuals not primarily in the degree of femininity or masculinity they possess, but in the extent to which their self-concepts and behaviors are organized on the basis of gender rather than some other dimension. Many individuals who are not sex typed may describe themselves as, say, nurturant or dominant without implicating the concepts of femininity or masculinity. When sex-typed individuals so describe themselves, however, it is precisely the gender connotations of the attributes or behaviors that are presumed to be salient for them.

As a real-life example of what it means to be gender schematic, consider how a particular college student at Cornell might go about deciding which new hobby to try out from among the many possibilities available. Among other things, he or she could ask how expensive each possibility is, whether it can be done in cold weather, whether it can be done between classes, exams, and term papers, and so forth. Being gender schematic, however, means having a readiness to look at this decision through the lens of gender and thereby to ask first: What sex is the hobby? What sex am I? Do they match? If so, then the hobby will be considered further. If not, then it will be rejected without further consideration.

This is not to say, however, that gender-schematic individuals are consciously aware of their own gender schematicity. Quite the contrary. Just as the fish is unaware that its environment is wet (after all, what else could it be?), so too are most people unaware that their perceptions are (but need not be) organized on the basis of gender. The child learns to utilize certain dimensions rather than others as cognitive organizing principles but does not typically become aware that there were alternative dimensions that might have been used instead. The dimensions chosen as cognitive organizing principles thus function as a kind of nonconscious ideology, an underlying or deep cognitive structure influencing one's perceptions without conscious awareness. Such is the nature of schematic processing generally. Such, in particular, is the nature of gender-schematic processing.

A HISTORICAL COMMENT ON PSYCHOLOGICAL ANDROGYNY

My research on gender schema theory began in the early 1970s with the concept of psychological androgyny. At that time the field of psychology shared with the larger culture the assumption that being sex typed was not only the normal, but also the desirable, outcome of human development. This assumption was reflected in the field's instruments for assessing masculinity and femininity, most of which classified the individual in bipolar fashion as either like the typical male or like the typical female, as either "sex typed" or "sex reversed." The concept of an androgynous individual, an individual who does not rely on gender as a cognitive organizing principle and whose personality therefore combines both masculine and feminine elements, was undefined and unarticulated.

Within the field of psychology, androgyny was clearly a concept whose time had come, as indicated by the fact that several of us independently began to question the field's psychometric and conceptual assumptions about masculinity and femininity at approximately the same time. My own research program on androgyny began in 1971 with the development of the Bem Sex Role Inventory (Bem, 1972, 1974). Two years later, in 1973, Jeanne Block published an insightful article about androgyny in the *American Psychologist* based on her research (Block, 1973), and Ann Constantinople published a review article in the *Psychological Bulletin* criticizing the bipolarity assumption of traditional masculinity-femininity scales (Constantinople, 1973). In 1974 Janet Taylor Spence, Robert Helmreich, and Joy Stapp published their instrument for assessing androgyny, the Personal Attributes Questionnaire, or PAQ (Spence, Helmreich, & Stapp, 1974).

The idea that an androgynous or "blended" personality might provide a feminist alternative to our society's sex-typed definitions of mental health probably accounted for the instant success of the androgyny concept, both inside and outside the field of psychology. As evidence of how receptive psychologists were to the idea of androgyny as a new definition of mental health, consider that over 100 studies have been carried out during the past eight years relating various measures of mental health to various measures of androgyny, even though there is no real theoretical reason for expecting androgynous individuals to score higher on such measures than sex-typed individuals in the context of a sex-typed society.

It should be noted that this literature was recently reviewed both by Taylor and Hall (1982) and by Whitley (1983), who conclude that although the data now compel us to reject the conventional assumption that healthy functioning necessarily implies masculinity for men and femininity for women, they also compel us to conclude that it is not just androgynous individuals—but masculine individuals as well—who score high on virtually all indexes of mental health. In other words, it is psychological masculinity—not androgyny—that is associated with mental health in both sexes.[1] Another conventional assumption in this general area, of course, is that because masculine

---

1. With respect to the strong relationship that has been found in many studies between masculinity and self-esteem in particular, I share the concern expressed by

men and feminine women complement each other they make good marriage partners. Like the conventional assumption that mental health requires masculinity in men and femininity in women, however, this bit of conventional wisdom is also beginning to be challenged empirically (e.g., Antill, 1983; Ickes, 1981; Ickes & Barnes, 1978).

Although this early enthusiasm for the concept of androgyny was very exciting in some ways, it tended—unfortunately—to emphasize the surface attributes of the androgynous individual rather than the underlying process that permitted both stereotypically masculine and stereotypically feminine attributes to coexist within the same individual. In so doing, moreover, this early enthusiasm also obscured my original rationale for wanting to bring the concept of androgyny into focus.

Ironically, one of my major purposes in highlighting androgyny in the first place was to clarify the process of sex typing, to emphasize that the important characteristic of the sex-typed individual is not the possession of sex-typed attributes, but the readiness to sort information on the basis of gender rather than other available dimensions. The concept of androgyny provided precisely the right contrast group to highlight this aspect of sex typing. For the first time, sex-typed individuals could now be contrasted with a group whose thinking and behavior were relatively unconstrained by cultural stereotypes of gender appropriateness. For the first time, sex-typed individuals could also be contrasted with a group whose very existence challenged the dominant assumption that to be anything other than conventionally sex typed was evidence of pathology.

Empirical Research on Gender Schema Theory[2]

At the broadest level, my empirical research on gender schema theory to date has had two major goals: (a) To demonstrate that sex-typed individuals do, in fact, spontaneously engage in gender-schematic processing to a greater extent than other individuals and

---

Nichols, Licht, and Pearl (1982) that the amount of item equivalence on tests used to measure these two concepts may be so great as to render this particular finding more artifactual than substantive.

2. Most of the research to be described here was supported by grants I received from the National Science Foundation (Grant BNS-78-22637) and the National Institute of Mental Health (Grant 5-R01-MH-21735).

thereby to suggest that gender-schematic processing may be neither a necessary nor a desirable outcome of human development; and (b) to demonstrate that individuals who engage in a high level of gender-schematic processing also engage in a high level of gender-stereotyped behavior and thereby to suggest that many gender differences are themselves derived from gender-schematic processing.

It should be noted that these goals imply a particular research strategy, namely, the investigation of individual differences in sex typing as a means for demonstrating both the existence of gender-schematic processing and its consequences. My interest is thus not in individual differences per se, but in the underlying psychological processes that such differences can reveal and illuminate.

THE BEM SEX ROLE INVENTORY

The first step in implementing this overall strategy was to construct the Bem Sex Role Inventory (BSRI; Bem, 1974, 1977, 1979, 1981a), a new assessment instrument that would enable us to identify both sex-typed individuals and the newly conceived contrast group of androgynous individuals. The BSRI is a paper-and-pencil self-report instrument that asks the respondent to indicate on a 7-point scale how well each of 60 attributes describes him or her. Although it is not apparent to the respondent, 20 of the attributes reflect the culture's definition of masculinity (e.g., assertive, independent), 20 reflect the culture's definition of femininity (e.g., tender, understanding), and 20 are fillers. Each respondent receives both a masculinity score and a femininity score. Those who score above the median on the sex-congruent scale and below the median on the sex-incongruent scale are defined as sex typed. Those who show the opposite pattern are defined as cross-sex-typed. Those who score above the median on both scales are defined as androgynous. Those who score below the median on both scales are defined as undifferentiated.[3]

Although gender schema theory had not yet been fully developed at the time the BSRI was being constructed, nevertheless the construction of the BSRI was based upon two specific theoretical assumptions that are consistent with gender schema theory: (a) Largely as a

---

3. A shortened form of the BSRI (Bem, 1981a) has not proved comparable to the original BSRI, and hence its use is no longer advised (Frable & Bem, in press).

result of historical accident, the culture has clustered a rather heterogeneous collection of personality attributes into two mutually exclusive categories, each category considered by the culture both more characteristic of and more desirable for one or the other of the two sexes. These cultural expectations and prescriptions are well known by virtually all members of the culture. (b) Individuals differ from one another in the extent to which they utilize these cultural definitions of gender appropriateness as idealized standards of masculinity and femininity against which to evaluate their own personality and behavior. In particular, sex-typed individuals are highly attuned to these definitions and are motivated to keep their behavior consistent with them, a goal they accomplish both by selecting behaviors and attributes that are consistent with their gender and by avoiding behaviors and attributes that are inconsistent with it. In contrast, androgynous individuals are less attuned to these cultural definitions of masculinity and femininity and are less likely to regulate their behavior in accordance with them.

An important distinction should be made at this point between what the individual members of a given culture themselves define as masculine or feminine, and what they all believe to be the prevailing definitions of masculinity and femininity in the culture at large. In the context of the BSRI and gender schema theory, it is the latter—that is, what everyone believes the prevailing definitions of masculinity and femininity to be in the culture at large—that is critical, serving both as the criterion for item selection on the BSRI and as the presumed criterion for the gender conformity of the sex-typed individual.

The strategy used in constructing the BSRI followed directly from these several assumptions, with items for the BSRI selected on the basis of judges' ratings of the culturally defined desirability of various attributes for each of the two sexes. More specifically, undergraduate judges were asked to rate the desirability in American society generally of approximately 200 personality attributes either "for a woman" or "for a man." A personality characteristic was then defined as feminine or masculine (and hence eligible for the Femininity and Masculinity scales of the BSRI) if, and only if, it was judged significantly more desirable in American society for one sex than for the other by four independent samples of judges. The consistency of the ratings across four independent samples both in our original research and in a later replication by other investigators (Walkup & Abbott, 1978) is strong evidence that the BSRI is tapping widely known and relatively enduring cultural definitions of gender-appropriate behavior, as stipulated by the theory.[4]

The BSRI was thus designed to assess the extent to which the culture's definitions of gender appropriateness are incorporated into an individual's self-description. Put somewhat differently, the BSRI was designed to present an individual with a heterogeneous collection of attributes and then to assess the extent to which he or she clusters this collection into the two categories designated by the culture as masculine and feminine.

In contrast to common psychometric practice, no attempt was made during the development of the BSRI to specify the full set of attributes that constitute the domains of masculinity and femininity or to construct unidimensional measures of those domains, because to do so would have been to put the methodological cart before the theoretical horse. As noted earlier, the theory underlying the BSRI asserts that sex-typed individuals will conform to whatever definitions of masculinity and femininity the culture happens to provide. Hence it would be of no special interest to specify the particular contents of these definitions, for these will vary from culture to culture. Likewise the theory also asserts that masculinity and femininity are nothing more than heterogeneous collections of attributes arbitrarily clustered together by the culture. Moreover, the very concept of gender-schematic processing is itself a positive statement that these arbitrary clusters of apples and oranges need not—and for some individuals do not—"hang together." To force them to be unidimensional for all individuals would thus violate the theory. (For further discussion of this methodological issue see Bem, 1979; Pedhazur & Tetenbaum, 1979.)

Like the strategy used in constructing the BSRI, the original

4. Recently several critics of the BSRI have subjected the items on the BSRI to new empirical tests and have argued on the basis of those tests that the items do not tap widely known cultural definitions of masculinity and femininity (e.g., Edwards & Ashworth, 1977; Myers & Gonda, 1982a, 1982b; Pedhazur & Tetenbaum, 1979). In each of these cases, however, the new test failed to focus on the respondent's beliefs about the culture's definitions of masculinity and femininity, and hence the data are irrelevant to the specific issue the critics claim to be addressing. This is not to say, however, that no methodology other than the original could legitimately be used to demonstrate the culturally defined masculinity and femininity of the relevant items on the BSRI. Quite the contrary. Virtually any question that asked about the *culture's* beliefs with respect to these items would be a good candidate; for example, how the respondent thinks American society would rate each item on a scale ranging from "very masculine" to "very feminine."

method for scoring the BSRI was also theoretically based. When the BSRI was first developed, an individual was defined as either sex-typed, androgynous, or cross-sex-typed on the basis of the *t*-ratio between his or her self-rating of masculine and feminine attributes, with small *t*-ratios indicating androgyny and with large *t*-ratios (significant differences) indicating either sex-typing or cross-sex-typing. This method of scoring the BSRI follows directly from the theory because it distinguishes between those individuals who cluster the attributes on the BSRI into masculine and feminine categories and those who do not. The later emergence of differences in social behavior and self-esteem between those who score high on both the Femininity and the Masculinity scales (the androgynous high-highs) and those who score low on both (the "undifferentiated" low-lows)—even though both groups achieve small *t*-ratios—led to the suggestion that the BSRI be scored on the basis of a median split on both scales, a scoring procedure yielding four distinct groups rather than three. For empirical purposes this was an entirely sensible proposal, and we have adopted it in our own research. However, it did tend to obscure the original theoretical rationale behind the BSRI.

In principle, then, the BSRI should be fully adequate to identify individuals who are spontaneously inclined to organize information—especially information about the self—on the basis of gender. Because they spontaneously sort the items on the BSRI into gender categories when describing themselves, sex-typed individuals should be highly gender schematic. In contrast, because they do not spontaneously sort the items on the BSRI into gender categories when describing themselves, both androgynous and undifferentiated individuals should be much less gender schematic. Unfortunately, no such unambiguous statement can be made about cross-sex-typed individuals. Like sex-typed individuals, cross-sex-typed individuals do spontaneously sort the items on the BSRI into masculine and feminine categories, but unlike sex-typed individuals, they also rate the sex-incongruent set as more self-descriptive. Hence no clear prediction can be made about the gender schematicity of this group.

A COMMENT ON THE SPENCE-HELMREICH VIEW OF THE BSRI

Before proceeding to discuss the empirical studies that have used the BSRI to test the major propositions of gender schema theory, I want to comment briefly on Spence and Helmreich's claim (Bem, 1981c; Spence, in press; Spence, this volume; Spence & Helmreich, 1981) that neither the BSRI nor their own instrument, the PAQ, can legitimately be viewed as diagnostic of anything at all about the individual's gender psychology, including such things as the individual's level of masculinity or femininity, sex-role orientation, or— most important—readiness to organize information on the basis of gender. Rather, they argue, such tests can legitimately be viewed as measuring only what many of their items specifically denote, namely, the much more limited personality traits of instrumentality and expressiveness. Their reasoning seems to be as follows: If such tests tapped anything about gender, they should readily predict a wide variety of gender-related attitudes and behaviors across a wide variety of settings. In fact, however, "the journals are littered with dozens of" failed attempts to predict such things from these tests (Spence, this volume). Hence there is no justification for viewing these tests as measures of any abstract construct related to gender.

Like Spence and Helmreich, I too believe that the literature is littered with failed attempts to use the BSRI and the PAQ to predict a wide variety of gender-related attitudes and behaviors. Like Spence and Helmreich, I also believe (and have always believed) that it is not reasonable to expect all facets of an individual's gender psychology to hang together in a coherent package that can be indexed by a single paper-and-pencil instrument. If we have learned anything at all in personality psychology in the past two decades, it is to question the global generality of personality dispositions. Spence and Helmreich's major contribution here is thus to restate in the domain of gender the lesson we learned long ago in personality psychology generally: Assume nothing is glued together unless proved otherwise.

But Spence and Helmreich are wrong to assume that just because the BSRI cannot predict everything about an individual's gender psychology it cannot predict anything about it. Moreover, contrary to what Spence and Helmreich imply, gender schema theory is not a global theory that claims to predict every facet of an individual's gender psychology. Rather, gender schema theory proposes only that individuals come to match the template defined as sex appropriate by their culture—that is, they become sex typed—in part because they have learned to sort information into equivalence classes, to evaluate their adequacy as persons, and to regulate their behavior on the basis of gender rather than other available dimensions. The theory thus predicts that individuals identified as sex typed on the BSRI should differ from others not on every possible dependent measure related to gender, but in highly specific ways. In particular, they should have a lower threshold for spontaneously organizing information—including information about the self—into gender-based equivalence classes, and they should be more motivated to conform to the culture's definitions of masculinity and femininity. Only a tiny fraction of the voluminous literature utilizing the BSRI (or the PAQ) tests these hypotheses. Hence the bulk of that literature is irrelevant for assessing either the ability of the BSRI to tap gender-schematic processing or the validity of gender schema theory.

Much of the research that is relevant has been done in our own laboratories, and hence I should now like to discuss eight of our own studies in some detail while also noting relevant studies by other investigators whenever appropriate. The first four of these studies ask whether individuals identified as sex typed by the BSRI do, in fact, spontaneously engage in gender-schematic processing to a greater extent than either androgynous or undifferentiated individuals. The last four ask whether sex-typed individuals also engage in gender-stereotyped behavior to a greater extent than androgynous or undifferentiated individuals. Because sex-typed individuals are seen as differing from others not in their *ability* to organize information on the basis of gender but in their *threshold* for doing so *spontaneously*, all these studies present subjects with a multidimensional stimulus array in which gender is but one of many ways to organize the available information. Likewise, all these studies take great care to ensure that the experimental situation does not itself elicit or reinforce the use of gender in particular as a cognitive organizing principle.

STUDY 1: GENDER-SCHEMATIC PROCESSING OF THE SELF-CONCEPT

By definition, sex-typed individuals rate the sex-congruent attributes on the BSRI as more self-descriptive than the sex-incongruent attributes. But are the gender connotations of these attributes especially salient to sex-typed individuals, as gender schema theory implies? That is, do sex-typed individuals have a readiness to decide on the basis of gender which personality attributes are to be associated with their self-concepts and which are to be dissociated?

This hypothesis was tested in a doctoral dissertation by Girvin

(1978), reported in Bem (1981b). Subjects were 48 male and 48 female undergraduates preselected on the basis of a median split on the BSRI as sex typed, cross sex typed, androgynous, or undifferentiated. During each of the individual experimental sessions, the 60 attributes from the BSRI were projected on a screen one at a time, and the subject was requested to push one of two buttons, "ME" or NOT ME," to indicate whether the attribute was or was not self-descriptive. Of interest was the subject's response latency, that is, how long it took to make a decision about each attribute.

Gender schema theory predicts and the results of this study confirm that sex-typed subjects are significantly *faster* than any of the other three groups when endorsing sex-appropriate attributes and rejecting sex-inappropriate attributes. These results suggest that when deciding whether a particular attribute is or is not self-descriptive, sex-typed individuals do not bother to go through the time-consuming process of recruiting behavioral evidence from memory and then judging whether the evidence warrants an affirmative answer—which is presumably what other individuals do. Rather, sex-typed individuals "look up" the attribute in the gender schema. If the attribute is sex appropriate, they quickly say yes; if the attribute is sex inappropriate, they quickly say no.

Occasionally, of course, even sex-typed individuals must admit to possessing an attribute that is sex inappropriate or to lacking an attribute that is sex appropriate. Because such admissions conflict with cultural definitions of gender appropriateness, however, gender schema theory predicts and the results of this study confirm that, on those occasions, sex-typed subjects are significantly *slower* than any of the other three groups. This pattern of rapid delivery of gender-consistent self-descriptions and slow delivery of gender-inconsistent self-descriptions supports the central hypothesis of gender schema theory that sex typing is accompanied by a readiness to process information about the self in terms of the culture's definitions of maleness and femaleness, and it further indicates that the attributes on the BSRI are themselves processed in this fashion by sex-typed individuals.

The results of this study further indicate that there was no tendency whatever for either androgynous or undifferentiated subjects to differentiate in latency between masculine, feminine, and neutral attributes, confirming that neither of these groups is spontaneously inclined to process information about the self in terms of gender. In contrast, the results for cross-sex-typed subjects were mixed, leaving open the question of whether such individuals are or are not gender schematic.

Two studies whose methodologies were very similar to this study were independently carried out by Markus, Crane, Bernstein, and Siladi (1982) and by Mills (1983). Although there is some disagreement about precisely how the Markus et al. (1982) data are to be interpreted (Bem, 1982; Crane & Markus, 1982), the results of both these studies clearly replicate the latency findings reported here and thereby confirm the hypothesis that sex-typed individuals do have a greater readiness than androgynous or undifferentiated individuals to process information about the self in terms of gender. As still further evidence for this hypothesis, when subjects in the Mills (1983) study were later asked to recall the attributes that had been presented to them, the sex-typed subjects were significantly more likely than anyone else to recall more of the gender-congruent attributes than the gender-incongruent attributes.

STUDY 2: GENDER-SCHEMATIC PROCESSING OF INFORMATION UNRELATED TO THE SELF

If an individual is spontaneously inclined to encode and organize information on the basis of some underlying schema or network of associations, then thinking of one schema-related item should enhance the probability of thinking of another schema-related item. Similarly, if an individual is given a number of items to memorize and is then asked to recall them in whatever order they happen to come to mind, the sequence of recall should reveal runs or clusters of items that were linked in memory via the gender schema. In keeping with this logic, this study (Bem, 1981b) examines the amount of gender clustering in an individual's free recall in order to test the hypothesis that sex-typed individuals are more likely than non-sex-typed individuals to process information not related to the self in terms of gender.

Subjects in this study were 48 male and 48 female undergraduates preselected on the basis of a median split on the BSRI as sex typed, androgynous, undifferentiated, or cross sex typed. During the experimental session, subjects were presented with a sequence of 61 words in random order. These words included 16 proper names, 15 animal names, 15 verbs, and 15 articles of clothing. Half the proper names were male and half were female. One third of the items within each of the other categories had been consistently rated by undergraduate judges as masculine (e.g., gorilla, hurling, trousers), one third as feminine (e.g., butterfly, blushing, bikini), and one third as neutral (e.g., ant, stepping, sweater). The words were presented on slides at 3-sec intervals, and subjects were told that their recall would later be tested. Three seconds after the presentation of the last word, they were given 8 min to write down on a sheet of paper as many words as they could remember, in whatever order they happened to come to mind.

Other categories besides gender were incorporated into the structure of the list both to mask the presence of gender and also to ensure that strategies other than the use of gender would be available to facilitate maximum task performance. Were no such other strategies available, the situation itself could readily prompt highly motivated subjects to encode items on the basis of gender regardless of the individual's own threshold for doing so spontaneously, thereby swamping the very individual differences that the study was designed to reveal.[5]

Gender schema theory predicts and the results of this study confirm that sex-typed individuals are significantly more likely to cluster words on the basis of gender than androgynous, undifferentiated, or cross-sex-typed individuals, who did not differ from one another in this regard. That is, once having recalled a feminine item, sex-typed individuals were significantly more likely than anyone else to recall another feminine item next rather than a masculine or a neutral item. The same was true for masculine items. In contrast, sex-typed and non-sex-typed individuals did not differ either in the total number of items they recalled overall or in the extent to which they clustered items that belonged to the same semantic category (e.g., animals, articles of clothing). Taken together, these results provide strong support for gender schema theory's contention that sex-typed individuals have a spontaneous readiness to encode even information that is unrelated to the self in terms of the sex-linked associations that constitute the gender schema.

5. A cognitive paradigm to which this problem seems endemic is release from proactive inhibition following a shift from masculine to feminine or from feminine to masculine. Because the only systematic strategy for doing well on this task involves the use of the gender schema, the finding by Mills and Tyrrell (1983) that sex-typed and non-sex-typed subjects do not differ on this task is not inconsistent with gender schema theory's claim that the groups differ in their thresholds for using the gender schema spontaneously.

Still further support for this contention comes from two studies by Lippa (1977, 1983), which asked whether subjects classsified as sex-typed on the BSRI make more highly differentiated judgments on the basis of gender than other subjects, as they should if they are more gender schematic. In the first of these studies, sex-typed subjects differentiated among handwriting samples significantly more than androgynous subjects when rating the samples on a dimension of masculinity-femininity, and they also weighted the dimension of masculinity-femininity more heavily when making similarity judgments on those same samples (Lippa, 1977). In the second study, sex-typed subjects classified significantly more body outline drawings as either "male" or "female" than androgynous or undifferentiated subjects, who classified more of the outlines as "uncertain" (Lippa, 1983).

STUDY 3: GENDER-SCHEMATIC PROCESSING OF OTHER PEOPLE

The results of the previous studies indicate that sex-typed individuals are more likely than androgynous, undifferentiated, and cross-sex-typed individuals to organize information into masculine and feminine categories. This study (Frable & Bem, in press) asks whether sex-typed individuals are also more likely to organize *other people* into masculine and feminine categories.

It should be noted that the results of two previous studies are consistent with this hypothesis. In the first study, Deaux and Major (1977) found that sex-typed subjects differentiate between males and females significantly more than androgynous subjects when asked to segment each person's videotaped sequence of behaviors into units that seem natural and meaningful for them. In the second study, Taylor and Falcone (1982) found that when asked to recall "who said what" after listening to a group discussion, sex-typed (and cross-sex-typed) subjects were significantly more likely than androgynous subjects to make "within-sex" rather than "cross-sex" errors, that is, to confuse women with women and men with men.

This study constitutes both a replication and an extension of the study by Taylor and Falcone (1982). Subjects were again 48 male and 48 female undergraduates preselected on the basis of a median split on the BSRI as sex typed, androgynous, undifferentiated, and cross sex typed. During the experimental session, subjects listened to a tape recording of a carefully scripted and rehearsed discussion in which three males and three females talked about various universal aspects of college life. As each person spoke on the tape, his or her photograph was simultaneously projected on a screen. At the end of the slide-and-tape show, subjects were asked to match each statement from the tape with the appropriate photograph, that is, to recall "who said what." Of interest was not how many errors the subject made overall, but how much the subject erroneously attributed male statements to other males rather than to females and female statements to other females rather than to males. Such "within-sex" errors indicate that the subject is confusing the members of a given sex with one another. Put somewhat differently, such errors indicate that the subject is sorting people into equivalence classes on the basis of gender rather than on the basis of some other available dimension.

In contrast to the results reported by Taylor and Falcone (1982), this study found that sex-typed subjects were significantly more likely than androgynous and undifferentiated subjects to confuse only the members of the *opposite* sex in particular. For sex-typed males, in other words, female speakers were especially likely to be confused with one another and thereby treated as equivalent. For sex-typed females, in contrast, male speakers were especially likely to be confused with one another. Although it is not clear why sex-typed subjects were not also more likely than androgynous or undifferentiated subjects to confuse the members of their own sex with one another, these results support the contention of gender schema theory that sex-typed individuals are spontaneously inclined to organize other persons into equivalence classes on the basis of gender. As in the previous studies, there were no differences between androgynous and undifferentiated subjects.

This is not to say, however, that sex-typed subjects were the *most* likely to confuse the members of the opposite sex with one another. Quite the contrary. That distinction belonged to the *cross-sex-typed* subjects, who were significantly more likely than even the sex-typed subjects to do so. This finding is pertinent to the recurring question of whether cross-sex-typed individuals, like sex-typed individuals, have a greater readiness than androgynous or undifferentiated individuals to encode and organize information on the basis of gender. On the basis of the data from this study, it seems that cross-sex-typed individuals may well have a greater readiness than androgynous or undifferentiated individuals to organize at least some kinds of information (in particular, information about other people) on the basis of gender. Despite this and other similarities, however, the fact is that sex-typed individuals have a history of gender conformity whereas cross-sex-typed individuals have a history of gender deviance. Accordingly, even when sex-typed and cross-sex-typed individuals both appear to be gender schematic (as they did in this study), it may be inappropriate to think of them as being gender schematic in exactly the same way or for exactly the same reasons.

It should be noted that the "who said what" study also included a condition in which the speakers on the tape were three blacks and three whites rather than three males and three females. This control condition was included so that we could discover whether the greater schematicity of sex-typed individuals is specific to gender, as gender schema theory implies, or whether sex-typed individuals tend toward schematic processing generally. In contrast to the gender condition, however, no significant differences emerged in the race condition between sex-typed, androgynous, undifferentiated, and cross-sex-typed subjects. Accordingly, we may conclude that the greater schematicity of sex-typed individuals does seem to be specific to gender and does not reflect a content-independent cognitive style.

STUDY 4: GENDER-SCHEMATIC PROCESSING OF PHYSICAL ATTRACTIVENESS

Gender schema theory asserts that sex-typed individuals are highly attuned to cultural definitions of gender appropriateness and that they use those definitions as prescriptive. Because one must not only act a certain way but also look a certain way to satisfy these standards, however, it seems likely that sex-typed individuals would also be highly attuned to the culture's gender-specific definitions of physical attractiveness.

To test this hypothesis, Andersen and Bem (1981) conducted a study that asked whether sex-typed individuals are more likely than androgynous individuals to differentiate between people who are consensually defined as physically attractive and people who are consensually defined as physically unattractive. In that study, sex-typed and androgynous subjects of both sexes engaged in getting-acquainted telephone conversations with four different partners. The subjects were led to believe that each of their partners was either physically attractive or physically unattractive, a belief manipulated by means of a Polaroid snapshot allegedly taken of the partner a few moments before. Each subject conversed with one allegedly attractive and one unattractive partner of his or her own sex as well as with one allegedly attractive and one unattractive partner of the opposite sex. The partners in this study were all naive, not confederates, and all were strangers to the subjects with whom they conversed. Each conversation lasted approximately 8 min and was totally uncontrived. Three independent judges—all blind with respect to the subject's BSRI category as well as to the partner's sex and alleged physical attractiveness—later listened to the subject's half of each conversation and rated him or her on a number of dimensions.

The results of this study indicate that, as predicted, sex-typed individuals were significantly more likely than androgynous individuals to differentiate between attractive and unattractive partners, displaying greater animation, enthusiasm, and interest toward those represented as more attractive. These results indicate that sex-typed individuals are attuned to the culture's gender-specific definitions of physical attractiveness, as predicted by the theory.

Interestingly, the finding that sex-typed individuals were more likely than androgynous individuals to differentiate between attractive and unattractive partners was especially pronounced in interactions with partners of the *opposite* sex. Taken together with the finding from the previous study that sex-typed individuals also have a hard time distinguishing one member of the opposite sex from another, this suggests that sex-typed individuals may have a readiness to encode all members of the opposite sex in terms of physical attractiveness rather than in terms of other dimensions that are more individuating or more relevant to the situational context. This, of course, is precisely what is implied when feminists object to the ubiquitous sexual coloring of cross-sex interaction.

Still further evidence that sex-typed individuals are attuned to the culture's gender-specific definitions of physical attractiveness comes from a study cited earlier, by Lippa (1983), which found, among other things, that when asked to select the particular body outlines they considered most attractive for a male and for a female, sex-typed subjects selected body outlines that were significantly more divergent from one another physically than those selected by either androgynous or undifferentiated subjects.

STUDY 5: THE AVOIDANCE OF GENDER-INAPPROPRIATE
BEHAVIOR

The several studies described thus far collectively confirm the first major contention of gender schema theory that sex-typed individuals are especially likely to encode and to organize information—including information about the self—in terms of gender. The remaining studies test the second major contention of gender schema theory that individuals who engage in a high level of gender-schematic processing also engage in a high level of gender-stereotyped behavior.

Gender schema theory asserts that sex-typed individuals engage in a high level of gender-stereotyped behavior because they are motivated to keep their behavior consistent with the culture's definitions of gender appropriateness. But is gender-inappropriate behavior motivationally problematic for sex-typed individuals, as gender schema theory implies, or would sex-typed individuals be perfectly willing to engage in such behavior if the situation were structured to encourage it? Put somewhat differently, do sex-typed individuals actively avoid activities just because those activities happen to be stereotyped as more appropriate for the other sex, and, if they have to perform a gender-inappropriate activity for some reason, does it cause them discomfort to do so? This study (Bem & Lenney, 1976) was designed to test these hypotheses in a situation where some of the more obvious barriers to gender-inappropriate behavior had been removed.

Subjects in this study were 24 sex-typed, 24 androgynous, and 24 cross-sex-typed undergraduates of each sex preselected on the basis of the *t*-ratio between their masculine and feminine ratings on the BSRI. During the individual experimental sessions, each subject was told that we were preparing to do a study to find out whether people make different personality judgments about an individual as a function of the particular activity he or she happens to be seen performing, and that we therefore needed pictures of the same person performing many different activities. The activities were arranged in pairs, and each subject was asked to select the one activity from each pair that he or she would prefer to perform during the photography session that was to follow immediately.

Although it was not apparent to the subject, fifteen of the pairs required the subject to choose between activities that differed in their gender connotations. Of these, five pitted neutral activities (e.g., playing with a yo-yo; peeling oranges) against masculine activities (e.g., oiling squeaky hinges on a metal box; attaching artificial bait to a fishhook); five pitted neutral activities against feminine activities (e.g., preparing a baby bottle by mixing powdered formula with water; ironing cloth napkins); and five pitted masculine and feminine activities against each other. In all of these gender conflict pairs, moreover, it was always the gender-inappropriate activity that paid more. (In the remaining fifteen pairs, both activities were either masculine, feminine, or neutral, and one activity was arbitrarily assigned to be the higher paying.) Immediately after making their choices, the subjects proceeded to perform three masculine, three feminine, and three neutral activities while the experimenter pretended to photograph them, and they indicated how they felt after each activity on a series of rating scales.

In an attempt to get the purest possible measure of preference, unconfounded by the effects of competence at or familiarity with the various activities, great care was taken to assure the subjects that we were not at all interested in how well they could perform each activity or, indeed, if they had ever done it before. For example, they were explicitly told that they would be given only one minute or so for each activity, because all we really wanted was for them to become sufficiently involved in each activity for a convincing photograph to be taken. They were also assured that simple written instructions would be available for each of the activities they selected. In addition, to prevent subjects from becoming overly self-conscious about how their pictures would look, they were assured that the later study would be done at a different university and that no one they knew would ever be likely to see their pictures. Finally, no emphasis whatever was placed on having the pictures reflect the "true" personality of the individual subject. If anything, what was implied was that we needed each subject to perform as wide a variety of activities as possible.

Gender schema theory predicts and the results of this study confirm that sex-typed individuals are significantly more likely to choose behaviors that are consistent with their own gender than are androgynous or cross-sex-typed individuals, who do not differ from one another in this regard. More specifically, sex-typed individuals are significantly more likely to select gender-appropriate activities and to reject gender-inappropriate activities, even in a situation where many of the external barriers to gender-inappropriate activity have been removed and even if such choices cost them money.

Likewise, gender schema theory also predicts and the results of this study also confirm that sex-typed individuals feel significantly worse after performing gender-inappropriate activity than androgynous or cross-sex-typed individuals, who do not differ from one another in this regard. More specifically, sex-typed subjects reported feeling more nervous and peculiar after performing gender-inappropriate activities than anyone else did; they reported feeling less likeable and less attractive than anyone else did; they reported feeling less masculine (if they were male) and less feminine (if they were female) than anyone else; and they reported that they had enjoyed themselves less.

Taken as a whole, the results of this study thus demonstrate that gender-inappropriate behavior is motivationally problematic for sex-typed individuals and so they actively avoid it. That is, sex-typed individuals are motivated to restrict their behavior in accordance with cultural definitions of gender appropriateness, as gender schema theory implies.

A conceptual replication of the Bem and Lenney study was later carried out by Helmreich, Spence, and Holahan (1979) using the PAQ rather than the BSRI to classify subjects and also using a somewhat different set of experimental procedures. Despite the many methodological differences between the two studies, the central finding that sex-typed subjects are significantly more likely than other subjects to prefer gender-appropriate activities was replicated, though only for males.[6]

Still further support for gender schema theory's claim that subjects classified as sex typed on the BSRI are especially motivated to keep their behavior consistent with cultural definitions of gender appropriateness comes from two studies that asked whether sex-typed in-

---

6. In contrast, the finding that sex-typed subjects have more negative feelings about doing gender-inappropriate activities was not replicated. However, given that the affect data in the Helmreich, Spence, and Holahan study were derived from a procedure in which subjects read quickly through a list of hypothetical activities and indicated how comfortable or uncomfortable they imagined they might feel while performing each activity, it is not surprising that the ratings merely revealed once again what has already been reported in numerous other studies, namely, that masculine and androgynous subjects report feeling more comfortable about themselves in a wide variety of settings than feminine and undifferentiated subjects. In the Bem and Lenney study, by contrast, subjects rated their feelings about each activity in the context of actually doing the activity; hence the experiential difference between doing a gender-appropriate activity and doing a gender-inappropriate activity was salient enough to overcome the global individual differences in self-esteem that must be surmounted if the effect of gender appropriateness is to be made visible.

dividuals are more gender stereotyped than androgynous individuals in their expressive style, that is, in their nonverbal or paralinguistic behaviors or both. In the first of these studies (Lippa, 1978),
sex-typed and androgynous males and females were videotaped
while enacting a standardized behavior in a standardized situation,
and the soundless videotapes were then rated by naive judges for
how much masculinity or femininity they conveyed. As anticipated,
sex-typed women were rated as more feminine than androgynous
women, and sex-typed men were rated as more masculine than
androgynous men, which implies that the nonverbal behavior of sex-
typed individuals is more gender stereotyped than the nonverbal behavior of androgynous individuals.

In the second study (LaFrance, 1981; LaFrance & Carmen, 1980),
trained observers counted every spontaneous occurrence of four specific paralinguistic behaviors while the subject was engaged in a
dyadic interaction. Of these four, two were more typical of males
than of females (filled pauses and interruptive statements) and two
were more typical of females than of males (gaze while speaking and
smile while not speaking). The results indicated not only that sex-
typed subjects were significantly more likely than androgynous subjects to exaggerate gender-congruent behaviors and to avoid gender-
incongruent behaviors, but also that there was significantly more
gender-based cohesiveness among the four paralinguistic behaviors
for sex-typed subjects than for androgynous subjects.

STUDIES 6–8: GENDER SCHEMATICITY AND GENDER
DIFFERENCES

The results of the Bem and Lenney study demonstrate that sex-typed
individuals are motivated to avoid activities stereotyped as inappropriate for their sex. But is this pattern of avoidance restricted to
relatively trivial activities of the sort sampled in that study, or does it
also extend to more complex social behaviors like, say, being nurturant or being independent? More specifically, does this pattern of
avoidance restrict the sex-typed male's ability to nurture other human beings? Likewise, does it restrict the sex-typed female's ability to
behave independently? To test this hypothesis (and, simultaneously, to demonstrate the relative freedom from gender constraints of the
androgynous individual in particular), three separate laboratory
studies were carried out, two designed to evoke the stereotypically

feminine behavior of nurturance (Bem, Martyna, & Watson, 1976) and one designed to evoke the stereotypically masculine behavior of independence (Bem, 1975). In the first of the two nurturance studies, subjects interacted with a human baby; in the second, they interacted with a lonely peer.

In the baby study, each subject was left alone with a 5-month-old baby for 10 min with the understanding that we would be observing the infant's reactions to a stranger through one-way glass. In fact, we were measuring the subject's responsiveness to the baby. Using time sampling procedures, we measured how much the subject smiled at the baby, talked to the baby, held the baby, kissed or nuzzled the baby, and played with the baby in a way that involved touching (e.g., tickling, patting, stretching). We then derived a global measure of the subject's overall responsiveness to the baby by adding together all these various behaviors.

In the lonely peer study, which was designed to evoke sympathetic and supportive listening on the part of the subject, two same-sex subjects (one of whom was actually an experimental assistant) participated in a study of "the acquaintance process." They appeared to draw lots to determine who would take the role of "talker" and who the role of "listener," but in fact the experimental assistant always served as the talker and the subject always served as the listener. The talker began with relatively impersonal background information, but he or she soon became more personal, describing himself or herself as a recent and rather lonely transfer student. The talker did not sound neurotic, just somewhat isolated and rather pleased to have this opportunity to share some of his or her feelings with another person. In contrast, the subject—as listener—was allowed to ask questions and to make comments but was instructed never to shift the focus of the conversation to himself or herself. As in the baby study, we observed the interaction from behind one-way glass and recorded a number of the subjects' behaviors, such as how much responsiveness they showed in their facial expressions, how many times they nodded, how many comments they made, and how positively they reacted to the talker's implicit request for further contact. After the conversation, we also asked both the talker and the experimenter to rate how nurturant the subject had seemed to them. We then derived a global responsiveness score for each subject by adding together these various measures.

In the independence study, which was an adaptation of Asch's conformity paradigm, four males or four females were brought to the lab simultaneously and asked to rate a series of cartoons for funniness. The cartoons had previously been rated by a set of independent judges, with half of them judged very funny and half judged very unfunny. Of interest was how the subject responded when he or she was the last to be called upon and everyone else had already given a preprogrammed false response, agreeing either that a particular cartoon was funny when it was not or that a particular cartoon was not funny when it was. We gave subjects this somewhat subjective task of judging cartoons for funniness—rather than judging the length of lines or the like—so that false norms could impose pressure to conform without appearing to be bizarre.

When these three studies were originally reported in the literature, what was most emphasized about their results was that they demonstrated the androgynous individual's freedom from gender stereotypes. More specifically, what was most emphasized was that whereas masculine subjects were low in nurturance (in both studies) and feminine subjects were low in independence, only androgynous subjects showed both high levels of independence in the face of group pressure to conform and high levels of nurturance in interaction with both a baby and a lonely peer.

From the perspective of gender schema theory, of course, it is the behavior of the sex-typed (or gender-schematic) individual that is of the greatest interest. Two things are especially noteworthy in this regard. First, the results indicate that the sex-typed individual's pattern of avoiding gender-inappropriate activity is not restricted to relatively trivial activities but extends to complex social behaviors like independence and nurturance. Second, a reanalysis of the data reveals a significant sex by sex type interaction in all three studies, with the difference between males and females being significantly greater among sex-typed subjects than among androgynous or cross-sex-typed subjects. This same pattern was also found in a recent study of bystander intervention by Senneker and Hendrick (1983). Taken together with the finding that sex-typed individuals are especially motivated to avoid gender-inappropriate activities, this finding of a correlation between gender schematicity and gender difference constitutes evidence for the contention of gender schema theory that gender schematicity is itself responsible for creating and / or enhancing many gender differences that currently exist in our society.

Put somewhat differently, this finding brings into focus the possibility that many of the stereotyped differences in behavior, motivation, and self-concept that psychologists and laypersons alike typically call "sex" differences (and that I have been referring to here as "gender" differences) are not really sex differences at all but "sex-type" differences, that is, differences between sex-typed males and sex-typed females that emerge as a direct result of their being gender schematic. These "sex-type" differences can be perceived even when unselected males and females are compared with one another—and are thereby misperceived as "sex" differences—only because sex-typed males and females so predominate not only in our society at large but also in any sample of unselected subjects that we study.

The Antecedents of Gender-Schematic Processing

The results of these several empirical studies demonstrate that sex-typed individuals do have a readiness to organize information in general, and their self-concepts in particular, in terms of gender. But how and why do sex-typed individuals develop such a readiness? Because gender-schematic processing is considered a special case of schematic processing, this specific question is superseded by the more general question of how and why individuals come to organize information in terms of any social category, that is, how and why a social category becomes transformed into a cognitive schema.

Gender schema theory proposes that the transformation of a given social category into the nucleus of a highly available cognitive schema depends upon the nature of the social context within which the category is embedded, not on the intrinsic nature of the category itself. Given the proper social context, then, even a category like eye color could become a cognitive schema. More specifically, gender schema theory proposes that a category will become a schema if: (a) The social context makes it the nucleus of a large associative network, that is, if the ideology and/or the practices of the culture construct an association between that category and a wide range of other attributes, behaviors, concepts, and categories; and (b) the social context assigns the category broad functional significance—that is, if a broad array of social institutions, norms, and taboos distinguishes between persons, behaviors, and attributes on the basis of this category.

This latter condition is most critical, for gender schema theory presumes that the culture's insistence on the functional importance of the social category is what transforms a passive network of associations into an active and readily available schema for interpreting reality. We all learn many associative networks of concepts throughout life—many potential cognitive schemata—but it is the centrality or functional importance assigned by society to particular categories and distinctions that animates their associated networks and gives these schemata priority and availability over others.

From the perspective of gender schema theory, then, gender has come to have cognitive primacy over many other social categories because the culture has made it so. Nearly all societies teach the developing child two crucial things about gender: first, as noted earlier, they teach the substantive network of sex-related associations that can come to serve as a cognitive schema; second, they teach that the dichotomy between male and female has intensive and extensive relevance to virtually every domain of human experience. The typical American child cannot help observing, for example, that what parents, teachers, and peers consider appropriate behavior varies as a function of sex; that toys, clothing, occupations, hobbies, the domestic division of labor—even pronouns—all vary as a function of sex.

Gender schema theory thus implies that children would be far less likely to become gender-schematic and hence sex typed if the society were to limit the associative network linked to sex and temper its insistence on the functional importance of the gender dichotomy. Ironically, even though our society has become sensitive to negative sex stereotypes and has begun to expunge them from the media and from children's literature, it remains blind to its gratuitous emphasis on the gender dichotomy itself. In elementary schools, for example, boys and girls line up separately or alternately; they learn songs in which the fingers are "ladies" and the thumbs are "men"; they see boy and girl paper doll silhouettes alternately placed on the days of the month in order to learn about the calendar. Children are not lined up separately or alternately as blacks and whites; fingers are not "whites" and thumbs "blacks"; black and white dolls do not alternately mark the days of the calendar. Our society seeks to deemphasize racial distinctions but continues to exaggerate sexual distinctions.

Because of the role that sex plays in reproduction, perhaps no society could ever be as indifferent to sex in its cultural arrangements as it could be to, say, eye color, thereby giving the gender schema a sociologically based priority over many other categories. For the same reason, it may even be, as noted earlier, that sex has evolved to be a basic category of perception for our species, thereby giving the gender schema a biologically based priority as well. Be that as it may, however, gender schema theory claims that society's ubiquitous insistence on the functional importance of the gender dichotomy must necessarily render it even more cognitively available—and available in more remotely relevant contexts—than it would be otherwise.

Gender schema theory's claims about the antecedents of gender-schematic processing have not yet been tested empirically. Hence it is not possible at this point to state whether individual differences in gender-schematic processing do in fact derive from differences in the emphasis placed on gender dichotomy in individuals' socialization histories, or to describe concretely the particular kinds of socialization histories that enhance or diminish gender-schematic processing. Nevertheless, I should like to set forth a number of plausible strategies that are consistent with gender schema theory for raising a gender-aschematic child in the midst of a gender-schematic society.

This discussion will, by necessity, be highly speculative. Even so, it will serve to clarify gender schema theory's view of exactly how gender-schematic processing is learned and how something else might be learned in its place. That is, it will serve to clarify how the priorities of other schemata might be elevated relative to the gender schema. As we shall see, many of the particular strategies recommended for raising gender-aschematic children are strategies that have already been adopted by feminist parents trying to create what is typically called a nonsexist or gender-liberated form of child rearing. In these cases, what gender schema theory provides is a new theoretical framework for thinking about the psychological impact of various child-rearing practices. Sprinkled throughout the discussion will be examples taken from my own home. These are meant to be illustrations and not systematic evidence that such strategies actually decrease gender-schematic processing.

Raising Gender-Aschematic Children

Feminist parents who wish to raise gender-aschematic children in a gender-schematic world are like any parents who wish to inculcate in their children beliefs and values that deviate from those of the dominant culture. Their major option is to try to undermine the dominant ideology before it can undermine theirs. Feminist parents are thus in a difficult situation. They cannot simply ignore gender in their child rearing as they might prefer to do, because the society will then have free rein to teach their children the lessons about gender that it teaches all other children. Rather, they must manage somehow to inoculate their children against gender-schematic processing.

Two strategies are suggested here: First, parents can enable their children to learn about sex differences initially without their also learning the culture's sex-linked associative network by simultaneously retarding their children's knowledge of sex's cultural correlates and advancing their knowledge of sex's biological correlates. Second, parents can provide alternative or "subversive" schemata that their children can use to interpret the culture's sex-linked associative network when they do learn it. This step is essential if children are not simply to learn gender-schematic processing somewhat later than their counterparts from more traditional homes. Whether one is a child or an adult, such alternative schemata "build up one's resistance" to the lessons of the dominant culture and thereby enable one to remain gender aschematic even while living in a gender-schematic society.

TEACHING CHILDREN ABOUT SEX DIFFERENCES

The Cultural Correlates of Sex. Children typically learn that gender is a sprawling associative network with ubiquitous functional importance through their observation of the many cultural correlates of sex existing in their society. Accordingly, the first step parents can take to retard the development of gender-schematic processing is to retard the child's knowledge of these cultural messages about gender. Less crudely put, parents can attempt to attenuate sex-linked correlations within the child's social environment, thereby altering the basic data upon which the child will construct his or her own concepts of maleness and femaleness.

In part, parents can do this by eliminating sex stereotyping from their own behavior and from the alternatives they provide for their children, just as many feminist parents are already doing. Among other things, for example, they can take turns making dinner, bathing the children, and driving the car; they can ensure that all their children—regardless of sex—have both trucks and dolls, both pink and blue clothing, and both male and female playmates; and they can arrange for their children to see women and men in nontraditional occupations.

When children are quite young, parents can further inhibit cultural messages about gender by censoring books and television programs whose explicit or implicit message is that the sexes differ on nonbiological dimensions. At present this tactic will eliminate many children's books and most television programming. Ironically, it will also temporarily eliminate a number of feminist books designed to overcome sex stereotypes; even a book that insists it is wrong for William not to be allowed to have a doll by implication teaches a child who has not yet learned the associative network that boys and dolls do not normally go together.

To compensate for this censorship, parents will need to seek out—and create—materials that do not teach sex stereotypes. With our own children, my husband and I got into the habit of doctoring books whenever possible so as to remove all sex-linked correlations. We did this, among other ways, by changing the sex of the main character; by drawing longer hair and the outline of breasts onto the illustrations of previously male truck drivers, physicians, pilots, and the like; and by deleting or altering sections of the text that described females or males in a sex-stereotyped manner. When reading children's picture books aloud, we also chose pronouns that avoided the ubiquitous implication that all characters without dresses or pink bows must necessarily be male: "And what is this little piggy doing? Why, he or she seems to be building a bridge."

All of these practices are designed to permit very young children to dwell temporarily in a social environment where, if the parents are lucky, the cultural correlations with sex will be attenuated from, say, .96 to .43. According to gender schema theory, this attenuation should retard the formation of the sex-linked associative network that will itself form the basis of the gender schema. By themselves, however, these practices teach children only what sex is not. But children must also be taught what sex is.

The Biological Correlates of Sex. What remains when all the cultural correlates of sex are attenuated or eliminated, of course, are two of the undisputed biological correlates of sex: anatomy and reproduction. Accordingly, parents can make these the definitional attributes of femaleness and maleness. By teaching their children that the genitalia constitute the definitive attributes of females and males, parents help them to apprehend the merely probabilistic nature of sex's cultural correlates and thereby restrict sex's associative sprawl. By teaching their children that whether one is female or male makes a difference only in the context of reproduction, parents limit sex's functional significance and thereby retard gender-schematic processing. Because children taught these lessons have been provided with an explicit and clear-cut rule about what sex is and when sex matters, they should be predisposed to construct their own concepts of femaleness and maleness based on biology rather than on the cultural correlates to which they have been exposed. And to the extent that young children tend to interpret rules and categories rigidly rather than flexibly, this tendency will serve to enhance their belief that sex is to be narrowly defined in terms of anatomy and reproduction rather than to enhance a traditional belief that every arbitrary gender rule must be strictly obeyed and enforced. Thus there may be an irony, but there is no inconsistency, in the fact that an emphasis on the biological differences between the sexes should here be advocated as the basis for feminist child rearing.

The liberation that comes from having an unambiguous genital definition of sex and the imprisonment that comes from not having such a definition are nicely illustrated by the story of what happened to our son Jeremy, then age four, the day he decided to wear barrettes to nursery school. Several times that day, another little boy told Jeremy that he, Jeremy, must be a girl because "only girls wear barrettes." After trying to explain to this child that "wearing barrettes doesn't matter" and that "being a boy means having a penis and testicles," Jeremy finally pulled down his pants as a way of making his point more convincingly. The other child was not impressed. He simply said, "Everybody has a penis; only girls wear barrettes."

In the American context, children do not typically learn to define sex in terms of anatomy and reproduction until quite late, and as a result they—like the child in the example above—mistakenly treat many of the cultural correlates of sex as definitional. This confusion is facilitated, of course, by the fact that the genitalia themselves are not usually visible and hence cannot be relied on as a way of identifying someone's sex.

Accordingly, when our children asked whether someone was male or female, we frequently denied certain knowledge of the person's sex, emphasizing that without being able to see whether there was a penis or a vagina under the person's clothes, we had no definitive information. Moreover, when our children themselves began to utilize nonbiological markers as a way of identifying sex, we gently teased them about that strategy to remind them that the genitalia— and only the genitalia—constitute the definition of sex: "What do you mean that you can tell Chris is a girl because Chris has long hair? Does Chris's hair have a vagina?"

We found Stephanie Waxman's picture book *What Is a Girl? What Is a Boy?* (Waxman, 1976) to be a superb teaching aid in this context. Each page displays a vivid and attractive photograph of a boy or a girl engaging in some behavior stereotyped as more typical of or more appropriate for the other sex. The accompanying text says such things as, "Some people say a girl is someone with jewelry, but Barry is wearing a necklace and he's a boy." The book ends with nude photographs of both children and adults, and it explicitly defines sex in terms of anatomy.

These particular lessons about what sex is, what sex is not, and when sex matters are designed to make young children far more naive than their peers about the cultural aspects of gender and far more sophisticated about the biological aspects of sex. Eventually, of course, their naiveté will begin to fade, and they too will begin to learn the culture's sprawling network of sex-linked associations. At that point, parents must take steps to prevent that associative network from itself becoming a cognitive schema.

PROVIDING ALTERNATIVE SCHEMATA

Let us presume that the feminist parent has successfully produced a child who defines sex in terms of anatomy and reproduction. How is such a child to understand the many sex-linked correlations that will inevitably begin to intrude upon his or her awareness? What alternative schemata can substitute for the gender schema in helping the child organize and assimilate gender-related information?

The Individual Differences Schema. The first alternative schema is simply a child's version of the time-honored liberal truism used to counter stereotypic thinking in general, namely, that there is remarkable variability of individuals within groups compared with the small mean differences between groups. To the child who says that girls do not like to play baseball, the feminist parent can thus point out that although it is true that some girls do not like to play baseball, it is also true that some girls do (e.g., your Aunt Beverly and Alissa who lives across the street) and that some boys do not (e.g., your dad and Alissa's brother Jimmy). It is, of course, useful for parents to supply themselves with a long list of counterexamples well in advance of such occasions.

This individual differences schema is designed to prevent children from interpreting individual differences as sex differences, from assimilating perceived differences among people to a gender schema. Simultaneously, it should also encourage children to treat as a given that the sexes are basically similar to one another and, hence, to view all glib assertions about sex differences as inherently suspect. And it is with this skepticism that feminist consciousness begins.

The Cultural Relativism Schema. As the child's knowledge and awareness grow, he or she will gradually begin to realize that his or her family's beliefs and attitudes about gender are at variance with those of the dominant culture. Accordingly, the child needs some rationale for not simply accepting the majority view as the more valid. One possible rationale is cultural relativism, the notion that "different people believe different things" and that the coexistence of even contradictory beliefs is the rule in a pluralistic society rather than the exception.

Children can (and should) be introduced to the schema of cultural relativism long before it is pertinent to the domain of gender. For example, our children needed the rationale that "different people believe different things" in order to understand why they, but not the children next door, had to wear seat belts; why our family, but not the family next door, was casual about nudity in the home. The general principle that contradictory beliefs frequently coexist seems now to have become a readily available schema for our children, a schema that permits them to accept with relative equanimity that they have different beliefs than many of their peers with respect to gender.

Finally, the cultural relativism schema can solve one of the primary dilemmas of the liberal feminist parent: how to give one's children access to the riches of classical literature—as well as to the lesser riches of the mass media—without abandoning them to the forces that promote gender-schematic processing. Happily, the censorship of sex-stereotyped materials that is necessary to retard the initial growth of the sex-linked associative network when children are young can end once children have learned the critical lesson that cultural messages reflect the beliefs and attitudes of the persons who created those messages.

Accordingly, before we read our daughter her first volume of fairy tales, we discussed with her the cultural beliefs and attitudes about men and women that the tales would reflect; and while reading the tales, we frequently made such comments as, "Isn't it interesting that the person who wrote this story seems to think that girls always need to be rescued?" If such discussions are not too heavy-handed, they can provide a background of understanding against which the child can thoroughly enjoy the stories themselves while still learning to discount the sex stereotypes within them as irrelevant both to their own beliefs and to truth. The cultural relativism schema thus brings children an awareness that fairy tales are fairy tales in more than one sense.

The Sexism Schema. Cultural relativism is fine in its place, but feminist parents will not and should not be satisfied to pretend that they think all ideas—particularly those about gender—are equally valid. At some point they will feel compelled to declare that the view of women and men conveyed by fairy tales, by the mass media, and by the next-door neighbors is not only different, but wrong. It is time to teach one's children about sexism.

Moreover, it is only by giving children a sexism schema, a coherent and organized understanding of the historical roots and the contemporaneous consequences of sex discrimination, that they will truly be able to comprehend why the sexes appear to be so different in our society: why, for example, there has never been a female president of the United States; why fathers do not stay home with their children; and why so many people believe these sex differences to be the natural consequence of biology. The child who has developed a readiness to encode and to organize information in terms of an evolving sexism schema is a child who is prepared to actively oppose the gender-related constraints that those with a gender schema will inevitably seek to impose.

The development of a sexism schema is nicely illustrated by our daughter Emily's response to Norma Klein's book *Girls Can Be Anything* (Klein, 1973). One of the main characters is Adam Sobel, who insists that "girls are always nurses and boys are always doctors" and that "girls can't be pilots, . . . they have to be stewardesses." After reading this book, our daughter, then age four, spontaneously began to label with contempt anyone who voiced stereotyped beliefs about gender an "Adam Sobel." Adam Sobel thus became for her the nucleus of an envolving sexism schema, a schema that enables her now to perceive—and also to become morally outraged by and to oppose—whatever sex discrimination she meets in daily life.

Many feminist parents might wish to raise their children with neither a gender schema nor a sexism schema. At this historical moment, however, that is not an option. Rather, they must choose either to have their children become gender schematic and hence sex typed or to have their children become sexism schematic and hence feminists. We have chosen the latter for our children.

The Politics of Gender Research

As Kuhn (1962) has pointed out, "normal science" is practiced within a prevailing paradigm or set of assumptions that defines the discipline's problem areas, guides its formulation of research questions, and shapes the methods by which those questions are addressed. Because the paradigm is widely shared, its presence is usually unacknowledged and its nonrational influence on the scientific process unappreciated. A prevailing paradigm thus operates on the scientific process in much the same way as a political ideology or a set of value assumptions. Although the influence of a paradigm is widely regarded as legitimate and the influence of a political ideology or a set of value assumptions is widely regarded as illegitimate, in fact the scientific process is equally vulnerable to compromise from either source. It is most likely to be compromised, moreover, if underlying assumptions of either kind remain implicit and unexamined.

Research on gender provides a textbook case of how implicit cultural assumptions have shaped the scientific process. As I noted earlier, the field of psychology has traditionally shared with the larger culture the implicit assumption that being sex typed is not only the normal, but also the desirable, outcome of human development. This assumption shaped both the field's bipolar conception of masculinity-femininity and the instruments designed to assess it. This assumption also led naturally and inevitably to research questions on the antecedents of "successful" and "unsuccessful" sex-role socialization. For example, does father absence retard the development of masculinity in boys? Is the mother's working outside the home likely to cause sex-role confusion? An important point to note here is that such research was never considered "political," because it shared rather than challenged the prevailing ideology of both the field and the culture. In fact, of course, reinforcing the status quo is just as political an act as challenging it; it is just less likely to be perceived as such.

In contrast, my research on androgyny and gender schema theory has been perceived as political, and correctly so, because it has explicitly challenged the prevailing assumptions about gender held by psychologists and laypersons alike. Thus, as part of a scientific analysis of how gender differences emerge, the research not only generates and tests specific empirical hypotheses, but also attempts to shift the dominant paradigm within psychology from one that implicitly treats the cognitive and emotional primacy of gender as the given, the unmarked norm, the baseline, to one that explicitly views the primacy of gender as marked, as problematic, as requiring explanation. Simultaneously, as part of a feminist analysis that advocates social change, the research also attempts to persuade the layperson that masculinity and femininity are merely social constructions and that gender may have cognitive and emotional priority over other dimensions only because certain modifiable cultural practices have given it that priority. In the realm of science, such an attempt to transform perception is known as paradigm shifting; in the realm of politics, it is known as consciousness raising. The difference between the two is less than most people suppose.

THE CONCEPT OF ANDROGYNY RECONSIDERED

As I noted earlier, the concept of androgyny appeared in the early 1970s to provide a liberated and more humane alternative to the traditional, sex-biased standards of mental health. And it is true that this concept can be applied equally to both women and men and that it encourages individuals to embrace both the feminine and the masculine within themselves. But advocating the concept of androgyny can also be seen as replacing a prescription to be masculine or feminine with the doubly incarcerating prescription to be masculine and feminine. The individual now has not one but two potential sources of inadequacy to contend with.

Even more important, however, the concept of androgyny is problematic from the perspective of gender schema theory because it continues to presuppose that there is a feminine and a masculine within us all, that is, that the concepts of "femininity" and "masculinity" have an independent and palpable reality rather than themselves being cognitive constructs derived from gender-schematic processing. A focus on the concept of androgyny thus fails to prompt serious examination of the extent to which gender organizes both our perceptions and our social world.

In contrast, the concept of gender-schematic processing directs our attention to the promiscuous availability of the gender schema in contexts where other schemata ought to have priority. Thus, if gender schema theory has a political message, it is not that the individual should be androgynous. Rather, it is that the network of associations constituting the gender schema ought to become more limited in scope and that society ought to temper its insistence on the ubiquitous functional importance of the gender dichotomy. In short, human behaviors and personality attributes should no longer be linked with gender, and society should stop projecting gender into situations irrelevant to genitalia.

Were this to occur, we might then come to accept as a given the fact that we are male or female as unselfconsciously as we now accept as a given the fact that we are human. Our maleness or femaleness would be self-evident and nonproblematic; rarely would we be prompted to ponder it, to assert that it is true, to fear that it might be in jeopardy, or to wish that it were otherwise. The gender distinctions that remained would still be perceived—perhaps even cherished—but they would not function as imperialistic schemata for organizing everything else, and the artificial constraints of gender on the individual's unique blend of temperament and behavior would be eliminated. The feminist prescription, then, is not that the individual be androgynous, but that the society be gender aschematic.

REFERENCES

Andersen, S. M., & Bem, S. L. (1981). Sex typing and androgyny in dyadic interaction: Individual differences in responsiveness to physical attractiveness. *Journal of Personality and Social Psychology, 41,* 74–86.

Antill, J. K. (1983). Sex role complementarity versus similarity in married couples. *Journal of Personality and Social Psychology, 45,* 145–155.

Bem, S. L. (1972). Psychology looks at sex roles: Where have all the androgynous people gone? Paper presented at the UCLA Symposium on Sex Roles.

Bem, S. L. (1974). The measurement of psychological androgyny. *Journal of Consulting and Clinical Psychology, 42,* 155–162.

Bem, S. L. (1975). Sex role adaptability: One consequence of psychological androgyny. *Journal of Personality and Social Psychology, 31,* 634–643.

Bem, S. L. (1977). On the utility of alternative procedures for assessing psychological androgyny. *Journal of Consulting and Clinical Psychology, 45,* 196–205.

Bem, S. L. (1979). The theory and measurement of androgyny: A reply to the Pedhazur-Tetenbaum and Locksley-Colten critiques. *Journal of Personality and Social Psychology, 37,* 1047–1054.

Bem, S. L. (1981a). *Bem Sex Role Inventory professional manual.* Palo Alto, CA: Consulting Psychologists Press.

Bem, S. L. (1981b). Gender schema theory: A cognitive account of sex typing. *Psychological Review, 88,* 354–364.

Bem, S. L. (1981c). The BSRI and gender schema theory: A reply to Spence and Helmreich. *Psychological Review, 88,* 369–371.

Bem, S. L. (1982). Gender schema theory and self-schema theory compared: A comment on Markus, Crane, Bernstein, and Siladi's "Self-schemas and gender." *Journal of Personality and Social Psychology, 43,* 1192–1194.

Bem, S. L. (1983). Gender schema theory and its implications for child development: Raising gender-aschematic children in a gender-schematic society. *Signs: Journal of Women in Culture and Society, 8,* 598–616.

Bem, S. L., & Lenney, E. (1976). Sex typing and the avoidance of cross-sex behavior. *Journal of Personality and Social Psychology, 33,* 48–54.

Bem, S. L., Martyna, W., & Watson, C. (1976). Sex typing and androgyny: Further explorations of the expressive domain. *Journal of Personality and Social Psychology, 34,* 1016–1023.

Block, J. (1973). Conceptions of sex role: Some cross-cultural and longitudinal perspectives. *American Psychologist, 28,* 512–526.

Bronfenbrenner, U. (1960). Freudian theories of identification with their derivatives. *Child Development, 31,* 15–40.

Cazden, C. B. (1968). The acquisition of noun and verb inflections. *Child Development, 39,* 433–448.

Chodorow, N. (1978). *The reproduction of mothering: Psychoanalysis and the sociology of gender.* Berkeley: University of California Press.

Clark, H. H., & Clark, E. V. (1977). *Psychology and language: An introduction to psycholinguistics.* New York: Harcourt Brace Jovanovich.

Constantinople, A. (1973). Masculinity-femininity: An exception to the famous dictum? *Psychological Bulletin, 80,* 389–407.

Crane, M., & Markus, H. (1982). Gender identity: The benefits of a self-schema approach. *Journal of Personality and Social Psychology, 43,* 1195–1197.

Damon, W. (1977). *The social world of the child.* San Francisco: Jossey-Bass.

Deaux, K., & Major, B. (1977). Sex-related patterns in the unit of perception. *Personality and Social Psychology Bulletin, 3,* 297–300.

Edwards, A. L., & Ashworth, C. D. (1977). A replication study of item selection for the Bem Sex Role Inventory. *Applied Psychological Measurement, 1,* 501–507.

Frable, D. E. S., & Bem, S. L. (In press). If you're gender-schematic, all members of the opposite sex look alike. *Journal of Personality and Social Psychology.*

Freud, S. (1959a). Some psychological consequences of the anatomical distinction between the sexes (1925). In E. Jones (Ed.), *Collected papers of Sigmund Freud* (Vol. 5). New York: Basic Books.

Freud, S. (1959b). The passing of the Oedipus complex (1924). In E. Jones (Ed.), *Collected papers of Sigmund Freud* (Vol. 5). New York: Basic Books.

Girvin, B. (1978). *The nature of being schematic: Sex-role self-schemas and differential processing of masculine and feminine information.* Unpublished doctoral dissertation, Stanford University.

Helmreich, R. L., Spence, J. T., & Holahan, C. K. (1979). Psychological androgyny and sex role flexibility: A test of two hypotheses. *Journal of Personality and Social Psychology, 37,* 1631–1644.

Ickes, W. (1981). Sex-role influences in dyadic interaction: A theoretical model. In E. Mayo & N. M. Henley (Eds.), *Gender and nonverbal behavior.* New York: Springer-Verlag.

Ickes, W., & Barnes, R. D. (1978). Boys and girls together—and alienated: On enacting stereotyped sex roles in mixed-sex dyads. *Journal of Personality and Social Psychology, 36,* 669–683.

Kagan, J. (1964). Acquisition and significance of sex typing and sex role identity. In M. L. Hoffman & L. W. Hoffman (Eds.), *Review of child development research* (Vol. 1). New York: Russell Sage Foundation.

Klein, N. (1973). *Girls can be anything.* New York: E. P. Dutton.

Kohlberg, L. (1966). A cognitive-developmental analysis of children's sex-role concepts and attitudes. In E. E. Maccoby (Ed.), *The development of sex differences.* Stanford, CA: Stanford University Press.

Kuhn, T. S. (1962). *The structure of scientific revolutions.* Chicago: University of Chicago Press.

LaFrance, M. (1981). Gender gestures: Sex, sex-role, and nonverbal communication. In C. Mayo & N. M. Henley (Eds.), *Gender and nonverbal behavior.* New York: Springer-Verlag.

LaFrance, M., & Carmen, B. (1980). The nonverbal display of psychological androgyny. *Journal of Personality and Social Psychology, 38,* 36–49.

Lewis, M., & Brooks-Gunn, J. (1979). *Social cognition and the acquisition of self.* New York: Plenum.

Lippa, R. (1977). Androgyny, sex typing, and the perception of masculinity-femininity in handwriting. *Journal of Research in Personality, 11,* 21–37.

Lippa, R. (1978). The naive perception of masculinity-femininity on the basis of expressive cues. *Journal of Research in Personality, 12,* 1–14.

Lippa, R. (1983). Sex typing and the perception of body outlines. *Journal of Personality, 51,* 667–682.

Maccoby, E. E., & Jacklin, C. N. (1974). *The psychology of sex differences.* Stanford, CA: Stanford University Press.

Markus, H., Crane, M., Bernstein, S., & Siladi, M. (1982). Self-schemas and gender. *Journal of Personality and Social Psychology, 42*, 38–50.

Martin, C. L., & Halverson, C. F. (1981). A schematic processing model of sex-typing and stereotyping in children. *Child Development, 52*, 1119–1134.

McConaghy, M. J. (1979). Gender permanence and the genital basis of gender: Stages in the development of constancy of gender identity. *Child Development, 50*, 1223–1226.

Meigs, A. S. (1976). Male pregnancy and the reduction of sexual opposition in a New Guinea Highlands Society. *Ethnology, 15*, 393–407.

Mills, C. J. (1983). Sex-typing and self-schemata effects on memory and response latency. *Journal of Personality and Social Psychology, 45*, 163–172.

Mills, C. J., & Tyrrell, D. J. (1983). Sex-stereotypic encoding and release from proactive interference. *Journal of Personality and Social Psychology, 45*, 772–781.

Mischel, W. (1970). Sex-typing and socialization. In P. H. Mussen (Ed.), *Carmichael's manual of child psychology* (Vol. 2). New York: Wiley.

Moore, S. F. (1976). The secret of the men: A fiction of Chagga initiation and its relation to the logic of Chagga symbolism. *Africa, 46*, 357–370.

Mussen, P. H. (1969). Early sex-role development. In D. A. Goslin (Ed.), *Handbook of socialization theory and research.* Chicago: Rand McNally.

Myers, A. M., & Gonda, G. (1982a). Empirical validation of the Bem Sex Role Inventory. *Journal of Personality and Social Psychology, 43*, 304–318.

Myers, A. M., & Gonda, G. (1982b). Utility of the masculinity-femininity construct: Comparison of traditional and androgyny approaches. *Journal of Personality and Social Psychology, 43*, 514–523.

Neisser, U. (1976). *Cognition and reality.* San Francisco: Freeman.

Nichols, J. G., Licht, B. G., & Pearl, R. A. (1982). Some dangers of using personality questionnaires to study personality. *Psychological Bulletin, 92*, 572–580.

Pedhazur, E. J., & Tetenbaum, T. J. (1979). Bem Sex Role Inventory: A theoretical and methodological critique. *Journal of Personality and Social Psychology, 37*, 996–1016.

Rubin, G. (1975). The traffic in women: Notes on the "political economy" of sex. In R. Reiter (Ed.), *Toward an anthropology of women.* New York: Monthly Review Press.

Senneker, P., & Hendrick, C. (1983). Androgyny and helping behavior. *Journal of Personality and Social Psychology, 45*, 916–925.

Spence, J. T. (In press). Masculinity, femininity, and gender-related traits: A conceptual analysis and critique of current research. In B. A. Maher (Ed.), *Progress in experimental research in personality* (Vol. 13). New York: Academic Press.

Spence, J. T., & Helmreich, R. L. (1981). Androgyny versus gender schema: A comment on Bem's gender schema theory. *Psychological Review, 88*, 365–368.

Spence, J. T., Helmreich, R., & Stapp, J. (1974). The Personal Attributes Questionnaire: A measure of sex-role stereotypes and masculinity-femininity. *JSAS Catalog of Selected Documents in Psychology, 4,* 43–44, MS617.

Taylor, M. C., & Hall, J. A. (1982). Psychological androgyny: A review and reformulation of theories, methods, and conclusions. *Psychological Bulletin, 92,* 347–366.

Taylor, S. E., & Crocker, J. (1981). Schematic bases of social information processing. In E. T. Higgins, C. P. Herman, & M. P. Zanna (Eds.), *The Ontario Symposium on Personality and Social Psychology* (Vol. 1). Hillsdale, NJ: Erlbaum.

Taylor, S. E., & Falcone, H. (1982). Cognitive bases of stereotyping: The relationship between categorization and prejudice. *Personality and Social Psychology Bulletin, 8,* 426–432.

Ullian, D. Z. (1981). The child's construction of gender: Anatomy as destiny. In E. K. Shapiro & E. Weber (Eds.), *Cognitive and affective growth: Developmental interaction.* Hillsdale, NJ: Erlbaum.

Walkup, H., & Abbott, R. D. (1978). Cross-validation of item selection on the Bem Sex Role Inventory. *Applied Psychological Measurement, 2,* 63–71.

Waxman, S. (1976). *What is a girl? What is a boy?* Culver City, CA: Peace Press.

Whitley, B. E. (1983). Sex role orientation and self-esteem: A critical meta-analytic review. *Journal of Personality and Social Psychology, 44,* 765–778.

Perinatal Psychoactive Drug Use: Effects on Gender, Development, and Function in Offspring[1]

Joan C. Martin

University of Washington, Seattle

*B*ehavioral teratology is the study of modified function in offspring following maternal, and sometimes paternal, exposure to noxious extrinsic agents before and during the perinatal period.

I shall discuss the effects of selected sedative and stimulant psychoactive drugs of abuse in animal models—specifically nicotine, alcohol, barbiturates, and the amphetamines. All these psychoactive drugs are used and abused by large segments of the United States population, including pregnant women. Since my own research on animal models has dealt primarily with such agents, I have firsthand knowledge of the literature, design problems, and potential applications to humans.

Drugs can be characterized and grouped in many ways, for example, by similarity of chemical structure, by neurophysiological or neurochemical mechanisms of action, or by the way they affect function. Here I shall use the functional grouping. Julien (1981) listed five classes of psychoactive drugs by function. I will be concerned with only two of these: the sedative-hypnotic compounds and the stimulants and convulsants. Under the sedative-hypnotics Julien listed

1. Funding for our research has come from a variety of public and private sources including the American Medical Association, the National Foundation/March of Dimes, NIAAA/ADAMHA, NICHHD/NIH, and NIA/NIH. In addition, both Duke University and the University of Washington have contributed funds for pilot projects. A number of my colleagues have been directly involved in the animal studies reported here. I would particularly like to express my appreciation to R. Fred Becker, Bruce Mackler, and Donald C. Martin.

228

barbiturates, nonbarbiturate hypnotics, antianxiety agents (tranquilizers), and alcohol. He included the amphetamines, clinical antidepressants, cocaine, convulsants, caffeine, and nicotine in the stimulant category.

Extent of the Problem

The United States population, including gravid women, is overmedicated and over self-medicated. Hill, Craig, Chaney, Tennyson, and McCulley (1977) reported that pregnant women in their sample took an average of 6.4 prescription drugs and 3.2 nonprescription (over-the-counter) drugs during pregnancy. This confirmed earlier reports of overuse in this country (Peckham & King, 1963) and Scotland (Forfar & Nelson, 1973), who noted that 21% of pregnant United States women had taken more than five drugs and that 65% of Scottish women were self-medicated and 85% were taking prescribed medication.

Chambers and Hunt (1977) found that their sample of 30,000 women were above average in their use of barbiturates, the major and minor tranquilizers, antidepressants, and the amphetamines. In addition, 57% of the 18–34-year-old women in the sample were drinkers and 52% took amphetamines, either as pep pills or as a dietary aid. Women in this cohort tended to use multiple drugs along with alcohol, a practice of critical concern for its potential effects on offspring.

The National Institutes of Health (NIH) collaborative study of over 50,000 prospective births reported that 54% of white women and 42% of black women smoked during pregnancy (Niswander & Gordon, 1972). Less education and lower social class are positively correlated with smoking in United States women. Streissguth, Martin, Martin, & Barr (1981a) found that 25% of well-educated, predominately middle-class pregnant women were smokers, and Hill et al. (1977) noted that in a similar middle to high socioeconomic class, 23% were smokers and 68% were drinkers. A recent midwestern study found a much higher percentage of smokers in a sample of women that delivered at two university-affiliated hospitals: 44% smoked cigarettes, and 13% smoked marijuana (Rayburn, Wible-Kant, and Bledsoe, 1982). These figures are above recent national norms for cigarette smoking but perhaps are typical for the Midwest.

The total number of smokers in this country has declined since 1972 from 43% to 35%, but the decline is smaller for women than for men (Gallup Report, 1981). This discrepancy has been attributed to the greater freedom in role choices now available to women and the increasing number of women who pursue careers and in doing so adopt many of the cultural mores of males. Twenty percent of United States pregnancies in 1979 were in women below the age of 20 (Bowerman, 1980). The age of onset of smoking as well as alcohol use has been steadily dropping, and in 1981 24% of teenage females smoked compared with 20% of teenage males (Gallup Report, 1981). This, coupled with the rise in teenage pregnancies, places the fetuses that are already at most risk in even greater jeopardy.

Possible Mechanisms for Fetal Effects

Drugs and other extrinsic agents affect the fetus through the mother either before pregnancy or at any time during pregnancy. Such effects may be genetic, through alteration of the chromosomal structure or cytoplasm (Larsson, 1973), or they may be environmental through direct action of the toxic agent on the fetus or by altering the oxygen-carrying capacity of the blood or other maternal organs. Paternal use of the agent may exert deleterious effects genetically by altering the sperm or indirectly by exerting a toxic effect on the germ cell. Unlike maternal effects, these effects can occur only at the time of conception or through earlier action on the sperm (Evans, Fletcher, Torrance, & Hargreave, 1981).

All agents except the large plasma protein molecules pass through the placental barrier, and many agents including alcohol and nicotine pass into the semen and may alter various aspects of spermatogenesis (Soyka & Joffe, 1980). Smoking, alcohol, and amphetamine all have anorectic effects and may cause undernutrition in utero. The genetic background of the mother and father partially determine the extent to which the fetus will be affected. Only 20% of thalidomide users delivered infants with the gross limb deformities considered typical of that tranquilizer. Unfortunately, there is no current method to determine in advance whether an infant will be protected by its genetic constitutents. For example, a case was reported of fraternal twins of whom one was born with fetal alcohol syndrome (FAS) while the other was only slightly affected (Christoffel & Salafsky, 1975).

Psychoactive Drugs and the Human Fetus

Heinonen, Slone, and Shapiro (1977) further analyzed data from the NIH collaborative study of over 50,000 births and noted a significant increase in cardiovascular malformations in the infants of women who took barbiturates during the first 4 months of pregnancy. They also reported an increased rate of central nervous system malformations in infants whose mothers had smoked more than 15 cigarettes daily. There was no increased risk for the users of amphetamines, and no questions were asked about alcohol use. However, Jones, Smith, Streissguth, & Myrianthopoulos (1974) analyzed data from that study for women whose doctors had reported that they were alcohol abusers. Compared with matched controls, 70% of their children were two to three standard deviations below the mean on the Wechsler intelligence Scale for Children (WISC). The excessive use of alcohol during pregnancy results in a recognized syndrome of malformation and mental retardation (Streissguth, Landesman-Dwyer, Martin, and Smith, 1980). Smaller amounts of alcohol cause partial expression of the syndrome (Hanson, Streissguth, & Smith, 1978), including functional deficits (Martin, Martin, Streissguth, & Lund, 1977, 1979; Landesman-Dwyer, Keller, & Streissguth, 1978). The cognitive deficits may be irreversible. Alcohol is the most abused drug in the country today, and according to the Department of Health and Human Services an estimated nine million Americans have an alcohol problem.

Eriksson, Larsson, & Zetterstrom (1981) and Eriksson & Zetterstrom (1981) followed 69 Swedish amphetamine addicts prospectively throughout their pregnancies. They reported an increased rate of preterm deliveries, a higher perinatal mortality rate, and a higher rate of congenital malformations. The malformations included omphalocele, which the authors considered unique to amphetamine abuse. Milkovich and Van den Berg (1977), who prospectively studied women prescribed anorectic drugs during pregnancy, found an excess of oral clefts if the drugs were taken during the first trimester. No other anomalies were found at the clinical drug levels used by this group.

In summary, there is sufficient clinical and correlational evidence to implicate tobacco, alcohol, and amphetamines as human teratogens. The evidence for the barbiturates is less clear. At lower doses, the maternal use of tobacco and alcohol is linked with perinatal mortality and with problems in growth, development, and behavior in the surviving children. There have to my knowledge been no long-term behavioral studies involving the children of amphetamine or barbiturate users.

Rationale for Using Animal Models in Behavioral Teratology

Since drug use by humans is a matter of self-selection, inferences from human studies are always correlational, not causal. For ethical and legal reasons one cannot assign women to drug or nondrug conditions, then wait until pregnancy occurs and follow the offspring after birth. Therefore the argument can be, and has been, made that it is not the drug which causes deficits in the human offspring but the physiological, biological, and genetic predisposition of the woman (Yerushalmy, 1972).

Using animal models extricates us from this difficulty. Animals from the same genetic pool, of the same age, size, and nutritional background, can be randomly assigned to either drug or control conditions and impregnated by the same males, and causal inferences can be made from the outcome of the study. The rat is a useful model for studies of central nervous system development and function, since the rat brain continues to mature for 30 days postnatally and thus is available for chemical manipulation. As is true of other extrinsic agents, chemicals primarily affect developing organ systems rather than mature systems (Hudson, Merrill, & Sands, 1974).

There are several other advantages to animal models. The timing, dose, total period, and pattern of drug administration can all be varied. The greatest effect occurs while an organ system is developing (Wilson, 1977), and there is less effect later in development. Acute, or episodic, access (binges) may have greater effects on the fetus than the same amount of the drug administered chronically (Bowden et al., 1983). The period during which the drug is ingested is important and can be varied in an animal model. There is some evidence that the growth retardation so characteristic of infants of smoking women does not occur if the mother stops smoking before the 4th month of pregnancy (Butler, Goldstein, & Ross, 1972). This is apparently not the case with alcohol, since there are indications that the damage is done early in pregnancy, before the woman is even certain she is pregnant (Streissguth, Landesman-Dwyer, Martin, & Smith, 1980), although there is some evidence that reducing alcohol consumption during pregnancy may ameliorate the effects (Rosett, Ouellette, Weiner, & Owen, 1978).

The advantages of an animal model are as follows:

1. The amount, concentration, and combination of drugs can be exactly controlled.

2. Exposure periods can be selected, and the periods of greatest vulnerability can be determined for each system.

3. Genetic factors can be controlled.

4. The agents can be administered maternally, paternally, or both.

5. The environment can be held constant, with food, handling, lighting, noise level, and temperature kept identical for all animals.

6. Dams can be assigned randomly to treatment conditions, so causal inferences can be made.

Principles of Teratology

Although teratology (the science or study of monsters) is largely a misnomer when applied to deficits of growth and function, the term was adopted from the anatomical and biological nomenclature by behaviorists when they entered the field in the late 1950s with fetal irradiation studies. Since cognitive, affective, and perceptual deficits following intrauterine exposure to extrinsic agents do not necessarily involve morphological alterations, a term such as behavioral fetotoxicology might be more accurate. However, the term behavioral teratology is probably here to stay.

The field of teratology was begun by Josef Warkany in the 1940s when he called attention to the fact that environmental factors could adversely affect intrauterine development and that the placenta was not an impervious shield, as had previously been assumed (Warkany & Nelson, 1940).

Teratology is based upon relatively few principles, which have been most ably expounded by James Wilson and his colleagues (Wilson, 1977):

1. Susceptibility depends upon the genotype of the conceptus. For example, the gross morphological alterations in fetuses whose mothers took thalidomide occurred in relatively few cases.

2. Susceptibility varies with the developmental stage at exposure; the system that is developing at the time of drug exposure is most at

risk. This is the "critical moments" hypothesis (Stockard, 1921), or "critical periods" hypothesis (Dobbing, 1974; Goldman, 1980). For the behaviorist, the last trimester and the early neonatal period are of the most interest, since the central nervous system is experiencing its greatest growth at those times.

3. There are nine mechanisms by which pathogenesis can occur regardless of the agent.

4. There is a continuum of severity of reproductive deficit: death, malformation, growth retardation, and functional disorder. The last is of most interest to behaviorists.

5. Deviant development increases as the dosage of the agent increases. Pasamanick and his colleagues postulated a similar continuum for behavioral deficits, moving in decreasing severity from cerebral palsy, epilepsy, mental retardation, affective disorders, and minor behavioral problems (Pasamanick & Lilienfeld, 1955; Pasamanick, Rogers, & Lilienfeld, 1956).

Implicit in the critical periods hypothesis is the concept of irreversibility—that once the organ system is damaged the behavioral anomaly is fixed immutably. Studies of fetal alcohol syndrome and cerebral palsy lend support to this deduction, since children suffering from such disorders exhibit little improvement even with heroic rehabilitation efforts. Lesser amounts of a stressor, and hence less damage, may allow other areas of the brain to compensate to a greater degree than is possible with FAS or cerebral palsy. Though such compensation would not be possible in the visual cortex, it would be in brain areas not serving perceptual functions. For example, Sugioka (1983) found no evidence for functional deficits at maturity in animals in which the hippocampus had been bilaterally lesioned at birth, even though the hippocampal syndrome (hyperactivity) had been present in these animals as weanlings and juveniles.

An additional troubling concept that has been neither proven nor disproven is that of biological thresholds (Vorhees, 1983), which assumes that there is an amount of a stressor above which damage occurs and below which there is no effect on the organism. If this were true, there would be a "safe" amount of all agents which could be ingested with no untoward effects on the fetus. Any investigator who has ever lectured on alcohol consumption during pregnancy is inevitably asked, "How much can I drink and not harm the baby?" At this point this question is unresolved, but I submit that it has little meaning, since the phenomenon is not an either or matter but a continuum shading from severe mental retardation to small deficits in one cognitive area. The problem is further complicated by the interaction of maternal genotype and paternal genotype, timing of drug ingestion, amount crossing the placenta, health and nutritional status of the mother, prior paternal drug use, and a host of other individual factors which do not readily allow for a general statement about a safe quantity.

Experimental Design Considerations

There is usually good agreement across laboratories concerning experimental design. Obviously an experimenter would like to exert as much control over the design as possible in order to rule out alternative interpretations of the results. Just as obviously, this is not always possible.

SUBJECT SELECTION

Ideally the females are all the same age and weight and from the same genetic background. They should be acclimated to the laboratory for a week to 10 days prior to impregnation and drug treatment. The same studs should be used across treatment conditions, and the females should be randomly assigned to a given treatment. In our own studies we have with rare exceptions received the females on day 1 after impregnation the night before and they perforce have received no acclimation to the laboratory. The exception to this modus operandi is the barbiturate studies I will report.

DRUG AMOUNT

A range of doses should be explored, from a level at which no measurable functional effect is expected in the offspring to a level at which severe deficits are observed, with possible drug-related fetal and neonatal death. Since function is being studied, it is important not to exceed the dosage at which performance is impaired; otherwise it is difficult to determine whether the animal performs inadequately to physical or neural impairment or both.

ROUTE OF ADMINISTRATION

Since the ostensible goal of using animal models for behavioral teratology is to approximate the human condition, the ideal drug route is
that used by the gravid woman. This is usually oral, though exceptions do exist, as in cocaine and heroin use. It goes without saying that
the control group of dams receive the vehicle in which the drug or a
placebo is given by the same route to control for stress due to handling
and administration. There are studies which demonstrate effects on
litter size, neonatal viability, and function in offspring caused just by
the stress of maternal handling or saline injection (Wiener & Levine,
1983; Becker & Martin, 1971; Dubin, Baros, Cox, & King, 1979; Weir &
DeFries, 1963).

MATERNAL NUTRITION

This is usually not a problem in animal studies, since the same diet is
fed to all and the drug exposure period is short enough that biological
systems are not impaired. The exception may be alcohol, which prevents utilization of some nutrients (Wiener, 1980).

PAIR FEEDING OF DAMS

Toxic agents may interfere with maternal nutrition in two ways: by
interfering with the absorption of vital nutrients, and by decreasing
appetite to the point that the fetus may be undernourished. Control
dams are usually fed the same amount on a given day of gestation as is
consumed by drug-exposed dams. A control dam may be paired
according to weight on Day 1 of pregnancy with a drug-exposed dam,
or the mean amount consumed by all drug-exposed dams may be fed
to all control dams. The latter is easier to implement and seems to
work as well as the individual pairing providing the animals are
matched for weight before being assigned to groups.

FOSTERING AND CROSS-FOSTERING OF OFFSPRING

To separate intrauterine from extrauterine factors, the offspring should be fostered at birth to other than their natural mothers. There are several ways to accomplish this, including fostering all offspring to nontreated dams (Martin, Martin, Sigman, & Radow, 1978), fostering across all treatments (cross-fostering), and fostering some litters and leaving others to be raised by their natural mothers as a control. All such methods are time consuming, expensive, and fraught with difficulties, which is probably the reason these excellent procedures are not performed more often. After the initial study to separate prenatal from postnatal effects, it is probably not worth the time, effort, and expense to use the fostering technique in succeeding studies with the same drug.

OFFSPRING SUBJECT SELECTION

No more than two newborns (one male and one female) should be randomly selected from a litter for any single postweaning outcome measure (Vorhees, 1983). This reduces confounding of genetics and maternal caretaking to a minimum.

STATISTICAL CONSIDERATIONS

The unit of analysis should be based upon the litter rather than the number of individual animals if more than one male and one female per litter are tested, such as usually occurs with measures of growth and development. There are three reasons for this caveat: (1) Performance of individuals within a litter cannot be presumed to be independent of common genetic and intra- and extrauterine factors; (2) such common effects could either enhance or attenuate treatment effects; and (3) a large number of individual offspring from a small number of litters could result in a statistically significant result which would be not generalizable to the overall population. See Jensh, Brent, & Barr (1970), Weil (1970, 1975), Palmer (1975), and Holson, Scott, Gaylor, & Wilson (1976) for discussions of this issue.

METHODS OF TEST SELECTION

Clinical observation is based upon deficits observed in children or infants whose mothers ingested the agent during pregnancy. The problem is that multiple drug use is the rule with humans, and it may be difficult to isolate the effects of one drug. Correlation with neurochemical or neurophysiological deficits is based upon laboratory measurements that implicate a particular area of the brain, such as the hippocampus. If it is suspected that more than one functional system will be impaired or if no clinical or neural hypotheses are forthcoming, then a behavioral screen which samples different systems of behavior may be the choice. Although such a system has little scientific validity, it is pragmatic and may yield much useful information. Vorhees (1983) describes such techniques, which may sample reflexes, developmental milestones, sensory systems, activity, and simple and complex learning. Our own research has utilized both clinical observation and neurophysiological clues.

Psychoactive Drugs and Animal Models

The research I am going to describe is limited to two drugs from each of two pharmacological classes: nicotine and amphetamine, which are both central nervous system stimulants and antidepressants; the barbiturates, which are classed as sedative-hypnotics or anticonvulsants and central nervous system depressants, and alcohol, which is also a sedative-hypnotic.

NICOTINE

Nicotine is the most toxic of the more than 1,500 components of tobacco and is the addictive agent in cigarettes (Jarvik, 1973; Henningfield & Jasinski, 1983). It is a classic cholinergic agonist that has marked effects on the central nervous system owing to its close structural similarity to the neurochemical transmitter acetylcholine (Domino & Jasinski, 1983). It readily crosses the placenta to accumulate in fetal tissues (Mosier & Jansons, 1972). Fetal and placental concentrations are high up to 60 min postinjection and drop to a very low level again by 4 hr (Tjalve, Hansson, & Schmiterlow, 1968). Nicotine is excreted in mammalian milk, and the nursing infant is thereby doubly compromised (Perlman & Dannenberg, 1942). Nicotine induces a marked and protracted reduction in blood flow in the oviduct and uterus which may alter the amount of oxygen available to the fetus (Hammer & Mitchell, 1979).

Amphetamine, a psychomotor stimulant, is a sympathomimetic drug which exerts its effects by releasing the neurotransmitter noradrenaline from stores and blocking its re-uptake into neurons (Caldwell, 1980). In addition, at higher concentrations it releases dopamine and 5-hydroxytryptamine and blocks their re-uptake. The latter effect may result in hallucinations and psychotic behavior (Weiner, 1972). Since amphetamine has an anorectic effect, it has been prescribed for weight loss during pregnancy (Milkovich & Van den Berg, 1977).

Transplacental studies have documented transient increases in brain catecholamines (Middaugh, Blackwell, and Zemp, 1971) and increased numbers of anomalies at high doses (Kasirsky & Tansy, 1971). In addition to increases in brain catecholamines and anomalies, functional deficits observed in rodent offspring include increased voluntary activity (Middaugh et al., 1971; Seliger, 1973; Martin & Martin, 1981). Adams et al. (1982) reported increased sensitivity to later challenge doses of the drug and slower maze learning.

Alcohol is the oldest known drug of the sedative-hypnotic class and has its most marked effect on the central nervous sytem. It is a profound CNS depressant with some initial stimulatory properties, especially at low doses. With increased doses, the disruption of the inhibitory centers is followed by depression of excitatory centers in the cortex. Alcohol is oxidized almost exclusively by the liver, and blood levels in the rat have returned to zero within 4 hr at a moderate dose (2.5 g/kg) and by 7.5 hr at 5.0 g/kg (Wendell & Thurman, 1979). It readily crosses the placenta, and high blood levels are achieved more rapidly in gravid than in nongravid rats. It is also eliminated more rapidly by pregnant than by nonpregnant animals, and levels are negligible after 1 hr. The fetal concentrations peak more slowly than maternal levels but are excreted as rapidly (Kaufman & Woollam, 1981).

Barbituric acid was first synthesized in 1864, and there are now 2,500 derivatives of that compound. These barbiturates are usually classified by the duration of their action. The "ultrashort" acting ones include sodium thiamylal (Surital) and sodium thiopental (Pentothal), which are used primarily as anesthetics. The "short to intermediate" acting drugs are amobarbital (Amytal), sodium pento-barbital (Nembutal), and secobarbital (Seconal), which are used as sedative-hypnotic agents. The "long" acting barbiturates are pheno-barbital (Luminal) and methabarbital (Gemonil), and these are used principally as anticonvulsant agents (National Institute of Mental Health, 1974). Those in the last group are most likely to be prescribed for pregnant women.

Phenobarbital is partly metabolized and partly excreted un-changed in urine. In humans its half-life for disappearance from plas-ma is from 53 to 140 hr (Maynert, 1972). The drug accumulates in the body due to its slow rates of biotransformation and renal clearance.

Although anticonvulsant drugs readily cross the placenta and there is good evidence that diphenylhydantoin and trimethadione are teratogenic in humans, the evidence for phenobarbital and pento-barbital is not compelling except at doses 3–18 times therapeutic levels (Schardein, 1976; Sullivan and McElhatton, 1977).

A reduction in the numbers of Purkinje cells in cerebellum and hippocampus have been found in the immature young of rodents which received phenobarbital during pregnancy (Yanai, Woolf, & Feigenbaum, 1982). The same laboratory also noted mitochondrial and myelin sheath degeneration in the brains of these offspring and postulated a hormonal causal factor (Fishman, Ornoy, & Yanai, 1983). Gupta, Yaffe, & Shapiro (1982) exposed rats to phenobarbital during the late prenatal period and found decreased testosterone in the males during the fetal, postnatal, pubertal, and adult periods. Their conclusion was that altered programming in the brain may re-sult in permanent changes in testicular function.

Studies from Our Laboratory

NICOTINE

In 1967 Duke University anatomist Fred Becker and I began a series of studies using rats to investigate the behavioral consequences to offspring of maternal nicotine exposure during pregnancy. To date we have published 11 reports in this area. Although the experimental parameters have varied to some extent, our methodology has varied little over the years, except in the early studies where we were estab-lishing dose response curves, timing parameters, and performance measures. We were primarily interested in a maternal dose that would mimic the physiological and morphological changes found in the newborn infants of women who smoke heavily, including lighter weight newborns, an increased likelihood of stillbirth and neonatal death, and developmental delay (Becker, Little, & King, 1968; Becker & Martin, 1971). Since rats are considerably less sensitive to the effects of nicotine than are humans, we found it necessary to administer larger doses than human smokers received to achieve the same effects. The dose we empirically determined to yield these same physiological effects was 3.0 mg/kg twice daily, which we administered for the entire 21-day gestational period. Increasing the dose to conform to weight gain during pregnancy had no additional effect on offspring viability and maternal caretaking and hence was discontinued after the first study (Becker & Martin, 1971). Maintaining a constant dose also more nearly approximated the human condition, since a pregnant smoker does not increase her intake as her weight increases over pregnancy. Indeed, there is evidence that some women smoke fewer cigarettes during this period (Hook, 1976).

Studies of the vital and developmental effects of maternal nicotine absorption on Sprague-Dawley rats performed five years and a continent apart yielded remarkably similar results. Nicotine administered either during pregnancy or during pregnancy and the nursing period increased gestational length: typically to 24 or 25 days rather than the normal 22-day period found with saline-exposed controls. Smaller maternal weight gain and significantly lighter individual birth and neonatal weights were found as well (Martin & Becker, 1971; Martin, Martin, Radow, & Sigman, 1976). There were fewer liveborn young and an increased neonatal death rate in the studies at Duke, but not in the replications at the University of Washington, although the trend was in the same direction. The discrepancy may have been partially due to the superior housing conditions at the latter site, where the rooms are equipped with separate cubicles, each with its own temperature and humidity controls and air-exchange system. This greatly lessened the chance of airborne infections and provided more uniform conditions.

We found increased locomotor activity in prepubertal male offspring whose dams received nicotine during gestation and nursing. These were short sessions over a 10-day period. During the second 5-day period, the control offspring acclimated to the activity wheel and reduced their activity level, but the nicotine-exposed rats increased their activity and showed no evidence of habituation (Martin & Becker, 1970). A second study examined locomotor activity over the life span in these offspring beginning at maturity (90 days of age) and continuing at monthly intervals until 35 months of age or death. The animals were confined overnight in the wheels. The nicotine-exposed offspring were slightly but not significantly more active over the life span than saline-exposed controls. On the other hand, methamphetamine-exposed offspring exhibited significantly greater activity over the entire life span than either nicotine- or saline-exposed control rats. This study is discussed below in the section on amphetamines. We found increased activity as a result of intrauterine and neonatal exposure to nicotine to be a transient phenomenon which disappeared at maturity.

We performed one long-term sensory study on male rats whose mothers had received either nicotine or methamphetamine during the perinatal period. The offspring were tested on six concentrations of saccharin solution, each paired with plain water, over 36 months. Both drug treatments permanently altered the pattern of choice for the saccharin solutions. The amount of fluid consumed was not affected. These changes were not due to handling or injection per se, since the offspring of saline-injected dams did not differ in their choices from offspring whose mothers had not been injected. The mechanism for such irreversible changes is not known. Since there were no differences in life span as a consequence of perinatal treatment, the results could not be ascribed to the rats' being sick or moribund (Martin, Martin, Sigman, & Day-Pfeiffer, 1983).

Reflex development, motor control, and normal maturation were measured in newborns from birth to Day 28 in the Washington study. These measures were always taken blind by two individuals not involved in caretaking duties, since many of the tests require subjective evaluation. Although Krsiak (1973) had found some developmental delay in nicotine-exposed offspring, the significant changes in our study were in the methamphetamine-exposed group.

We tested the rat offspring on several simple appetitive schedules in environmental chambers beginning at 6 weeks of age and continuing through maturity. An animal had to press and release one or two bars to receive a food reward. The amount of work expended on such schedules and the satiation level are influenced by body weight, which in turn may be altered by prenatal drug exposure. Nicotine- and amphetamine-exposed offspring usually weigh less than saline-exposed animals, and in the case of methamphetamine animals the decrement may be irreversible. Weight should not be a factor, however, on schedules which require a slowed rate of response (DRL) or pauses (VI). In our studies, the rats whose dams had received nicotine during gestation and lactation were slower to learn a schedule which required a response on the particular bar that was paired with a distinctive tone and light. It is possible that it took them longer to learn to attend to multiple stimuli. Subsequently they learned to perform as well as controls, but when the stimuli were reversed so that the tone and light previously associated with the right bar were now associated with the left bar and vice versa, the nicotine-exposed offspring made fewer appropriate responses and hence received fewer reinforcements. They tended to perseverate with the old, now unrewarded responses. Similar inflexibility has been found with brain-damaged organisms. These rats did in time learn to reverse the response on these schedules (Martin & Becker, 1971).

A result from our earlier study at Duke that was not replicated in the more nearly germ-free environment at Washington was a shorter life span in both groups of nicotine-exposed offspring. Half the animals exposed to nicotine during gestation and nursing had succumbed by 54 weeks of age, compared with a mean of 67 weeks for those that were exposed to nicotine during gestation only and 69 weeks for saline-exposed control offspring. All animals exposed to nicotine during gestation plus nursing periods were dead at 90 weeks of age, and all exposed during gestation only by 100 weeks. At 100 weeks, when the experiment was terminated, one third of the saline-treated control rats were still alive (Martin and Becker, 1972).

METHAMPHETAMINE

Repeated administration of methylamphetamine or d-amphetamine reportedly produces long-lasting decreases in central nervous system levels of dopamine and serotonin when administered to adult animals (Lucot, Wagner, Schuster, and Seiden, 1982). In an early study we had noted that maternal weight gain over the gestation period was negatively correlated with drug dose and that drug-exposed dams delivered their litters significantly earlier than did control animals (Martin, 1975). Erikkson in 1981 found that Swedish amphetamine addicts delivered prematurely. In our rat study, litter size decreased as a function of increasing drug dose, and eye opening was delayed in drug-exposed offspring. The rats whose dams had received the highest dose of methamphetamine, 5.0 mg/kg twice daily, made more avoidance responses, but not more escape responses, in the shuttle box than did either lower-dose drug-exposed rats or control rats. Since escape and avoidance responses are correlated— an avoidance response precludes an escape response on that trial— the results could equally well be attributed either to better learning of the contingencies or to hyperactivity. The 5.0 mg/kg dose is subteratogenic in the rat, as in the mouse and rabbit (Kasirsky and Tansy, 1971).

The longitudinal study performed at Washington and discussed in the section on nicotine included methamphetamine as one of the perinatal treatments. The amount injected into the gravid rat was 5.0 mg/kg twice daily, which was the effective subteratogenic dose in that earlier study. We replicated the shorter gestations and lower maternal weight gain found earlier. In addition, the methamphetamine-exposed offspring remained underweight from birth through weaning and late maturity. Eye opening was delayed, which we had also found earlier. Methamphetamine-exposed offspring were significantly more active in the wheel than were either nicotine- or saline-exposed offspring. Differences were found starting at 3 months of age and thereafter at monthly intervals, with a few exceptions up to 36 months, at which time few animals remained alive (Martin, Martin, Radow, & Sigman, 1976). Differences in voluntary locomotor activity were especially evident in late maturity from 13 to 36 months, since activity had dropped off markedly in the control group (Martin and Martin, 1981).

Free-feeding littermates of these animals were weighed monthly from birth to death. Methamphetamine-exposed offspring remained significantly underweight from 5 to 16 months of age, after which differences no longer were significant (Martin, Martin, Radow, & Day, 1979). The mechanism for this long-lasting increase in activity has been linked to a hypothesized irreversible change in the concentration of brain catecholamines. Tonge (1973) found increased noradrenaline and dopamine in hippocampus, hypothalamus, and cortex in 9-month-old Wistar rats whose mothers had received methamphetamine during pregnancy. Middaugh, Blackwell, and Zemp (1971) found higher levels of norepinephrine in the brains of 30-day-old mice whose dams received d-amphetamine during the latter part of gestation. The young mice were characterized by bursts of nondirected activity and increased grooming behaviors. Nasello and Ramirez (1978) found increased catecholamine turnover but no increase in catecholamine levels in similarly treated male rat offspring. In summary, although the direction of behavioral and biochemical change is not always consistent in the cited studies, all have found that administering amphetamine during pregnancy alters some facet of brain catecholamines and thus affects activity.

The methamphetamine-exposed offspring in our study developed significantly more tumors in middle and late maturity than did either the nicotine-exposed, saline-exposed, or untreated offspring. The group which went to autopsy was small, and these results should be replicated before much faith is placed in them.

Taste preferences for sweet solutions were altered in nicotine- and methamphetamine-exposed offspring in middle and late maturity (15 to 36 months) relative to the two control groups. The trauma of maternal injection per se also had some effect, since the saline-exposed rats differed from the stock offspring whose dams had been weighed daily as had all other dams but had never been injected. That was the first study to our knowledge which has shown lifetime alterations in sensory choices as a function of perinatal treatment (Martin, Martin, Sigman, & Day-Pfeiffer, 1983).

In summary, maternal methamphetamine exposure appears to exert an even greater effect on development, growth, and function in offspring than does nicotine exposure, at least under the conditions which prevailed in these studies. These changes appear to be irreversible.

BARBITURATES

Our barbiturate studies have been limited to phenobarbital (Luminal) and pentobarbital (Nembutal), selected as representative of the longer- and shorter-acting barbiturates. Sodium phenobarbital inhibits mitochondrial oxidative energy metabolism, and such drugs have been found to produce congenital malformations (Mackler et al., 1975).

We initially studied sodium phenobarbital alone at maternal doses of 0, 40, and 80 mg/kg/day with injections begun on Day 9 of pregnancy to insure that implantation had occurred. The two drug-exposed groups delivered a day later than saline controls. Nicotine-injected dams have always delivered significantly later as well, whereas methamphetamine dams deliver earlier.

We found an interesting U-shaped function on some of the developmental measures, with the lower-level phenobarbital-exposed offspring developing more rapidly than controls, which in turn developed more rapidly than offspring exposed to the higher drug dose. Middaugh, Santos, and Zemp (1975) found a similar inversion in activity measures in mouse offspring which received the same drug doses we used. Other investigators have found similar performance inversions at low levels of alcohol (Vincent, 1958) and handling (Dennenberg & Karas, 1960). This bidirectional relationship, in which lesser amounts of a maternal stressor result in faster or more efficient performance in the offspring, is a curious and not always replicable phenomenon that has been attributed to "lessened emotionality." There is little direct evidence for that attribution.

Escape, but not avoidance, responses in the shuttle box were negatively correlated with increasing phenobarbital dose. Since methamphetamine-exposed offspring in one of our earlier studies had made a significantly greater number of responses in the same paradigm, it is possible that the results may be specific to the class of drugs, that is, activators versus sedatives (Martin, Martin, Lemire, & Mackler, 1979).

The offspring were tested on fixed-ratio concurrent schedules (FR-10/20) on which reinforcement was available on both bars but with a different ratio requirement on each. Both the drug- and saline-exposed offspring initially spent 70–75% of the time on the low-ratio bar. When the ratio between the bars was reversed, the drug-exposed groups raised their time on the low ratio bar to 80–90% whereas the saline-exposed offspring dropped to 64%. In spite of this, the saline-exposed offspring garnered as many reinforcements as the drug-exposed offspring. One might hypothesize that the drug renders the animals less able to expend effort so they are motivated to seek easier routes. The saline-exposed offspring may also have been obtaining all the reinforcements they could consume with the 60/40 division between bars and were not motivated to change. The offspring exposed to high drug doses were significantly less able to inhibit early responses on the DRL schedules, which reward a slow response rate, and as a consequence they made more late responses as well. Inability to inhibit responses has been linked to brain damage.

The next study added pentobarbital as a treatment condition, since it is a shorter-acting barbiturate. This study was designed to expand upon the previous one, which found a dose-response function in the conditioned avoidance paradigm (shuttle box) following maternal phenobarbital administration. We hypothesized that adult offspring which had been prenatally exposed to barbiturates might be less able to tolerate stress (shock).

There were procedural differences between the two studies. Since pentobarbital in utero, but not phenobarbital, results in underweight offspring relative to controls, we decided to pair-feed all groups to the high-dose pentobarbital-exposed dams to maintain identical conditions between treatments. The dose-response avoidance curve was obtained with pentobarbital in the shuttle box, with escape responses negatively correlated with increasing drug dose. The higher dose of phenobarbital resulted in decreased numbers of escapes as well, but the low-level phenobarbital-exposed group did not differ significantly from controls, so this facet was not replicated from the first study.

We attempted to separate learning from performance factors with the two-way conditioned avoidance task described above, which measured learning (acquisition), and two operant schedules which measured steady-state behavior (performance). The discriminated Sidman avoidance schedule with tone and light cues was similar to the shuttle box in that both measured escape and avoidance to experimenter-initiated cued shock. The punishment schedule had the same shock levels as the modified Sidman, but it measured appetitive behavior with subject-initiated shock. The rat had to initiate shock in order to have access to pellet reinforcers.

The high-dose phenobarbital-exposed offspring made the fewest escape responses on the Sidman initially, whereas the low-dose phenobarbital-exposed and the saline-exposed offspring made the greatest number. All four drug groups outperformed the controls on the punishment schedule at the higher levels of shock. As a consequence they received more shock-contingent reinforcement.

These results seem to suggest that intrauterine exposure to barbiturates alters responsivity to shock and that it is performance, not learning, that is affected. In addition, the value of food reinforcement may be higher for the drug-exposed animals, since they initiated more shock-on periods than controls on the punishment schedule, whereas they had performed more poorly in escaping the same shock levels on the other two tasks. The brains were removed and weighed at the completion of the study when the rats were almost a year old. The two pentobarbital groups had significantly lower brain body weight ratios on a blind analysis. There were no differences between the two phenobarbital-exposed groups and controls. The phenobarbital-exposed offspring were the only animals that had a significant number of neonatal deaths, and it is possible that only the most nearly normal animals with normal brains survived to maturity.

In summary, the shorter-acting barbiturate, pentobarbital, resulted in lighter brains compared with body weight, early transient hyperactivity, and lowered efficiency in escaping environmentally initiated shock. The longer-acting phenobarbital resulted in poorer neonatal survival and a higher rate of activity which seemed to be a permanent alteration (Martin et al. 1984).

ALCOHOL

Ethanol is not a concentrated drug as are nicotine, methamphetamine, and the barbiturates, and injection alone is not a feasible method of administration. Alcohol has been administered to gravid animals by intubation or gavage, by injection, and in various dietary solutions as well as in plain and sweetened water. It is difficult to administer more than 8–10 g/day by injection, which amounts to 9–10 K/cal of alcohol. In addition subcutaneous injections cause depilation and sores at the site of needle entry. Intubation is limited to a 20–25% ethanol solution, since gastric hemorrhage has resulted with higher concentrations. This limits the total amount which can be administered, since the procedure itself is stressful and two intubations a day is enough. We have managed 8.5 g/kg, or 20 K/cal, by this method. Alcohol in a 0.1% saccharin solution is palatable to the rat at concentrations of 3–10% and drinkable at a concentration of 20%. We have achieved 11.9 g/kg or 28.3 K/cal by offering ethanol in a saccharin solution as the sole fluid source. When 10% ethanol is given in a total liquid diet such as Ensure, Metrecal, or Sustacal, large amounts of alcohol are consumed steadily over the day (14.6 g/kg or 27.6 K/cal). The liquid diet should be supplemented with vitamins and minerals if one of the diets designed for human use is selected (Martin, Martin, Radow, & Sigman, 1978).

The method of administration should be chosen to fit the study objectives. If episodic or "binge" drinking is the goal, then intubation is preferable to giving oral solutions of ethanol in drinking water or total liquid diets. The rats ingest the ethanol solutions more slowly, resulting in lower blood alcohol levels with little evidence of addiction as defined by withdrawal symptoms. Consumption of the total liquid diet is more evenly dispersed throughout the 24-hr period (Martin, Martin, Radow, & Sigman, 1978), although consumption of both oral solutions is somewhat elevated at night. Binge drinking at moderate rather than high consumption levels can be studied by any method by simply limiting access to specified time periods.

Alcohol ingestion during pregnancy retards delivery in the rat. We have never failed to replicate this result. This is not unexpected, because alcohol has been used to retard premature labor in the human (Castr, Gummerous, & Saarikoski, 1975). Administering alcohol in the drinking water or in a liquid diet results in smaller maternal weight gains and underweight offspring (Martin, Martin, Radow, & Sigman, 1978; Martin, Martin, Sigman, & Radow, 1977), but this is not true of the intubation method (Martin, Martin, Sigman, & Radow, 1978). It is a good idea to pair-feed the control dams to the ethanol dams when the oral methods are used so as to have equal degrees of fetal undernutrition. This method does not control for the effects of undernutrition: that would require an ad lib control group of dams.

One of our studies which employed pair-feeding examined the effects of ethanol during gestation and lactation and during lactation alone. As might have been expected, offspring exposed to alcohol during gestation and nursing (AGN offspring) were the most affected functionally. This could have been because they were exposed to more alcohol than were those exposed only during nursing (AN offspring). Both ethanol groups experienced greater neonatal mortality and were significantly underweight compared with their pair-fed controls at 72 days of age. All the offspring had been placed on free-feeding at weaning on Day 23.

Eye opening was delayed in the two alcohol groups, and even with weight co-varied these animals initially obtained fewer reinforcements on fixed-ratio schedules. The AGN offspring also performed more poorly on the continuous reinforcement (FR-1) schedule, but they outperformed the other groups initially on a schedule that required a slowed rate of response (DRL). A striking difference was found on the punishment schedule, on which the animals initiated shock-on periods to obtain access to reinforcement. At the highest level of shock, which at 0.25 mA was not very high, the AGN rats ceased to discriminate the contingencies and responded to the food bar during shock-off periods. They had responded appropriately at lower shock levels, but the higher shock level disrupted their behavior.

We found failure to thrive and some developmental delay as a consequence of alcohol administration both during the entire perinatal period and during nursing alone. The AGN offspring were also slower to learn simple appetitive schedules, although they caught up later, and their behavior broke down completely on subject-initiated shock at higher levels (Martin, Martin, Sigman, & Radow, 1977).

One striking feature of Fetal Alcohol Syndrome children is their excessive and inappropriate activity level. We administered ethanol or saline solution to pregnant rats, then fostered half the offspring at birth to nonhandled dams which had delivered a litter within a day or two of the other two groups. Both the cross-fostered and the naturally reared offspring were significantly more active at 60 days of age than were the equivalent two groups whose mothers had received saline intubation. Offspring showed no significant weight differences either at birth or thereafter, probably because the mothers received relatively small amounts of ethanol with this method. This was direct evidence that intrauterine alcohol exposure was responsible for the early hyperactivity of the offspring, rather than any difference in maternal caretaking (Martin, Martin, Sigman, & Radow, 1978).

Fetal exposure to alcohol resulted in quite different offspring behaviors than exposure to barbiturates even though both are classified as sedatives. Alcohol exposure results in underweight offspring which were the product of longer gestations and that showed hyperactivity as juveniles, slower learning on simple appetitive tasks— with the exception of the DRL, which they learned more rapidly— and poorer tolerance of one form of stress (shock). The barbiturate-exposed offspring also were delivered later, but development proceeded faster at the lower dosage of phenobarbital. The barbiturate-exposed offspring performed more poorly on the DRL, showing an inability to delay the response, but performed at a higher level than controls on subject-initiated shock schedules. Since alcohol is a known teratogen whereas phenobarbital and pentobarbital have not been proven to be, ethanol may cause greater and more lasting central nervous system deficits at subteratogenic levels.

DRUG INTERACTIONS

Almost 23% of women who were classified as moderate to heavy drinkers also smoked cigarettes in a Seattle sample of 1,500 unselected pregnancies at two hospitals (Streissguth, Martin, Martin, & Barr, 1981b). As I stated earlier, multiple drug use is the norm rather than the exception for pregnant women. We designed a study to examine the interactive effects of nicotine and alcohol exposure in utero in the rat. The nicotine was injected, and the ethanol was given as 10% of a total liquid diet (Ensure). The alcohol-, nicotine-, and saline-exposed groups were pair-fed to the nicotine-alcohol-exposed (NIC-

ALC) dams during gestation. The offspring were studied until 15 months of age, which is middle maturity in the rat.

The NIC-ALC group suffered significantly more stillbirths and neonatal deaths than did the other three groups. The surviving NIC-ALC offspring were developmentally accelerated on several neonatal measures, including ear opening, righting from a vertical drop, eye opening, and forward movement. They were also more active on an activity platform neonatally, as were the alcohol-exposed litters. The nicotine- and saline-exposed offspring did not differ in activity level.

This hyperactivity of the NIC-ALC offspring was reversed at maturity, and they made significantly fewer voluntary turns in the activity wheel from 6 to 15 months of age, particularly during the last three months of that test.

The animals were trained on an operant punishment schedule when they were 4–6 months of age, and the NIC-ALC rats initiated fewer shock-on periods and hence obtained fewer reinforcements. They caught up to the other rats by the fourth week on this schedule. Nicotine, a drug which excites central nervous system neurons, and alcohol, which depresses neural firing, when combined and administered maternally caused effects that were not predictable for either alone. Since pregnant women tend to take combinations of drugs, additional studies of animal models of drug interactions are needed. These should employ a variety of levels of the drugs which are commonly combined by women. Caffeine, nicotine, and alcohol are abused together, as are marijuana and nicotine and barbiturates and amphetamines ("downers" and "uppers").

In summary, as I stated previously, alcohol administered in utero causes underweight offspring which exhibit hyperactivity, slower learning on simple tasks, and poorer tolerance to stress (shock). When nicotine is added to the alcohol, the hyperactivity in early life becomes hypoactivity at maturity, concomitant with a lessened ability to perform on subject-initiated shock schedules (Martin, Martin, Chao, & Shores, 1982).

To summarize our studies on the four drugs, gestation periods are lengthened after administration of the three sedatives and nicotine, thus increasing the probability of fetal distress. There are increased numbers of neonatal deaths with all drugs except pentobarbital, where we found no change from control levels. Neonatal growth was retarded with all drugs except phenobarbital. This measure is highly correlated with maternal weight gain, and phenobarbital is the only drug we tested that did not have a detrimental effect on either appetite or food absorption. Growth of offspring is still retarded at maturity after methamphetamine and alcohol exposure. The nicotine-exposed animals catch up with controls. Neonatal development is retarded on some or all measures for all drugs except nicotine. There is an indication that low doses of phenobarbital enhance development so that the offspring reach developmental milestones sooner. Neonatal hyperactivity was found for all drugs except phenobarbital. Mature hyperactivity was especially evident in methamphetamine- and alcohol-exposed offspring. Nicotine- and pentobarbital-exposed offspring outgrew the high activity levels they had exhibited neonatally.

Offspring exposed to methamphetamine, phenobarbital, pentobarbital, and alcohol offspring were tested on environmentally controlled shock. All except the latter group had difficulty coping with the shock. The alcohol-exposed groups did have trouble with subject-initiated shock schedules. It may well be that one of the major effects of drugs in utero is to lessen the ability of the offspring to cope with stress. If replicable in humans, these results could have profound implications for children exposed to such drugs in utero.

In addition, our nicotine- and alcohol-exposed offspring initially had greater difficulty in learning simple schedules with food as a reinforcer. It is not clear whether this slowed rate of learning is due to motivational factors or to slight intellectual deficits. Since the alcohol-exposed offspring performed better initially on schedules which rewarded a slower rate of response, it may be that they were physically less well coordinated than control animals, which in most learning situations would result in apparent learning deficits. Table 1 lists the results of our studies for all drugs.

In conclusion, it is difficult to find any merit for the ingestion of even moderate quantities of the psychoactive drugs nicotine, alcohol, and amphetamine during pregnancy. Phenobarbital had less obvious detrimental effects and was the only drug of the five, if one includes pentobarbital, whose clinical usefulness may outweigh the possible fetal problems. There is of course no clinical justification for the first three drugs.

Sex Ratio Change following Perinatal Drug Exposure

This topic never fails to stimulate controversy whenever it is reported. Theoretically, a shift in sex ratio could occur through either

Table 1
Comparison of Effects of Maternal Drug Exposure

	Nicotine	Methamphetamine	Phenobarbital	Pentobarbital	Alcohol
Maternal measures					
Weight gain	<	<	<, No	<, No	<
Gestation length	>	<	>, No	No	>
Neonatal measures					
Stillbirths	>	N.A.	>	No	No
Birth weight	<	<	<, No	No	<
Litter size	<, No	<, No	No	No	No
Sex ratio	No	No	No, >	No	No
Deaths (1–4 days)	>, No	No	>	No	No
Deaths (4–28 days)	>, No	No	>	No	>
Growth	<	<	<, No	<	<
Development	No	<	>	>	>
Activity	N.A.	N.A.	>, No	>	>
Mature measures (3–24 months)					
Activity	>	>	>	No	N.A.

Table 1 *continued*

	Nicotine	Methamphetamine	Phenobarbital	Pentobarbital	Alcohol
Mature measures (3–24 months)					
Appetitive					
CRF–FR	<	N.A.	>	N.A.	<
DRL	No	N.A.	<	N.A.	>
VI	<	N.A.	N.A.	N.A.	N.A.
Aversive					
CAR	N.A.	>	<	<	N.A.
SID	N.A.	N.A.	<	<	No
PUN	N.A.	N.A.	>	>	<
Other	Change, taste preference	Change, taste preference	No	<, brain/ body weight	No
Old mature (24–36 months)					
Activity	No	>	N.A.	N.A.	N.A.
Perceptual	Change, taste preference		N.A.	N.A.	N.A.
Pathology	No	> tumors	N.A.	N.A.	N.A.
Life span	<, No	No	N.A.	N.A.	N.A.

maternal or paternal use of psychoactive drugs. In male exposure the drug could affect spermatogenesis, and Hemsworth (1981) demonstrated this result following prolonged nicotine exposure in the male rodent. Ethanol causes dominant lethal mutations at different stages of spermatogenesis (Bariliak & Kozachuk, 1981). There have been few studies on paternal drug use and consequences to offspring, and even fewer of these have reported the sex ratio as a measure. One genetic theory states that the same-sex offspring will be least affected by the exposure of either the mother or the father to noxious agents (Miller, 1969). If the same-sex offspring are least affected by exposure to noxious agents, then women who take drugs during all or part of pregnancy will tend to deliver more live female offspring.

It is known that adverse environmental conditions and declining maternal condition are correlated with fewer male births in humans and in deer (Trivers & Willard, 1973). The male fetus is also at greater risk and more likely to be aborted (Stevenson, 1966). Toivanen & Hirovnen (1970) found a preponderance of males born to women suffering from toxemia in pregnancy and postulated histoincompatibility of the male fetus and the mother as the cause. The authors studied only live births; presumably in the cases where toxemia was severe enough to result in habitual miscarriage, the only fetuses carried to term would be female, since histoincompatibility would not be a factor.

Sex ratios are not always reported in either human or animal studies of maternal drug ingestion, and the differences when reported do not always reach statistical significance. Considering the myriad factors that can affect sex ratios, this is not surprising. Some of the contingent variables include the predisposition of the male partner, whose X or Y chromosome determines the sex of the offspring; the health of the mother; the amount of drug ingested; and the mother's tendency to abort a fetus at risk.

The following studies which reported sex ratios were found in a recent search of the human and animal literature. A bibliography follows the discussion for those interested in the topic.

NICOTINE OR TOBACCO PRODUCTS

There were eight human and three animal studies in which mothers absorbed tobacco products during pregnancy. Fewer male than female births were reported in all eight of the human studies. This difference is even greater than it appears, since the human ratio is not 50/50 but is skewed slightly in favor of male births, with approximately 105 live males to every 100 females born in the United States. This result was also found in two of the three animal studies. Litters should be sexed at birth for this purpose, but sexing is not always done at that time.

ALCOHOL

Nine rodent studies reported sex ratios, and in seven of these fewer males were born. Prasad, Kaufman, & Prasad (1978), who combined diethylstilbestrol (DES) with alcohol, reported increased numbers of male mice (0.63 to 0.46). The only study on rabbits reported more male births rather than fewer. This may be a species difference. The one human study that reported the sex ratio noted that in a sample of 64 women drinkers the sex ratio was heavily skewed toward female births (0.34) (Qazi & Masakawa, 1976). Two of the reported studies contained some of the same children; when these were removed from the sample the differences were no longer significant, but the ratio was still in favor of females at 0.38. Abel (1979) totaled the results from 39 human studies on FAS and found a less impressive ratio, but one still in favor of females at 0.47.

AMPHETAMINE

We found fewer male births among methamphetamine-exposed offspring than among controls (0.49 to 0.53). I have located no other studies, animal or human, which reported the sex ratio.

OPIATES

Three human and two animal studies with heroin or methadone or both as agents all noted fewer male births. Two additional human studies included only drug addicts, with no control groups. One had a very low male/female ratio (0.29), and the other was within normal limits (0.54).

BARBITURATES

I found four studies using the rat as a model. Three of these reported fewer male births. The study that found fewer males with pentobarbital administration also found slightly more males with sodium barbital (0.70 to 0.68) (Armitage, 1952). We found a higher male/female ratio in one of our studies, but we also had very few males in the control group (0.39), so the results may not be reliable. In no cases have researchers reported on the usual ratio found for the strain of animals used in their laboratories. This is of crucial significance in these studies, since the results for any given study could be due to transient effects on the control group.

MULTIPLE DRUG USE

Two human reports on street drug abusers reported significantly lower numbers of male births (Poland, Wogan, & Calvin, 1972; Aase, Laestadius, & Smith, 1970). Poland studied 183 women and found a male/female ratio of 0.34 for drug users compared with 0.55 for controls. The second study was a clinical one of 10 LSD users, all of whom delivered female infants.

PATERNAL DRUG USE BEFORE PREGNANCY

Two early studies reported the effects of administering alcohol to male mice, and in both instances increased numbers of males were born, the expected result if the theory described earlier is true (Bluhm, 1924; Danforth, 1926). Klassen & Persaud (1976) also found an increased male/female ratio in rat offspring whose sires had received alcohol for 2–5 weeks before mating. Underwood, Kesler, O'Lane, & Callagan (1967) reported fewer male births in a human sample when both parents smoked, and Ravenholt, Levinski, & Nellist (1966), conversely, found fewer male births when the father smoked. Last, Weathersbee, & Lodge (1974) administered caffeine to male hamsters and found fewer male offspring instead of more.

Fetal viability and sex ratio can be influenced in several ways through paternal drug ingestion. There could be a direct mutagenic effect, a change in sperm motility resulting in differential effects on X and Y chromosomes, effects on various aspects of spermatogenesis, or a direct effect on the ovum to systemic drug absorption through the seminal fluid (Soyka & Joffe, 1980).

The rather inconclusive evidence indicates an alteration of the sex ratio in favor of females when the gravid animal or human ingests drugs. The evidence for paternal effects is much weaker. The difficulty with all the studies reported is that the sex ratio has seldom been an end in itself, but merely has been reported as additional information. Carefully controlled studies designed to examine sex ratio as a consequence of different drugs and drug combinations across a range of doses in several animal models are needed before any firm conclusions can be drawn.

The references include the studies from which the statistics above are taken, plus additional articles of interest.

REFERENCES

Sex Ratios

Aase, J. M., Laestadius, N., & Smith, D. W. (1970). Children of mothers who took LSD in pregnancy. *Lancet, 1,* 100–101.

Abel, E. L. (1979). Sex ratio in fetal alcohol syndrome [Letter to the Editor]. *Lancet,* 2:105.

Abrams, C. A. L. (1975). Cytogenic risks to the offspring of pregnant addicts. *Addictive Diseases: An International Journal, 2,* 63–77.

Armitage, S. G. (1952). Effects of barbiturates on the behavior of rat offspring as measured in learning and reasoning situations. *Journal of Comparative Physiology and Psychology, 45,* 146–152.

Bariliak, I. R. , & Kozachuk, S. I. (1981). Effect of ethanol on the genetic apparatus of mammalian germ cells. *Tsitologiya i Genetica, 15,* 29–32.

Becker, R. F. & Martin, J. C. (1971). Vital effects of chronic nicotine absorption and chronic hypoxic stress during pregnancy and the nursing period. *American Journal of Obstetrics and Gynecology, 110,* 522–533.

Bluhm, A. (1924). Über einige Versuche, bei Säugetieren das Zahlenverhältnis der Geschlechter zu beeinflussen [some experiments designed to influence the sex ratio in mammals]. *Arch. Rass. -u GesBiol., 16,* 1–28.

Buckalew, L. W. (1977). Developmental and behavioral effects of maternal and fetal neonatal alcohol exposure. *Research Communications in Psychology, Psychiatry and Behavior, 2,* 179–191.

Chen, J. J., & Smith, E. R. (1979). Effects of perinatal alcohol on sexual differentiation and open-field behavior in rats. *Hormones and Behavior, 13,* 219-231.

Crawford, J. S. (1973). Pre-pregnancy oral contraceptives and respiratory distress syndrome. *Lancet, 1,* 858-860.

Danforth, C. H. (1926). Alcohol and the sex ratio in mice. *Proceedings of the Society for Experimental Biology, 23,* 305-308.

Dinges, D. F., Davis, M. M., & Glass, P. (1980). Fetal exposure to narcotics: Neonatal sleep as a measure of nervous system disturbance. *Science, 209,* 619-621.

Fraumeni, J. F., Jr., & Lundin, F. E., Jr. (1964). Smoking and pregnancy, *Lancet, 1,* 173.

Frazier, J. M., Davis, G. H., Goldstein, H., & Goldberg, I. D. (1961). Cigarette smoking and prematurity: A prospective study. *American Journal of Obstetrics and Gynecology, 81,* 988-996.

Harper, R. C., Solish, G. I., Purow, H. M., Sang, E., & Panepinto, W. C. (1974). Effect of a methadone treatment program upon pregnant heroin addicts and their newborn infants. *Pediatrics, 54,* 300-305.

Harrison, K. L. & McKenna, H. (1977). Effect of maternal smoking on cord blood erythrocytes. *Australian and New Zealand Journal of Obstetrics and Gynaecology* 17, 160-162.

Hemsworth, B. N. (1981). Deformation of the mouse foetus after ingestion of nicotine by the male. *IRCS Journal of Medical Science, 9,* 728-729.

Herriot, A., Billewicz, W.Z., & Hytten, F. E. (1962). Cigarette smoking in pregnancy. *Lancet, 1,* 771-773.

Ikeda, H. (1982). Pharmacological studies on the functional development of the CNS in first generation rats born to phenytoin-treated mothers. *Folia Pharmacologia Japonica, 79,* 65-76.

Kerseru, T. L., Maraz, A., & Szabo, J. (1974). Oral contraception and sex ratio at birth [Letter to the Editor]. *Lancet, 1,* 369.

Kizer, S. (1967). Influencia del habito de fumar sobre el embarazo, parto y recien nacido. *Revista de Obstetricia y Ginecologia de Venezuela, 27,* 595-643.

Klassen, R. W., & Persaud, T. V. N. (1976). Experimental studies on the influence of male alcoholism on pregnancy and progeny. *Experimental Pathology, 12,* 38-45.

Krishna, K. (1978). Tobacco chewing in pregnancy. *British Journal of Obstetrics and Gynaecology, 85,* 726-728.

Lodge, A., Marcus, M. M., & Ramer, C. M. (1975). Behavioral and electrophysiological characteristics of the addicted neonate. *Addictive Diseases: An International Journal, 2,* 235-255.

MacMahon, B., Alpert, M., & Salber, E. J. (1966). Infant weight and parental smoking habits. *American Journal of Epidemiology, 82,* 247-261.

Martin, J. C., Martin, D. C., Lemire, R., & Mackler, B. (1979). Effects of maternal absorption of phenobarbital upon rat offspring development and function. *Journal of Neurobehavioral Toxicolology and Teratology, 1,* 49-55.

Martin, J. C., Martin, D. C., Radow, B., & Sigman, G. (1976). Growth, development and activity in rat offspring following maternal drug exposure. *Experimental Aging Research, 2,* 235–252.

Martin, J. C., Martin, D. C., Sigman, G., & Radow, B. (1977). Offspring survival, development, and operant performance following maternal ethanol consumption. *Developmental Psychobiology, 10,* 435–446.

McGinty, J. F., & Ford, D. H. (1976). Effects of maternal morphine or methadone intake on growth, reflex development and maze behavior of rat offspring. In D. H. Ford & D. H. Clovet (Eds.), *Tissue responses to addictive drugs* (pp. 611–629). New York: Spectrum.

Miller, R. W. (1969). Delayed radiation effects in atomic-bomb survivors. *Science, 166,* 569–574.

Peters, D. A. V., & Tang, S. (1982). Sex-dependent biological changes following prenatal nicotine exposure in the rat. *Pharmology, Biochemistry and Behavior, 17,* 1077–1082.

Poland, B. J., Wogan, L., & Calvin, J. (1972). Teenagers, illicit drugs and pregnancy. *Canadian Medical Association Journal, 107,* 955–958.

Prasad, R., Kaufman, R. H., & Prasad, N. (1978). Effect of maternal alcohol exposure on fetal ovarian lactate dehydrogenase. *Obstetrics and Gynecology, 52,* 318–320.

Qazi, Q. H., & Masakawa, A. (1976). Altered sex ratio in fetal alcohol syndrome. *Lancet, 2,* 42.

Ravn, J. (1974–75). Pregnancy and progeny after long-term contraceptive treatment with low-dose pregestogens. *Curr. Med. Res. Opin., 2,* 616–619.

Rementeria, J. L., & Lotoghkum, L. (1977). The fetus of the drug-addicted woman: Conception, fetal wastage, and complications. In *Drugs of abuse in pregnancy and neonatal effects* (pp. 3–18). St. Louis: C. V. Mosby.

Russell, C. S., Taylor, R., & Law, C. E. (1968). Smoking in pregnancy, maternal blood pressure, pregnancy outcome, baby weight and growth, and other related factors. *British Journal of Preventive and Social Medicine, 22,* 119–126.

Schwetz, B. A., Smith, F. A., & Staples, R. E. (1978). Teratogenic potential of ethanol in mice, rats, and rabbits. *Teratology, 18,* 385–392.

Sherwin, B. T., Jacobson, S., Troxwell, S. L., Rogers, A. E., & Pelham, R. W. (1980). A rat model (using a semi-purified diet) of FAS. In M. Galanter (Ed.), *Currents in alcoholism: Recent advances in research and treatment* (pp. 15–29).

Soyka, L. F., & Joffe, J. M. (1980). Male mediated drug effects on offspring. In H. Schwarz & S. Yaffe (Eds.), *Drugs and chemical risks to the fetus and newborn,* (pp. 49–66). New York: Alan Liss.

Stevenson, A. C. (1966). Sex chromatin and the sex ratio in man. In K. L. Moore (Ed.), *The sex chromatin.* Philadelphia: Saunders.

Terris, M., & Gold, E. M. (1969). An epidemiologic study of prematurity. I.

Relation to smoking, heart volume, employment and physique. *American Journal of Obstetrics and Gynecology, 103*, 358-370.

Toivanen, P., & Hirvonen, T. (1970). Sex ratio of newborns: Preponderance of males in toxemia of pregnancy. *Science, 170*, 187-188.

Trivers, R. L., & Willard, D. E. (1973). Natural selection of parental ability to vary the sex ratio of offspring. *Science, 179*, 90-92.

Underwood, P. B., Kesler, K. F., O'Lane, J. M., & Callagan, D. A. (1967). Parental smoking empirically related to pregnancy outcome. *Obstetricis and Gynecology, 29*, 1-8.

Weathersbee, P. S., & Lodge, J. R. (1974). Caffeine and Chinese hamster reproduction. *Journal of Animal Science, 39*, 995.

Weiner, N. (1972). Neurotransmitter systems in the central nervous system. In A. Veriiadakis & N. Weiner (Eds.), *Drugs and the developing brain* (pp. 121-125). New York: Plenum Press.

Younoszai, M. K., Kacic, A., & Haworth, J. C. (1968). Cigarette smoking during pregnancy: The effect upon the hematocrit and acid-base balance of the newborn infant. *Canadian Medical Association Journal, 99*, 197-200.

General

Adams, J., Buelke-San, J., Kimmel, C. A., & LaBorde, J. B. (1982). Behavioral alterations in rats prenatally exposed to low doses of d-amphetamine. *Neurobehavioral Toxicology and Teratology*, 4:63-70.

Becker, R. F., Little, C. R. D., & King, J. E. (1968). Experimental studies on nicotine absorption in rats during pregnancy. III. Effect of s.c. injections of small, chronic doses upon mother, fetus and neonate. *American Journal of Obstetrics and Gynecology, 100*, 957-968.

Becker, R. F., & Martin, J. C. (1971). Vital effects of chronic nicotine absorption and chronic hypoxic stress during pregnancy and the nursing period. *American Journal of Obstetrics and Gynecology, 110*, 522-533.

Bowden, D. M., Weathersbee, P. S., Clarren, S. K., Fahrenbruch, C. E., Goodlin, B. L., & Caffery, S. A. (1983). A periodic dosing model of FAS in the pig-tailed macaque (*Macaca nemestrina*). *American Journal of Primatology*, 4, 143-157.

Bowerman, J. (1980). Teenage pregnancy: The national picture. *Healthwise, 2*, 1-3.

Butler, N. R., Goldstein, H., & Ross, E. M. (1972). Cigarette smoking in pregnancy: Its influence on birth weight and perinatal mortality. *British Medical Journal, 2*, 127-130.

Caldwell, J. (1980). The metabolism of amphetamines and related stimulants in animals and man. In J. Caldwell (Ed.), *Amphetamines and related stimulants: Chemical, biological, clinical, and sociological aspects* (pp. 30-46). Boca Raton: CRC Press.

Castr, E. O., Gummerous, M., & Saarikoski, S. (1975). Treatment of imminent premature labor. *Acta Obstetrica et Gynecologia Scandinavica, 54,* 95–100.

Chambers, C. D., & Hunt, L. G. (1977). Drug use patterns in pregnant women. In J. L. Rementeria (Ed.), *Drug abuse in pregnancy and neonatal effects* (pp. 73–81). St. Louis: C. V. Mosby.

Christoffel, K. K., & Salafsky, I. (1975). Fetal alcohol syndrome in dizygotic twins. *Journal of Pediatrics, 87,* 963–967.

Denenberg, V. H., & Karas, G. G. (1960). Interactive effects of age and duration of infantile experience on adult learning. *Psychological Reports, 7,* 313–322.

Dobbing, J. (1974). The later growth of the brain and its vulnerability. *Pediatrics, 53,* 2–6.

Domino, E. F., & Jaskinski, D. R. (1983). Neuropsychology of nicotine and tobacco smoking: Tobacco smoking as a dependence disorder. *Psychopharmacology Bulletin, 19,* 398–401.

Dubin, N. H., Baros, N. A., Cox, R. T., & King, T. M. (1979). Implantation and fetal survival in the rat as affected by intrauterine injection of normal sterile saline. *Biology of Reproduction, 21,* 47–52.

Eriksson, M., Larsson, G., & Zetterstrom, R. (1981). Amphetamine addiction and pregnancy. II. Pregnancy, delivery and the neonatal period. Socio-medical aspects. *Acta Obstetrica et Gynecologia Scandinavica, 60,* 253–259.

Eriksson, M., & Zetterstrom, R. (1981). The effect of amphetamine addiction on the fetus and child. *Teratology, 24,* 39A (Abstract).

Evans, H. J., Fletcher, J., Torrance, M., & Hargreave, T. B. (1981). Sperm abnormalities and cigarette smoking, *Lancet, 1,* 627–629.

Fishman, R. H. B., Ornoy, A., & Yanai, J. (1983). Ultrastructural evidence of long-lasting cerebellar degeneration after early exposure to phenobarbital in mice. *Experimental Neurology, 79,* 212–222.

Forfar, J. O., & Nelson, M. M. (1973). Epidemiology of drugs taken by pregnant women that may affect the fetus adversely. *Clinical Pharmacology and Therapeutics, 14,* 632–642.

Gallup Report. (1981). Gallup smoking audit: Percentage of Americans who smoke lowest in 37 years. Perceptions of health hazards may explain decline. *Gallup Report,* No. 190, 2–17.

Goldman, A. S. (1980). Critical periods of prenatal toxic insults. In R. Schwarz & S. Yaffe (Eds.), *Drugs and chemical risks to the newborn* (p. 31). New York: Alan Liss.

Gupta, C., Yaffe, S. J., & Shapiro, B. H. (1982). Prenatal exposure to phenobarbital permanently decreases testosterone and causes reproductive dysfunction. *Science, 216,* 640–642.

Hammer, R. E., & Mitchell, J. (1979). Nicotine reduces embryo growth, delays implantation and retards parturition in rats. *Proceedings of the Society for Experimental Biology and Medicine, 162,* 333–336.

Hanson, J. W., Streissguth, A. P., & Smith, D. W. (1978). Effects of moderate alcohol consumption during pregnancy on fetal growth and morphogenesis. *Journal of Pediatrics, 92,* 457–460.

Heinonen, O. P., Slone, D., & Shapiro, S. (1977). *Birth defects and drugs in pregnancy.* Littleton, MA: Publishing Sciences Group.

Henningfield, J. E., & Jasinski, D. R. (1983). Human pharmacology of nicotine. Psychopharmacology Bulletin, 19, 413–415.

Hill, R. M., Craig, J. P., Chaney, M. D., Tennyson, L. M., & McCulley, L. B. (1977). Utilization of over-the-counter drugs during pregnancy. *Clinical Obstetrics and Gynecology, 20,* 381–394.

Holson, J. F., Scott, W. J., Gaylor, D. W., & Wilson, J. G. (1976). Reduced interlitter variability in rats resulting from a restricted mating period, and reassessment of the "litter effect." *Teratology, 14,* 135–142.

Hook, E. B. (1976). Changes in tobacco smoking and ingestion of alcohol and caffeinated beverages during early pregnancy: Are these consequences, in part, of feto-protective mechanisms diminishing maternal exposure to embryotoxins? In S. Kelly, E. B. Hook, D. P. Janerich, & I. H. Porter (Eds.), *Birth defects: Risks and consequences* (pp. 173–183). New York: Academic Press.

Hudson, D. B., Merrill, B. J., & Sands, L. A. (1974). Effects of prenatal and postnatal nicotine administration on biochemical aspects of brain development. In A. Vernadakis & N. Weiner (Eds.), *Drugs and the developing brain* (pp. 243–256). New York: Plenum Press.

Jarvik, M. E. (1973). Further observations on nicotine as the reinforcing agent in smoking. In W. L. Dunn, Jr. (Ed.), *Smoking behavior: Motives and incentives* (pp. 33–50). New York: John Wiley & Sons.

Jensh, R. P., Brent, R. L., & Barr, M., Jr. (1970). The litter effect as a variable in teratologic studies of the albino rat. *Journal of Anatomy, 128,* 185–192.

Jones, K. L., Smith, D. W., Streissguth, A. P., & Myrianthopoulos, N. C. (1974). Outcome in offspring of chronic alcoholic mothers. *Lancet, 1,* 1267–1271.

Julien, R. M. (1981). *A primer of drug action* (3rd ed.). San Francisco: W. H. Freeman.

Kasirsky, G., & Tansy, M. F. (1971). Teratogenic effects of methamphetamine in mice and rabbits. *Teratology, 4,* 131–134.

Kaufman, M. H., & Woollam, D. H. M. (1981). The passage to the foetus and liquor amnii of ethanol administered orally to the pregnant mouse. *British Journal of Experimental Pathology, 62,* 357–361.

Krsiak, J. E. M. (1973). The effect of nicotine administration during pregnancy on the postnatal development of offspring. *Activitas Nervosa Superior (Praha), 15,* 148.

Landesman-Dwyer, S., Keller, L. S., & Streissguth, A. P. (1978). Naturalistic observations of newborns: Effects of maternal alcohol intake. *Alcoholism: Clinical and Experimental Research, 2,* 121–127.

Larsson, K. S. (1973). Contributions of teratology to fetal pharmacology. In L. Boreus (Ed.), *Fetal pharmacology* (pp. 401–415). New York: Raven Press.

Lucot, J. B., Wagner, G. C., Schuster, C. R., & Seiden, L. S. (1982). Decreased sensitivity of rat pups to long-lasting dopamine and serotonin depletions produced by methylamphetamine. *Brain Research, 247,* 181–183.

Mackler, B., Grace, R., Tippit, D., Lemire, R. J., Shepard, T. H., & Kelley, V. C. (1975). Studies of the development of congenital anomalies in rats. III. Effects of inhibition of mitochondrial energy systems on embryonic development. *Teratology,* 12: 291–296.

Martin, D. C., Martin, J. C., Streissguth, A. P., & Lund, C. (1979). Sucking frequency and amplitude in newborns as a function of maternal drinking and smoking. In M. Galanter (Ed.), *Currents in alcoholism,* vol. 5, pp. 359–366). New York: Grune & Stratton.

Martin, J. C. (1975). Effects on offspring of chronic maternal methamphetamine exposure. *Developmental Psychobiology 8,* 397–404.

Martin, J. C., & Becker, R. F. (1970). The effects of nicotine administration in utero upon activity in the rat. *Psychonomic Science, 19,* 59–60.

Martin, J. C., & Becker, R. F. (1971). The effects of maternal nicotine absorption or hypoxic episodes upon appetitive behavior of rat offspring. *Developmental Psychobiology, 4,* 133–147.

Martin, J. C., & Becker, R. F. (1972). The effects of chronic maternal absorption of nicotine or hypoxic episodes upon the life span of the offspring. *Psychonomic Science, 29,* 145–146.

Martin, J. C., & Martin, D. C. (1981). Voluntary activity in the aging rat as a function of maternal drug exposure. *Neurobehavioral Toxicology and Teratology, 3,* 261–264.

Martin, J. C., Martin, D. C., Chao, S., & Shores, P. (1982). Interactive effects of chronic maternal ethanol and nicotine exposure upon offspring development and function. *Neurobehavioral Toxicology and Teratology, 4,* 293–298.

Martin, J. C., Martin, D. C., Lemire, R., & Mackler, B. (1979). Effects of maternal absorption of phenobarbital upon rat offspring development and function. *Neurobehavioral Toxicology, 1,* 49–55.

Martin, J. C., Martin, D. C., Mackler, B., Grace, R., Shores, P., & Chao, S. (1984). Maternal barbiturate administration and offspring response to shock. (In press, *Psychopharmacology*).

Martin, J. C., Martin, D. C., Radow, B., & Day, H. E. (1979). Lifespan and pathology in offspring following nicotine and methamphetamine exposure. *Experimental Aging Research, 5,* 509–522.

Martin, J. C., Martin, D. C., Radow, B., & Sigman, G. (1976). Growth, development and activity in rat offspring following maternal drug exposure. *Experimental Aging Research, 2*, 235–251.

Martin, J. C., Martin, D. C., Radow, B., & Sigman, G. (1978). BAL and caloric intake in the gravid rat as a function of diurnal period, trimester and vehicle. *Pharmacology, Biochemistry, and Behavior, 8*, 421–427.

Martin, J. C., Martin, D. C., Sigman, G., & Day-Pfeiffer, H. (1983). Saccharin preferences in food deprived aging rats are altered as a function of perinatal drug exposure. *Physiology and Behavior, 30*, 853–858.

Martin, J. C., Martin, D. C., Sigman, G., & Radow, B. (1978). Maternal ethanol consumption and hyperactivity in crossfostered offspring. *Physiological Psychology, 6*:352–365.

Martin, J. C., Martin, D. C., Streissguth, A. P., & Lund, E. (1977). Maternal alcohol ingestion and cigarette smoking and their effects upon newborn conditioning. *Alcohol: Clinical and Experimental Research, 1*:243–247.

Maynert, E. W. (1972). Phenobarbital, mephobarbital, and metharbital: Biotransformation. In D. M. Woodbury, J. K. Penry, & R. P. Schmidt (Eds.), *Antiepileptic drugs.* New York: Raven Press.

Middaugh, L. D., Blackwell, L. A., & Zemp, J. W. (1971). Effects of prenatal administration of DAMS on activity and brain catecholamine levels in mice. In *Proceedings of First Annual Meeting of the Society for Neuroscience*, Los Angeles, CA (Abstract).

Middaugh, L. D., Santos, C. A., & Zemp, J. W. (1975). Phenobarbital during pregnancy alters operant behavior of offspring in C57BL16J mice. *Pharmacology, Biochemistry, and Behavior, 3*, 1137–1139.

Milkovich, L. & Van den Berg, B. J. (1977). Effects of antenatal exposure to anorectic drugs. *American Journal of Obstetrics and Gynecology, 129*, 637–642.

Mosier, H. D., Jr., & Jansons, R. A. (1972). Distribution and fate of nicotine in the rat fetus. *Teratology, 6*, 303–311.

Nasello, A. G., & Ramirez, O. A. (1978). Brain catecholamine metabolism in offspring of amphetamine treated rats. *Pharmacology, Biochemistry, and Behavior, 9*, 17–20.

National Institute of Mental Health. (1974). *Downers: The central nervous system depressant drugs.* Madison, WI: Stash Press.

Niswander, K. R., & Gordon, M. (1972). Cigarette smoking. In *The women and their pregnancies: The collaborative perinatal study of NINCDS.* Philadelphia: W. B. Saunders.

Palmer, A. K. (1975). Statistical analysis and choice of sample units [Letter to the Editor]. *Teratology, 10*, 301–302.

Pasamanick, B., & Lilienfeld, A. M. (1955). Association of maternal and fetal factors with the development of mental deficiency. I. Abnormalities of the prenatal and paranatal periods. *Journal of the American Medical Association, 159*, 155–160.

Pasamanick, B., Rogers, M. E., & Lilienfeld, A. M. (1956). Pregnancy experience and the development of behavior disorders in children. *American Journal of Psychiatry, 112,* 613–618.

Peckham, C. H., and King, R. W. (1963). A study of intercurrent conditions observed during pregnancy. *American Journal of Obstetrics and Gynecology,* 87:609–624.

Perlman, H. H., & Dannenberg, A. M. (1942). The excretion of nicotine in breast milk and urine from cigarette smoking. *Journal of the American Medical Association, 120,* 1003–1009.

Ravenholt, R. T., Lovinski, M. J., & Nellist, D. J. (1966). Effects of smoking upon reproduction. *American Journal of Obstetrics and Gynecology,* 96:207–281.

Rayburn, W., Wible-Kant, J., & Bledsoe, P. (1982). Changing trends in drug use during pregnancy. *Journal of Reproductive Medicine, 27,* 569–575.

Rosett, H. L., Ouellette, E. M., Weiner, L., & Owens, E. (1978). Therapy of heavy drinking during pregnancy. *Obstetrics and Gynecology, 51,* 41–46.

Schardein, J. L. (1976). Anticonvulsants. In *Drugs as teratogens* (chap. 15). Cleveland, OH: CRC Press.

Seliger, D. (1973). Effect of prenatal maternal administration of d-amphetamine on rat offspring activity and passive avoidance learning. *Physiological Psychology,* 1:273–280.

Soyka, L. F., & Joffe, J. M. (1980). Male mediated drug effects on offspring. In R. H. Schwarz & S. J. Yaffe (Eds.), *Drug and chemical risks to the fetus and newborn* (pp. 49–66). New York: Alan Liss.

Stockard, C. R. (1921). Developmental rate and structural expression: An experimental study of twins, "double monsters," and single deformities, and the interactions among embryonic organs during their origin and development. *American Journal of Anatomy, 28,* 115–227.

Streissguth, A. P., Landesman-Dwyer, S., Martin, J. C., & Smith, D. (1980). Teratogenic effects of alcohol in humans and laboratory animals. *Science, 209,* 353–361.

Streissguth, A. P., Martin, D. C., Martin, J. C., & Barr, H. (1981a). A longitudinal prospective study on the effects of intrauterine alcohol exposure in humans. In S. Mednick & M. Harvey (Eds.), *Longitudinal research in the United States.* Boston: Martinus Nijhoff.

Streissguth, A. P., Martin, D. C., Martin, J. C., & Barr, H. (1981b). The Seattle longitudinal prospective study on alcohol and pregnancy. *Neurobehavioral Toxicology and Teratology, 3,* 223–233.

Sugioka, K. (1983). Perinatal brain damage and behavioral disorders: Analysis of compensatory behavior after perinatal hippocampal lesions. *Teratology, 28,* 5A (Abstract).

Sullivan, F. M., & McElhatton, P. R. (1977). A comparison of the teratogenic activity of the antiepileptic drugs carbamazepine, clonazepam, ethosuximide, phenobarbital and primidone in mice. *Toxicology and Applied Pharmacology, 40,* 365–378.

Tjalve, H., Hansson, E., & Schmiterlow, C. G. (1968). Passage of 14C-nicotine and its metabolites into mice foetuses and placentae. *Acta Pharmacologica et Toxicologica, 26*, 539–555.

Tonge, S. R. (1973). Permanent alterations in catecholamine concentrations in discrete areas of brain in offspring of rats treated with methylamphetamine and chlorpromazine. *British Journal of Pharmacology, 47*, 425–427.

Vincent, N. M. (1958). The effects of prenatal alcoholism upon motivation, emotionality, and learning in the rat. *American Psychologist, 13*, 401 (Abstract).

Vorhees, C. V. (1983). Behavioral teratogenicity testing as a method of screening for hazards to human health: A methodological proposal. *Neurobehavioral Toxicology and Teratology, 5*, 469–474.

Warkany, J., & Nelson, R. C. (1940). Appearance of skeletal abnormalities in the offspring of rats reared on a deficient diet. *Science, 92*, 383–384.

Weil, C. S. (1970). Selection of the valid number of sampling units and a consideration of their combination in toxicological studies involving reproduction, teratogenesis or carcinogenesis. *Food and Cosmetics Toxicology, 8*, 177–182.

Weil, C. S. (1975). Choice of the number of sampling units in teratology [Letter to the Editor]. *Teratology, 10*, 301.

Weir, M. W., & DeFries, J. C. (1963). Blocking of pregnancy in mice as a function of stress. *Psychological Reports, 13*, 365–366.

Wendell, G. D., & Thurman, R. G. (1979). Effect of ethanol concentration on rates of ethanol elimination in normal rats in vivo. In V. M. Galanter (Ed.), *Currents in alcoholism: Biomedical issues and clinical effects of alcoholism*, (pp. 81–89). New York: Grune & Stratton.

Wiener, S. J. (1980). Nutritional considerations in the design of animal models of FAS. *Neurobehavioral Toxicology, 2*, 175–179.

Wiener, S. J., & Levine, S. (1983). Influence of perinatal malnutrition and early handling on the pituitary-adrenal response to noxious stimuli in adult rats. *Physiology and Behavior, 31*, 285–291.

Wilson, J. G. (1977). Current status of teratology: General principles and mechanisms derived from animal studies. In *Handbook of teratology. Vol. I. General principles and etiology* (pp. 47–74). New York: Plenum Press.

Yanai, J., Woolf, M., & Feigenbaum, J. J. (1982). Autoradiographic study of phenobarbital's effect of development of the central nervous system. *Experimental Neurology, 78*, 439–449.

Yerushalmy, J. (1972). Infants with low birth weight born before their mothers started to smoke cigarettes. *American Journal of Obstetrics and Gynecology, 112*:277–284.

Women and Weight: A Normative Discontent

Judith Rodin, Lisa Silberstein, and Ruth Striegel-Moore

Yale University

*F*or an overwhelming number of women in our society, being a woman means feeling too fat. For many women, chronic dieting has become a way of life (Herman & Polivy, 1975). In 1978 a Nielsen survey found that 56% of all female respondents between ages 24 and 54 were on a diet (Nielsen, 1979), and the number of women dieting appears to have increased significantly over the past decade (Nylander, 1971). Concerns about dieting are significantly greater for women than for men and are not well correlated with the women's actual weight (Drewnowski, Riskey, and Desor, 1982; Rodin and Stoddard, 1981). This concern appears to influence even male and female children differentially (Dwyer, Feldman, Seltzer, & Mayer, 1969; Hawkins, Turell, & Jackson, 1983; Nylander, 1971). In this chapter we will explore the nature of women's preoccupation with weight and consider some possible reasons underlying this phenomenon.

Beyond the "normative" worry about weight and dieting exhibited by most women in our society, a rapidly increasing number of women are being diagnosed as having eating disorders such as anorexia nervosa and bulimia (Garner, Olmstead, & Polivy, 1983; Halmi, Falk, & Schwartz, 1981; Hawkins & Clement, 1980; Jones, Fox, Babigian, & Hutton, 1980; Stangler & Printz, 1981). We will argue that these eating disorders lie on a continuum with women's "normal" concerns with weight and eating. Indeed, there is considerable overlap between clinical populations of women with eating disorders and "normal" women in terms of eating behaviors and attitudes toward body and weight. For example, even apparently normal female college students differ from their male peers on several subscales of the Eating Disorder Inventory, a questionnaire developed to assess psychological and behavioral characteristics associated with bulimia and anorexia nervosa. Women scored significantly higher than men on the subscales "Drive for Thinness," "Body Dissatisfaction," and "Bulimia" (Garner et al., 1983).

We will also consider women's concerns with weight and dieting in the context of the dramatically changed fabric of women's lives in the past two decades. While women are increasingly striving for thinness and are developing eating disorders with rising prevalence, they are at the same time expanding, challenging, and discarding sex-role stereotypes on many frontiers. Are these serendipitous co-occurrences, or are they related? The magazines and newspapers that herald women's diversifying professional accomplishments also present fashion models chosen to match a template of abnormal thinness, along with new diets to attain it. Do women experience broadening choices in careers but not in appearance? The media constantly promote new diets, new exercise regimens, new beauty treatments to correct or hide physical flaws and to delay and mask aging. Are these messages to women inconsistent with exhortations to achieve professionally and personally, or are the two closely intertwined?

While daily conversations and the popular press clearly indicate the importance of weight in women's lives, psychological research has largely neglected the issue. Perhaps the phenomenon is so pervasive and so close to all of us, men and women alike, that it is difficult to see. As Sandra and Daryl Bem (1976) have commented about other feminist topics, "We are like the fish who is unaware that his environment is wet." Perhaps, as Blumstein and Schwartz (1983) suggest, "Since most scholars overvalue the power of the mind, they tend to denigrate or even ignore the power of the body." Or perhaps, as Orbach (1978) comments, "It seems . . . almost like a travesty—feminists concerned about how they look!"

Hatfield and Sprecher (in press) report that Kinsey and his coworkers, in their survey of sexual practices in America, found that women were more embarrassed when asked their weight than when asked "How often do you masturbate?" or "Have you ever had a homosexual affair?" The relationship of women to their bodies and, in particular, to their weight is clearly a highly charged issue and one worthy of attention from psychologists.

In this chapter we will attempt to bring together insights from social psychology, the literature on the biology of weight regulation, the recent clinical literature on eating disorders, and the expanding theoretical and empirical work on the psychology of women and gender. Because relatively little research has directly addressed women's concerns about weight, many gaps exist in our initial map of this terrain. We will, for now, hypothesize about the bridges that may connect diverse areas, but we also appeal to future investigators to explore this understudied domain.

To consider why legions of women pursue thinness like a career, we will first examine cultural attitudes about obesity, thinness, and beauty and explore how and why women and men may be differentially affected by these attitudes. Second, we will discuss the biological factors of weight regulation that may influence and be altered by women's pursuit of the thin ideal. Third, we will examine the relationship women have with their bodies and how it differs from men's, and finally we will consider the roles that body image and weight play in women's lives. This review will lead us to assert that weight concerns and dieting are normative for most women, at least in Western society, and that eating disorders may be best understood as a likely consequence of this "normative" behavior when taken to extremes.

Throughout this analysis, let us be sensitive to the potential cohort-specific nature of the phenomenon we are examining. This is a time of rapid social change, and our hypotheses must be understood within the context of the specific cohorts from which these data have been taken. Sex-role socialization is bound by historical moment. Feelings about achievement and appearance and the type of appearance that is especially valued change with historical period, and so do the types of disorders they precipitate. We will try to characterize what seems particular to this cohort and what is more generalizable, and to extract clues that may help us generate hypotheses to the challenging question, "Why now?"

Cultural Attitudes

In asking why women strive so greatly to be thin, we must first consider current cultural norms and stereotypes. This provides a much-needed context for understanding individual behavior.

OBESITY IS A STRONGLY STIGMATIZED CONDITION

From a very early age, children learn that obese people are to be stigmatized. Numerous studies suggest that children of both sexes develop clear preferences for lean bodies and concomitant rejection of chubby ones (Lerner, 1973; Lerner & Gellert, 1969). Indeed, two reports (Goodman, Richardson, Dornbusch, & Hastorf, 1963; Richardson, Goodman, Hastorf, & Dornbusch, 1961) suggest that children have a more negative attitude toward obese children than toward children with a wide range of handicaps, such as being in a wheelchair, missing a hand, or having a facial disfigurement. In keeping with these results, Matthews and Westie (1966) report that high-school students preferred to be at greater "social distance" from an obese classmate than from a handicapped one. When children with juvenile diabetes were asked whether they would "trade" their chronic illness for obesity, clearly a medically less threatening problem, most diabetic children said no (Davis, Shipp, & Pattishall, 1965).

The stereotype of the obese that children develop early includes a long list of negative traits. Staffieri (1967, 1972) found that boys of all body types attributed uniformly unfavorable traits to silhouettes of endomorphic children (e.g., cheats, is dirty, argues, is lazy, sloppy, mean, stupid), and girls attributed an even greater number of negative characteristics to the obese body build than did the boys.

It therefore seems compellingly clear that children learn there is something dreadful about being overweight. Wooley, Wooley, and Dyrenforth (1979) suggest that not only is the impact of this hatred on the overweight child probably irreversible, but the antifat attitudes learned in childhood most likely figure into nonoverweight people's fears of becoming overweight. In the best-selling *Beverly Hills Diet*, Mazel (1981) summarizes, "Being fat is an obscenity—we are shunned, scorned, and ridiculed. A failure for all to see—and mock." The obese are not only psychologically stigmatized and interpersonally distanced, but are discriminated against in educational and vocational settings (e.g., Canning & Mayer, 1966; Larkin & Pines, 1979). It has even been reported that in the early 1900s Sweden levied a tax on individuals based on the number of pounds they were overweight (cited in Allon, 1975).

Hence society imposes strong sanctions against obesity for both men and women—but is this equally true for both sexes? Canning and Mayer (1966) reported that in a sample of high-school graduating classes, 52% of the nonobese females went to college after graduation while only 32% of the obese females did. The obese and nonobese women did *not* differ either on objective measures of intellectual ability and achievement or on the percentage who applied for college admission. Among male high-school seniors, 53% for the nonobese men went on to college and 50% of the obese men did—a statistically nonsignificant difference. As the authors suggest, education is a crucial variable in determining social class, and college-admission discrimination against the obese may thus initiate a downward spiral in social mobility.

Such a view seems to be corroborated by a study done on a large sample of women and men in Midtown Manhattan (Goldblatt, Moore, & Stunkard, 1965). Compared with nonobese women, overweight women were much less likely to achieve a higher socioeconomic status than their parents and much more likely to achieve a lower status. No such relationship was found among the men studied. Furthermore, whereas the percentage of thin men was the same in each of the three social classes (10%, 9%, and 12% for low, middle, and high SES), the percentage of thin women was positively related to social class level (9%, 19%, and 37% for low, middle, and high SES).

In our society, therefore, obesity is met with punishment—psychological, social, and economic—and the sanctions appear to be more severe for females than for males. Surely one root of women's fear of overweight lies in the harsh negative views of society toward obesity—particularly toward obesity in women.

BEING ATTRACTIVE IS EXTREMELY IMPORTANT IN OUR SOCIETY

A basic issue underlying women's concern with their weight is that physical appearance matters in our society. Let us step back for a moment from the weight issue per se and consider the role of physical appearance in the lives of women and men.

In general there is high interrater agreement about which stimulus persons are most attractive, suggesting the operation of strongly shared social norms regarding attractiveness (Unger, Hilderbrand, & Madar, 1982). Complementing the "fat is bad" stereotype there is a "what is beautiful is good" stereotype (Dion, Berscheid, & Walster, 1972), and developmental research has documented that this stereotype also develops early. Preschool children view attractive peers as friendlier and smarter than unattractive peers (Dion, 1973), and physical attractiveness is significantly correlated with sociometric rank within the preschool classroom (Vaughn & Langlois, 1983). Researchers have also consistently observed that preschool and elementary school teachers rate attractive children more favorably and build higher expectations about an attractive child's likely performance (Adams & Cohen, 1976a, 1976b; Clifford, 1975; Clifford & Walster, 1973).

Attractive people are perceived to have virtually every character trait that is socially desirable to the perceiver. This includes being interesting, strong, poised, kind, socially outgoing, and sexually warm. Attractive persons are also believed to live more successful and fulfilling lives (Berscheid & Walster, 1974). A study measuring the effects of changes in attractiveness accomplished by cosmetic surgery showed subjects "before" and "after" photographs. Stimulus persons were rated as significantly kinder, warmer, more responsive, and happier after becoming more attractive (Kalick, 1977).

Physically attractive individuals appear to have a distinct advantage over less attractive individuals in interpersonal situations. They are more likely to receive help (Benson, Karabenick, & Lerner, 1976; West & Brown, 1975) and are more able to elicit cooperation in conflict situations (Sigall, Page, & Brown, 1971). Attractive applicants may have a better chance of getting a job, and they tend to be hired at a higher starting salary (Dipboye, Arvey, & Terpstra, 1977; Dipboye, Fromkin, & Wibach, 1975). Attractive individuals also benefit from more positive outcomes in simulated jury cases, being deemed guilty less often and seen as worthy of milder punishments (Efran, 1974) and awarded more favorable judgments (Stephan & Tully, 1977) than less attractive individuals.

Following from these striking findings about the effects of physical attractiveness is, again, a question central to our present inquiry: Are these effects differentially significant for males and females? The answer, again, is yes and is evident from an early age. In their study of preschool children, Vaughn and Langlois (1983) found the relationship between attractiveness and higher sociometric status to be stronger for girls than for boys. From their review of the developmental literature on sex differences, Maccoby and Jacklin (1974) suggest that boys with the greatest status and power, as well as reasonably good looks, interest the most attractive girls—while the most alluring, beautiful girls interest the highest-status boys.

Research on dating and mate selection corroborates this view of the differential importance of attractiveness for men and women (Berscheid, Dion, Walster, & Walster, 1971; Janda, O'Grady, & Barnhort, 1981; Krebs & Adinolfi, 1975; Stroebe, Insko, Thompson, & Layton, 1971). Traditional sex-role definitions specify very different sources of status for men and women. For men, easily quantifiable criteria of successful functioning are available, such as income or value of possessions. Since women have traditionally lacked such criteria, beauty has been a central asset that has helped a woman to gain access to a man's resources. Men, conversely, benefit from marrying a beautiful woman. Presenting subjects with all possible combinations of pictures of attractive and unattractive men and women as couples, Bar-Tal and Saxe (cited in Bar-Tal & Saxe, 1976) found that an unattractive male married to an attractive female received the most favorable ratings of any of the stimulus persons, while the ratings of an unattractive female were unaffected by the attractiveness of her husband. Thus, marrying a beautiful woman may improve a man's status, whereas marrying an attractive man does not affect the woman's status.

Similar evidence emerges from Blumstein and Schwartz's (1983) recent large-scale study of American couples. The heterosexual women in their sample resented it when their husbands or boyfriends were relatively more attractive to others than they were, while men did not resent the relatively greater attractiveness of their wives or girl friends. Consistent with the Bar-Tal and Saxe (1976) study, a man viewed a relatively more attractive female mate as a positive reflection on him. Interestingly, Blumstein and Schwartz (1983) observed that although their subjects tended to assume that physical appearance would diminish in importance to the couple as the relationship progressed, looks continued to be critical. Most particularly, they noted that wives were keenly aware of the importance of their looks to their husbands. They found that attractive women experience better sex lives and may have more faithful partners. While the authors did not explicitly separate out weight from other dimensions of physical appearance, their case reports suggest that weight gain is a central, and perhaps *the* central, way physical appearance changes over time.

We have seen that attractiveness seems more important to females than to males even as young children, but what happens in later life? If being thin and attractive figures more prominently in a woman's life than in a man's, we would expect the effects of the aging process on appearance in general and its tendency to promote weight gain in particular to be more of a problem for women than for men. Indeed, in a current longitudinal study of elderly people, we have found that the second greatest personal concern expressed by women in the sample, following memory loss, was change in body weight. Weight concerns were not expressed by men in the sample (Rodin, 1984b).

Sontag (1972) has argued that women's concerns about aging reflect a veridical perception of the double standard of aging that distinguishes men from women. Whereas women are judged less worthwhile as their youth fades, men are not. This is probably partly because men are judged throughout the life cycle on the basis of their achievements rather than their looks. But in addition, society affords males some possibilities for remaining attractive when older (e.g., "distinguished" looks), whereas the beauty ideal for women seems restricted to youthfulness. Hatfield and Sprecher (in press), for example, report preliminary data that suggest both young and old individuals judge old women as relatively less attractive than old men. Women appear to have a more narrowly defined template to match— in terms of age as well as appearance.

In addition to making a woman more valued to her partner and to society, attractiveness figures prominently into a woman's feelings of self-worth. While there is evidence that attractiveness relates to self-acceptance for both sexes (Adams, 1977), attractiveness and body attitudes are a more salient component of self-concept for females than for males (Lerner & Karabenick, 1974). Simmons and Rosenberg (1975) found that adolescent girls tended to be more concerned with their looks than were their male peers and also perceived themselves as less attractive than did the boys. Significantly, those girls who perceived themselves to be less good-looking had lower self-esteem scores than girls who were more satisfied with their appearance.

It is not possible to discern from the current literature the precise nature of the relationship between a female's self-perceived attractiveness and her self-esteem. The high value society places on female appearance surely serves to enhance an attractive female's self-confidence and to challenge seriously a relatively unattractive female's self-worth. The research suggests that the more attractive woman is likely to have been more liked and reinforced as a child and to have had a relatively easier time being successful in school, career, and intimate relationships. Perhaps, then, the external contingencies of attractiveness serve as mediating variables between degree of attractiveness and self-worth. On the other hand, perhaps women who suffer from low self-esteem view themselves as deficient in all areas relevant to their self-definition, including their appearance.

As will become further evident as we continue our discussion, it is important for researchers, in order to understand such issues, to distinguish by whose eye the beauty is beheld: Is attractiveness judged by the self, by a significant other, by a panel of judges? Quite beautiful women may feel flawed, just as statistically slim women may feel fat (Rodin & Stoddard, 1981). In addition, there has been a relative absence of efforts to objectify beauty in the social science literature. Hence very little is known about what specific features result in others' judging individuals to be attractive. Social psychological research on physical attractiveness overwhelmingly utilizes head-and-shoulders "yearbook" pictures as stimuli. Yet while portraits of males in the arts, in newspapers, and even in casual drawings by research participants do tend to emphasize the face, women are more likely to be shown in full figure (Archer, Iritani, Kimes, & Barrios, 1983). We might conjecture that the greater salience of the face in the portrayal of men suggests that faces are more important in evaluating a man's attractiveness. For women, the body may be more crucial in determining attractiveness.

THE FEMALE SEX-ROLE STEREOTYPE PRESCRIBES PREOCCUPATION WITH AND PURSUIT OF BEAUTY

For centuries, beauty has been considered a feminine attribute, and its pursuit a feminine responsibility. In fact the word beauty itself reflects the intimate connection between beauty and femininity. Derived from the Latin word *bellus*, a diminutive of *bonus* (good), beauty was originally used only in reference to women and children (Banner, 1983). Even the most recent revision of *Webster's New World Dictionary* (1982) has as one of its definitions of beauty "a very good looking woman." Thus we postulate that women's preoccupation with their appearance is consistent with the feminine sex-role stereotype.

As Banner (1983) points out, there are at least two additional aspects of beauty that may fuel women's efforts to emulate their culture's beauty ideal. First, beauty often is associated with moral goodness, with being virtuous. The social-psychological research we reviewed earlier clearly documents this "what is beautiful is good" stereotype (Dion et al., 1972). Second, beauty can contribute to being powerful. History provides many examples of women who, because of their physical attractiveness, were able to exert political influence. Our analysis of the attractiveness literature showed that beauty gives a woman power in terms of having more access to resources (e.g., being able to attract and marry high-status men) and of being more favorably treated in social contexts.

SOCIETY HAS LONG DICTATED WAYS FOR WOMEN TO ALTER THEIR BODIES TO ACHIEVE "UNNATURAL" BEAUTY IDEALS

Brownmiller (1984) suggests that dieting resembles foot binding and corseting in that all of these represent instances in a long history of women's mutilating their bodies for the sake of beauty. Let us take as an example the 19th century, in which attaining the beautiful female body required wearing a corset. As Ehrenreich and English (1978) describe, among the short-term results of tight-lacing were shortness of breath, constipation, weakness, and a tendency to violent indigestion, while long-term effects included bent or fractured ribs, displacement of the liver, and uterine prolapse. Despite these ghastly "side effects" of wearing corsets, physicians promoted their use because women's bodies were thought to be too weak to sustain themselves without support. Similarly, in current times dieting has been strongly advocated by the medical profession as a safe means of reducing weight, despite a number of potential negative effects.

Is it possible that dieting has replaced the corset (Brownmiller, 1984; Squire, 1983)? Once women were finally freed of corsets, girdles, and stiff bras, internal constraint may have taken the place of the external constraints, in compliance with the belief that the female body is deficient and in need of reshaping (Brownmiller, 1984).

Implicit in the discussion to this point has been a relationship between weight and attractiveness, and specifically, a correlation between obesity and unattractiveness, and between thinness and attractiveness. Let us now directly examine this premise.

BEING THIN IS A CENTRAL FEATURE OF THE CONTEMPORARY IDEAL OF FEMALE ATTRACTIVENESS

Although the features that lead to being perceived as attractive are not all well specified, it is certainly true that our society equates thinness with beauty in women. Beauty ideals are highly culture bound and have, at least in Western cultures, undergone many changes over the centuries (Banner, 1983; Beller, 1977; Brownmiller, 1984; Rudofsky, 1971). For example, the fleshy, rounded models in Rubens's paintings reflect the beauty ideal of his era, whereas today they would be viewed as too plump.

In recent decades Western cultures have experienced a marked trend toward an increasingly thin beauty ideal for women. Comparing measurements of contestants in the Miss America Pageant between 1959 and 1979, Garner, Garfinkel, Schwartz, and Thompson (1980) documented a significant decrease in body weight and measurements over the 20-year period. Furthermore, since 1970 the winners have been significantly thinner than the other contestants. These investigators also found body sizes of *Playboy Magazine* centerfold models to have decreased over recent years. During the same time period, however, women under 30 years of age have increased in body weight, according to the average weight statistics from the Society of Actuaries (1980) and Metropolitan Life Insurance Company (1983; see Table 1). Thus, over the past 25 years young women have actually become heavier, while the beauty ideal for this same age group has become lighter.

Let us consider now our conjecture that the body might be more salient for defining attractiveness in women than in men. This view seems consistent with the literature reviewed earlier, which indicates that obesity is more severely punished in women than in men—for if the body is more central to determining a woman's attractiveness, then a body type deemed unattractive will be proportionately more important (more damaging) in an overall view of the appearance of a woman than of a man.

We were unable to locate, however, any empirical studies that directly investigated the relative importance of body weight and shape in determining perception of one's *own* degree of physical attractiveness. Hence we tested a random sample of male and female undergraduates and found that weight and body shape constituted the *central* determinants of a woman's perception of her physical attractiveness. For men, weight and body shape were important but not central in perceived attractiveness (Rodin & Striegel-Moore, 1984).

Following from the premise discussed earlier that self-perceived attractiveness and self-esteem are correlated for women, we would expect, in particular, that a woman's body weight and her satisfaction with it would be important variables in her overall satisfaction with herself. While no definitive research has explored this tenet, in a recent large-scale survey of *Glamour* magazine readers, Wooley and

Table 1
Metropolitan Height and Weight Tables for Women, 1959 and 1983

WOMEN

Weight in Pounds (Without Clothing)

Height (Without Shoes)		SMALL FRAME		Change Since 1959		Percent Change		MEDIUM FRAME		Change Since 1959		Percent Change		LARGE FRAME		Change Since 1959		Percent Change	
Feet	Inches	1959	1983					1959	1983					1959	1983				
4	9	90- 97	99-108	9	11	10	11	94-106	106-118	12	12	13	11	102-118	115-128	13	10	13	8
4	10	92-100	100-110	8	10	9	10	97-109	108-120	11	11	11	10	105-121	117-131	12	10	11	8
4	11	95-103	101-112	6	9	6	9	100-112	110-123	10	11	10	10	108-124	119-134	11	10	10	8
5	0	98-106	103-115	5	9	5	8	103-115	112-126	9	11	9	10	111-127	122-137	11	10	10	8
5	1	101-109	105-118	4	9	4	8	106-118	115-129	9	11	8	9	114-130	125-140	11	10	10	8
5	2	104-112	108-121	4	9	4	8	109-122	118-132	9	10	8	8	117-134	128-144	11	10	9	7
5	3	107-115	111-124	4	9	4	8	112-126	121-135	9	9	8	7	121-138	131-148	10	10	8	7
5	4	110-119	114-127	4	8	4	7	116-131	124-138	8	7	7	5	125-142	134-152	9	10	7	7
5	5	114-123	117-130	3	7	3	6	120-135	127-141	7	6	6	4	129-146	137-156	8	10	6	7

Table 1: *continued*

WOMEN

Weight in Pounds (Without Clothing)

Height (Without Shoes) Feet Inches	SMALL FRAME		Change Since 1959		Percent Change		MEDIUM FRAME		Change Since 1959		Percent Change		LARGE FRAME		Change Since 1959		Percent Change	
	1959	1983					1959	1983					1959	1983				
5 6	118-127	120-133	2	6	2	5	124-139	130-144	6	5	5	4	133-150	140-160	7	10	5	7
5 7	122-131	123-136	1	5	1	4	128-143	133-147	5	4	4	3	137-154	143-164	6	10	4	6
5 8	126-136	126-139	0	3	0	2	132-147	136-150	4	3	3	2	141-159	146-167	5	8	4	5
5 9	130-140	129-142	−1	2	−1	1	136-151	139-153	3	2	2	1	145-164	149-170	4	6	3	4
5 10	134-144	132-145	−2	1	−1	1	140-155	142-156	2	1	1	1	149-169	152-173	3	4	2	2

Wooley (1984a) found that for 63% of the young women in their sample, weight often affected how they felt about themselves; 33% reported that weight sometimes affected how they felt about themselves, and only 4% stated that it never did. Despite the potential sampling problems with this survey, the data are based on 33,000 respondents, which suggests the prevalence of weight-related concerns and their importance to young women.

Are men spared from the "thinness equals attractiveness" premise of modern society? Our fitness-conscious culture has surely affected both men and women and propelled members of both sexes to seek hard, firm bodies. We have already reviewed evidence that appearance in general matters relatively less in men's lives, however, and that obesity, while incurring considerable negative sanctions in both sexes, is more allowable in men than in women. Furthermore, while males aspire to the mesomorphic build, females prefer the ectomorphic body type. These particular preferences prove to be more of a problem for females than for males, an argument we will now substantiate by examining the biology of weight regulation.

Biological Aspects of Weight Regulation

THE CONTEMPORARY BEAUTY IDEAL OF "THINNESS EQUALS ATTRACTIVENESS" PRESCRIBES A BODY WEIGHT THAT FOR MOST WOMEN IS UNREALISTICALLY LOW DUE TO BIOLOGICAL FACTORS

Implicit in the cultural legislation of a uniform, and uniformly thin, body ideal for women seems to be an assumption that a woman can choose and is responsible for her body type and weight. However, body size and weight include a large genetic contribution, an important fact in our consideration of women's concerns with weight and their pervasive dieting behavior.

The research on heredity and weight has documented that identical twins have closely related body weights, over twice as similar as those of fraternal twins or siblings. When identical twins are reared apart, they show a somewhat larger weight variation than do identical twins reared together (Bray, 1981; Newman, Freeman, & Holzinger, 1982; Withers, 1964). Hence environmental factors are clearly involved in one's ultimate weight. Importantly, however, identical twins reared apart evidenced weights that were far more similar than either nonidentical twins or siblings reared together. These data suggest that, on average, one's genes may be more powerful than environmental factors in determining one's weight (Bray, 1981).

One path by which heredity may influence weight is by determining how food is metabolized and therefore affecting one's ability to store fat. Consequently, the level of overeating necessary to gain weight is far less for some people than for others. In a now-classic study, Rose and Williams (1961) investigated people whose caloric intake varied greatly from one to another, ranging from 1,600 to 7,400 calories per day, yet whose weights remained stable. In subject pairs matched for sex, weight, age, and activity level, often one member of the pair was eating twice as many calories as the other while both were maintaining the same body weight. Extraordinary as they may seem, these findings suggest that in different individuals, the identical type and quantity of food eaten may not be stored or expended in the same way given equal activity levels. Individual differences in metabolic rate appear extremely significant in determining the efficiency of caloric expenditure (Rimm & White, 1979). Hence, in light of our present discussion, it is significant that while one individual may be genetically predisposed to a thin body build, another would "naturally" have a heavier build without necessarily eating more than the first.

Clearly pertinent to our current discussion is the fact that there are sex differences in metabolic rate. On the average, females have lower basal metabolic rates than males. This is in part a function of difference in body size, but it is also due to differences in the ratio of lean to fat tissue. Fat tissue is more metabolically inert than lean tissue, and, as we will elaborate below, females are biologically disposed to have a higher proportion of fat to lean tissue than males. Thus women are genetically programmed to have a proportionately higher fat composition than men and lower resting metabolic rates.

Sex-linked hormones seem to play a major role in stimulating fat storage and perhaps even fat cell development. As we will discuss in the following section, each of the milestones in the course of women's biological development—puberty, pregnancy, and menopause—has the potential to increase fat. The sex-linked hormones appear to be important factors in each of these functions.

FEMALE BIOLOGICAL DEVELOPMENTAL MILESTONES TEND TO INCREASE FAT

For women, the natural course of development involves several milestones that tend to induce increased fat storage. At puberty, pregnancy, and menopause, the physiological changes women undergo make weight gain possible. It appears that men do not experience analogous milestones in terms of increased fat.

Even before puberty, girls have 10% to 15% more fat than boys, and after puberty girls have almost twice as much as boys (Angel, 1949). While the weight spurt accompanying adolescence in females is primarily due to an increase in adipose tissue, boys gain their weight at puberty as muscle and bone (Beller, 1977; Cheek, 1974; Tanner, 1974).

Although hormonal changes at puberty seem strongly implicated in weight gain in females, the precise role of the sex hormones in weight regulation is still not fully understood. Progesterone may play an important lipogenic (fat-making) role, and it has been shown to affect weight gain (Dalvit-MacPhillips, 1983; Dippel & Elias, 1980). High levels of progesterone also increase the perceived palatability of sweet foods (Dippel & Elias, 1980; Rodin, 1984a). Since progesterone level varies greatly throughout the menstrual cycle, the increase in appetite that some women experience during the last week before menstruation or during pregnancy may reflect this effect of increased progesterone.

Estrogen has been shown to both increase and decrease weight, and what seems clear from an otherwise confused set of studies is that estrogen acting in concert with insulin has a more potent effect on fat deposition than either estrogen or insulin alone. It is probably this powerful combination of estrogen and insulin that is at the root of the pregnant woman's unwanted weight gain. Estrogen production clearly increases throughout pregnancy. Furthermore, insulin output in the mother has to go up a little almost each day just to keep pace with the ever-increasing demand for blood sugar from the developing fetus. Beller (1977) has suggested that as the normal day-by-day escalation of insulin supply occurs, in concert with increased estrogen production, added fat storage seems especially likely.

On the average, a healthy woman gains 25 to 30 lb during pregnancy. Of this weight gain, 5 to 11 lb are due to fat storage (Committee on Dietary Allowances, 1974; Hytten & Leitch, 1971; Pitkin, 1976). Although excess adipose tissue is biologically important for the mother and the fetus, women often have difficulty losing it even well after the baby is born (Beller, 1980; Cederlöf & Kaij, 1970; Helliovaara & Aromaa, 1981). Indeed, this may be due to increased insulin output in response to carbohydrate-containing meals. One interesting speculation is that every time the new mother eats a meal containing starches and sugars, thus flooding her bloodstream with glucose, the beta cells of the pancreas respond by secreting a surplus of insulin. Without a fetus to utilize the excess glucose and to titrate this feedback cycle, the mother's response can lead to continued weight gain. Weight gain in pregnancy is not inevitable and varies widely in different cultures and different time periods, but fat deposition even with a relatively stable weight gain is a definite occurrence in pregnancy.

The aging process itself has important implications for weight regulation. Basal metabolic rate declines with age, along with a decrease in lean body mass and an increase in body fat. Young and co-workers (Young, Blondin, Tensuan, & Fryer, 1963; Young, Martin, Chihan, McCarthy, Mannielo, Harmuth, & Fryer, 1961), for example, reported body fat data in a sample of 94 normal-weight women between 16 and 70 years old. Mean body fatness increased after the 40th year; percentage of fat in the body was 23.1% at 40–50 years, 46% at 50–60 years, and 55.3% at 60–70 years. While men also experience body-composition changes, women experience a larger increase in fat with age than men and seem to undergo a relatively greater slowdown of their metabolism (Bray, 1976; Forbes & Reina, 1970; Parizkowa, 1973; Wessel, Ufer, Van Huss, & Cederquist, 1963).

In light of the role sex hormones seem to play in determining women's body fat content, menopause is another event in female adulthood that is likely to affect body weight and composition. Though medical textbooks report weight gain as one of the possible symptoms of menopause (e.g., Lanson, 1975; Weideger, 1976), we were unable to locate a longitudinal study of women in midlife that investigated weight change as a dependent variable. In a cross-sectional study, McKinlay and Jefferys (1974) surveyed more than 600 women between 45 and 54 years of age. Those who were undergoing menopause at the time of the survey reported weight gain more frequently than did pre- or postmenopausal women.

In sum, then, females start out in life with more fat than males do, and this difference increases over the life cycle. Furthermore, there are certain developmental junctures in women's lives, but apparently not in men's, that produce rapid and marked changes in body-weight regulation systems. The young girl encounters the first of these at adolescence, and with increased estrogen and progesterone levels at puberty, she develops the biological machinery that increases her fat-making capacity at precisely the time when she is becoming most concerned with her appearance. The convergence of these biological and psychosocial events can lead to the excessive dieting behavior documented as pervasive among adolescent girls (Hawkins et al., 1983; Nylander, 1971). For some reason we do not yet understand, dieting at the time the sex hormones are being established and regulated may be especially destructive for normal bodyweight regulation. We also speculate that dieting efforts after pregnancy and at menopause may have a similar disregulating effect.

Thus women's bodies are equipped with physiological and endocrine mechanisms promoting the development of fat cells and the storage of body fat, and the influence of these mechanisms tends to increase over the life cycle. Regardless of cultural, ethnic, or social factors, women are fatter than men. Assuming that body size and weight are normally distributed, only a minority of women can be expected to "naturally" match the extremely thin ideal; the great majority will have varyingly heavier bodies.

In light of these biological factors, we may also conjecture yet another answer to our question of why women are more concerned than men about their weight. In addition to the sociocultural explanations offered earlier, we now suggest a concrete biological reality. Men are genetically programmed to resemble, to a high degree, the male build society sees as ideal—the mesomorph, with little fat. While the aging process slows down the male's metabolic rate, it does so less than for women; and there are no male developmental milestones analogous to female puberty, pregnancy, and menopause that may reduce large increases in fat. Thus the body most men naturally assume is synchronous with society's ideal male figure, whereas for most women there is a much greater discrepancy between "natural" and "ideal." Furthermore, this discrepancy increases throughout the female life cycle.

WOMEN'S REPEATED WEIGHT-REDUCTION ATTEMPTS SERVE TO DISREGULATE THEIR METABOLIC SYSTEMS AND MAKE ATTAINMENT OF THE THIN IDEAL EVEN MORE UNLIKELY

Before leaving the discussion of the biological aspects of weight, let us briefly consider the biological effects of dieting. Were achieving thinness merely a matter of conditioning oneself to eat less than would be "natural," we might expect more women to be successful in achieving the svelte ideal. However, decreasing one's caloric intake greatly suppresses metabolism (Apfelbaum, 1975; Garrow, 1978). When few calories are taken in, the human system becomes more efficient; to accommodate the decrease in incoming fuel, resting metabolic rate slows down. Such a response represents an important homeostatic mechanism, for the fat stores are protected from quick depletion. While adaptive biologically, however, this effect is clearly not in the interest of dieters aiming for weight loss.

Studies also show that this effect is strongest in people who begin with the lowest basal metabolic rate (Wooley et al., 1979). Since women in general have lower metabolic rates than men, they are particularly likely to find that despite their dieting attempts, they cannot lose as much weight as they would like. Their relatively low metabolic rates become even lower as they reduce their caloric intake. Furthermore, this effect appears to increase with each successive dieting attempt (Garrow, 1978). Therefore a vicious cycle is triggered, in which increasingly stringent dieting efforts are mounted, only to produce further metabolic slowdown.

When people stop dieting and resume normal caloric intake, their metabolism does not immediately rebound to its normal pace. The longer the period of underfeeding, the longer the body takes to return to a normal metabolic rate (Even & Nicolaidis, 1981). Hence, during the time following a diet when the metabolism remains sluggish, an individual would be especially likely to gain weight, especially when there is binge eating after a period of dieting. Therefore "normal" eating or overeating after a diet will tend to produce weight gain, which typically leads to yet another dieting attempt.

Data also suggest that those who have patterns of repeated dieting and overeating or dieting alone may not be as biologically able to cope with even small bouts of overeating. Individuals who have a history of dieting demonstrate a lower thermogenic response to food—that is, the amount of energy expended by the body immediately following a meal in order to digest food (Armitage, Harris, Hervey, & Tobin, 1981; James & Trayhurn, 1981). It may be that people with long dieting histories are able to eat far fewer calories relative to their equal-weight peers who have not engaged in comparable dieting.

In sum, because she is genetically predisposed to a heavier body size than the sociocultural thin ideal, the average woman often feels compelled to go on a diet. In doing so, and especially in doing so repeatedly, she disregulates her metabolic system and finds it increasingly difficult to achieve her target weight. The biological side of dieting is, of course, complemented by a psychological dimension. Typically, the dieter feels deprived of favorite foods and, upon "going off" the diet, is likely to overeat (Herman & Mack, 1975). As described above, the on the diet/off the diet cycle and the accompanying wide variance in caloric intake are particularly likely to promote weight gain and metabolic disregulation.

Women's Relationships to Their Bodies

FEMALES INTERNALIZE SOCIETY'S MESSAGE THAT THEY SHOULD CARE A GREAT DEAL ABOUT HOW THEY LOOK

Females learn society's expectations and emphasis on attractiveness early in life. Developmental studies have shown that girls are more concerned than boys about having an attractive appearance (Coleman, 1961, Douvan & Adelson, 1966). Parents, teachers, and peers all depict girls as being more focused on their looks than are boys, and girls' fantasies also reflect this interest (Nelsen & Rosenbaum, 1972; Wagman, 1967). While boys tend to choose toys involving physical and mechanical activity, girls select toys centering on adornment and nurture (Ambert, 1976; Oakley, 1972).

The media message, continually endorsing women's need to be attractive, clearly influences children and adults alike. From their survey of children's readers, Women on Words and Images (1972) found that girls in these primers were constantly concerned about how they looked, while boys never were. Indeed, attending to one's appearance was a major activity for the girl characters, ranking with cooking, sewing, and looking on while the boys did everything, such as solving problems and playing hard. Television programs and commercials, according to Mamay and Simpson (1981), represent only three female roles: maternal, housekeeping, and decorative. Analyzing over 500 television commercials, they found that women were depicted as relentlessly indulgent servants to their husbands and children and as in need of expert advice to perfect these roles. In contrast, women were seen as competent in the domain of self-beautification, and in fact television commercials promote a view that women are experts *only* in the decorative role. It is interesting that the relative frequency of magazine advertisements depicting women in a decorative role has actually increased over the past 20 years (Venkatesan & Losco, 1975; Weinberger, Petrosius, & Westin, 1979).

WOMEN POSSESS HIGHLY DIFFERENTIATED CONCEPTS BOTH OF THEIR OWN BODIES AND OF THE IDEAL FEMALE FIGURE, AND DISCREPANCIES BETWEEN THE TWO INVOKE SELF-CRITICISM

Given this persistent indoctrination into sociocultural attitudes toward female appearance, it is not surprising that females develop very specific barometers for measuring their own bodies. In a sample of college students, Kurtz (1969) found that women possessed a more clearly differentiated body concept—that is, they discriminated more finely among various features of the body—than men.

Similarly, females have clearly defined "templates" of the ideal, extremely thin female figure (Fallon & Rozin, 1984; Jourard & Secord, 1955) and show much less variability than males in their view of acceptable size and weight (Harris, 1983). Young girls assume an association between femininity and smallness as early as age 3 (Katcher & Levin, 1955).

With these two images in mind—their own body image and the ideal body image—females begin, surely by adolescence and possibly much sooner, to measure self against ideal. Given the biological realities of women's bodies as discussed above, most women emerge from such comparisons with discrepancies—which are viewed as flaws and as worthy of self-criticism. Dornbusch, Carlsmith, Duke, Gross, Martin, Ritter, and Siegel-Gorelick (1984) concluded from their national survey of adolescents that normal development produces dissatisfaction with body weight for *most* adolescent females. Similarly, Jourard and Secord (1955) found no woman in a sample of 60 college females who rated all of her body parts positively. With one exception (the bust), they concluded that women wished to be smaller in all body parts. In their *Glamour* magazine survey, Wooley and Wooley (1984a) found that women pervasively experienced dissatisfaction with their bodies, particularly the fat-bearing areas of thighs, hips, and waist. Fallon and Rozin (1984) asked a sample of men and women to locate their actual figure as well as their ideal figure on a display of different body shapes. For females, there was a significant discrepancy between their current figure and their ideal, with the ideal always thinner. For males, there was no significant difference between self and ideal.

Again, we hark back to our discussion of the biological factors involved in weight. Reviewing that literature, we concluded that the male "ideal" body of current society more closely resembles the "natural" body most men assume, while the female "ideal" is far thinner than the "natural" female figure. Hence, from both biological and psychosocial perspectives, it is not surprising to find a discrepancy between self and ideal for women but not for men.

At the same time, however, there is evidence that this discrepancy may be exaggerated for women—not only because of the increasingly thin standards that constitute the "ideal" but also because women tend to overestimate their body size. Many studies document women's consistent exaggeration of body size, both of the figure as a whole and of specific body parts—typically the fat-bearing areas such as waist and hips. These estimation differences appear specific to the female subjects' own bodies, for they accurately judge the body size of other people and physical objects (Button, Fransella, & Slade, 1977; Casper, Halmi, Goldberg, Eckert, & Davis, 1979; Crisp & Kalucy, 1974; Fries, 1975; Garner, Garfinkel, Stancer, & Moldofski, 1976; Halmi, Goldberg, & Cunningham, 1977). There have been no studies comparing the estimation errors of men and women, but we hypothesize that men would be as likely to err in the direction of underestimation as overestimation.

The Meaning of Weight for Women

We would now like to consider the role weight plays in women's lives. As will be apparent, this is largely an area with few empirical data. We will draw from our clinical experience in treating women in weight control programs and eating disorder clinics, as well as women seeking psychotherapy, who, in large numbers, spontaneously discuss concerns with their weight and body image as intricately interwoven with other personal issues. We will try to extrapolate insights about women and weight from the literature on the psychology of women, although little direct attention has been given to the topic. We broach this section as conjectural and hope to offer hypotheses that may be submitted to empirical investigation.

THE DIFFERENCES IN HOW FEMALES AND MALES VIEW THEIR BODIES ARE ANALOGOUS TO THEIR DIFFERENT ORIENTATIONS TO THE WORLD IN GENERAL

Females, Chodorow (1978) asserts, define themselves primarily in relation and in connection to other people, while males are more oriented toward individuation and their own sense of agency. Gilligan (1982) found that this framework accounted for sex differences in moral reasoning. We would like to propose that there is an analogous difference in the way men and women view their bodies. Whereas men primarily view their bodies as actively functional, as tools that need to be in shape and ready for use, women primarily see their bodies as commodities, their physical appearance serving as an interpersonal currency. Some support for this hypothesis is provided by Kurtz (1969), who found that college women rated their bodies more extremely on the "evaluative" dimension of the semantic differential than men, while men saw their bodies as more "potent" and more "active" than women did. Similarly, a study of adolescent males and females found that girls' self-concepts were more strongly related to their body attractiveness, whereas boys' self-concepts derived from perceptions of physical instrumental effectiveness (Lerner, Orlos, & Knapp, 1976).

Concomitant with their greater relational orientation, women tend to be field dependent, while men tend to be field independent (Witkin, Lewis, Hertzman, Machover, Meissner, & Wagner, 1954). Females typically demonstate a higher need for approval from others (Crandall & Rabson, 1960; Hoffman, 1972; Simmons & Rosenberg, 1975). Given our earlier discussion of the importance of a woman's appearance in achieving interpersonal and societal success, it is not surprising that women view appearance and weight as high priorities in their lives. Women are socialized to be oriented to others, to need their approval—and society, they quickly learn, metes out rewards to women with thin bodies.

WOMEN'S PURSUIT OF THINNESS IS A FORM OF COMPETITION AND ACHIEVEMENT BEHAVIOR

It is possible that something as hard for most women to achieve as the thin ideal comes to be more valued precisely because it is so difficult to attain. In a time of affluence, thinness has become a status symbol for women.

In addition, the arenas of physical attractiveness and weight may be the chief and most wholeheartedly sanctioned competitive domains in which women are encouraged to contend with each other (Boskind-White & White, 1983; Brownmiller, 1984). For most women, the subjective experience of dieting is clearly marked not only by success vis-à-vis their own weight goals but also by comparison with women friends, colleagues, and relatives. Issues about weight, we find, constitute a central core around which other issues revolve in many mother-daughter, sister-sister, friend-friend, colleague-colleague relationships. For many women, weight is a quick and concrete barometer by which to measure oneself and one's worth—how well one is doing as a woman. Many women report that upon entering a room they automatically sweep their gaze across the female occupants and assess where they rank: who is thinner, who is fatter.

Brownmiller (1984) also argues for another competitive aspect of femininity and thinness, the female-against-female competition produced by the effort to attract and secure men. Fallon and Rozin's (1984) recent study, however, suggests that women's pursuit of extreme thinness may not derive simply from an attempt to please men. Undergraduate men and women were asked to select the figure representing their perception of what is attractive to the opposite sex. The ideal female figure aspired to by women subjects was significantly thinner than their estimates of what is most attractive to males. For males, their ideal figure and the figure they thought was attractive to women were not significantly different. Furthermore, the female figure that women rated as most attractive to males was significantly thinner than the figure male raters actually preferred. On the other hand, male judgments of the male figure most attractive to females were significantly heavier than female ratings of the same. Thus both males and females are misinformed about what the opposite sex finds attractive; however, these errors are in opposite directions, with females underestimating and males overestimating the body size desired by the other sex. In terms of women's relationship to their own weight, the results are striking: women want to be thinner than they think men want them to be, and even their estimate of what men want is significantly lower than men's actual preferences.

WEIGHT HAS COME TO BE A METAPHOR FOR WOMEN

The results of the Fallon and Rozin (1984) study suggest that women do not pursue extreme thinness merely to attract men. When asked what would make them happiest among four possible alternatives, 42% of the women respondents in the *Glamour* magazine survey (Wooley and Wooley, 1984a) reported that it would be losing weight, versus 22% who endorsed success at work, 21% a date with a man they admired, and 15% hearing from an old friend. One wonders how losing weight has become such a desired end in itself. White and Boskind-White (1981) comment on the common fantasy in women with eating disorders that their lives would be totally transformed if only they were thin. There is, as Bruch (1978) notes, a "thinness = femininity = happiness" life equation.

Women talk about losing "the weight"—those pounds on specific locales of the body that stand between them and the thin ideal—as if it were not really a part of them. For many women, their weight history is a handle on their past and their hoped-for future; weight is the lens through which experience is viewed. A bad day or a bad year is one in which they felt fat; a New Year's resolution to lose weight is virtually the same as a wish for a happy year, for thinness and happiness are nearly synonymous.

The Wooleys (1980) postulate some reasons why weight control has become such an important metaphor in so many women's lives. The challenge is sufficiently difficult that it commands respect; the effects are visible and highly valued. Indeed, the high chances of failure and the resultant attribution of personal shortcomings may reinforce its importance.

WOMEN'S CONCERNS WITH WEIGHT SEEM NOT TO DIMINISH AS THEY CAST OFF OTHER SEX-ROLE TRADITIONS

As the societal changes wrought by the women's movement take hold, many cultural stereotypes of women are being challenged and are changing. Are the many women who can now be valued by society on the basis of occupational success and financial independence less focused on weight and bodily appearance?

There are as yet no complete empirical data to answer this question, and competing hypotheses might be postulated. On one hand, the diversification of arenas in which women today can feel competent and productive might diminish the salience of weight and physical appearance in their sense of self and well-being. A study of female undergraduates (Kimlicka, Cross, & Tarnai, 1983) found that women high on androgyny and masculinity had higher body satisfaction and overall self-esteem than subjects high on femininity or with an undifferentiated gender orientation. Birnbaum (1975) found from a study of women in midlife that homemakers felt significantly less attractive than did married professional women. In general, research is suggesting that women with "multiple roles"—women who work outside the home as well as have a family life—enjoy an enhanced sense of well-being (Baruch, Barnett, & Rivers, 1982; Crosby, 1982; Kessler & MacRae, 1982; Thoits, 1983). But further research is needed to assess the relationship among a general sense of well-being, self-esteem, and body satisfaction and to examine specifically the effects of "multiple roles" on women's body image.

The competing hypothesis would posit that as the demands on and expectations for women have proliferated, they feel compelled to be "both beautiful and smart" (Selvini-Palazzoli, 1974). In other words, weight control may be a persistent "role" for women, on top of which they may or may not add an occupational role. The working woman today may wish to achieve the proper weight, along with her other accomplishments on the job and at home. Banner (1983) has suggested that being attractive makes women feel powerful and virtuous as well as feminine. It may be that in striving to be thin and beautiful, a woman may both be feminine, thus pleasing society, and experience a sense of agency and control. Furthermore, women who are successful in previously male-dominated professions often feel simultaneous needs to minimize their female status and to retain it. Given that attractiveness is largely defined as thinness, and that attractiveness increases perceived femininity (Cash, Gillen, & Burns, 1977; Gillen, 1981; Gillen & Sherman, 1980), aspiring to thinness may be a way for women in traditionally male occupations to maintain a feminine identity. Beck, Ward-Hull, and McLear (1976) found that women who value nontraditional roles and greater options for women prefer a smaller, thinner female body, associating a more ample form with a view of woman as "wife and mother." Thus, professional women who ascribe to many nontraditional views of women may experience a tension between a philosophical sense that perhaps appearance should not matter and a conviction that weight and appearance do matter, both to themselves and to others.

Indeed, might it be that women who aspire to greater occupational success actually experience a greater need to "achieve" thinness as well? Our data suggest that women who have perfectionist standards and high expectations for personal performance tend to be more dissatisfied with their own bodies and feel fatter regardless of actual weight than less achievement-oriented women of identical weight (Rodin & Striegel-Moore, 1984). It may be that dissatisfaction with weight and striving for achievement are positively related, and that women who have a high need to be professionally successful also have a great need to experience success in weight control.

SHAME IS A SALIENT EMOTION IN WOMEN'S RELATION TO THEIR BODIES

Although other affects are surely discernible (e.g., anger, pride), shame occupies a central place in women's relationships to their bodies. Intense shame is triggered by childhood obesity and the accompanying teasing, ostracism, and hate. Women feel ashamed of their unsuccessful dieting attempts, of feeling fat, and of feeling stared at. A repetitive theme in this chapter has been that the shame evoked by dissatisfaction with one's body is intricately interwoven with low self-esteem and a general sense of personal inadequacy.

Lewis (1971) has explored the affect of shame and its counterpart guilt. Shame, she argues, involves feeling bad about who one is, with the entire self the target of hostility, whereas guilt comprises negative feelings about what one does or has done. In shame one experiences one's self, rather than merely one's behavior, as faulty; one's self-concept plummets, and one feels worthless. Lewis has found that shame is experienced more by women than by men, while guilt is more man's lot.

The general depiction of shame by Lewis (1971) fits well with the picture we have been compiling of women's scrutinizing, evaluating, and criticizing their bodies, which almost universally fall short of the ideal, resulting in painful, derogatory conclusions about the adequacy of the self. Lewis points out that shame, because it is largely imagistic and hence primitive and irrational, is difficult to deal with rationally. Often, she notes, one is ashamed of being ashamed. It is our sense that women do experience shame frequently and powerfully with respect to their weight and bodies—and that they also experience shame about their shame. We would like to suggest that it is partly this double tier of shame that has made women's relationship with their bodies a highly charged, even almost taboo topic for inquiry.

Conclusion

All the data we have reviewed suggest that women in general, more than men, spend a great deal of time and energy worrying about appearance and feeling too fat. In the now-classic study by Broverman, Broverman, Clarkson, Rosenkrantz, and Vogel (1970), the healthy adult woman, as compared with a man, was seen as "more conceited about [her] appearance." We contend, after our study of the literature, that women are not "conceited" about their appearance in the sense of viewing their bodies with "pride" or "overvaluation." Rather, in response to a cultural imperative that women be attractive—that is, thin—and given that thinness is not, for many women, their natural body build, women appear vain because they persistently expend much effort and attention in the pursuit of the svelte ideal. Thus it is not vanity or conceit, but shame and social pressure that lead to women's preoccupation with their appearance. This preoccupation and the behaviors it engenders have serious psychological consequences and considerably affect physical health as well.

Many of the psychological consequences have been reviewed in this chapter. They include decreased self-esteem for failure to meet the thin idealized body type, distorted body image, feelings of helplessness and frustration in response to unsuccessful dieting efforts, and becoming preoccupied and even victimized by consumerism (Banner, 1983; Boskind-White & White, 1983; Garner & Garfinkel, 1981–1982; Wooley & Wooley, 1984b). We believe the psychological consequences of weight concerns and chronic body dissatisfaction may also be among the causes of depression in many women.

In addition to these often serious psychological outcomes, physical health may also be affected by women's weight-control efforts. Repeated dieting may produce changes in metabolic rate and in lipid and glucose metabolism (Apfelbaum, 1975; Even & Nicolaidis, 1981; Howard, Grant, Challand, Wraight, & Edwards, 1978). Extremes in dieting behaviors, including purging, use of laxatives, and starvation, are associated with renal and liver problems, gastrointestinal disorders, and in some severe cases with death (Beumont, George, &

Smart, 1976; Dally, 1969; Garfinkel & Garner, 1982; Hsu, Crisp, & Harding, 1979; Theander, 1970; Williams, 1958). However, many dieters believe—and certainly the diet industry wishes to promote this belief—that the pursuit of thinness is the pursuit of better health.

The assumption that thinner equals healthier is now the focus of increasing skepticism. Keys (1980) reviewed 13 prospective studies on obesity and mortality and concluded that risk of early death increased only at the extremes of under- and overweight, with weight having no impact on the health of women in the middle 80%. In fact, data from the Framingham study indicated that underweight was more dangerous than overweight and revealed no association between fatness and mortality for women in the middle 60% of the weight range (Sorlie, Gordon, & Kannel, 1980). Thus the association between thinness and health may be illusory, and the unrelenting quest for the thin ideal may be the real health risk.

Another significant consequence of women's concern about attaining an idealized weight and appearance may be the development of eating disorders. Several authors have suggested that the current preoccupation with thinness and dieting may have contributed to the great increase in eating disorders in the past decade (Boskind-Lodahl, 1976; Bruch, 1981; Chernin, 1981; Garner & Garfinkel, 1980; Orbach, 1978; Schwartz, Thompson, & Johnson, 1982; Selvini-Palazzoli, 1974; Thompson & Schwartz, 1982). In this chapter we have tried to ask systematically, and based on empirical data, *why* women are so preoccupied with thinness and dieting and to suggest several testable hypotheses where no data are currently available. On the basis of this review, we propose that weight concerns and efforts to be thin are at present so normative that a large majority of women may be at risk for developing an eating disorder. Indeed, we believe that for many women today, eating and dieting patterns are dangerous candidates for pathological disruption. Although this assertion may seem extreme, estimates of the prevalence of binge eating among women on college campuses now range from 35% to 60% (Halmi et al., 1981; Hawkins & Clement, 1980; Nevo, 1984; Ondercin, 1979). An extensive survey of 1,268 high-school females between 13 and 19 years of age documented the high incidence of bulimic behavior in this relatively young population (Johnson, Lewis, Love, Lewis, & Stuckey, in press). Twenty-one percent reported binge eating episodes at least once each week. Seven percent of this sample were using purging (vomiting or laxative abuse) as a way of controlling their weight.

In a survey of more than 1,300 college freshman, Pyle, Mitchell, Eckert, Halverson, Neuman, and Goff (1983) compared bulimic with nonbulimic students and found that fear of being fat was so pervasive among the nonbulimic women that its usefulness as a differentiating variable was negligable. Thompson and Schwartz (1982) compared female anorexic students, students with anorexic-like attitudes and behaviors, and healthy students. All three groups reported with almost identical frequency that they were "always on a diet." Similarly, anorexic and healthy students alike reported that they constantly exerted willpower to restrain their food intake and that they experienced their hunger as exaggerated and obscene. While body-image distortion has traditionally been recognized as a central feature of the anorexic female (Bruch, 1973), body-size overestimation is, as we reported earlier, characteristic of women in general (Button et al., 1977; Casper, Halmi, Goldberg, Eckert, & Davis, 1979; Crisp & Kalucy, 1974; Fries, 1975; Garner et al., 1976).

A different category of support for the importance of sociocultural determinants of eating disorders among women may be obtained by examining those sociocultural subgroups that value thinness the most. Presumably such subcultures would place females at even greater risk for eating disorders. A few sources of data suggest that this may be true. Dancers, a subgroup known to emphasize and even demand extreme thinness, have a notoriously high rate of anorexia nervosa, and what is informative to us is that most of these women develop the disorder *after* joining the dance world and experiencing its pressures to be thin (Garner & Garfinkel, 1980).

We also hypothesize that current sociocultural influences teach women not only what the ideal body looks like, but also how to try to attain it, including dieting, purging, and other disregulating behaviors. These rituals are nearly prescribed by the mass-market weight control industry. For example, the 1981 best-seller—outselling the nearest competition more than two to one—was the *Beverly Hills Diet*, in which Mazel advocates a form of bulimia in which binges are "compensated" by eating massive quantities of raw fruit to induce diarrhea (Wooley & Wooley, 1982). In addition to the mass media's making available what one might call manuals for "how to develop an eating disorder," women more directly teach each other how to diet, and how to binge and purge and starve. Schwartz, Thompson, and Johnson (1981) found that a college woman who purges almost always knows another who purges, while a woman who does not purge rarely knows someone who does.

A positive feedback loop is thus established: the more women there are with disordered eating, the more likely there are to be even more women with disordered eating. We certainly do not mean to imply that psychopathology is merely learned behavior—but we would like to suggest that the public's heightened awareness of the eating disorders and a young woman's likelihood of personal exposure to the behaviors may be a significant factor in the increase in eating disorders over the past several years.

On the basis of this review, we urge that empirical studies of eating disorders, and clinical interventions for them, take into account the variables we have proposed. Equally important is our recommendation that investigators interested in the psychology of women focus greater attention on women's feelings and concerns about bodily appearance. Such data will elucidate the determinants and consequences of what we believe is a profound and almost universal experience among women in contemporary Western societies.

REFERENCES

Adams, G. R. (1977). Physical attractiveness research. *Human Development,* 20, 217–239.
Adams, G. R., & Cohen, A. S. (1976a). An examination of cumulative folder information used by teachers in making differential judgments of children's abilities. *Alberta Journal of Educational Research, 22,* 215–225.
Adams, G. R., & Cohen, A. S. (1976b). Characteristics of children and teacher expectancy. An extension to the child's social and family life. *Journal of Educational Research, 70* (2), 87–90.
Allon, N. (1975). The stigma of overweight in everyday life. In G. A. Bray (Ed.), *Obesity in perspective* (Vol. 2). DHEW Publication No. NIH 75-708. Washington, DC: U.S. Government Printing Office.
Ambert, A. M. (1976). *Sex structure.* Don Mills: Longman Canada.
Angel, J. L. (1949). Constitution in female obesity. *American Journal of Physical Anthropology, 7,* 433–471.
Apfelbaum, M. (1975). Influence of level of energy intake on energy expenditure in man: Effects of spontaneous intake, experimental starvation and experimental overeating. In G. A. Bray (Ed.), *Obesity in perspective* (Vol. 2). DHEW Publication No. NIH 75-708). Washington, DC: U.S. Government Printing Office.
Archer, D., Iritani, B., Kimes D. D., & Barrios, M. (1983). Face-ism: Five studies of sex differences in facial prominence. *Journal of Personality and Social Psychology, 45,* 725–735.
Armitage, G., Harris, R. B. S., Hervey, G. R., & Tobin, G. (1981). Energy-

expenditure of Zucker rats in relation to environmental temperature. *Journal of Physiology*, 310, 33–34.

Banner, L. (1983). *American beauty*. Chicago: University of Chicago Press.

Barnett, R. C., & Baruch, G. K. (1980). *The competent woman: Perspectives on development*. New York: Irvington.

Bar-Tal, D., & Saxe, L. (1976). Physical attractiveness and its relationship to sex-role stereotyping. *Sex Roles*, 2, 123–133.

Baruch, G. K., Barnett, R. C., & Rivers, C. (1982). *Lifeprints*. New York: McGraw-Hill.

Beamon, A. L., & Klentz, B. (1983). The supposed physical attractiveness bias against supporters of the women's movement: A meta-analysis. *Personality and Social Psychology Bulletin*, 9, 544–550.

Beck, J. B., Ward-Hull, C. J., & McLear, P. M. (1976). Variables related to women's somatic preferences of the male and female body. *Journal of Personality and Social Psychology*, 34, 1200–1210.

Beller, A. S. (1977). *Fat and thin: A natural history of obesity*. New York: Farrar, Straus and Giroux.

Beller, A. S. (1980). Pregnancy: Is motherhood fattening? In J. R. Kaplan (Ed.), *A woman's conflict*. Englewood Cliffs, NJ: Prentice-Hall.

Bem, S., & Bem, D. (1976). Case study of a nonconscious ideology: Training the woman to know her place. In S. Cox (Ed.), *Female psychology: The emerging self*. Chicago: Science Research Associates.

Benson, P. L., Karabenick, S. A., & Lerner, R. M. (1976). Pretty pleases: The effects of physical attractiveness, race, and sex on receiving helping. *Journal of Experimental Social Psychology*, 12, 409–415.

Berscheid, E., Dion, K. K., Walster, E., & Walster, G. (1971). Physical attractiveness and dating choice: A test of the matching hypothesis. *Journal of Experimental Social Psychology*, 7, 173–189.

Berscheid, E., & Walster, E. (1974). Physical attractiveness. In L. Berkowitz (Ed.), *Advances in experimental social psychology* (Vol. 7). New York: Academic Press.

Beumont, P. J., George, G. C., & Smart, D. E. (1976). "Dieters" and "vomiters and purgers" in anorexia nervosa. *Psychological Medicine*, 6, 617–622.

Birnbaum, J. A. (1975). Life patterns and self-esteem in gifted family oriented and career committed women. In M. Mednick, L. W. Hoffman, & S. Tangri (Eds.), *Women and achievement: Social and motivational analyses*. New York: Halstead Press.

Blumstein, P. W., & Schwartz, P. (1983). *American couples: Money, work, and sex*. New York: William Morrow.

Boskind-Lodahl, M. (1976). Cinderella's stepsisters. *Signs: Journal of Women in Culture and Society*, 2, 342–358.

Boskind-White, M., & White, W. C. (1983). *Bulimarexia: The binge/purge cycle*. New York: W. W. Norton.

Bray, G. A. (1976). *The obese patient*. Philadelphia: Saunders.

Bray, G. A. (1981). The inheritance of corpulence. In L. A. Cioffi, W. P. T. James, & T. B. Van Itallie (Eds.), *The body weight regulatory system: Normal and disturbed mechanisms.* New York: Raven Press.

Broverman, I. K., Broverman, D. M., Clarkson, F. E., Rosenkrantz, P. S., & Vogel, S. R. (1970). Sex-role stereotypes and clinical judgments of mental health. *Journal of Consulting and Clinical Psychology, 34,* 1–7.

Brownmiller, S. (1984). *Femininity.* New York: Simon and Schuster.

Bruch, H. (1973). *Eating disorders: Obesity, anorexia nervosa and the person within.* New York: Basic Books.

Bruch, H. (1978). *The golden cage: The enigma of anorexia nervosa.* Cambridge: Harvard University Press.

Bruch, H. (1981). Developmental considerations of anorexia nervosa and obesity. *Canadian Journal of Psychiatry, 26,* 212–217.

Button, E. J., Fransella, F., & Slade, P. D. (1977). A reappraisal of body perception disturbance in anorexia nervosa. *Psychological Medicine, 7,* 235–243.

Canning, H., & Mayer, J. (1966). Obesity—its possible effect on college acceptance. *New England Journal of Medicine, 275,* 1172–1174.

Cash, T. F., Gillen, B., & Burns, D. S. (1977). Sexism and "beautyism" in personnel consultant decision making. *Journal of Applied Psychology, 62,* 301–310.

Casper, R. C., Eckert, E. D., Halmi, K. A., Goldberg, S. C., & Davis, J. M. (1980). Bulimia: Its incidence and clinical importance in patients with anorexia nervosa. *Archives of General Psychiatry, 37,* 1030–1035.

Casper, R. C., Halmi, K. A., Goldberg, S. C., Eckert, E. D., & Davis, J. M. (1979). Disturbances in body image estimation as related to other characteristics and outcome of anorexia nervosa. *British Journal of Psychiatry, 134,* 60–66.

Cederlöf, R., & Kaij, L. (1970). The effect of childbearing on body weight: A twin control study. *Acta Psychiatrica Scandinavica, 46* (Suppl. 219), 47–49.

Cheek, D. B. (1974). Body composition, nutrition, and adolescent growth. In M. M. Grumbach, G. D. Grave, and F. E. Mayer (Eds.), *Control of the onset of puberty.* New York: John Wiley.

Chernin, K. (1981). *The obsession.* New York: Harper and Row.

Chodorow, N. (1978). *The reproduction of mothering: Psychoanalysis and the sociology of gender.* Berkeley: University of California Press.

Clifford, M. M. (1975). Physical attractiveness and academic performance. *Child Study Journal, 5,* 201–209.

Clifford, M. M., & Walster, E. (1973). The effect of physical attractiveness on teacher expectations. *Sociology of Education, 46,* 248–258.

Coleman, J. S. (1961). *The adolescent society.* New York: Free Press.

Committee on Dietary Allowances. (1974). *Recommended dietary allowances* (8th rev. ed.). Washington, DC: Food and Nutrition Board, National Research Council, National Academy of Sciences.

Crandall, V. J., & Rabson, A. (1960). Children's repetition choices in an intellectual achievement situation following success and failure. *Journal of Genetic Psychology, 97,* 161–168.

Crisp, A. H., & Kalucy, R. S. (1974). Aspects of the perceptual disorder in anorexia nervosa. *British Journal of Medical Psychology, 47,* 349–361.

Crosby, F. J. (1982). *Relative deprivation and working women.* New York: Oxford University Press.

Dally, P. J. (1969). *Anorexia nervosa.* New York: Grune and Stratton.

Dalvit-MacPhillips, S. P. (1983). The effect of the human menstrual cycle on nutrient intake. *Physiology and Behavior, 31,* 209–212.

Davis, D. M., Shipp, J. C., & Pattishall, E. G. (1965). Attitudes of diabetic boys and girls towards diabetes. *Diabetes, 14,* 106–109.

Dion, K. K. (1973). Young children's stereotyping of facial attractiveness. *Developmental Psychology, 9,* 183–188.

Dion, K. K., Berscheid, E., & Walster, E. (1972). What is beautiful is good. *Journal of Personality and Social Psychology, 24,* 285–290.

Dipboye, R. L., Arvey, R. D., & Terpstra, D. E. (1977). Sex and physical attractiveness of raters and applicants as determinants of resume evaluations. *Journal of Applied Psychology, 62,* 228–294.

Dipboye, R. L., Fromkin, H. L., & Wibach, K. (1975). Relative importance of applicant sex, attractiveness and scholastic standing in evaluations of job applicant resumes. *Journal of Applied Psychology, 60,* 39–43.

Dippel, R. L., & Elias, J. W. (1980). Preferences for sweets in relationship to use of oral contraceptives in pregnancy. *Hormones and Behavior, 14,* 1–6.

Dornbusch, S. M., Carlsmith, J. M., Duke, P. M., Gross, R. T., Martin, J. A., Ritter, P. L., & Siegel-Gorelick, B. (1984). The desire to be thin among adolescent females as a form of conspicuous consumption: An empirical test in a national sample. Unpublished manuscript, Stanford University, CA.

Douvan, E., & Adelson, J. (1966). *The adolescent experience.* New York: John Wiley.

Drewnowski, A., Riskey, D., & Desor, J. A. (1982). Feeling fat yet unconcerned: Self-reported overweight and the restraint scale. *Appetite: Journal for Intake Research, 3,* 273–279.

Dwyer, J. T., Feldman, J. J., Seltzer, C. C., & Mayer, J. (1969). Body image in adolescents: Attitudes toward weight and perception of appearance. *American Journal of Clinical Nutrition, 20,* 1045–1056.

Efran, M. G. (1974). The effect of physical appearance on the judgment of guilt, interpersonal attraction, and severity of recommended punishment in a simulated jury task. *Journal of Research in Personality, 8,* 45–54.

Ehrenreich, B., & English, D. (1978). *For her own good: 150 years of the experts' advice to women.* New York: Anchor/Doubleday.

Even, P., & Nicolaidis, S. (1981). Changes in efficiency of ingestants are a major factor of regulation of energy balance. In L. A. Cioffi, W. P. T. James, & T. B. Van Itallie (Eds.), *The body weight regulatory system: Normal and disturbed mechanisms*. New York: Raven Press.

Fallon, A. E., & Rozin, P. (1984). *Sex differences in perceptions of body shape*. Manuscript submitted for publication.

Forbes, G., & Reina, J. C. (1970). Adult lean body mass declines with age: Some longitudinal observations. *Metabolism, 19*, 653–663.

Fries, H. (1975). Anorectic behavior: Nosological aspects and introduction of a behavior scale. *Scandinavian Journal of Behaviour Therapy, 4*, 137–148.

Garfinkel, P. E., & Garner, D. M. (1982). *Anorexia nervosa: A multidimensional perspective*. New York: Brunner/Mazel.

Garner, D. M., & Garfinkel, P. E. (1980). Socio-cultural factors in the development of anorexia nervosa. *Psychological Medicine, 10*, 647–656.

Garner, D. M., & Garfinkel, P. E. (1981–1982). Body image in anorexia nervosa: Measurement, theory and clinical implications. *International Journal of Psychiatry in Medicine, 12*, 1263–1283.

Garner, D. M., Garfinkel, P. E., Schwartz, D., & Thompson, M. (1980). Cultural expectations of thinness in women. *Psychological Reports, 47*, 483–491.

Garner, D. M., Garfinkel, P. E., Stancer, H. C., & Moldofski, H. (1976). Body image disturbances in anorexia nervosa and obesity. *Psychosomatic Medicine, 38*, 327–336.

Garner, D. M., Olmstead, M. P., & Polivy, J. (1983). Development and validation of multidimensional eating disorder inventory for anorexia nervosa and bulimia. *International Journal of Eating Disorders, 2*, 15–35.

Garrow, J. (1978). The regulation of energy expenditure. In G. A. Bray (Ed.), *Recent advances in obesity research* (Vol. 2). London: Newman.

Gillen, B. (1981). Physical attractiveness: A determinant of two types of goodness. *Personality and Social Psychology Bulletin, 7*, 277–281.

Gillen, B., & Sherman, R. C. (1980). Physical attractiveness and sex as determinants of trait attributions. *Multivariate Behavioral Research, 15*, 423–437.

Gilligan, C. (1982). *In a different voice: Psychological theory and women's development*. Cambridge: Harvard University Press.

Goldblatt, P. B., Moore, M. E., & Stunkard, A. J. (1965). Social factors in obesity. *Journal of the American Medical Association, 192*, 1039–1044.

Goodman, N., Richardson, S. A., Dornbusch, S. M., & Hastorf, A. H. (1963). Variant reactions to physical disabilities. *American Sociological Review, 28*, 429–435.

Halmi, K. A., Falk, J. R., & Schwartz, E. (1981). Binge-eating and vomiting: A survey of a college population. *Psychological Medicine, 11*, 697–706.

Halmi, K. A., Goldberg, S., & Cunningham, S. (1977). Perceptual distribution of body image in adolescent girls: Distortion of body image in adolescence. *Psychological Medicine, 67*, 253–257.

Harris, M. B. (1983). Eating habits, restraint, knowledge and attitudes toward obesity. *International Journal of Obesity, 7*, 271–288.

Hatfield, E., & Sprecher, S. (in press). *Mirror, mirror on the wall: A revealing report on the importance of good looks.* New York: SUNY Press.

Hawkins R. C., II, & Clement, P. F. (1980). Development and construct validation of a self-report measure of binge eating tendencies. *Addictive Behaviors, 5*, 219–226.

Hawkins R. C., II, Turell, S., & Jackson, L. J. (1983). Desirable and undesirable masculine and feminine traits in relation to students' dietary tendencies and body image dissatisfaction. *Sex Roles, 9*, 705–724.

Helliovaara, M., & Aromaa, A. (1981). Parity and obesity. *Journal of Epidemiology and Community Health, 35*, 197–199.

Herman, C. P., & Mack, D. (1975). Restrained and unrestrained eating. *Journal of Personality, 43*, 647–660.

Herman, C. P., & Polivy, J. (1975). Anxiety, restraint and eating behavior. *Journal of Abnormal Psychology, 84*, 666–672.

Hoffman, L. W. (1972). Early childhood experiences and women's achievement motives. *Journal of Social Issues, 28*, 129–156.

Howard, A. N., Grant, A., Challand, G., Wraight, E. P., & Edwards, O. (1978). Thyroid metabolism in obese subjects after a very low calorie diet. *International Journal of Obesity, 2*, 391–392.

Hsu, L. K., Crisp, A. H., & Harding, B. (1979). Outcome of anorexia nervosa. *Lancet, 1*, 61–65.

Hytten, F. E., & Leitch, I. (1971). *The physiology of human pregnancy.* Oxford: Blackwell.

James, W. P., & Trayhurn, P. (1981). Thermogenesis and obesity. *British Medical Bulletin, 37*, 43–48.

Janda, L. H., O'Grady, K. E., & Barnhort, S. A. (1981). Effects of sexual attitudes and physical attractiveness on person perception of men and women. *Sex Roles, 7*, 189–199.

Johnson, C., Lewis, C., Love, S., Lewis, L., & Stuckey, M. (in press). Incidence and correlates of bulimic behavior in a female high school population. *Journal of Youth and Adolescence.*

Jones, D. J., Fox, M. M., Babigian, H. M., & Hutton, H. E. (1980). Epidemiology of anorexia nervosa in Monroe County, New York: 1960–1976. *Psychosomatic Medicine, 42*, 551–558.

Jourard, S. M., & Secord, P. R. (1955). Body-cathexic and the ideal female figure. *Journal of Abnormal Social Psychology, 50*, 243–246.

Kalick, S. M. (1977). *Plastic surgery, physical appearance, and person perception.* Unpublished doctoral dissertation, Harvard University, Cambridge.

Katcher, A., & Levin, M. M. (1955). Children's concept of body size. *Child Development, 26*, 103–110.

Kessler, R. C., & McRae, S. (1982). The effect of wives' employment on the mental-health of married men and women. *American Sociological Review,* *47*, 216–227.

Keys, A. (1980). Overweight, obesity, coronary heart disease and mortality. *Nutrition Review, 38,* 297–307.

Kimlicka, T., Cross, H., & Tarnai, J. (1983). A comparison of androgynous, feminine, masculine, and undifferentiated women on self-esteem, body satisfaction, and sexual satisfaction. *Psychology of Women Quarterly, 7,* 291–295.

Krebs, D., & Adinolfi, A. A. (1975). Physical attractiveness, social relations, and personality style. *Journal of Personality and Social Psychology, 31,* 245–253.

Kurtz, R. M. (1969). Sex differences and variations in body attitudes. *Journal of Consulting and Clinical Psychology, 33,* 625–629.

Lanson, L. (1975). *From woman to woman.* New York: Knopf.

Larkin, J. C., & Pines, H. A. (1979). No fat persons need apply—experimental studies of the overweight stereotype and hiring preference. *Sociology of Work and Occupations, 6,* 312–327.

Lerner, R. M. (1973). The development of personal space schemata toward body build. *Journal of Psychology, 84,* 229–235.

Lerner, R. M., & Gellert, E. (1969). Body build identification, preference, and aversion in children. *Developmental Psychology, 5,* 456–462.

Lerner, R. M., & Karabenick, S. A. (1974). Physical attractiveness, body attitudes, and self-concept in late adolescents. *Journal of Youth and Adolescence, 3,* 307–316.

Lerner, R. M., Orlos, J. B., & Knapp, J. R. (1976). Physical attractiveness, physical effectiveness and self-concept in late adolescents. *Adolescence, 11,* 313–326.

Lewis, H. B. (1971). *Shame and guilt in neurosis.* New York: International Universities Press.

Maccoby, E. E., & Jacklin, C. N. (1974). *The psychology of sex differences.* Stanford: Stanford University Press.

Mamay, P. D., & Simpson, R. L. (1981). Three female roles in television commercials. *Sex Roles, 7,* 1223–1232.

Matthews, A. M., & Westie, C. (1966). A preferred method for obtaining rankings: Reactions to physical handicaps. *Amercian Sociological Review, 31,* 851–854.

Mazel, J. (1981). *The Beverly Hills diet.* New York: Macmillan.

McKinlay, S., & Jeffreys, M. (1974). The menopausal syndrome. *British Journal of Preventive and Social Medicine, 28,* 108–115.

Metropolitan Life Insurance Company. (1983). *Statistical Bulletin, 64,* 2–9.

Millman, M. (1981). *Such a pretty face: Being fat in America.* New York: W. W. Norton.

Nelsen, E. A., & Rosenbaum, E. (1972). Language patterns within the youth subculture: Development of slang vocabularies. *Merril-Palmer Quarterly*, *18*, 273–285.

Nevo, S. (1984). *Bulimic symptoms: Prevalence and ethnic differences among college women*. Paper presented at the 5th annual meeting of the Society of Behavioral Medicine, Philadelphia.

Newman, H. H., Freeman, F. N., & Holzinger, K. J. (1982). *Twins: A study of heredity and environment*. Chicago: University of Chicago Press.

Nielsen, A. C. (1979). *Who's dieting and why?* Chicago: A. C. Nielsen.

Nylander, I. (1971). The feeling of being fat and dieting in a school population: Epidemiologic interview investigation. *Acta Sociomedica Scandinavica*, *3*, 17–26.

Oakley, A. (1972). *Sex, gender and society*. New York: Harper and Row.

Ondercin, P. A. (1979). Compulsive eating in college women. *Journal of College Student Personnel*, *20*, 153–157.

Orbach, S. (1978). *Fat is a feminist issue*. New York: Berkeley Press.

Parizkowa, J. (1973). Body composition and exercise during growth and development. In G. L. Rarick (Ed.), *Physical activity: Human growth and development*. New York: Academic Press.

Pitkin, R. M. (1976). Nutritional support in obstetrics and gynecology. *Clinical Obstetrics and Gynecology*, *19*, 489–513.

Pyle, R. L., Mitchell, J. E., Eckert, E. D., Halverson, P. A., Neuman, P. A., & Goff, G. M. (1983). The incidence of bulimia in freshman college students. *International Journal of Eating Disorders*, *2*, 75–85.

Richardson, S. A., Goodman, N., Hastorf, A. H., & Dornbusch, S. M. (1961). Cultural uniformity in reaction to physical disabilities. *American Sociological Review*, *26*, 241–247.

Rimm, A. A., & White, P. L. (1979). Obesity: Its risks and hazards. In G. A. Bray (Ed.), *Obesity in America* (103–124). NIH Publication No. 79-359. Washington, DC: U.S. Government Printing Office.

Rodin, J. (1984a). *Gravid food behavior, infant responsiveness, and weight gain*. Unpublished grant proposal, Yale University, New Haven.

Rodin, J. (1984b). *Yale Health and Patterns of Living Study: A longitudinal study on health, stress, and coping in the elderly*. Unpublished progress report. Yale University, New Haven.

Rodin, J., & Stoddard, P. (1981). *Predictors of attitudes toward weight and eating*. Unpublished manuscript. Yale University, New Haven.

Rodin, J., & Striegel-Moore, R. H. (1984). Predicting attitudes toward body weight and food intake in women. Paper presented at the 14th Congress of European Association of Behavior Therapy in Brussels, September.

Rose, G. A., & Williams, R. T. (1961). Metabolic studies on large and small eaters. *British Journal of Nutrition*, *15*, 1–9.

Rudofsky, B. (1971). *The unfashionable human body*. New York: Doubleday.

Schwartz, D. M., Thompson, M. G., & Johnson, C. L. (1982). Anorexia nervosa and bulimia: The socio-cultural context. *International Journal of Eating Disorders, 1,* 20–36.

Selvini-Palazzoli, M. (1974). *Self-starvation.* London: Aronson.

Sigall, H., Page, R., & Brown, A. C. (1971). Effort expenditure as a function of evaluation and evaluator attractiveness. *Representative Research in Social Psychology, 2,* 19–25.

Simmons, R. G., & Rosenberg, F. (1975). Sex, sex roles, and self-image. *Journal of Youth and Adolescence, 4,* 229–258.

Society of Actuaries and Association of Life Insurance Medical Directors of America. (1980). *Build and blood pressure study 1979.* Chicago: Author.

Sontag, S. (1972). The double standard of aging. *Saturday Review, 54,* 29–38.

Sorlie, P., Gordon, T., & Kannel, W. B. (1980). Body build and mortality? The Framingham Study. *Journal of the American Medical Association, 243,* 1828–1831.

Squire, S. (1983). *The slender balance: Causes and cures for bulimia, anorexia, and the weight-loss/weight-gain seesaw.* New York: G. P. Putnam's Sons.

Staffieri, J. R. (1967). A study of social stereotype of body image in children. *Journal of Personality and Social Psychology, 7,* 101–104.

Staffieri, J. R. (1972). Body build and behavioral expectancies in young females. *Developmental Psychology, 6,* 125–127.

Stangler, R. S., & Printz, A. M. (1980). DSM-III: Psychiatric diagnosis in a university population. *American Journal of Psychiatry, 137,* 937–940.

Stephan, C., & Tully, J. C. (1977). Influence of physical attractiveness of a plaintiff on decisions of simulated jurors. *Journal of Social Psychology, 106,* 149–150.

Stroebe, W., Insko, C. A., Thompson, V. D., & Layton, B. D. (1971). Effects of physical attractiveness, attitude similarity, and sex on various aspects of interpersonal attraction. *Journal of Personality and Social Psychology, 18,* 79–91.

Tanner, J. M. (1974). Sequence and tempo in the somatic changes in puberty. In M. M. Grumbach, G. D. Grave, & F. E. Mayer (Eds.), *Control of the onset of puberty.* New York: John Wiley.

Theander, S. (1970). Anorexia nervosa: A psychiatric investigation of 44 female cases. *Acta Psychiatrica Scandinavica, 48* (Suppl. 214), 1–94.

Thoits, P. A. (1983). Multiple identities and psychological well-being: a reformulation and test of the social-isolation hypothesis. *American Sociological Review, 48,* 174–187.

Thompson, M. G., & Schwartz, M. (1982). Life adjustment of women with anorexia and anorexic-like behavior. *International Journal of Eating Disorders, 1,* 47–60.

Unger, R. K., Hilderbrand, M., & Madar, T. (1982). Physical attractiveness and assumptions about social deviance: Some sex-by-sex comparisons. *Personality and Social Psychology Bulletin, 8,* 293–301.

Vaughn, B. E., & Langlois, J. H. (1983). Physical attractiveness as a correlate of peer status and social competence in preschool children. *Developmental Psychology, 19*, 561–567.

Venkatesan, M., & Losco, J. (1975). Women in magazine ads: 1959–1971. *Journal of Advertising Research, 15*, 49–54.

Wagman, M. (1967). Sex differences in types of daydreams. *Journal of Personality and Social Psychology, 3*, 329–332.

Weideger, P. (1976). *Menstruation and menopause*. New York: Knopf.

Weinberger, M. G., Petrosius, S. M., and Westin, S. A. (1979). Twenty years of women in magazine advertising: An update. In N. Beckwith, M. Houston, R. Mittelstaedt, K. B. Monroe, & S. Ward (Eds.), *1979 Educators Conference Proceedings*. Chicago: American Marketing Association.

Wessel, J. A., Ufer, A., Van Huss, W. D., & Cederquist, D. (1963). Age trends of various components of body composition and functional characteristics in women aged 20–69 years. *Annals of the New York Academy of Science, 110*, 608–622.

West, S. C., & Brown, T. J. (1975). Physical attractiveness, severity of emergency and helping: Field experiment and interpersonal simulation. *Journal of Experimental Social Psychology, 11*, 531–538.

White, W. C., & Boskind-White, M. (1981). An experimental-behavioral approach to the treatment of bulimarexia. *Journal of Psychotherapy: Theory, Research, and Practice, 18*, 501–507.

Williams, E. (1958). Anorexia nervosa: A somatic disorder. *British Medical Journal, 2*, 190–195.

Withers, R. F. (1964). Problems in the genetics of human obesity. *Eugenics Review, 56*, 81–90.

Witkin, H. A., Lewis, H. B., Hertzman, M., Machover, K., Meissner, P. B., & Wagner, S. (1954). *Personality through perception*. New York: Harper and Row.

Women on Words and Images. (1972). *Dick and Jane as victims: Sex stereotyping in children's readers*. Princeton, NJ: Author.

Wooley, O. W., Wooley, S. C., & Dyrenforth, S. R. (1979). Obesity and women II: A neglected feminist topic. *Women Studies International Quarterly, 2*, 81–89.

Wooley, S. C., & Wooley, O. W. (1980). Eating disorders: Obesity and anorexia. In A. M. Brodsky & R. Hare-Mustin (Eds.), *Women and psychotherapy*. New York: Guilford Press.

Wooley, S., & Wooley, O. W. (1982). The Beverly Hills eating disorder: The mass marketing of anorexia nervosa. *International Journal of Eating Disorders, 1*, 57–69.

Wooley, S. C., & Wooley, O. W. (1984a). Feeling fat in a thin society. *Glamour*, February, 198–252.

Wooley, S. C., & Wooley, O. W. (1984b). Should obesity be treated at all? In

A. J. Stunkard & E. Stellar (Eds.), *Eating and its disorders*. New York: Raven Press.

Young, C. M., Blondin, J., Tensuan, R., & Fryer, J. H. (1963). Body composition studies of "older" women, thirty–seventy years of age. *Annals of the New York Academy of Science, 110*, 589–607.

Young, C. M., Martin, M. E. K., Chihan, M., McCarthy, M., Mannielo, M. J., Harmuth, E. H., & Fryer, J. H. (1961). Body composition of young women: Some preliminary findings. *Journal of the American Dietetic Association, 38*, 332–340.

Subject Index

312

Author Index

316